Jerusalem

JERUSALEM

A City and Its Future

Edited by
MARSHALL J. BREGER
and ORA AHIMEIR

A Publication of the Jerusalem Institute for Israel Studies

Syracuse University Press

Library of Congress Cataloging-in-Publication Data
Jerusalem : a city and its future / edited by Marshall J. Breger and Ora Ahimeir.—1st ed.
p. cm.—(Publication of the Jerusalem Institute for Israel Studies)
Includes bibliographical references (p.) and Index.
ISBN 0-8156-2912-5 (cl. : alk. paper)—ISBN 0-8156-2913-3 (pbk. : alk. paper)
1. Jerusalem. 2. Jerusalem—International status. 3. Jerusalem—Ethnic relations. 4. Jerusalem—
Politics and government—20th century. 5. Arab-Israeli conflict—1993—-Peace. I. Berger, Marshall J.
II. Ahimeir, Ora. III. Series.
DS109.9 .J453 2002
956.94'42—dc21
2002001561

This book is dedicated to the memory of Marshall Breger's mother, Beatrice Breger, who passed away during its preparation.

Marshall Breger is professor of law at the Columbus School of Law, the Catholic University of America. From 1999–2001 he was an adjunct fellow for the Center for Strategic and International Studies and is presently a regular contributor to *Moment* magazine. He serves as vice president of the Jewish Policy Center, a public policy think tank in Washington, D.C. During the Bush administration, he served as Solicitor of Labor, the chief lawyer of the Labor Department. From 1985 to 1991, Breger was chairman of the Administrative Conference of the United States. From 1983 to 1985, he was a special assistant to President Reagan and his liaison with the Jewish community. He is the author of *Jerusalem's Holy Places and the Peace Process* (with Thomas A. Indinopulos, 1998).

Ora Ahimeir has been the director of the Jerusalem Institute for Israel Studies for the past twenty years. She has edited many publications on current-day Jerusalem, the state of women in Israel, and Israeli cultural issues. She initiated and organized (together with Dr. Maya Choshen) the Jerusalem Institute's think tank for peace arrangements in Jerusalem. Her most recent book, together with Haim Beer, is *One Hundred Years of Cultural Creativity in Eretz Israel* (2000).

Contents

Illustrations

Figures

Maps

Tables

Acknowledgments

The publication of this book was made possible by funds granted by the Charles H. Revson Foundation. The statements made and the views expressed, however, are solely the responsibility of the authors. The editors wish to thank Professor Abraham (Rami) Friedman, the head of the Jerusalem Institute for Israel Studies, for his support of this project.

Early versions of some of these essays were delivered at a conference titled "Jerusalem: Then and Now," at the Columbus School of Law, the Catholic University of America, and published in the *Catholic University Law Review.* We thank the law school as well as Dean Bernard Dobranski and Interim Dean Robert Destro for their continued support for the study of legal issues of concern to the Jewish community.

Contributors

Qasem Abdul-Jaber teaches at al-Quds University, Jerusalem, in the Department of Applied Earth and Environmental Sciences. He received his Ph.D. from the University of Munster, Germany, in natural sciences. He has also been a consultant for the Palestinian Water Authority.

Amir Cheshin served as advisor to the mayor of Jerusalem on Arab affairs from 1984 until 1994. A sixth-generation Jerusalemite, he now runs a consulting company that operates throughout the Middle East. He is also the coauthor of *Separate and Unequal: The Inside Story of Israeli Rule in East Jerusalem* (1999), with Bill Hutman.

Maya Choshen holds a Ph.D. in geography from the Hebrew University in Jerusalem. Senior researcher at the Jerusalem Institute for Israel Studies, especially in the sphere of demographic trends in the Jerusalem and metropolitan area. Dr. Choshen is the editor of the *Jerusalem Statistical Yearbook,* a lecturer in the School of Education at the Hebrew University in Jerusalem, and a planner for the Jerusalem metropolitan area master plan, the Tel-Aviv metropolitan master plan, and other plans.

Silvio Ferrari is professor of ecclesiastical law at the University of Milan and Leuven. He is also the editor of the *Quaderni di Diritto e Politica Eclesiastica* (Bologna) and a member of many organizations, including: the scientific committee of the *Anuario de Derecho Eclesiastico del Estado* (Madrid); the editorial council of the *Journal of Church and State* (Waco); the executive committee of the European Consortium for Church and State Research (Milan); the board of directors of the International Academy for Freedom of Religion and Belief (Washington); the research group on Droit et Religion *(Conseil National de Recherche Scientifique,* Strasbourg); and the Centre for Law and Religion (Cardiff). Professor Ferrari has written extensively on relations between the Vatican and Israel.

Abraham (Rami) Friedman is head of the Jerusalem Institute for Israel Studies. He is also a professor at the Jerusalem Business School at the Hebrew University. He has taught as a visiting professor at New York University, the University of Chicago, the University of Minnesota, and the University of California at Berkeley. Professor Friedman served as the civil service commissionaire for the State of Israel. He is and was chairperson and member of many "blue ribbon" government task forces in the Ministry of the Treasury, the Prime Minister's Office, the Ministry of Labor and Welfare, the Ministry of Interior, the Ministry of Education, and several municipalities. He is a leading authority in Israel on labor relations, management of human resources, and public administration.

Menachem Friedman is a professor of sociology at Bar-Ilan University. He is also Israel's leading scholar of ultraorthodoxy in Judaism and author of numerous studies of *haredi* society.

Rotem M. Giladi is an international lawyer specializing in the Oslo Peace Process. A former employee of the Ministry of Foreign Affairs, he was a member of the Israeli delegation to the talks on the Israeli-Palestinian Interim Agreement (Oslo II). Giladi serves as legal adviser to the Tel Aviv delegation of the International Committee of the Red Cross (ICRC).

Shlomo Hasson is a member of the Jerusalem Institute for Israel Studies task team for the future of Jerusalem. He is also a professor at the Hebrew University. He has conducted extensive research on neighborhood government in the city, has served as a board member and consultant on various development projects, and has published two books on urban social movements.

Moshe Hirsch is a lecturer in International and European Law at the Faculty of Law, the Hebrew University of Jerusalem; and researcher at the Jerusalem Institute for Israel Studies. He has published extensively on the legal status of Jerusalem, European Union-Israel relations, and international environmental law.

Bill Hutman has written extensively on Jerusalem. From 1992 until 1996, he was the Jerusalem beat reporter for the *Jerusalem Post* newspaper. His articles on Jerusalem have also appeared in the *New York Times* and the *London Times.* His recent book on Jerusalem, *Separate and Unequal: The Inside Story of Israeli Rule in East Jerusalem* (with Amir Chesin), was published in 1999.

Menachem Klein is a research fellow at the Jerusalem Institute for Israel Studies and a senior lecturer in the Department of Political Science at Bar-Ilan University, Israel. He has published several monographs and articles about the Palestine Liberation Organization's policy and ideology, including "Competing Brothers: The Web of Hamas-PLO Relations," in *Terrorism and Political Violence;* "Quo-Vadis: Palestinian Dilemmas of Ruling Authority Building Since 1993," in *Middle Eastern Studies;* and "Between Right and Realization: The PLO Dialectics of 'The Right of Return,'" in *Journal of Refugee Studies.* His book *Doves over Jerusalem's Sky: The City and the Peace Process* was published in 2000.

Ruth Lapidoth is a professor of international law in the Faculty of Law and the Department of International Relations at the Hebrew University of Jerusalem; a member of the Permanent Court of Arbitration; and senior researcher at the Jerusalem Institute for Israel Studies. Professor Lapidoth was formerly the legal adviser of the Ministry of Foreign Affairs of Israel and Israeli member of the Arbitral Tribunal that decided the Taba case between Egypt and Israel.

Ambassador (Ret.) Reuven Merhav served in the Prime Minster's Office and in the Ministry of Foreign Affairs in Ethiopia, Kenya, Iran, Lebanon, and Hong Kong. He devoted much of this time to nursing contacts with Muslim and East Asian nations, mainly China, eventually serving as director general of the Ministry of Foreign Affairs. Since 1995, he has served on the boards of various academic bodies and public companies.

Deborah F. Mir is currently director of Sviva Technologies Ltd., an environmental consulting firm. She has taught a course on environmental issues in Jerusalem at Hebrew University. She is also an environmentalist for ATAT Ltd., working on environmental impact statements and analysis for the Jerusalem area.

Charalambos K. Papastathis is professor of ecclesiastical law at the Faculty of Law of the Aristotle University of Thessaloniki. He is vice president of the Hellenic Association for Slavic Studies and secretary-general of the Macedonia-Thrace Union of Fulbrighters; member of the European Consortium for Church-State Research, the International Association of Canon Law, the Society of the Law of Oriental Churches, the Jean Bodin Society for the Comparative History of Institutions; fellow of the International Academy for Freedom of Religion and Belief; and secretary-general of cults at the Ministry of Education and Cults (1987–88). He is author of *The Legislative Work of the Cryillo-Methodian Mission in Great Moravia* (1978); *On the Administrative Organization of the Church of Cyprus* (1981); *The Characters of Orthodox Communities of the Ottoman Empire* (1984); *The Nomocanon of George Trapezountios* (1985); *The Status of Monks at Mount Athos* (1988); *A Handbook of Ecclesiastical Law* (2d ed., 1994); and more than ninety articles and reports in various reviews and symposia.

Amnon Ramon holds an M.A. in history from the Hebrew University in Jerusalem. He currently works as a researcher for the Jerusalem Institute for Israel Studies and for Yad Izhak Ben-Zvi. His focus is the history of Jerusalem in the modern era and religions in contemporary Jerusalem. He has published several essays, including "Christian Views on the Jerusalem Question" and "The Attitude of the State of Israel and the Jewish Public to the Temple Mount."

Yitzhak Reiter is a lecturer at the Hebrew University of Jerusalem, Department for Islamic and Middle Eastern Studies. Dr. Reiter, who received his Ph.D. from the Hebrew University, has done extensive research in the fields of Islamic institutions and law, modern Middle East history, and the Arabs in Israel. He is a research fellow at both the Truman Institute and the Jerusalem Institute for Israel Studies. Formerly the deputy prime minister's advisor on Arab affairs, he was also nominated in 1993 by the Israeli government to head a public committee for integrating the Arabs into the civil service.

Geoffrey R. Watson is associate professor of law at the Columbus School of Law at the Catholic University of America. Previously he was an associate professor of law at the Seattle University School of Law and served as an attorney-adviser at the Office of the Assistant Legal Adviser for Near Eastern and South Asian Affairs in the U.S. Department of State.

Abbreviations

CBS	Central Bureau of Statistics (Israel)
CSCE	Council on Security and Cooperation in Europe
EIA	environmental impact assessment
HCJ	High Court of Justice
IDF	Israeli Defense Forces
JDEC	Jerusalem Dictrict Electric Company
JEA	Jerusalem Education Authority
JIIS	Jerusalem Institute for Israel Studies
JMA	Jerusalem metropolitan area
JNF	Jewish National Fund
JWU	Jerusalem Water Undertaking
MCM	million cubic meters
MOE	Ministry of Environment (Israel)
MSW	metropolitan solid waste
NGOs	nongovernmental organizations
NIS	new Israeli shekels
NRP	National-Religious Party
NWC	National Water Carrier
OIC	Organization of the Islamic Conference
PCBS	Palestinian Central Bureau of Statistics
PLO	Palestine Liberation Organization
UN	United Nations
WBWD	West Bank Water Department
WSSA	Water Supply and Sewerage Authority

Jerusalem

Introduction

Marshall J. Breger

The different aspects of Jerusalem's social geography cannot be clearly delineated on a map. In poet Yehuda Amichai's words, "The city plays hide-and-seek among her names: Yerushalayim, al Quds, Salem, Jeru, Yesu" (Amichai 1995). Neither secular and mainstream Orthodox neighborhoods nor areas of *haredi* and Arab residence are fixed entities. *Haredi* neighborhoods push out into formerly secular districts, such as Ramot. Jewish enclaves spring up between Palestinian villages. Jewish construction in east Jerusalem neighborhoods such as Gilo and Pisgat Zeev has left Arabs a minority in their east Jerusalem hinterland. Indeed, the notion that Jerusalem can be easily divided up is ridiculous to anyone who actually walks its metes and bounds. The different Jerusalems are so intertwined that they can be disentangled only in utopian visions. How they interact will do more to determine the future of Jerusalem than all the posturing of Israel or Palestinian politicians, not to speak of the final-status negotiations between Israel and the Palestinian Authority.

The Navel of the World

For medieval Christians, Jerusalem was the *umbilicus mundi*—the navel of the world—and indeed, for centuries, European maps of the world used it as their center. The city has been the focus of Christian pilgrimage since the fourth century. It contains the reputed sites of the crucifixion, burial, and resurrection of Jesus Christ, including the Church of the Holy Sepulcher, the churches marking the stations of the cross along the Via Dolorosa, the Garden of Gethsemane, and the Church of the Ascension. The city, moreover, has been the underlying metaphor for the Christian notion of heavenly Jerusalem—where humans live out of time in God's good and fulsome grace.

For Jews, Jerusalem is the "mountain of the Lord," the very core of the Jewish people for three thousand years. Indeed, the *mishnah,* the second-century law code composed by Judah Ha-Nasi, tells us that the *shekhinah,* the Divine Presence, has never left the Western Wall. It is the symbol of both spiritual and national revival. The "Hatikvah," the Jewish national anthem, speaks of the yearning for the "return to Zion and Jerusalem." In daily prayers, three times a day, the religious Jew entreats the Lord to "return in mercy to thy City Jerusalem."

Throughout history, Jerusalem has been the center of Jewish consciousness. In medieval times, elderly Jews traveled to Jerusalem to be buried in its hallowed ground. Throughout the centuries, Jews came to live in spiritual piety. By 1844, they constituted the largest single religious group in the city. In the 1870s, they were an absolute majority and have remained so ever since.

For Jews, then, Jerusalem is not a city that encompasses holy places. Rather, it is the earthly city itself that is holy, both the land and, as former Chief Rabbi Abraham Isaac Kook told us, even the air. Jerusalem is synonymous with Judaism's entrenchment in the land of Israel. It is the very center of that engagement. For Jews, political control over the part of Jerusalem that it deems holy is intrinsic to its holiness. The religion itself "requires its political control as the capital of the Jewish Commonwealth" (Reisman 1970, 73).

At the same time, as Professor Werblowsky has underscored, "the sanctity of Jerusalem in Islam is a fact" (1988, 2). It is the original direction for Islamic prayer, *'ula al-qublatheyn,* and the *al-mi'radj haqq,* the place from which the Prophet ascended (some say on a winged mount) to heavenly spheres. It is, moreover, the place according to Muslim tradition where those eschatological events harkening the end of the world will commence. Those who try to suggest that al-Quds is less holy to Islam than to Judaism simply are incorrect. The construction of comparative hierarchies of holiness between religious faiths is a fruitless exercise.

It also must be recognized, however, that, as Saul Cohen points out, "At no time in the thirteen centuries of Islamic rule was Jerusalem part of let alone synonymous with, a national entity" (1977, 109). The Umayyids in the seventh century chose Ramle, not Jerusalem, as the administrative capital of the country. The Ottomans ruled Palestine from Damascus. Indeed, some twelfth-century Muslim leaders were prepared to trade the city of Jerusalem for Dammietta (now Dumyat), a then-important port on the Egyptian coast.

A Clash of Symbols

To make matters even more complex, this earthly Jerusalem has become a symbol for the nationalist political aspirations of both Israelis and Palestinians. For Israelis, whether religious or secular, it is "Jerusalem of Gold," a united Jerusalem, the "eternal capital of Israel now and forever."

And, for their part, Palestinians find it difficult to imagine a Palestinian entity that does not encompass some part of Jerusalem. These competing political aspirations create a belief among many that Jerusalem, like the baby in the Judgment of Solomon, presents a zero-sum problem in which, of necessity, winners must be offset by losers. The intertwining of religious and nationalist imagery and symbolism makes finding a solution even that much more difficult.

Israel's East Jerusalem Policy

Israeli municipal policy toward the Arabs between 1967 and 1993 became closely associated with the city's former mayor, Teddy Kollek, who served for twenty-eight years, from 1965 to 1993. Essentially, he sought to guarantee Israel's sovereignty over Jerusalem and believed that moderate and humane policy, sensitive to social rights, would convince the Arabs to live in peace and to prosper. The kernel of Kollek's policy was to secure Jewish-Arab coexistence by fostering autonomy, equality in service provision, and positive contacts between different groups (Kollek 1988–89).

Kollek quite often likened Jerusalem to a "cultural mosaic," where each unit is assumed to have a high degree of control over its life. This notion, which closely resembles the Ottoman's millet system, held that local autonomy in cultural and service affairs could lead to good citizenship, responsibility, and democratization. Kollek even suggested that self-administered neighborhood councils may come to play an important role in the solution of the Jerusalem problem (Kollek 1988–89).

Kollek's political style has been described as pragmatic, open, active, fair, and humane (Romann and Weingrod 1991, 203). Arab mukhtars (community patrons) occasionally mentioned that "his door is always open." In everyday politics, he relied on principles historically developed in ethnically mixed Middle Eastern cities. These principles, as Romann and Weingrod demonstrate (1991), entailed urban government based on cooperation with the social and economic elite and on a strong reliance on mukhtars. The local elite with whom Kollek cooperated included key figures in the Arab community: heads of churches (some of them appointed to their office by the Vatican), heads of the Waqf (Muslim religious trust), and heads of the Chamber of Commerce—all of whom maintained close connections with Jordan. Through informal negotiations approved by the Jordanian government, Kollek and these notables were able to pursue broad public issues concerning social and cultural life in the city.

Occasionally Kollek acted as a bridge between the notables and the Israeli government. Thus, for instance, he played an important role in seeing that the Holy Places would be controlled by the religious authorities without any governmental intervention. Similarly, he supported the Arabs in their demand that they administer the educational system by themselves (Kollek 1988–89).

For more than twenty years, ethnic relations in Jerusalem never erupted into substantial strife and violent action, though occasional outbursts did occur. Kollek supported the government's policy of strengthening the Jewish majority in the city, but he differed on certain details. On some occasions, he openly criticized the central government's activities, sometimes supporting the local Arab communities in their struggle against confiscations and housing demolition, and condemned Jewish extremist groups that moved into Arab neighborhoods.

Aware of the tension between appearance and reality, Kollek tended to blame the central government for suppressing his initiatives. As he remarked, "Power is left in the hands of the central government, not the municipality. The relationship between the local government and the central government is roughly the same as it was in the colonial period" (1993, 102). It is true that Israel is in general characterized by an excessively centralized governmental and bureaucratic system, with the result that Jerusalem's municipality has lacked the authority and resources to guarantee full-scale development of the self-management neighborhood councils.

Behind all this is Jerusalem *Shel Maalah* (the spiritual Jerusalem) often contending with the needs of Jerusalem *Shel Matah* (the earthly Jerusalem). The city has a relatively weak economic base (average family income is 11 percent lower than in Tel Aviv and 18 percent lower than in Haifa), and without private-sector jobs, secular youth won't stay there. Much of Jerusalem's core housing stock is owned by foreigners who come on "pilgrimages" but a few weeks a year. The need for economic growth is at odds with the need to maintain the spiritual character of the city.

The issue of Jerusalem, however, is not simply one of sacred space. Jerusalem is a city of the living, who need housing, industry, roads, and infrastructure. It is the center of government for the Jews, and the intellectual and economic center of the Palestinian West Bank. It is a city of approximately 646,000 persons, with 436,000 Jews and 203,000 Arabs joined, as it were, at the hip, living together separately in stippled fashion.

Thus, it is no surprise that Israel's conscious policy since 1967 has been to "limit the growth of the Arab population of the city" (Cheshin, Hutman, and Melamed 1999, 31; see also Hutman and Cheshin in this volume).[1] This policy has been carried out both by promoting Jewish migration to the eastern part of the city, and "by setting a strict limit on new homes built in [Arab] neighborhoods" (Cheshin, Hutman, and Melamed 1999, 30). As Cheshin, Hutman, and Melamed show in devastating detail, "the zoning plans for east Jerusalem were in no way based on a coherent vision for the neighborhood.

---

1. This attitude continues. Mayor Ehud Olmert has said, "Let there be no mistake. I do not want to enhance the Arab population in Jerusalem. It should not grow. . . . I wish the Arab minority in Jerusalem would shrink" (cited in Bollens 2000, 65).

They were based solely on preventing Arab population growth. Thus Arab building was to be allowed only in already built up areas" (1999, 37).

Israel's harsh application of its residence requirements also served to reduce Arab in-migration. Following the 1967 Israeli victory, Palestinians living within the newly defined Jerusalem were classified as permanent residents, not citizens. Permanent-resident permits were revoked for those who moved outside of Israel (even to the West Bank!) for seven years, including university studies. The Interior Ministry further adopted a "center-of-life" policy by which the ministry can revoke a permit when it determines that a resident's "center of life" is no longer in Jerusalem, even when all other applicable legal criteria are met. This policy also pertains to spouses from outside Jerusalem (again including the West Bank), who must apply through a lengthy bureaucratic process for possible family unification privileges.

Indeed, as one work has suggested, "Israel wanted Jews to be a majority in east as well as west Jerusalem, hoping this demographic reality would prevent the city from being divided again between Israel and an Arab state" (Cheshin, Hutman, and Melamed 1999, 34).

Separate but Equal?

Another source of tension appeared at the level of service provision. Although Kollek claimed to support the principle of equal access to municipal resources, as far as the Palestinian sections of east Jerusalem are concerned, "the municipality never provided more than 4% of its development budget for infrastructure in roads, sewage, water, electricity, and schools" (Amirav 1992, 41). Responding to the charges in this sphere, Kollek said, "As the Arabs are not in the Council, it was difficult to allocate funds for expenditure . . . [for] Arabs. . . . They pay their taxes fully, and they are right, to a certain extent, that not all their tax money was spent on Arab districts. . . . This too is influenced by the fact that they are not represented on the Council" (Kollek 1993, 102, 114). This state of affairs is a clear indication that Palestinians did not share equal rights with the Israelis in Jerusalem and that their rights were not genuinely championed during Kollek's long-standing regime.

There can be little doubt that Palestinians in Jerusalem have never received their full share of municipal benefits from Israel. Walk across the 1967 divide, and clear differences in housing stock and city services, if not in the quality of life, become obvious immediately. However, this problem not only stems from bias, which certainly exists, but comes more from the decision by nearly all Jerusalem Arabs to boycott municipal elections, resulting in their lack of political representation. Had Palestinians participated, they would likely have emerged as the swing voting bloc in the city council, and they would have been amply and practically rewarded for their vote.

The incumbent mayor Ehud Olmert has a clear vision of a united Jerusalem with no distinctions between Arab and Jewish sectors. To that end, he has continuously chastised Kollek for the shabby condition of East Jerusalem. He has promised new funding to move toward equality. Indeed, he has asserted that there can be no united Jerusalem without equality of service. Yet, like Kollek, Olmert has never delivered on these promises. Olmert's vision of an undivided Jerusalem runs directly up against the reality of east Jerusalem poverty. The differences in public services between both sides of the city are stark and obvious to any observer who travels across the imaginary line that separates Jewish from Arab Jerusalem. It runs up as well against the demands of Jewish neighborhoods, particularly the *haredi*, for municipal services.

Olmert presented his vision for Jerusalem in a government report on June 18, 1998. The proposal said not one word about local autonomy. Instead, it proposed expanding Jerusalem borders into the West Bank (see chapter 15 of this volume). Since that time, little has been done to face the challenge of providing equal resources to both parts of the city.

Any proposal for retaining a united Jerusalem that does not attack the problem of unequal resources is doomed to fail.

The "Trading Range"

The mere fact that both Israelis and Palestinians seek practical instead of ideological solutions is itself a sign of progress. Any discussion of the future of Jerusalem must recognize that a very narrow "trading range" exists in which the parties can bargain. No Israeli government will give the city back. Efforts to prove that Israel has no rights in Jerusalem under international law, whether correct or not, will have little if any effect on the practical discussions over the city's future. Similarly, proposals to divide the city in two are likely nonstarters. Of course, we must recognize that the trading range itself is evolving as intercommunal confidence ebbs and flows. Nevertheless, possibilities meriting discussion include notions of devolution of power, such as decentralized boroughs (talked up but rarely acted on by former mayor Teddy Kollek [1988–89, 156; 1981, 1041]); some form of a Vatican-type solution; and the idea that an enlarged "Greater Jerusalem" can in some way accommodate the political and religious needs of both communities.

One suggestion that builds on Kollek's borough concepts is the so-called Beilin-Abu Mazen plan.[2] As regards Jerusalem and the Holy Places, the plan would:

> Establish a Palestinian capital in Abu Dis (an Arab village just outside Jerusalem), where a future Palestinian parliament might be situated. Abu Dis would be renamed al-Quds (Arabic for Jerusalem);
> Leave the Temple Mount as is, under de facto Palestinian control, while formally suspending Israeli sovereignty to reflect that reality. As a result, the Palestinian flag would be allowed to fly on the Mount;
> Leave practical control over the entire city in Israeli hands; and
> Incorporate the closed-in West Bank Jewish city of Ma'ale Adumim into Israel's capital.

Beilin and Abu Mazen apparently did not agree on the matter of de jure sovereignty for eastern Jerusalem (which some call the Old City) and agreed with de jure control for Israel but wide-ranging Palestinian autonomy (see, generally, Schiff 1996; Makovsky 1996).[3]

Other proposals for power sharing have been made, many intimated in this book. The challenge, of course, as Moshe Hirsch makes clear in his cre-

2. So-called because the plan was never publically released and has been disseminated by various leaks. One member of Beilen's team told me proudly that the United States was not given the plan in writing until spring 2000.

3. The exact text of the Beilin-Abu Mazin plan was not leaked to the press until fall 2000 and was made available in *Newsweek*. See Michael Hirsch, "The Lost Peace Plan: The 1995 Document That Paved the Way to Camp David, and Perhaps Beyond," *Newsweek,* Sept. 25 (2000): 46.

ative contribution (chapter 3, this volume) is to put forward proposals that do not reflect a zero-sum game but rather meet in some way the interests and needs of all the parties. The essays in this book both underscore how difficult a task that is and intimate some paths that might be traveled toward that goal.

Boundaries and *Kedusha*

One question regarding Jerusalem is addressed only obliquely in these essays: how to define the city's boundaries. The Jordanians, when they controlled Jerusalem, had planned to stake out new municipal boundaries but were interrupted by the Six Day War. For its part, Israel, after its 1967 victory, dramatically enlarged the city dimensions. And proposals for further enlargement continue to appear. Indeed, it is worth noting that the 1947 United Nations (UN) proposals for internationalization had a different geographical configuration in mind—one that enlarged the city to achieve relative parity between the Jewish and Arab populations.

The notion of geographically "relativizing" Jerusalem adds to the possibilities for creative diplomacy. To do this, however, negotiators need to reflect on what geographical boundaries specifically encompass the holiness—in Hebrew, the *Kedusha*—of Jerusalem for Muslims, Christians, and Jews, as well as on what geographical boundaries symbolize these groups' respective nationalist aspirations. This exercise may well prove instructive to Arabs and Jews alike.

A Hegemonic Consensus?

Until recently, the national Israeli consensus regarding a united Jerusalem as an integral and indivisible part of Israel was hegemonic. Yielding up any portion of Jerusalem was inconceivable. Yet, as Asher (Alan) Arian has recognized, "public opinion in Israel on security questions is malleable" (1995, 1). Attitudes in Israel already have begun to change. Arian's 1994 survey of Israeli political attitudes indicates that only 14 percent of Israelis approved of the inclusion of the status of Jerusalem on the peace talks agenda (1994, 11). Yet a 1995 Gallup poll found "less than two-thirds (65 percent) of the Israeli

Jewish public voiced full support for exclusive Israeli sovereignty over all of Jerusalem" ("Israelis May Be More Flexible" 1995; see also Pfaff 1995).

Recent Events

As is well known, Prime Minister Barak began concrete discussion of Jerusalem at the July 2000 Camp David Summit.[4] Although exact parameters of what was on the table remains unclear, it appears that Barak offered up compromises on Jerusalem that provided the Palestinians some foothold in the city, and Arafat has intimated that he would accept some form of shared sovereignty on the Temple Mount.[5] These efforts were revived in late December 2000 after the commencement of the so-called al-Aqsa Intifada in fall 2000. Indeed, the parties appear to be discussing detailed plans that could lead to a substantial sharing of the city between Jews and Arabs.

These negotiations moved the debate to practical questions such as content of traffic, education, and sewage. Some of the contributors to this volume were directly involved in the Camp David talks.[6] It was generally understood, however, that the theoretical background work that led to the ability even to talk about flexible "options" was undertaken by the Jerusalem Institute of Israel Studies.[7] In earlier iterations, many of the essays of this volume were shared with policymakers and formed the core of the institute's work.

4. Laria Lahoud, "Israelis, Palestinians, and Americans Strain Toward Jerusalem Agreement," *Jerusalem Post*," July 19, 2000.

5. Jacob Lefkovits Dala, "On Forms of Sovereignty over the Temple Mount," *Jerusalem Post*, Sept. 15, 2000, 3. But see "U.S. Working on New Bridging Paper," *Mideast Mirror*, Sept. 18, 2000 ("Barak completely rules out Palestinian or Islamic sovereignty over Temple Mount").

6. Reuven Merhav was brought to Camp David by Prime Minister Barak. Menachem Klein served as an advisor to Israel's then acting foreign minister Shlomo Ben Ami. See Associated Press, "Experts Preparing Jerusalem, *Deseret News* (Salt Lake City, Utah), Aug. 20, 2000, A6.

7. See Vered Kleiner, "Institute in the News," *Kol Ha'ir*, Aug. 7, 2000, 58.

When the question was put pointedly in May 2000, only 71 percent of Israelis opposed handing over east Jerusalem to the Palestinians in a final peace settlement (Agence France Presse 2000). And even after the al-Aqsa Intifada, a majority of Israelis were prepared to make severe compromises over Jerusalem in the context of a peace agreement.[8]

We must remember that early Zionists saw Tel Aviv, not Jerusalem, as the symbol of Jewish renewal. Few in 1948 assumed Jerusalem would be the capital, and in the early years of the state it was a backwater town visited only by schoolchildren on class trips and by Israelis who had specific business with the government. Only with the "miracle" of Jerusalem's reunification in 1967 did "Jerusalem of Gold" become the center of Israeli national hopes and aspirations.

As the interests of Judaica and Secularia diverge in Jerusalem, the rest of secular Israel may begin to see the city as the home of religious zealots—not *their* kind of Jews. Will it remain the symbol of national identity for which they are prepared to lay down their lives? Already approximately a majority of the population is prepared to talk about dividing the city if that is the price of peace.[9] To that extent, supporters of Jewish Jerusalem may be lucky that the final-status talks have begun rather than waiting until the gulf between secular and religious Jerusalem in some measure erodes the Israeli commitment to the Holy City.

Playing for Time

With the collapse of the Camp David 2000 and Taba Summits and the continuing violence and terror occasioned by the al-Aksa intifada, residents of Jerusalem find that they are playing for time, waiting for the constant struggle between communal hope and communal fear to play itself out, recognizing that both the Jewish and the Palestinian communities fear the other side's

---

8. Herb Keinon, "The Temple Mount Factor," *Jerusalem Post,* Dec. 29, 2000, 1 *(Yediot Achronot* poll shows that 60 percent will agree to transfer of Arab areas of Jerusalem to Palestinians, albeit 57 percent are opposed to transferring the Temple Mount).

9. Ibid.

ultimate intentions.[10] The Israelis fear that the Palestinians adhere to a "salami strategy" in which their protestations of peace will ultimately pressure Israel to give up strategic advantage (e.g., land), thus allowing the city, in its weakened state, to be dismembered slice by slice. For their part, the Palestinians fear that what they consider Israeli imperialism will force them into the equivalent of Middle Eastern Bantustans.

The example of Trieste reminds us that time can be a palliative. After World War II, Trieste was organized as a free state, or in UN language, a *corpus separatum*. In 1954, Britain and the United States negotiated the London Agreement, a resolution of the Trieste dispute, which awarded the city itself to Italy and divided some of the outlying area (the so-called Zone A and Zone B) between Italy and Yugoslavia. In this resolution, "neither Italy nor Yugoslavia formally renounced its claims to the Free Territory. For the Great Powers, however, the territorial settlement was final" (Novak 1970, 460). Whereas the Yugoslavs "preferred to look at the London Agreement as a final accord, the Italian legal experts underlined its provisional character" (Novak 1970, 463).[11] In particular, it never referred to the imposition of Yugoslav or Italian sovereignty over the disputed zones because Italian public opinion in particular would not accept forfeiture of their sacred land. Some twenty years later, however, the Council on Security and Cooperation in Europe (CSCE), in a conference in Helsinki (July 30-August 1, 1975), proposed a treaty to resolve the border dispute, which took less than three months to negotiate (Unger and Šegulja 1990, 39; *New York Times* Nov. 11, 1975, 34).

10. With his usual pithiness, Samuel Lewis notes that "if diplomats and politicians could only place the word, 'sovereignty,' in a deep freeze somewhere for several decades, a workable and politically acceptable arrangement for the Holy City would become infinitely more achievable" (1996, 695).

11. The British negotiator Sir Geoffrey Harrison has pointed out: "The Yugoslavs wanted it to be a final settlement, but we knew that this would be quite unacceptable to the Italians; that any solution we took to the Italians which suggested that the solution would be final would not stand a chance of acceptance. So I think we did devise a formula in the end which worked, which was that the U.S. government and Her Majesty's government would not support any further claims by either side in the area, and this satisfied the Yugoslavs and was acceptable to the Italians. There were doors and windows left open for the future, but no matter" (Campbell 1976, 52).

Ruth Lapidoth's extraordinary contribution to discussion of the future of Jerusalem is the wisdom that the focus on the emotive language of sovereignty has led only to conflict, in Moshe Hirsch's terms, zero-sum games in which one side wins and another side loses (see chapters 2 and 3). Far more useful is the effort to devise areas where one community can, in a functional manner, exercise power and control over aspects of their lives in ways that do not force a stark resolution of the sovereignty question. Thus, Lapidoth asks us to think through the implications of what she calls "functional sovereignty" and "suspended sovereignty" in treating Jerusalem's future. The contributors to this volume point the way toward developing the kind of innovative approaches that meet both Israeli needs and Arab sensibilities.

These efforts are not likely to succeed given the atmosphere of violence that followed the collapse of the Camp David 2000 and Taba Summits. While the road may be large and other parties wiser, there is little doubt that whenever Israelis and Palestinians finally sit down to discuss the matter of Jerusalem and whatever the range of issues on the table, these essays will provide a central empirical background and focus for those discussions. They are the facts and data out of which peace agreements must be made.

PART ONE

Issues of Law and Politics

1

Jerusalem in Our Time

Past, Present, Future

Maya Choshen

The purpose of this chapter is to acquaint the reader with the social, economic, demographic, and other day-to-day issues of the city of Jerusalem.[1] Jerusalem is known by many names, most of them spiritual. Called the Holy City in literature and by the media, Jerusalem is yearned for by multitudes of believers. But Jerusalem is not only a holy city that exists "for the sake of believers" or only the name of a political-diplomatic issue. It is also the largest city in Israel, home to approximately 650,000 residents. It is a complex, fascinating city of exquisite treasures and numerous historical and religious sites, which are enhanced by the qualities of its magnificent physical setting. Jerusalem's earthly features are bound up with its spiritual ones; the dilemmas of managing the city and its surroundings and of planning future development for the benefit of the inhabitants must take into consideration that Jerusalem is the capital of Israel, bears a unique status for the three monotheistic religions, is of major geopolitical importance, and possesses singular historic and physical features.

Following its reunification in June 1967, Jerusalem, previously a city sit-

---

1. The origin of the data presented in this chapter, unless otherwise noted, is *The Statistical Yearbook of Jerusalem,* edited by Maya Choshen and Naama Shahar, and published annually by the Jerusalem municipality and the Jerusalem Institute for Israel Studies.

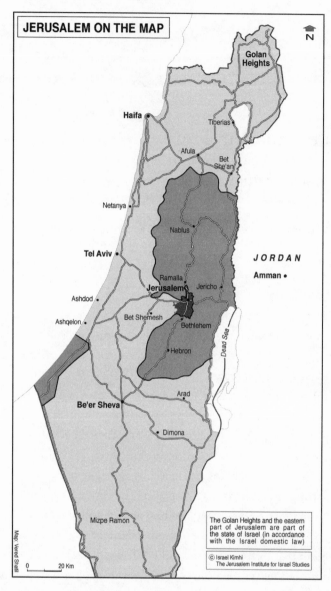

Map 1.1

uated on a hostile border at the eastern extremity of a narrow territorial corridor, found itself located at the center of an area containing a large number
of Jewish and Arab settlements (map 1.1).

Jerusalem is today Israel's largest city in area and in population, both of

Jews and non-Jews. However, it is not the country's major urban area, a distinction that belongs to metropolitan Tel Aviv.

The national policy of strengthening the capital, which had been pursued since the state's establishment, received added momentum following the city's reunification, which spurred physical, demographic, and economic growth. However, the development boom that began in the late 1960s tapered off in the 1980s. In recent years, the authorities have tried to restore the momentum by launching new initiatives in high-tech industry and infrastructure development, building modern commercial centers, promoting tourism, and accelerating housing construction.

The agenda of the peace process, specifically the "final-status" talks and the resolution of the "Jerusalem question," has again placed the city at the hub of national and international debates. The city's Jews and Arabs can do much to strengthen Jerusalem by exploiting its immense latent potential and by co-operating in projects of joint development that will lead it into an era of peace.

In early 1998, the question of expanding Jerusalem's municipal boundaries was raised once more and is currently on the agenda, following a government decision to bolster the city by means of economic, physical, and social measures such as the extension of its municipal boundaries westward, inside the Green Line (the Israeli-Jordanian border until June 1967). The reasons for the decision were basically the same as those cited a decade ago by the commission of inquiry on the boundaries of Jerusalem: the need to strengthen Jerusalem as Israel's capital while maintaining the current proportion of the Jewish population within the overall population despite a growing scarcity of available land for construction, without which the goals of population growth cannot be attained.

Area and Municipal Boundaries

Jerusalem is Israel's largest city in size and population. Its area within the municipal boundaries is 126 square kilometers. By comparison, the area of the second largest city, Tel Aviv, is 51 square kilometers. Since November 30, 1949, the date on which it was decided that the armistice lines are congruent with the lines determined in the Armistice Agreement signed at

Rhodes, Jerusalem's boundaries have been modified a number of times. The most substantial change was effected immediately after the city's reunification. A less-significant although still meaningful change occurred in 1993, and currently a move is under way to expand the city's boundaries significantly westward. In addition to the substantial changes that are discussed below, five minor boundaries changes were effected. Four of them took place before the city's reunification and brought about the incorporation of neighborhoods west of the city, which were in geographical proximity to it but had not been included within its area of jurisdiction. The fifth change occurred after the city's reunification and consisted mainly of mutual border rectifications involving the Matteh Yehuda Regional Council, which is located west of the city.

The point of departure for a discussion of the city's boundaries is the Partition Resolution adopted by the United Nations General Assembly on November 29, 1947, which recommended internationalization for Jerusalem. This change would have entailed the establishment of a special international regime for the city, making it a *corpus separatum* (separate body) (map 1.2).

The resolution triggered Israel's War of Independence, in which heavy fighting took place in the city and on its access roads. At the war's end, the Old City and east Jerusalem remained in the hands of the Jordanian army, whereas west Jerusalem was controlled by the Israel Defense Forces. Hostilities ended with a cease-fire agreement signed on November 30, 1948. Two lines were drawn on an accompanying map (scale of 1:20,000; see map 1.2) to show the positions of each side at the time. These lines were perpetuated in the Israel-Jordan armistice accord signed at Rhodes on April 3, 1949 (Hazan 1995). The area of west Jerusalem, under Israeli control, was 38 square kilometers, whereas the area of Jordanian-controlled east Jerusalem was only 6 square kilometers. Jerusalem's reunification following the Six Day War involved the most far-reaching and dramatic change in the city's area of jurisdiction, which was enlarged by some 70 square kilometers on June 28, 1967, in an accelerated legislative process. With an area of 108 square kilometers, the city now encompassed west Jerusalem, east Jerusalem, the Old City, and extensive additional areas mainly to the north and south, including twenty-eight villages, some of which were annexed completely,

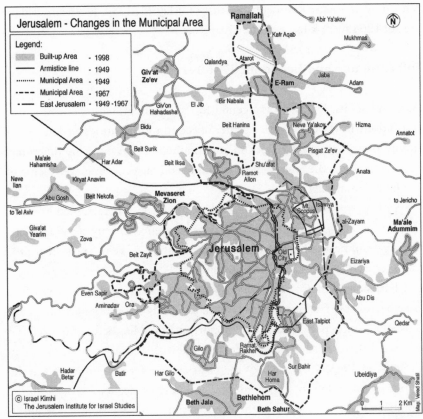

Map 1.2

though most only in part. In the late 1980s, the authorities reevaluated the city's boundaries.

On February 10, 1988, the director-general of the Interior Ministry, acting on the request of the mayor of Jerusalem, appointed a commission of inquiry to address the question of redrawing the boundaries. The Jerusalem municipality wanted to annex to the city another 30 square kilometers, all lying west of the city on the Israeli side of the former Green Line to avoid diplomatic and international problems (Hazan 1995). Annexation of territory in the west would also serve the municipality's policy of not only enlarging the city's Jewish majority but also strengthening it by adding a more economically established population. Ultimately the boundaries were extended by 15 square kilometers, so that on May 11, 1993, Jerusalem had an area of 126 square kilometers (see map 1.2).

Infrastructure and Economic Features

As a capital city, Jerusalem is a center for government, national, and public institutions; however, it is not a center of economic or business activity. Economic power in Israel resides in metropolitan Tel Aviv. This functional alignment affects the employment structure and the economic well-being of the Jerusalem residents.

In large measure, Jerusalem's economic profile is determined by three factors: the city's distinctive demographic makeup, lengthy periods of adverse geopolitical conditions, and a long tradition of being a city that provides services and acts as a religious center.

Jerusalem's employment structure and the type of work the city offers have been stable for the past generation, especially within the Jewish sector. Throughout this period, the large proportion of public-sector employers has remained the characteristic feature of the Jewish employment structure in the city. In 1968, 43 percent of the city's labor force was employed in the public sector, rising to 49 percent in 2000. A steep decline occurred in the number of Jews employed in the construction industry, from 9 percent in 1968 to 4 percent in 2000, their place being taken by Arabs. Similarly, fewer Jews are employed in industry, the decrease here being from 16 percent in 1968 to 9 percent in 2000. However, these data do not indicate a decline in the economic activity of the city's industrial sector or in the scope of industrial production for export.

The principal source of the data for the economic indicators of the population is the Labor Force Survey, which is conducted by the Central Bureau of Statistics and reflects accurately the workforce in Israel. However, in Jerusalem, the Arab population has cooperated only marginally with the survey since the beginning of the Intifada (Palestinian uprising) in December 1987, with the result that it does not reflect the situation of the workforce among the Arab population of east Jerusalem. As a result, the Central Bureau of Statistics has issued the following guideline:"Due to difficulties in assembling data on east Jerusalem from 1988 onwards, figures concerning

Arabs and others should be treated with reservation" (State of Israel 1997, 30). Consequently, the data cited in this chapter refer mainly to the Jews in the workforce.

The cross-section of employment in Jerusalem differs from that of Israel's other major cities (fig. 1.1). The proportion of public-service workers is twice that of Tel Aviv, but only half as many Jerusalemites are employed in the financial sector as compared with Tel Aviv. In industry, too, Jerusalem has a lower employment rate than either Tel Aviv or Haifa (if only the Jewish population is taken into account, the differences become even more stark).

There is also a difference between the Jewish and Arab populations in terms of the employment structure within Jerusalem itself, as there is in occupations, which reflect income potential better than the economic branches. In contrast to the high percentage of Jews employed in the public services and their high concentration in academic and scientific occupations, a strikingly high proportion of the Arab labor force is employed in industry, construction, commerce, and hospitality. As of the early 1990s, approximately 15 percent of Jerusalem's Arabs workforce were employed in construction (versus 3 percent of Jews), 24 percent in commerce and hospitality (12 percent among Jews), and 20 percent in public services, as compared with 45 percent of the Jewish workforce (Kimhi 1993, 13).

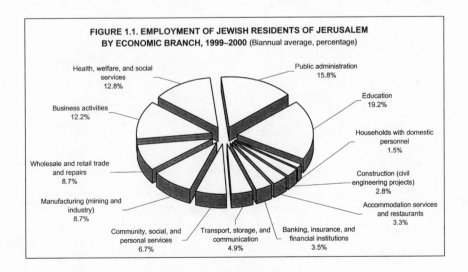

FIGURE 1.1. EMPLOYMENT OF JEWISH RESIDENTS OF JERUSALEM
BY ECONOMIC BRANCH, 1999–2000 (Biannual average, percentage)

Health, welfare, and social services 12.8%

Public administration 15.8%

Business activities 12.2%

Education 19.2%

Wholesale and retail trade and repairs 8.7%

Households with domestic personnel 1.5%

Manufacturing (mining and industry) 8.7%

Construction (civil engineering projects) 2.8%

Community, social, and personal services 6.7%

Transport, storage, and communication 4.9%

Banking, insurance, and financial institutions 3.5%

Accommodation services and restaurants 3.3%

Economic Status of the Population

Average income in Jerusalem is lower than in the other major cities in Israel, primarily owing to the city's employment structure and its distinctive population makeup. The Arabs and *haredi* (ultraorthodox) Jews tend to have large families and a relatively low rate of participation in the labor force, and many of those among them who do work hold low-paying jobs (fig. 1.2)—hence, the low economic status of the city and its residents, a situation clearly reflected in the poverty data for Jerusalem (fig. 1.3).

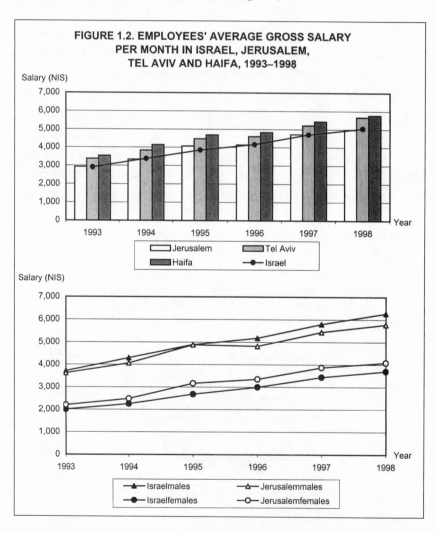

FIGURE 1.2. EMPLOYEES' AVERAGE GROSS SALARY PER MONTH IN ISRAEL, JERUSALEM, TEL AVIV AND HAIFA, 1993–1998

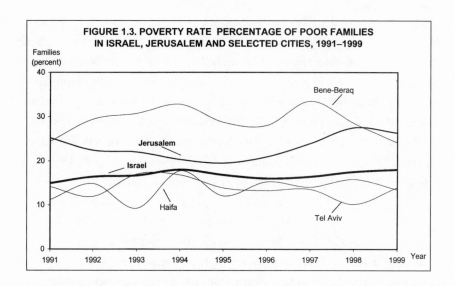

FIGURE 1.3. POVERTY RATE PERCENTAGE OF POOR FAMILIES IN ISRAEL, JERUSALEM AND SELECTED CITIES, 1991–1999

To conclude, the employment structure in Jerusalem—a low level of manufacturing and business activity—combined with the distinctive composition of the population and a low income level impair the city's social and economic resilience, and undermine its ability to strengthen its status as an economic center and a hub of services for the metropolitan area.

Tourism

Jerusalem is a religious center for the three monotheistic religions—Judaism, Christianity, and Islam. The remnants of the city's spectacular and important history draw many visitors, and Jerusalem is considered one of the world's most beautiful cities. As such, it is a tourist haven for Jews and Christians, especially pilgrims of both faiths. With the advent of full regional peace, it will undoubtedly attract Muslim tourism. The peace agreements with the Palestinians and with Jordan will make Jerusalem a major junction for tourists passing between Jordan and Israel and other Middle Eastern countries. Tourism, already an important component of the city's economy, could become even more significant in peacetime. Because the security situation has a major effect, prolonged calm and safety for local residents and for visitors will enhance Jerusalem's allure for both internal and external tourism.

On the eve of the city's reunification, tourism development in the form of hotels and rooms was under way primarily in the eastern section, where the main tourist attractions are located. The act of reunification and the concomitant growth in tourism potential brought about the development of a tourism infrastructure and a boom in hotel construction in west Jerusalem. The great majority of rooms for tourists are now located in west Jerusalem.

In 2000, there were seventy-one hotels with 9,107 rooms in Jerusalem, of which thirty-eight hotels containing 7,127 rooms were in west Jerusalem and thirty-three hotels with 1,980 rooms were in east Jerusalem.

Approximately one-fifth of all the hotel rooms in Israel are located in Jerusalem (fig. 1.4). In 2000, 1,211,600 guests stayed in Jerusalem, 74 percent of them tourists from abroad. Foreign tourists spent an average of 3.3 nights in Jerusalem, local tourists 1.6 nights. The advent of peace and the continuous growth of world tourism will increase the number of visitors to Jerusalem, and the Jerusalem municipality therefore intends to go on expanding and consolidating the city's tourism industry.

The Educational System in Jerusalem

The educational system in Jerusalem is Israel's largest and the most complex in terms of diversity of sectors. The large number of schoolchildren in the city is owing to the size of the population but more specifically to the fact

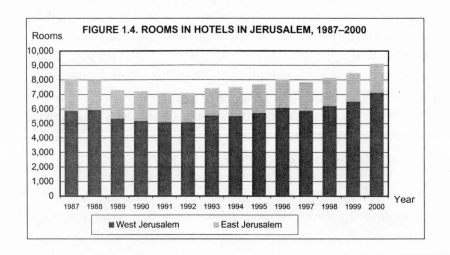

FIGURE 1.4. ROOMS IN HOTELS IN JERUSALEM, 1987–2000

that a substantial portion of the population—Arabs and *haredi* Jews—tend to have large families.

The educational system in Jerusalem is intricate and complex, mirroring in large degree the complexity of the city's population. The educational system in Jerusalem can be divided into four main currents:

1. state (secular) education, where the vast majority of the students are secular and traditionalist;

2. state-religious education, where the overwhelming majority of the students are religious and traditionalist Jews;

3. independent education—i.e., *haredi* education—where the overwhelming majority of the students come from ultraorthodox circles;

4. education in the Arab sector, which is divided between municipal education (under the auspices of the Jerusalem municipality) and private education, the latter largely religious in character and administered by the Waqf (Muslim religious trust) or by the Christian churches.

Until 1993, all the municipal educational services were concentrated in one municipal unit. Following a decision by the Municipal Council on November 29, 1993, the educational services were split: alongside Manhi (Jerusalem Education Authority), the Ultraorthodox Educational Division was established. Manhi is responsible for education services in the state, state-religious, and municipal Arab schools. The Ultraorthodox Educational Division is responsible for *haredi* education. State and state-religious education bear distinctive traits of public education, including a comprehensive inspection system and Education Ministry supervision of the curricula. The independent system is viewed as recognized but unofficial, entailing limited supervision by the Education Ministry and the local government. Those bodies generally do not determine or intervene in the curricula or in the teaching methods used in the schools of the independent educational system. In these schools, there is complete separation between boys and girls, who in fact attend different schools. There is a heavy emphasis on sacred studies, and most of the students do not sit for the matriculation exams, which are a condition for admission to the country's institutions of higher education.

Manhi, through its Arab Education Division, is responsible for the municipal educational services for the Arabs of east Jerusalem. In the 2000–2001 school year, there were 30,989 students in the Arab educational system, in addition to 13,955 students in the church-run private system and private schools and another 6,350 students in the private Waqf-run schools. Since 1994, the municipality, with extra governmental money budgeted for this purpose, has invested intensively in enhancing the Arab educational system, including the stepped-up building of classrooms and schools. This initiative has encountered considerable difficulties in addition to budgetary limitations. One of the most serious obstacles is the shortage of available public land on a scale large enough to build schools that meet the accepted standards of the educational system for the next century. It is also important to note that the students in the Arab municipal system follow the Jordanian curriculum and sit for the same matriculation exams as students in Jordan.

In the 2000–2001 school year, there were 192,000 pupils in the Jerusalem school system. Of them, 97,022 attended institutions administered by the Jerusalem Education Authority (JEA): 66,581 pupils in the Hebrew sector and 31,000 in the Arab sector. Approximately 74,000 pupils attended Ultraorthodox Educational Division schools, and about 20,000 pupils attended nonmunicipal schools in east Jerusalem.

Over the years, the proportion of *haredi* pupils in Jerusalem has risen steadily, whereas the share of students in state education has constantly declined. For example, in the 2000–2001 school year, there was an increase of 3 percent in the number of *haredi* pupils getting elementary education as compared with the previous year, but a 2 percent decline in the number of elementary-level pupils in the JEA's Hebrew sector (state nonreligious track).

Jerusalem takes pride in being the home of the Hebrew University, an institution of world renown. However, its allure has dimmed somewhat in recent years. At the end of the 1960s, students at the Hebrew University accounted for 36 percent of all students in Israeli universities, but this ratio fell to 25 percent in 1990–91 and to 19 percent in 2000–2001. The number of students at the Hebrew University increased from 12,600 in 1969–70 to 21,400 in 2000–2001, a growth of 70 percent (fig. 1.5); however, the number of university students in Israel rose in this period from 35,400 to 113,000— an increase of 220 percent. Also, in the 2000–2001 school year, there were 14,370 students in nonuniversity institutions of higher learning in Jerusalem.

In the 1999–2000–2001 academic year, the Hebrew University will for the first time open a Department of Technological Studies. From a first-year

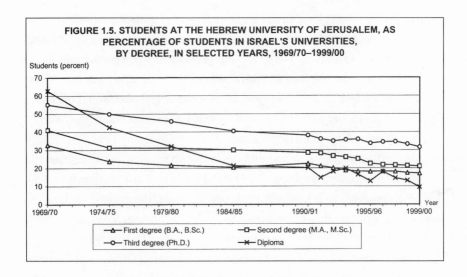

FIGURE 1.5. STUDENTS AT THE HEBREW UNIVERSITY OF JERUSALEM, AS PERCENTAGE OF STUDENTS IN ISRAEL'S UNIVERSITIES, BY DEGREE, IN SELECTED YEARS, 1969/70–1999/00

class of 100, it is projected to grow to about 3,000 students—a refreshing change in the university that followed many years of discussion. A major reason for establishing the department is to bolster participation in advanced industry, growth branches, and high-tech fields, and through them to strengthen the city's economy and attract a strong population. It is with the same goal that a technological college is planned to open soon in Jerusalem, which will train at the intermediate and some of the higher levels for the technological activity that will be developed in the city.

Planning and Construction

When Jerusalem was unified in 1967, no single master plan for the city existed. During the nineteen years of the city's partition, each side, the Israeli and the Jordanian, carried out planning based on its own conceptions, needs, and goals. An approach relating to a united city with one plan first emerged in 1968, with the completion of the master plan for Jerusalem. However, because this guideline lacked statutory force, it could not be utilized to issue building permits or to develop the infrastructure or public institutions as obligated by Israel's Planning and Construction Law. In fact, only 8 percent of the area that was annexed to the city was covered by an approved plan, dating from the period of Jordanian rule, and it referred solely to the Old City. west Jerusalem had an approved plan dating from 1959 that was inappropriate for the new situation in the wake of the city's reunification and expansion. Preparation of new plans proceeded lethargically mainly for two reasons: (1) the absence of a formal land settlement, which leaves land ownership unclear, and (2) the absence of a municipal planning tradition in the rural areas incorporated in Jerusalem's area of jurisdiction.

The desire to avoid infringing on the private property of the Arab population led to a decision against expropriating 40 percent of the private area for public needs, as permitted under the Planning and Construction Law. The Arab population is unused to expropriations on this scale, which are essential to supply public services such as education, health, culture, religion, roads, and other forms of infrastructure.

Land settlement is a key element for municipal planning and development, as well as for understanding the processes at work. Most of the areas that became part of the city when the municipal boundaries were extended had not undergone land settlement. Ownership had been arranged only in the tax books, not in the Land Registry Office. In most of the area annexed to Jerusalem, land was divided on an agricultural basis and as such precluded urban development. Urban planning and development required the consolidation and reparcelation of land, a difficult and protracted process even in a modern city and immeasurably more so among the rural, traditional Arab population of expanded Jerusalem (Kimhi forthcoming).

Jewish Building

The extension of Jerusalem's boundaries in June 1967 to incorporate large unbuilt areas enabled the building of new neighborhoods on the city's fringes. Reunification generated a building boom beginning in 1968–69 with the construction of the Ramat Eshkol and Givat Hamivtar neighborhoods. The next stage came in 1971–1972 in the form of new neighborhoods adjacent to Ramat Eshkol: Givat Shapira (French Hill), Maalot Dafna, and Sanhedriya Murhevet. The third wave of building—the major one in terms of the developing, growing, and shaping the city—was characterized by large-scale construction of neighborhoods on the periphery. Unlike the building from 1968 to 1971, which was contiguous with existing neighborhoods, the new, neighborhoods were established at the edges of the city's expanded municipal boundaries, at a considerable distance from previously built-up areas. These new neighborhoods were Gilo in the south, East Talpiot in the southeast, Neve Ya'akov in the north, and Ramat Allon in the northwest.

In the mid-1980s, construction began on the largest neighborhood in the eastern section of the city, Pisgat Zeev; in the western section, recent years have seen the establishment of the neighborhoods of Har Nof, Givat Masua, Manahat, and Ramat Beit Hakerem (map 1.3). The extensive establishment of new neighborhoods that characterized the 1970s has given way more recently to an effort to upgrade the city's infrastructure, with the emphasis on traffic arteries and the building of public institutions. Improvement of the transportation infrastructure became a critical necessity because of the high territorial dispersal of the population, the intensifying interrelations with the settlements around the city, and the greater level of motorization of the city's residents.

In November 1995, there were 169,149 residential units in Jerusalem: 136,775 in the Jewish areas and 32,374 in the Arab areas—a ratio of eighty to twenty. Of these units, 150,357 were inhabited: 120,594 in the Jewish areas (80 percent) and 29,763 in the Arab areas (20 percent). Of all the new units, 44,587 were built in the Jewish neighborhoods annexed to Jerusalem after 1967, constituting a third of the units added in the Jewish sector of Jerusalem during the last thirty years (State of Israel 1997).

Arab Building

Initially, the Arabs requested few building permits, and there was little pressure on the Jerusalem municipality from that sector in this regard.[2] However, as the Arab population increased rapidly, pressure mounted. In the first years after the city's reunification, the municipal planning system was not yet deployed to prepare master plans and detailed programs for the Arab sector at the requisite pace. The Arab population reacted by engaging in illegal building. In order to avoid turning Arab residents without housing solutions

2. Data on Arab building are derived from unpublished studies by Israel Kimhi of the Jerusalem Institute for Israel Studies.

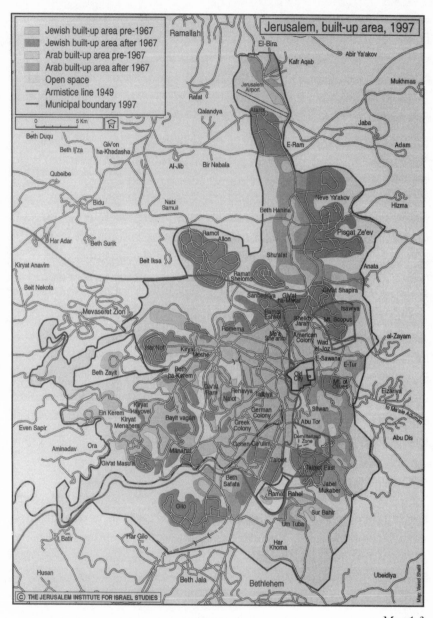

Jewish built-up area pre-1967
Jewish built-up area after 1967
Arab built-up area pre-1967
Arab built-up area after 1967
Open space
Armistice line 1949
Municipal boundary 1997

0   5 Km

Jerusalem, built-up area, 1997

© THE JERUSALEM INSTITUTE FOR ISRAEL STUDIES

Map: Vered Shatil

Map 1.3

into violators of the building regulations, the municipality applied special clauses in the Planning and Construction Law that make it possible to issue building permits during a plan's preparatory stages provided the construction will not harm overall planning. The idea was to enable residents to build adjacent to existing houses without infringing on the land reserves that would be needed for roads and public services in future development. At the same time, an attempt was made to plan the city in a manner that would allow public services to be provided and infrastructure work to proceed on roads, sewerage systems, and the like. The conditions for providing such services are adequate allocations for public needs and efficient, concentrated building.

The Arab population found this planning decision restrictive because it prevented them from building wherever they wished. In any event, despite the objective difficulties of development and building in the Arab sector, construction there has been—and continues to be—carried out on a massive scale. An analysis of aerial photographs taken over the same sites at different junctures between 1968 and 1995 and of data based on the granting of permits and the collection of residential property tax shows the existence of large-scale building in the Arab sector. Property tax figures, for example, indicate a growth of 122 percent in the number of Arab residential units from 1967 to 1995 (see map 1.3).

Housing Density

Overall, the Arab sector has a lower housing density (number of residential units per unit of area) than the Jewish, apart from the Muslim Quarter in the Old City and Shuafat, both areas of extremely high density. The density in the Arab sector is 1.9 residential units per dunam (4 dunams equals 1 acre), as compared with 5.9 units per dunam in the Jewish sector. (In the Muslim Quarter, the density is 86 residential units per dunam, and in Shuafat 32.)

Demographic Trends and Population Distribution

Rate of Population Growth

Jerusalem has had a Jewish majority since the middle of the nineteenth century. At the beginning of the British Mandate period, it was the most important city in Palestine and the most populous.

Between 1946 and 1967, Jerusalem's Jews outpaced the Arabs in rate of increase. The Jewish population increased by 99 percent, to 197,700, whereas the Arab population grew in the same period by only 75 percent, totaling 68,800.

In September 1967, the population of Jerusalem stood at 267,000: 197,700 Jews and 68,800 Arabs. In the thirty-three years between the city's reunification and the end of 2000, the population of Jerusalem grew by 147 percent; during this period, the Jewish population registered an increase of 127 percent and the Arab population an increase of 204 percent. The result was that the share of Jews in the city's population declined from 74 percent in 1967 to 68 percent today. The most rapid growth took place among Muslims, owing to their high rate of natural increase (the result of the difference between number of births and number of deaths).

Sources of Population Growth

Demographic processes reflect the fusion between the characteristics of the population at a given time and economic, social, and political processes in the state in general and in the specific city or region in particular. Demographic trends consist of natural movements, specifically natural-increase and migration movements (international migration, internal migration).

Population growth is the result of natural increase and the migration balance. If the migration balance declines, the natural-increase component in population growth assumes correspondingly greater importance.

Tables 1.1 and 1.2 and figures 1.6 and 1.7 show the rapid growth of the Arab population in Jerusalem as compared to the rate of Jewish increase. As these data show, the reality in the city conflicts with the declared govern-

TABLE I.I

Population and Population Growth in Jerusalem, 1967–2000

	Total		*Jews*		*Arabs & Others*	
Year	Population (thousands)	Population growth (in %)	Population (thousands)	Population growth (in %)	Population (thousands)	Population growth (in %)
1967	266.3	NA	197.7	NA	68.6	NA
1977	376.0	41.2	272.3	37.7	103.7	51.2
1987	482.6	28.4	346.1	27.1	136.5	31.6
1997	622.1	28.9	429.1	24.0	193.0	41.4
1998	657.5	NA	448.8	NA	208.7	NA
1967– 2000	NA	146.9	NA	127.0	NA	204.2

Source: Choshen and Shahar 2000, 52. NA = not applicable.

ment policy, since Jerusalem's reunification, of maintaining the demographic advantage of the Jewish population vis-à-vis the Arab population.

Natural increase. Natural increase is a major source of population growth in
Jerusalem. In 1967, the Jewish population's rate of natural increase was far
below that of the Arab population (fig. 1.8). The higher rate of the Arabs was
owing primarily to their higher birth rate. The past thirty years have seen
changes in the natural-increase rates of both Jews and Arabs. Among Arabs,
the rate of natural increase declined rapidly owing to a falloff in the number of
births. At the same time, the mortality rate among the Arab population also
underwent a rapid decline as a result of a significant improvement in the level
of health services, preventive medicine, and the general standard of living.
Among the Jewish population, the rate of natural increase also grew between
1967 and 1988. As a result of these two parallel processes, Jews and Arabs had
about the same natural-increase rate by the end of 1987. However, since 1988,
as a result of the Intifada (which had a baby boom effect), the birth rate among
the Arab population rose, inducing an increase in the rate of natural increase.

At present, annual population growth in Jerusalem as a result of natural
increase is about 8,500 Jews and 6,000 Arabs.

Birth rate. In 1967, the birth rate among Jerusalem's Arabs was 43 per
1,000, but by 1987 it had fallen dramatically by 30 percent, to 29.8 per

TABLE I.2

Population of Jerusalem by Groups, 1967–2000

Year	Total (in thousands)	Thousands		Percent	
		Jews	Arabs & Others	Jews	Arabs & Others
1967	266.3	197.7	68.6	74.2	25.8
1970	291.7	215.5	76.2	73.9	26.1
1972	313.8	230.3	83.5	73.4	26.6
1974	346.0	252.8	93.2	73.1	26.9
1976	366.3	266.0	100.3	72.6	27.4
1977	376.0	272.3	103.7	72.4	27.6
1978	386.6	279.4	107.2	72.3	27.7
1979	398.2	287.4	110.8	72.2	27.8
1980	407.1	292.3	114.8	71.8	28.2
1981	415.0	297.6	117.4	71.7	28.3
1982	424.4	304.2	120.2	71.7	28.3
1983	428.7	306.3	122.4	71.4	28.6
1984	447.8	321.1	126.5	71.7	28.2
1985	457.7	327.7	130.0	71.6	28.4
1986	468.9	336.1	132.8	71.7	28.3
1987	482.6	346.1	136.5	71.7	28.3
1988	493.5	353.9	139.6	71.7	28.3
1989	504.1	361.5	142.6	71.7	28.3
1990	524.5	378.2	146.3	72.1	27.9
1991	544.2	392.8	151.3	72.2	27.8
1992	556.5	401.0	155.5	72.1	27.9
1993	567.2	406.4	160.8	71.7	28.3
1994	578.8	411.9	166.9	71.2	28.8
1995	591.4	417.0	174.4	70.5	29.5
1996	602.1	421.2	180.9	70.0	30.0
1997	622.1	429.1	193.9	69.0	31.0
1998	633.7	433.6	200.1	68.4	31.6
1999	646.3	444.9	201.3	68.8	31.1
2000	657.5	448.8	208.7	68.3	31.7

Source: Choshen and Shahar 2000, 48.

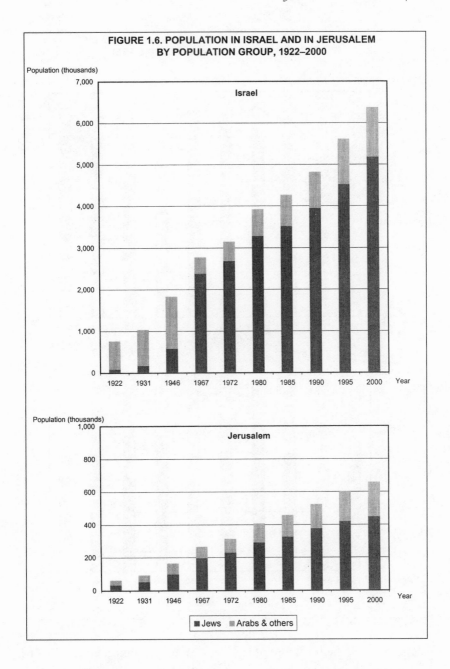

FIGURE 1.6. POPULATION IN ISRAEL AND IN JERUSALEM
BY POPULATION GROUP, 1922–2000

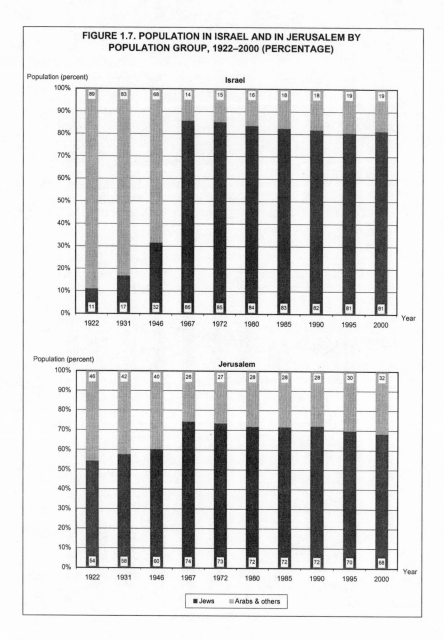

FIGURE 1.7. POPULATION IN ISRAEL AND IN JERUSALEM BY POPULATION GROUP, 1922–2000 (PERCENTAGE)

1,000. In 1988, the birth rate of Jews and Arabs was almost equal (28.8 per 1,000 among Jews, 29.8 among Arabs). By 2000, the birth rate among Arabs has risen to 36.4 per 1,000.

Although the birth rate among Jews in Jerusalem has declined gradually

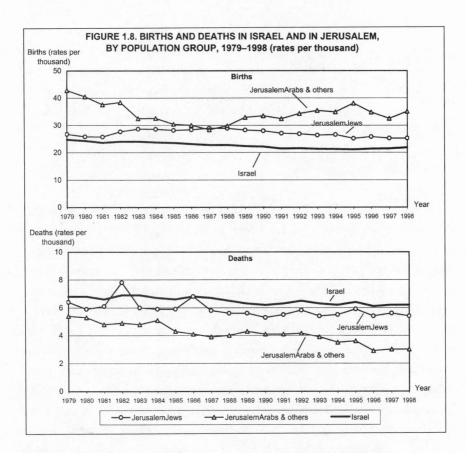

FIGURE 1.8. BIRTHS AND DEATHS IN ISRAEL AND IN JERUSALEM, BY POPULATION GROUP, 1979–1998 (rates per thousand)

in recent years, it has been, throughout the entire period being surveyed, considerably higher than that of the general countrywide rate for Jews (24.8 per 1,000 in Jerusalem as compared to a national rate of 18.5 per 1,000). The reason for this disparity is the high birth rate among *haredi* Jews in Jerusalem (where the average *haredi* family has six children).

Mortality. The mortality rate of the city's Arab and Jewish populations has also changed considerably since 1967. Among Arabs, it declined from 9 deaths per 1,000 to 3 per 1,000—a figure that has been maintained since 1988—representing a decrease of 67 percent.

At the beginning of the period, Jews had a lower mortality rate than Arabs. However, that rate declined more slowly, so that at present the Arab population has a lower mortality rate than the Jewish population, which, again, is owing to the improvement in the sanitation, health, and preventive medicine services among the Arab population, but also to the differential age structure of each group. The Jewish population is older, and if the health services available to two population groups are of an approximately equal level, the mortality rate will be higher within the older population group. At the same time, infant mortality remains lower among Jews than among Arabs in Jerusalem.

Migration Movements

Internal migration. The first decade after reunification was characterized by positive migration rates of Jews to the city; that is, more Jews moved to Jerusalem than left it. In the second decade, a low negative migration balance was recorded, whereas the third decade saw relatively high negative rates. Since 1988, Jerusalem has been losing about 5,000 to 8,000 residents a year, largely owing to an increase in the number of residents leaving the city. The proportion of former Jerusalem residents who are moving to the area around the city is on the rise, currently standing at about 50 percent of the migrants from the city. This trend has strengthened the settled area in the Jerusalem area and helped develop metropolitan Jerusalem.

The migration processes among the Arab population have not been studied adequately, and the available figures are unreliable. Nevertheless, it should be emphasized that such migration is taking place among the Arab population in Jerusalem as well as among West Bank Arabs. The result is the bolstering of the settled Arab areas around Jerusalem.

Figure 1.9 shows the long-term migration balance for Jerusalem. Research conducted in the Jerusalem Institute for Israel Studies found that housing factors are among the most important reasons that cause Jerusalem residents to leave the city (Choshen 2000). Approximately 41 percent of those who moved away cited housing, and particularly the high prices, as the most important factor that prompted them to leave. Of those who cited housing as the key factor, 88 percent noted the high cost of housing as the decisive cause.

Housing is the dominant factor for those who move to localities near Jerusalem but is less important for those who move farther away; its importance is particularly low for those who move to the area of Tel Aviv and the

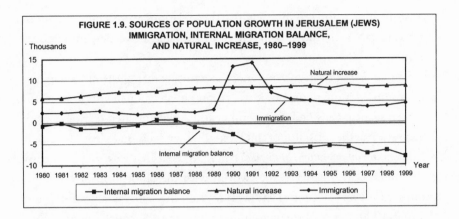

FIGURE 1.9. SOURCES OF POPULATION GROWTH IN JERUSALEM (JEWS) IMMIGRATION, INTERNAL MIGRATION BALANCE, AND NATURAL INCREASE, 1980–1999

center, which is economically the strongest section of the country. Of those who moved close to Jerusalem, 68 percent noted housing as the most important factor in their decision to leave the city, whereas the comparable figure for those moving to Tel Aviv and the center was only 12 percent.

As in other cities in Israel and elsewhere, housing prices decline as one moves away from the center. Thus, a move to a satellite locality enables the purchase of a larger dwelling—the transition from an apartment to a detached dwelling or from rental to home ownership. However, this transition entails giving up the advantages that accrue from living in the center.

Employment constitutes the second most important factor that induces Jerusalem residents to leave the city; 16 percent noted employment as the most important reason for their decision to move out.

In contrast to housing, the employment factor prompts mainly a move to areas farther from Jerusalem. Thus, 30 percent of those who moved to the area of Tel Aviv and the center and 18 percent of those who moved to Haifa and the north cited employment as the most important factor in their decision to leave Jerusalem. Only 3 percent of those who moved to a locality near Jerusalem cited the employment factor, which is not surprising because the great majority of those who move to metropolitan Jerusalem continue to work in the city.

Family reasons are the third most important factor for leaving Jerusalem, noted as such by 13 percent of those who move out of the city.

It is important to note that local factors that set Jerusalem apart are minor compared with the dominance of housing and employment in terms of motives for leaving. Jewish–Arab relations were rarely noted as a significant factor by those who left: less than half of one percent cited this reason.

Secular-*haredi* relations, and more specifically fear of the city's haredization prompted more people to leave. Approximately 2 percent of those who left cited secular-*haredi* relations, and nearly 7 percent cited fear of the city's haredization as the most important factor in their decision to leave Jerusalem.

International migration: immigration to Israel. Israel is a state that is receptive to immigrants; its history is interwoven with the absorption of immigrant groups from every corner of the world. From the state's establishment until the mid-1960s, most of the new immigrants arrived virtually destitute, and the state assisted them to obtain housing and education and to survive economically until their integration into the society. The responsible national institutions sent many of the new immigrants to localities that bore a high settlement priority at the time. Toward the end of the 1960s, the proportion of new immigrants from affluent countries increased. In contrast to their predecessors, these immigrants were economically independent and did not need state assistance, thus enabling them to choose their place of residence freely.

With its reunification, Jerusalem became a magnet for new immigrants, particularly those from affluent countries (figs. 1.9 and 1.10). In the 1980s,

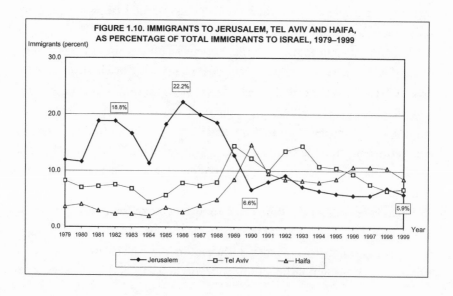

FIGURE 1.10. IMMIGRANTS TO JERUSALEM, TEL AVIV AND HAIFA, AS PERCENTAGE OF TOTAL IMMIGRANTS TO ISRAEL, 1979–1999

approximately 20 percent of all the immigrants to Israel chose to live in Jerusalem (about 3,000 a year). However, in the period of the mass immigration from the former Soviet Union, when most of the new arrivals lacked economic resources, Jerusalem's allure declined drastically. At present, only 4 percent of those who arrived in the 1990s from the former Soviet Union reside in Jerusalem. The high cost of housing in the city and the fact that employment opportunities are largely incommensurate with the needs of the new arrivals have vastly reduced the potential for their absorption in the city. As a result, since 1993 the negative migration rate has exceeded the number of new-immigrant arrivals in Jerusalem.

The new immigrants from the former Soviet Union who arrived in Israel during the 1990s are characterized by a high level of education: a large proportion have university degrees, in many cases postgraduate degrees. There are also a large number of musicians and intellectuals. Yet many of them specialize in fields unsuited to the Israeli labor market and have undergone vocational retraining to enable them to find work more easily. In Jerusalem, the absorption of these new immigrants in the labor market has been relatively difficult because of the language barrier; the city's potential places of employment consist largely of government ministries, public institutions, and institutions of higher learning, where a knowledge of Hebrew is a prerequisite.

The absorption of new immigrants from the former Soviet Union is of great importance for Jerusalem's growth and development. The addition of a working-age population characterized by a high level of education could contribute to the city's economy. Recent years have seen expanded development in high-tech and technologically advanced industries, in which the new immigrants can be absorbed with relative facility. Since 1998, the Jerusalem municipality has made special efforts to make the city more attractive to immigrants from the former Soviet Union by means of explanatory talks in their languages of origin, helping them adjust professionally and easing their integration into the labor market. Attempts are also being made to increase government housing assistance for these new immigrants.

Research studying migration from Jerusalem found that those leaving Jerusalem do not represent the entire population (Choshen 2000). They are in fact mainly young people age twenty-five to forty. Among Jews, the number of *haredim* leaving the city has increased recently, but the share of the general (non*haredi*) population among the leavers is higher. Those moving out of the city from the general population are mainly immigrants from the former Soviet Union and the middle or upper class. Their primary reasons for leaving are housing and employment. Those seeking better housing generally move to settlements near Jerusalem, which provide solutions of two types: for those who cannot afford the high price of housing in Jerusalem, but also for members of the middle and upper class who are seeking quality of life in the form of separate dwellings with land attached, such as is within reach in the city's satellite settlements. The second main group leaving the city—those in search of employment opportunities—moves farther afield, usually to the center of the country. If the strong population that moves to settlements in the Jerusalem area weakens the city by not contributing to municipal taxes, not sending its children to the local educational system, and eventually by reducing their economic, social, and cultural ties with the city. The second group severs its ties with Jerusalem almost completely.

Haredi Jews leaving the city are motivated primarily by less-expensive housing that has recently become available in the *haredi* towns of Betar Illit and Kiryat Sefer, both close to Jerusalem, and in *haredi* neighborhoods in the town of Beit Shemesh.

Population Distribution in the Urban Space

Jerusalem is characterized by a highly diversified population and a mosaic of neighborhoods. Contiguous Jewish and Arab neighborhoods and secular areas abutting *haredi* communities create a singular social and physical fabric. The way of life of each of these groups and the reciprocal relations between them have a profound impact on Jerusalem's day-to-day life and functioning. The city's demographic, social, and cultural complexity can be maintained only by preserving the balance among the diverse population groups.

The city's partition in 1949 separated Jews from Arabs, the former residing on the Israeli side, the latter on the Jordanian side. Jerusalem's reunification and expansion in 1967 again made Jews and Arabs urban neighbors. Most of the Arab population resides in the city's eastern section and is distributed along a north-south axis.

The processes of demographic change that the city experienced brought about a change in the numerical relationship between the different population groups, as well as shifts in their geographical distribution.

Dispersal of the Jewish Population

The city's expansion and the addition of new neighborhoods had a decisive impact on the directions the Jewish population spread (map 1.4). A deliberate policy of maintaining the Jewish-Arab demographic balance combined with a powerful desire to develop Jerusalem brought about the establishment of the new neighborhoods and the consolidation of Israel's hold throughout the entire expanded area of the city. These new neighborhoods were inhabited largely by a young population, most of whom came from the veteran neighborhoods, though some arrived from outside the city. The population in these neighborhoods is gradually aging.

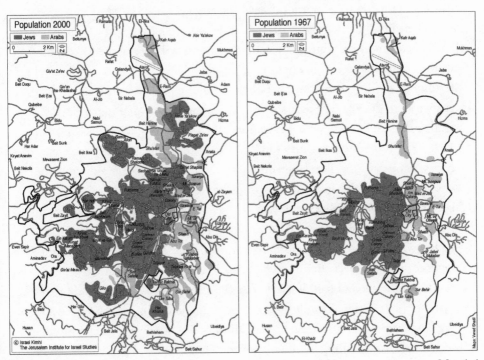

Map 1.4

At the end of 2000, approximately 165,500 Jews resided in Jewish neighborhoods in the areas annexed to the city in 1967, accounting for 38 percent of the city's total Jewish population. It should also be noted that in the areas annexed to the city after 1967, Jews constitute 45 percent of the overall population of the new neighborhoods.

The *Haredi* Space

According to Shilhav, "The haredi space in Jerusalem is undergoing a process of growth and expansion on the one hand, and insularity and segregation on the other. The growth and expansion are in the demographic and territorial realm, while the insularity and segregation exist primarily in the social-cultural sphere. These processes are leading Jerusalem's haredi population into a state of acute ghettoization" (1988, 82).

The *haredi* population has always inclined toward territorial insularity and closure, which indeed was the principal reason for the influx of the *haredim* to the old neighborhoods near the city center.

Their rapid demographic growth is caused by marriage at a young age and an extremely high birth rate. The natural-growth rate of the *haredi* population is the highest of any population group. Thus, for example, the total fertility rate—the average number of children to which a woman can expect to give birth during her lifetime—is 7.61 among the *haredi* population, 2.27 among the rest of the Jewish population, and 5.98 among Muslims (Berman 1998, 8). By comparison, the total fertility rate in the United States currently stands at 2.1. The large number of children in the family and the young age at which *haredim* marry brings about the addition of a large number of new *haredi* families every year. These families need housing, which in Jerusalem is very expensive. The large number of children per family, together with the low income level of *haredi* families, makes it even more difficult for young *haredi* families to purchase a home in Jerusalem.

Until the second half of the 1970s, their main thrust was in and proximate to the traditional *haredi* areas, a process marked by high-density building and a spread into adjacent neighborhoods, usually pushing out the secular and the traditionalist population and in some cases also the Orthodox (map 1.5). Gradually the *haredi* space expanded from the city center north-

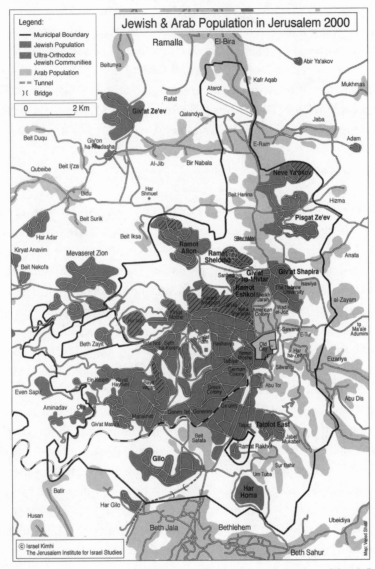

Map 1.5

ward. However, the dynamics of *haredi* demography and resulting housing crunch meant that the incremental crawl toward the north was insufficient to meet the needs of this sector. *Haredim* soon began moving into the new neighborhoods, particularly in the north—Sanhedriya Murhevet, Ramat

Allon, Neve Ya'akov—as well as Har Nof in the west. Until the current building of the Ramat Shelomo neighborhood on the Shuafat Ridge, no neighborhood had been especially designed for a religious and *haredi* population. Ramat Shelomo is the first neighborhood in Jerusalem to be planned for such a population, with all the special services this entails, such as a larger than usual number of ritual baths and synagogues, and apartments with special arrangements for the Sabbath and holidays.

The Arab Space

The Arab population of Jerusalem extends from north to south in a continuous built-up area, which is broken at the Mount Scopus-Givat Hamivtar line of hills by Jewish neighborhoods. The Arabs tend to have large families and a high rate of natural increase, producing rapid population growth. The result is a soaring demand for new residential units and the high-density expansion of built-up areas to meet the demands of young couples for housing. An analysis of developments in the Arab sector of Jerusalem shows the expansion and growth of Arab neighborhoods into empty areas in both the south and the north, together with high-density building in the rural areas annexed to the city in 1967. In recent years, these trends have also brought about a constant growth of the Arab settlements around Jerusalem. The Arab population is spilling over the municipal boundaries in the search for housing solutions but also for sites on which to establish businesses and institutions. Kimhi's complex, comprehensive study (1998) shows widespread building for the Arab population. In the first five years after the city's reunification, most of the Arab building took place within Jerusalem's area of jurisdiction. Since the mid-1980s, it has been concentrated in the settlements around the city. The major reason for the new trend is a shortage of available land within the city and a steep increase in the price of land in east Jerusalem. The difference between the Jewish and Arab sectors from this aspect is that Arab building abuts on existing urban or rural settlements and expands them, whereas Jewish building is concentrated primarily in urban locales, many of them new (see map 1.5).

Summary

In the past thirty years, the population of Jerusalem has undergone constant growth. In the 1970s, growth was rapid, propelled by massive building of outlying neighborhoods and a drive to bolster economic development. The housing supply created by the large-scale building, together with convenient prices, drew internal migrants to Jerusalem and reduced the numbers leaving the city. There was another relatively intensive spurt of growth in the early part of the 1990s, as immigrants who were part of the influx of immigration from the former Soviet Union settled in Jerusalem. Over the years, a discernible change has occurred in the causes of growth within and among the city's different population groups. The major cause of growth among the Arab population is rapid natural increase; among the Jews the natural-increase rate is significant and relatively stable. Changes have taken place in the components of demographic growth since 1985. About half of those who left moved to the settlements around the city, contributing to the consolidation of metropolitan Jerusalem. Simultaneously, the influx of immigrants that characterized the early 1990s dwindled, and beginning in 1993 Jerusalem's negative internal migration balance has exceeded the number of new immigrants who have settled in the city. In other words, the trend has been clearly toward a falloff in the growth rate of Jerusalem's Jewish population in the city.

Development Plans and Population Forecasts

The major influence in the Israel of the 1990s was the wave of mass immigration from the former Soviet Union and from Ethiopia. Within a nine-year period, Israel absorbed an addition of 18 percent to its population. Between 1990 and 1998, some 879,500 new immigrants arrived in Israel, of whom 714,100 were from the former Soviet Union. To illustrate the scale of this influx, if the United States absorbed 20 percent of its population in that same period, the number of new arrivals there would have totaled fifty million.

This vast inpouring of new immigrants resulted in upheavals in virtually every sphere of the public sector. Housing and employment, education, and social welfare were only a few of the areas in which the state had to provide solutions and quickly.

One immediate result of the immigration influx was renewed deployment and planning conceptualization in the relevant institutions at the national, municipal, and submunicipal (neighborhood) levels. A combined national master plan for building, development, and absorption (National Planning and Building Council 1991) was the first attempt to meet the problems raised by the arrival of new immigrants on this scale. The purpose of the plan was above all "to delineate a master plan accompanied by a combined physical-economic and social development plan with the aim of absorbing mass immigration, shaping the contours of its dispersal, and indicating the major spheres of activity, their mutual relationship, and the reciprocal relations between them" (National Planning and Building Council 1991, 1: 2b). This short-term program was slated to achieve its goals by 1995. It also marked the beginning of a series of national and metropolitan plans for the intermediate and long terms.

The planning wave did not omit Jerusalem and its surroundings. A development plan for metropolitan Jerusalem, a strategic plan for the city of Jerusalem, a development and conservation plan for the Jerusalem Hills (the hilly region west of Jerusalem inside the Green Line), and a conservation versus development plan in the area west of Jerusalem, including the Jerusalem Hills and the Judea Plain—all of them at the national level, including statutory, development, and strategic plans—posited the strengthening of Jerusalem as a paramount goal and endeavored to find the proper development policy that would achieve that aim.

A cornerstone of regional planning is a population forecast that tries to predict the size and characteristics of a city's population based on an analysis of the current data and of future trends. Of course, every planning endeavor contains an element of uncertainty that must be taken into account, owing primarily to changes in the basic factors—economic, social, cultural, demographic, technological—that affect a city's development, to which, in the case of Jerusalem, we must add political and diplomatic factors.

The complexity of Jerusalem gives rise to an equally complex population forecast; its interpretation is crucially important for planning the city and its surrounding area. As mentioned earlier, Jerusalem's various population groups have significantly different rates of natural increase. Among Arabs and *haredim,* the rate of natural increase is very high; among the religious Jewish population, it is intermediate to high; and among secular Jews and the Christian population, it is low. The natural-increase rate and the differential age structure of the various population groups influence the future rates of growth of each group. Because the numerical ratio among the three main population groups in Jerusalem—general Jews (non*haredi*), *haredi* Jews, and Arabs—has implications for the city's future, the population forecast must draw a distinction between the groups. Another key element in population change and growth is intersettlement migration movements. Future migration rates are largely a product of the housing supply in terms of cost and well-being in the city and in the nearby settlements. Other factors that influence migration balance are the city's economic status, the employment possibilities in and around it, and the quality of life it offers. Consequently, future population growth is also a function of the available housing in and around the city. A lower potential for adding residential units in a city drives up the price of housing and lowers the potential for population growth. In contrast, the possibility of obtaining less-expensive housing in areas around the city or of having a greater range of housing to choose from, perhaps a home with a garden in a small suburban settlement, also affects the migration balance.

Another factor that has an impact on population growth is the scope of international migration, in this case immigration to Israel, which is strongly influenced by the situation in countries where Jews reside. This factor is extremely difficult to forecast because it is bound up far more closely with changes for the worse in Diaspora conditions than with the shifting conditions in Israel.

A number of population forecasts, scenarios, and related programs for the city of Jerusalem have been undertaken in the past few years. The latest population forecast was made by DellaPergola as part of the strategic master plan for the city (1998). This forecast envisages that in the year 2020 the population of Jerusalem will be 50 percent larger than it is at present and will stand at 950,000. The Jewish population ratio will decline from its current 68 percent to 62 percent, and correspondingly the Arab population ratio will increase from its present 32 percent to 38 percent. The proportion of the *haredi* Jewish population, currently 30 percent, will remain stable because of the increasing migration of *haredi* Jews from Jerusalem to nearby localities. The major reason for this trend is the inability of *haredi* families, which tend to be large and have low per-capita incomes, to meet the high costs of housing in Jerusalem.

This forecast reinforces the position of those who advocate efforts to maintain the demographic balance between Jews and Arabs, and it constitutes the basis for the demand to extend the city's municipal boundaries to enable the growth of the Jewish population. However, many experts believe that the city's resilience is not dependent only on the size of its population in general and of its Jewish population in particular but on the strength of its population as such. A large Jerusalem with a lower socioeconomic-status population will be a weaker city than a smaller Jerusalem but one with a stronger population, characterized by a higher socioeconomic status, and economy. This difference of approach among the planners and experts is compounded by disagreement over the number of additional housing units that the city can realistically accommodate. One view holds that the land reserves for construction will not permit more than 40,000 to 50,000 new residential units in the Jewish sections of Jerusalem, whereas a different view speaks of 100,000 additional units. To this disagreement must be added the dilemma that confronts the city planners regarding ways to build within the framework of the strictures that exist to prevent damage to Jerusalem's distinctive landscape qualities: a prohibition on building in valleys, preservation of open areas, and limits on the height of buildings in various parts of the city (see chap. 15 of this volume).

Metropolitan Jerusalem

Jerusalem present and future is closely intertwined with its surroundings. It is impossible to separate developments in the city of Jerusalem proper from developments in the surrounding metropolitan area because Jerusalem is part of the broad, functional, geographic space that includes Jewish and Arab settlements linked by manifold mutual relations. Significant ties between Jerusalem and its surroundings take the form of economic activity, population movements (migration, commuting), cultural and religious activity, infrastructure, tourism, and so on. A continuous built-up area, Jewish and Arab, has emerged in the region around Jerusalem, which, spurred by the interrelations between its various parts, functions as one space for people choosing to reside there and engaged in day-to-day activities such as work and for firms considering the possibility of locating in the Jerusalem area, though not necessarily in the city. At the same time, it is important to note that this space is not uniform: there are disparities between different areas, in population type, in ethnoreligious affiliation, in economic level, and in some cases also in the level of infrastructure and available services.

Since the city's reunification, a continuous north-south built-up area of Arab villages and neighborhoods has emerged, linking, in territorial continuity, the Arab settlements outside the city's municipal boundaries with the Arab areas of Jerusalem. Jewish territorial dispersal is far more concentrated than that of the Arabs, and particularly notable in this regard is the large mass of Jews in the city of Jerusalem, home to 80 percent of the Jews in metropolitan Jerusalem.

It is equally important to point out that Jerusalem is no different from other big cities experiencing suburbanization—an outward slide of population and of economic activity, together with reciprocity involving surrounding settlements. Thus, despite the political and national struggle taking place in the city, it continues to function as the core of the evolving Jewish and Arab metropolitan area around it (map 1.6). However, it is differentiated from most other metropolitan areas in the world by the complexity of the relations and of the rifts between population groups, settlements, and neighborhoods.

From City to Metropolitan Jerusalem

The city of Jerusalem constitutes the core of the settled area around it and as such acts as the economic, social, cultural, and also political center for the Arab and Jewish communities both in and around the city.

The development of the Jerusalem area of settlement as one space, until its partition in 1948 and since its reunification in 1967, has brought into being a unitary urban system bearing a common infrastructure and strong attachments between the Israeli and Palestinian neighborhoods and settlements, particularly in the city proper and in the inner ring of surrounding settlements. A built-up physical area, the exposure of each side—Israeli and Palestinian—to the society and culture of the other, and each side's familiar-

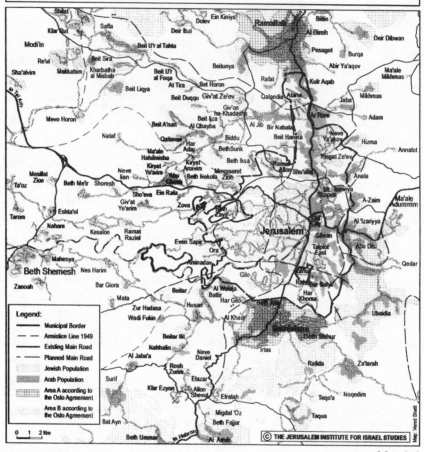

Map 1.6

ity with the other's institutional systems have engendered reciprocal relations and administrative mechanisms bearing the potential to produce cooperation in the future development of the city and its surrounding area of settlement. The origin of much of the population that currently resides in the settlements proximate to Jerusalem is in fact the city of Jerusalem. Both Arabs and Jews are migrating to the outlying localities. Many of those leaving the city are seeking less-expensive or more-spacious housing, but they continue to work and to avail themselves of services in the city.

Since 1967, as the area around Jerusalem has been modified, the Arab rural population around Jerusalem has experienced deep social changes. In fact, the major change has been its gradual transformation into an urban population, even while continuing to reside in villages. Overlaying this social shift is a process in which these Arab rural settlements are spreading out over broad areas, typically along existing roads. Over the years, the many roads built in the Jerusalem area have facilitated and accelerated the spread of Arab settlements. As a result, the typical model of the Arab village around Jerusalem is no longer closed in but spread out, its sprawl also reducing the possibilities of physical planning and development, such as road building and other aspects of infrastructure. More recently, a similar process has emerged in the Jewish sector. The urbanization of the rural settlements lying west of Jerusalem is seen in the rising demand for homes in these areas, the higher prices of land and housing, a significant decline in the numbers employed in agriculture, and a redesignation of land usage from farming to other purposes such as commerce and storage.

The heightened demand for housing around Jerusalem, parallel to the increase in the price of land and housing in Jerusalem proper, as well as the other processes that have been mentioned, notably infrastructure development, are the factors shaping the settlement system of the Jerusalem metropolitan area. These factors are producing a continuous built-up area in which travelers cannot tell when they cross municipal boundaries, such as the transition from north Jerusalem to al-Ram and Ramallah. This continuous built-up stretch is especially striking in Arab construction but is visible also in Jewish construction, notably between Jerusalem and Mevasseret Tzion.

Today, two political entities, Israel and the Palestinian Authority, coexist in geographical proximity in the Jerusalem area. Map 1.6 shows the built-up area that has been created between Jerusalem and the surrounding Jewish and Arab settlements. Also seen on the map is the built-up area that stretches between the city of Jerusalem and Areas A, B, and C as defined in the Israeli-Palestinian Interim Agreement (1995).

It should be noted, then, that because Jerusalem is umbilically bound to the area around it, any discussion of Jerusalem must take into account the fact that the strengthening of Jerusalem and the strengthening of the metropolitan area are intertwined and will benefit both the Jewish and the Arab populations in the city and around it. Developments in every part of the metropolitan area have implications for the other parts.

Boundaries

The boundaries of metropolitan Jerusalem are not demarcated by a clear line. Moreover, the boundaries of metropolitan Jerusalem change and expand in accordance with the development of the interrelations between the city and its surroundings. Generally, intensity of interrelations is a function of a settlement's proximity to the city. Hence, a distinction can be drawn between the inner ring of settlements, which lie close to the city and maintain the most intensive and diverse interrelations with it, and the outer ring of more distant settlements, with which less-intensive interrelations exist.

The ring around Jerusalem, covering a radius of approximately 20 kilometers from the city, contains the settlements between Ma'ale Adumim in the east, Beit Shemesh in the west, Ramallah in the north, and Bethlehem in the south.

It is important to emphasize that whereas the area of jurisdiction of the city of Jerusalem possesses statutory status like any other local government in Israel, the boundaries of metropolitan Jerusalem have no such status. Municipal boundaries, moreover, are absolute in character, contrary to the boundaries of metropolitan Jerusalem, which reflect one common though not uniform functional space that changes with time. An attempt is being made to demarcate the current functional boundaries of metropolitan Jerusalem, taking into account reciprocal relations such as commuting, migration—i.e., choice of place of residence—development of the built-up areas, and economic ties.

A committee on strengthening Jerusalem recently submitted a recommendation to the government calling for the establishment of an umbrella municipality for Jerusalem and the localities in the surrounding area. In 1998 and 1999, the Jerusalem municipality made major efforts to expand the city's boundaries westward into territory totally within the Green Line. The municipality views this expansion as an important step to strengthen the city by (1) adding territory on which to build tens of thousands of new residential units for the Jewish population, and (2) adding territory for economic activity that will create employment opportunities and increase the municipality's revenues from city taxes.

The municipality believes that these developments will also help solve two of the city's cardinal problems: (1) a decline in the proportion of the Jewish population and a concomitant rise in the proportion of the Arab population; and (2) the city's skewed employment structure.

The Jerusalem municipality together with the government of Israel reached the conclusion that the status of the capital should be upgraded. It was for this purpose that the government adopted Resolution 3913 on June 21, 1998, for the strengthening of Jerusalem. The resolution contained the following elements: (1) expansion of the city's area of jurisdiction in order to meet the needs of Jerusalem's development and prosperity (for which the minister of the interior is responsible); (2) establishment of an umbrella municipality for the Jerusalem area (to be headed by the mayor of Jerusalem); (3) encouragement of technology-intensive industries to bolster the city's economy and to absorb a young, educated population; (4) a meaningful increase in the supply of available land for construction and housing in the city; and (5) improvement of the transportation infrastructure to Jerusalem and in the city.

The government did not accept the municipality's proposal to effect the expansion of the city's boundaries by means of legislation, but adopted the usual procedure in which the interior minister appoints a committee to examine boundaries. The committee's brief is to determine the advantages and disadvantages of changing the municipal boundaries of a locality and present its recommendations to the interior minister, who is the final arbiter and decides whether the municipal boundaries will be changed and how.

The discussion on expanding the city westward is now under way. Among the major opponents of the municipality's conception are the settlements in the area being proposed for the expansion, and the Green organizations (the Greens in Israel are organized as nongovernmental organizations and not as a political party). The suburban settlements within the area of the proposed expansion want to preserve their distinctive character and to remain autonomous localities within the fabric of reciprocal relations that exists in metropolitan Jerusalem, but they do not wish to be part of the Jerusalem municipal entity.

The expansion of the city's boundaries and massive building in the areas to be added also threatens the growth of Beit Shemesh. Its boundaries were expanded in order to accommodate extensive building that will enable its growth from a small city with a population of slightly more than 20,000 to a large city of more than 100,000. Expansion of Jerusalem's boundaries and the resulting large-scale construction close to the city as presently constituted threaten the potential growth of Beit Shemesh.

The Greens vigorously oppose the city's expansion because it will take place on open, green land that is extremely important for the country. The areas in question, which serve as vacation and leisure sites, are very close to approximately half the country's population and in many cases possess unique landscape value. Their inclusion within the boundaries of Jerusalem for development and construction purposes will seriously affect their present status.

As of this writing, the struggle between the plans' supporters and opponents continues, and the decision has yet to be made.

Conclusion

The Jerusalem metropolitan area contains a highly diverse population—Jews and Arabs, Israelis and Palestinians, villagers and city dwellers, orthodox, ultraorthodox, traditionalists, and secularists. The majority of the Arab population in the area is Muslim and resides in Jerusalem and in areas that have been designated in the Interim Agreement as Areas A, B, and C. The Christian population is concentrated primarily in urban settlements, especially in Bethlehem and its satellites (Beit Jala and Beit Sahur), as well as in Ramallah and al-Birah. Jerusalem itself has a small Christian population of about 13,700. The majority of the Christians are Christian Arabs, though some, notably clerics, are not, and some are Christian newcomers from the former Soviet Union who immigrated to Israel, usually with Jewish relatives.

The distribution of the Jewish population in the metropolitan area differs from that of the Arab population. Most of the Jewish population is concentrated in areas where the spatial orientation runs from east to west, whereas the Arab population stretches along the ridge line from north to south. Whereas the great majority of the Jewish population (80 percent) in the Jerusalem metropolitan area is concentrated in the city of Jerusalem, the Arab population is more broadly dispersed, with approximately only 30 percent residing within Jerusalem's municipal boundaries.

The rate of population growth in the settlements around Jerusalem is more rapid than the rate within the city. The positive population growth in the city itself is owing mainly to natural increase, whereas in the areas around Jerusalem its principal cause is migration among the Jewish localities in contrast to both migration and natural growth among the Arab localities, a trend that will almost certainly continue into the future. Like their counterparts in other metropolitan areas around the world, residents of Jerusalem's core city are increasingly inclined to move elsewhere in the metropolitan area, thus increasing the relative proportion of the population in the outer rings of the conurbation as compared to the central city. Land is less expensive on the fringes of the metropolitan area than it is in the center, and, typically, better housing conditions are available in the periphery.

As the outlying sections of the metropolitan area become more attractive, the demand for housing there rises, and building is accelerated. The functional ties between Jerusalem and its suburbia have become stronger and more diversified over the years. A functional urban zone has sprung up, large parts of which are marked by a continuous built-up Jewish and Arab area. Commuting on a large scale takes place to Jerusalem from the Jewish and Arab settlements in the metropolitan area. *Today it is impossible to understand Jerusalem's urban and economic functional activity without considering that it is the core of a metropolitan area that has grown up around it.* As is the case elsewhere, negative migration rates are increasing in Jerusalem—a trend that encompasses all population groups. There is a growing demand in the Jerusalem area for high-quality suburban building and for the development of satellite towns.

A heightened process of out-migration from Jerusalem can be expected among secular Jews, *haredi* Jews, and Arabs. As in similar situations, in Israel and elsewhere, growth in the metropolitan area will result primarily from migration from the center to the periphery. Many city dwellers who move to the surrounding area continue to interact with the central city—in the present case, with Jerusalem. Such interaction generally bears an economic (especially business), social, or cultural character, though in Jerusalem it is sharper and more intense because of the city's unique religious dimension. The importance attaching to Jerusalem as a religious center and its large number of Jewish, Muslim, and Christian Holy Places heighten the interrelations between Jerusalem and the population in the surrounding settlements.

2

Jerusalem

Some Legal Aspects

Ruth Lapidoth

The title of this chapter raises a conceptual problem: Does the conflict about Jerusalem indeed have legal or jurisprudential aspects? Conflicts are usually classified as either political or legal. Whereas in a political conflict the parties disagree on what law to adopt, in a legal conflict the disagreement concerns the interpretation and application of existing law. Like most other aspects of the Arab-Israel conflict, the dispute about Jerusalem is primarily of a political nature.

Nevertheless, several reasons compel study of the legal dimension. First, though essentially of a political nature, the dispute does have some legal aspects. Second, the interested parties tend to define and justify their claims by relying on legal arguments. Finally, once a solution emerges, it will have to be formulated in legal terms and laid down in a legally binding document.

Legal considerations are relevant in four main spheres. First, Jerusalem is the subject of conflicting national claims of two peoples: Israelis and Pales-

An earlier version of this chapter appeared in 45 *Catholic University Law Review* 661 (1996) and is reprinted with permission. Some of the material included in this chapter was published previously (Lapidoth 1994, 1996a). This chapter was completed in November 2000 and partly updated in February 2002.

tinian Arabs. These claims raise the question of sovereignty over Jerusalem and the right of a state or another entity to determine the location of its own capital. Second, the problem of the Holy Places involves legal considerations, including the definition of Holy Places and who should supervise freedom of access and of worship. Moreover, some places are holy for two religions, thereby exacerbating tensions. Third, the municipal administration of this very heterogeneous city requires some legal analysis. Last but not least, cooperation and coordination between Jerusalem and its periphery have to be institutionalized. In this chapter, a brief examination of some relevant landmarks in the recent history of Jerusalem is followed by a short presentation of various opinions on the city's legal status and of its treatment in the peace process. A discussion of recent developments in the concept of sovereignty leads to some reflections on the city's future.

Some Relevant Landmarks in the History of Jerusalem

In 1517, soon after the end of the Middle Ages, Jerusalem, together with the rest of Palestine, came under Ottoman rule for a period of four hundred years. Since 1830, the majority of the city's population has been Jewish—at first merely a relative majority but subsequently an absolute one (Mohn 1950, 450).[1]

The Holy Places in the city have often been a source of conflicts (Berkovitz 1978, 8–30; Berkovitz 2000). In the eighteenth and nineteenth centuries, a bitter controversy arose when certain European countries extended their protection over various Christian communities in Palestine and over the places that were holy to them. In order to regulate the status of the various communities at the Holy Places, the Ottoman government promulgated a number of edicts *(firmans),* the most important one being that of 1852 (Zander 1971, 178–80). The 1852 edict concerned certain Christian Holy Places and determined the powers and rights of the various denominations regarding those places. This arrangement became generally known as

1. On the history of Jerusalem, see, e.g., Armstrong 1996; Bahat 1987; Ben-Arieh 1984, 1989; Gilbert 1985, 1994b, 1996; Idinopulos 1991, 306–37; Shaltiee 1981; Elon 1996; Wasserstein 2001.

the status quo[2] and has been applied to the Church of the Holy Sepulcher and its dependencies, the Deir al-Sultan, the Sanctuary of the Ascension (on the Mount of Olives), the Tomb of the Virgin Mary (near Gethsemane) in Jerusalem, the Church of the Nativity, the Milk Grotto, and the Shepherds' Field near Bethlehem. The status quo obtained international recognition at the 1856 Conference of Paris (after the Crimean War) and by the 1878 Treaty of Berlin. It has also been reconfirmed by the 1993 Fundamental Agreement between the Holy See and Israel (Article 4), as well as by the 2000 Basic Agreement between the Holy See and the Palestine Liberation Organization (Article 4).

Neither the Balfour Declaration made by Britain in 1917 (Lapidoth and Hirsch 1992) nor the Terms of the British Mandate for Palestine (Stoyanovsky 1928, 291–301) drafted by the Council of the League of Nations referred to Jerusalem. The Terms of the Mandate, however, did address the Holy Places (Lapidoth and Hirsch 1992, 28). The Mandatory Power was requested to preserve existing rights in those places and to ensure free access and worship, subject to requirements of public order and decorum. A commission was to be established that would "study, define and determine" the various rights and claims in connection with the Holy Places, but it was never established because of lack of agreement among the powers about its composition (Mohn 1950, 437–38). Shortly after the mandate came into force, Britain adopted the Palestine (Holy Places) Order in Council of 1924, under which "no cause or matter in connection with the Holy Places or religious buildings or sites or the rights or claims relating to the different religious communities in Palestine shall be heard or determined by any court in Palestine" (Drayton 1934, 2625). Although the text did not say so explicitly, these matters were to be handled by the British high commissioner (today the minister of religious affairs of Israel).

---

2. The term *status quo* is used in Israel in the religious context with three different meanings: first, the historical status quo mentioned in text (see, e.g., Berkovitz 1978, 35–45; Berkovitz 1997, 3; England 1994, 591–93; Mohn 1950, 438–42); second, the general situation of the various Holy Places and communities; third, the relations between secular and religious Jews in Israel—compromise arrangements on matters concerning the Jewish faith, such as respect for the precepts of Judaism in public places and in the army.

In 1947, after the Second World War, Britain asked the United Nations (UN) General Assembly to consider the Palestinian question, and on November 29, 1947, the General Assembly adopted its famous resolution on the future government of Palestine (United Nations General Assembly 1947). Part III of that resolution dealt with Jerusalem. The General Assem-

CITY OF JERUSALEM
BOUNDARIES PROPOSED
BY THE AD HOC COMMITTEE
ON THE PALESTINIAN QUESTION

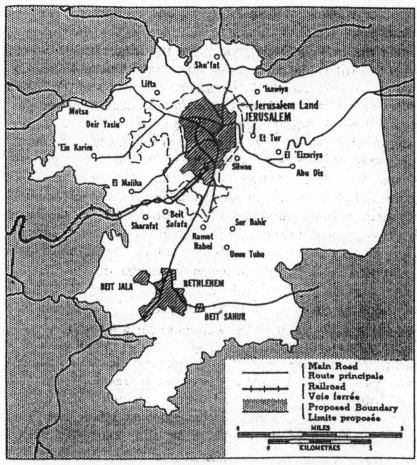

Map 2.1. United Nations map no. 104(b), courtesy of the United Nations.

bly recommended the establishment of a *"corpus separatum* under a special international regime." The UN Trusteeship Council and a governor appointed by it would administer the *corpus separatum.* In the economic sphere, the General Assembly recommended the establishment of an economic union between Jerusalem and the Jewish and Arab states that were to be established in Palestine.

The General Assembly resolution received the consent of the national leadership of the Jewish community of Palestine (see Lapidoth and Hirsch 1992, 55–56), but the Arabs categorically rejected it and immediately initiated attacks on Jewish towns and villages, including the Jewish neighborhoods in Jerusalem (see Lapidoth and Hirsch 1992, 57–60).

On May 14, 1948, when the British Mandate over Palestine was about to end, representatives of the Jewish community in Palestine proclaimed the establishment of the State of Israel. The declaration does not mention Jerusalem, but it declares that Israel "will safeguard the Holy Places of all religions" *(Laws of the State of Israel* 1948). Immediately after the establishment of the state, the armies of six Arab states invaded Israel. The armies of Jordan (or Transjordan as it then was called) and Egypt operated in the Jerusalem region (see Mohn 1950). The battle for Jerusalem was fierce, in part because, for a time, the Jewish areas were cut off from the coastal plain. The battle for the Old City ended with the surrender of the Jewish Quarter to the forces of the Jordanian Arab Legion (on May 28, 1948).

Even before the fighting abated, Jordan and Israel reached a special agreement under the auspices of the UN regarding the Jewish enclave on Mount Scopus (see Lapidoth and Hirsch 1992, 66–67). The parties agreed to neutralize this area as well as the adjoining area of the Augusta Victoria Hospital, which was under Jordanian control, and to assign these areas to UN protection.

When the fighting ended, Jordanian forces were in control of the eastern parts of the city, whereas the western sector was under Israeli control. In November 1948, a truce came into force throughout the city, and at the beginning of 1949 Jordan and Israel signed an armistice agreement (see Lapidoth and Hirsch 1992, 87–93). This agreement gave rise to various practical as well as legal questions (Rosenne 1951).

A proclamation made by the Israeli minister of defense on August 2,

1948 (see Lapidoth and Hirsch 1994b, 27–29), and the Area of Jurisdiction and Powers Ordinance of 5708–1948 *(Laws of the State of Israel* 1948) applied Israeli law to west Jerusalem. That ordinance provided that the law in force in the State of Israel should also apply to any part of Palestine that the minister of defense would designate by proclamation as under occupation of the Israel Defense Forces.

At the end of 1949, following the renewed debate on Jerusalem in the UN General Assembly, Prime Minister David Ben-Gurion of Israel announced in the Knesset (Israel's Parliament) that Jerusalem was an "inseparable part of the State of Israel" and its "Eternal Capital" (see Lapidoth and Hirsch 1994b, 81–84; see also Bialer 1985; Golani 1999, 582, 585–93). The Knesset approved this position.

In 1948 and 1949, a conference of dignitaries from areas conquered by Jordan in 1948 convened in Jericho. The participants expressed their wish to be part of Jordan, and consequently the king of Jordan and the Jordanian Parliament proclaimed the annexation (or unification, in their words) of the West Bank, including east Jerusalem, to the kingdom (see Lapidoth and Hirsch 1994b, 145–47).

During the years 1948–52, a number of debates took place at the UN on the future of Jerusalem, and the Trusteeship Council prepared a draft statute for the city (see Lapidoth and Hirsch 1994b, 117–34), but from 1952 until the Six Day War in 1967, no significant debates occurred.

When the Six Day War broke out, Jordan attacked west Jerusalem, despite Israel's promise that if Jordan refrained from attacking Israel, Israel would not attack Jordan. A few days later, Israel Defense Forces recovered the area taken by the Jordanian army ("Government House," formerly the seat of the British high commissioner) and expelled the Jordanian army from east Jerusalem and the West Bank. Opinions have differed between Israeli (and most Western) lawyers on the one hand and Arab lawyers on the other as to which party was the aggressor in the Six Day War (see Lapidoth 1994).

Soon after the fighting ceased, Israel sought to include east Jerusalem under its jurisdiction. The Knesset passed the Law and Administration Ordinance (Amendment No. 11) Law of 5727–1967, which authorizes the government to apply the law, jurisdiction, and administration of Israel to areas formerly part of Mandatory Palestine (see Lapidoth and Hirsch 1994b,

167). Similarly, the Municipalities Ordinance was amended to authorize the extension of the municipal boundaries where Israel's jurisdiction had been applied in accordance with the above amendment (see Lapidoth and Hirsch 1992, 130; Lapidoth and Hirsch 1994b, 167). The government of Israel issued an appropriate order to apply Israeli law to the eastern sector of Jerusalem, which also was included within the jurisdiction of the Jerusalem municipality. Israeli law and administrators, however, have granted east Jerusalemites certain facilities by establishing special arrangements, inter alia, by virtue of the Legal and Administrative Matters (Regulation) Law (Consolidated Version) of 1970. The most conspicuous examples of the differences between the principles applied in Israel and in east Jerusalem are the system of education and rules on foreign currency. Schools in the eastern neighborhoods have taught the Jordanian curriculum and later switched to the Palestinian one, and the Jordanian dinar constitutes legal tender along with the Israeli shekel (see Lapidoth 1999, chapter 4).

As to Israeli citizenship, it has not been imposed on the residents of east Jerusalem, but they can acquire it by applying for it in accordance with the rules of naturalization. So far, however, only a small number of residents of the eastern sector of the city have applied for Israeli citizenship. The participation in elections for the municipality is not limited to citizens of Israel, and hence the permanent residents of the eastern sector may vote in the municipal elections. Unfortunately, so far only few have actually cast their votes.

Israel has increased the municipal boundaries of Jerusalem to extend from Atarot in the north to a point not far from Rachel's Tomb in the south, and from Ein Kerem in the west to the eastern slopes of Mount Scopus (Hazan 1995).[3]

Various UN bodies have sharply criticized the measures Israel has taken in Jerusalem (see Lapidoth and Hirsch 1994b, 170). Did these acts constitute annexation of the eastern parts of Jerusalem? In July 1967, then-minister of

---

3. In 1993, the city was extended to the west (inside Israel). In 1998, proposals were submitted for a further extension of Jerusalem to the west and for the establishment of a greater Jerusalem cooperation unit, an umbrella municipality, which would also include certain areas in the West Bank (Shragai 1998c; Lapidoth 1999, chap. 4). The plan was approved in principle by the government on June 21, 1998, but by February 2002 it had not been implemented.

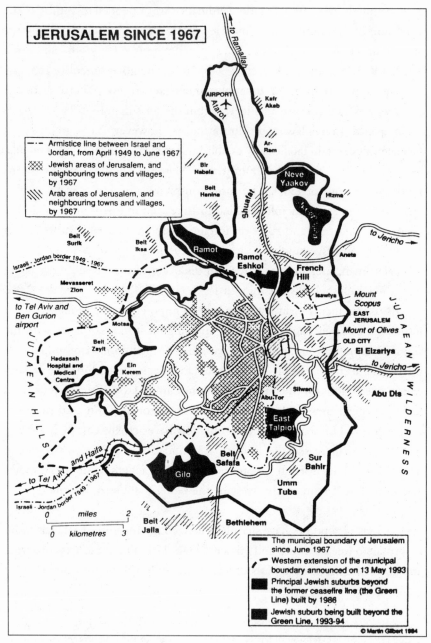

JERUSALEM SINCE 1967

- - - Armistice line between Israel and
Jordan, from April 1949 to June 1967

Jewish areas of Jerusalem, and
neighbouring towns and villages,
by 1967

Arab areas of Jerusalem, and
neighbouring towns and villages,
by 1967

to Ramallah

AIRPORT
Atarot

Kafr
Akab

Ar-
Ram

Bir
Nabela

Belt
Hanina

Neve
Yaakov

Htzma

Shuafat

to Jericho →

Belt
Surik

Belt
Iksa

Ramot

Ramot
Eshkol

French
Hill

Anata

Israeli - Jordan border 1949 - 1967

Mevasseret
Zion

Isawiya

Mount
Scopus

to Tel Aviv and
Ben Gurion
airport

Motsa

EAST
JERUSALEM

Mount of Olives

JUDAEAN WILDERNESS

Belt
Zayit

Hadassah
Hospital and
Medical
Centre

Ein
Kerem

OLD CITY

El Eizariya

to Jericho →

Abu-Tor

Silwan

Abu Dis

East
Talpiot

JUDAEAN HILLS

Belt
Safafa

Sur
Bahir

to Tel Aviv and Haifa

Gilo

Umm
Tuba

Israeli - Jordan border 1949 - 1967

0   miles   2

0   kilometres   3

Belt
Jalla

Bethlehem

The municipal boundary of Jerusalem
since June 1967

Western extension of the municipal
boundary announced on 13 May 1993

Principal Jewish suburbs beyond
the former ceasefire line (the Green
Line) built by 1986

Jewish suburb being built beyond the
Green Line, 1993-94

© Martin Gilbert 1994

Map 2.2

foreign affairs Abba Eban informed the UN secretary-general in writing that these acts did not constitute annexation but only administrative and municipal integration (see Lapidoth and Hirsch 1994b, 171–73; see also Lustick 1997). Israel's Supreme Court, however, has held, at first somewhat hesitantly, in a number of decisions that under Israeli law the eastern sectors of Jerusalem had become a part of the State of Israel.

Immediately after the fighting in Jerusalem ended in June 1967, Prime Minister Levi Eshkol convened the spiritual leaders of various communities and reassured them of Israel's intention to protect all Holy Places and to permit free worship (see Lapidoth and Hirsch 1994b, 163–64). A few days later, the Knesset passed the Protection of the Holy Places Law of 5727–1967, which ensures protection of the Holy Places against desecration as well as freedom of access thereto (see Lapidoth and Hirsch 1994b, 169).

Security Council Resolutions 242 and 338 of November 22, 1967, and October 22, 1973,[4] respectively, did not mention Jerusalem. Nor did Jerusalem feature in the 1978 Camp David Accords between Israel and Egypt (see Lapidoth and Hirsch 1992, 195–201) because of fundamental differences of opinion between the parties on the issue. Each of the participants in the Camp David conference, however, stated his position in a letter sent to the other via the president of the United States (see Lapidoth and Hirsch 1994b, 299–300).[5] Prime Minister Menachem Begin of Israel stated that, in accordance with legislation from 1967, "Jerusalem is one city, indivisible, the Capital of the State of Israel" (ibid., 300). President Anwar Sadat of Egypt, on the other hand, stated that "Arab Jerusalem is an integral part of the West Bank, . . .[and] should be under Arab sovereignty" (ibid., 299). At the same time, President Sadat determined that "[e]ssential functions in the City should be undivided, and a joint municipal council composed of an equal number of Arab and Israeli members can supervise the carrying out of these functions" (ibid., 299). He added that "in this way, the City shall be undivided."

In 1980, the Knesset adopted a new law concerning Jerusalem—the

4. Resolution 242 has been the subject of differing interpretations by the parties and of a great number of scholarly articles (see Abu Odeh et al. 1993 and Lapidoth 1992a).

5. The contents of the letter by President Carter is discussed later in this chapter.

Basic Law: Jerusalem, Capital of Israel (see Lapidoth and Hirsch 1994b, 322; see also Lapidoth 1999, chapter 4). This law states that "Jerusalem, complete and united, is the capital of Israel," that it is "the seat of the President of the State, the Knesset, the Government, and the Supreme Court." It states further that the Holy Places shall be protected and that the government and other authorities have to provide for the development and prosperity of Jerusalem. In fact, the contents of the law do not include any innovation. Although originally its provisions were not entrenched, in November 2000 two entrenched articles were added to the statute: the transfer of any powers, whether permanently or provisionally, concerning Jerusalem in its 1967 boundaries, requires the consent of a majority of the members of the Knesset (namely, sixty-one). This provision relates to any power entrusted by Israeli law to the government or to the municipality of Jerusalem.[6] The adoption of this law aroused resentment in the international community. The Security Council condemned it as "a violation of international law" (see Lapidoth and Hirsch 1994b, 351) and called on member states with embassies situated in Jerusalem to withdraw them from the city. Thirteen embassies left the city following that resolution. In 1982, however, the embassy of Costa Rica returned to west Jerusalem, followed in 1984 by that of El Salvador.

In his 1982 peace initiative, President Ronald Reagan of the United States declared, inter alia, that the status of Jerusalem should be determined through negotiations, that the Palestinian inhabitants of the eastern part of the city should be permitted to participate in the elections for the autonomous institutions of the West Bank and Gaza Strip, and that the city should remain undivided (see Lapidoth and Hirsch 1994b , 364–71).

In the early 1980s, Jordan requested to register the Old City and its walls in the World Heritage List, established under the 1972 UNESCO Convention for the Protection of the World Cultural and Natural Heritage

---

6. *Sefer Hahukim,* no. 1760 (5761 [2000–2001]), 28. See also the Law and Administration Ordinance (Abrogation of the Application of the Law, Jurisdiction, and Administration) Law, 5759 (1999), *Sefer Hahukim* no. 1703 (5759 [1998–99]), 86. For a discussion of Basic Laws, see Barak 1994, 355–38; Rubinstein and Medina 1996, 374–408; and C. Klein 1992, 1994.

(reprinted in *International Legal Materials* [1972], 11:1358–66). Although by that time Jordan was no more in control of the Old City, its request was granted (see Lapidoth and Hirsch 1994a, 358–61). The representative of Israel, which was in physical control of the area, was not given an opportunity to state his opinion at the meeting, allegedly because Israel was not a party to the convention. In 1999, Israel acceded to the convention.

In 1988, King Hussein of Jordan, who had declared in 1950 that he annexed the West Bank, including Jerusalem, announced that he intended to dismantle the legal and administrative links between the West Bank and Jordan (see Lapidoth and Hirsch 1992, 339–43). In the same year, the Palestine National Council of the Palestine Liberation Organization (PLO) proclaimed the establishment of the State of Palestine, with Jerusalem as its capital (see Lapidoth and Hirsch 1992, 344–56). Many states recognized this proclamation, but a mere proclamation, even if followed by large-scale recognition, is not sufficient for the establishment of a state unless the four prerequisites for the existence of a state are present: territory, population, effective government, and the ability to conduct international relations (Crawford 1990; Lapidoth and Calvo-Goller 1992; see also *Klinghoffer v. Achille Lauro* 1991 and Singer 1994a, 268, 270–71; but see Boyle 1990 and Salmon 1989).

Opinions on the Legal Status of Jerusalem

Many statespersons as well as experts in international law have expressed their opinions on the status of Jerusalem (see Lapidoth and Hirsch 1994a, 11–15; Hirsch, Housen-Couriel, and Lapidoth 1995, 15–24. This chapter reproduces only opinions of the *lex lata*. For the summary of various proposals *de lege ferenda*, see Hirsch, Housen-Couriel, and Lapidoth 1995, 25–144; Baskin 1994; Breger and Idinopulos 1998, 69–76; Chazan 1991; Eisner 1994, 260–75; Emmett 1996–97; Gilbert 1994b; Ginio 1980, 41–75; Gold 1995; Idinopulos 1991, 306–37; Khalidi 1996, 17–18; Musallam 1996, 119–32; Beilin-Abu Mazen Proposal 1995; Glaubach 1996; Pres. Clinton 2000). Only the most representative ones are presented here, and I only state those opinions, without analyzing the pros and cons. Because the western parts of Jerusalem have not changed significantly since 1949, I can analyze opinions on their status without a temporal division. The eastern sectors changed hands, however, in 1967, and therefore it may be useful to divide the discussion accordingly.

There have been four basic opinions on west Jerusalem. According to the first, Israel lawfully acquired sovereignty in 1948. When Britain left the area, a vacuum of sovereignty ensued that could be validly filled only by a lawful action. Because Israel acquired control of west Jerusalem in 1948 by a lawful act of self-defense, it was entitled to fill that vacuum and thus became the lawful sovereign (see, e.g., Gruhin 1980; E. Lauterpacht 1968; Schwebel 1970; Stone 1981).

Under a second opinion, sovereignty over Jerusalem has been suspended until a comprehensive settlement is agreed on (Bin Talal 1979, 24–27; see also Draper 1981, 154–56).

According to the third theory, the Palestinian Arab people have had and still have "legal sovereignty" over the whole of Palestine, including Jerusalem, since the mandatory period (Cattan 1976, 1981, 1988; Quigley 1996).

Proponents of the fourth opinion have maintained that the status of Jerusalem is still subject to the UN General Assembly resolution of 1947, which recommended the establishment of a *corpus separatum* under a special international regime and administered by the UN (Cassese 1981; Mallison and Mallison 1981; United Nations 1979).[7]

Most foreign nations have not adopted a clear-cut policy on the status of west Jerusalem.[8] Although their approaches differ, certain similarities emerge with regard to basic questions. Foreign states were not prepared to recognize the legality of Jordanian or Israeli rule over zones of Jerusalem under the latters' control. One manifestation of this attitude has been that foreign consuls stationed in the city have refused to apply to Jordan or Israel for permission to carry out their functions in the city. The refusal to recognize Israeli rule over the western sector was apparent for example in the 1952 civil case Jerusalem 208/52 *Heirs of Shababo v. Roger Heilen, the Con-*

---

7. According to Professor Willem J. M. van Genugten, the *corpus separatum* solution should be applied if the parties do not reach an agreement on a difficult solution (1999, 228–29).

8. For an analysis of the U.S. attitude, see Slonim 1998 and Feintuch 1987.

sulate General of Belgium and the Consul General of Belgium in Jerusalem. In that case, a driver of the Belgian consulate had been involved in a road accident that caused the death of Mr. Shababo. Family members of the deceased sued the driver, the consulate, and the consul general, claiming damages. The incident was the subject of several judgments of the Jerusalem District Court (Lauterpacht 1957). In the first hearing, the driver and his principals challenged the jurisdiction of the Israeli courts over the accident because it had taken place in Jerusalem. The court dismissed that argument.

Despite this nonrecognition of Israeli sovereignty, most states have nevertheless accepted the de facto applicability of Israeli law, and none has so far demanded that the laws of occupation, including the 1949 Fourth Geneva Convention Relative to the Protection of Civilian Persons in Time of War, be applied (see Lapidoth and Hirsch 1994b , 147–48, 447–49). The European Union supports the idea that Jerusalem is still subject to the *corpus separatum* status (see Eldar 1999; Lapidoth 2001).

There have also been four main opinions on the status of east Jerusalem for the period 1949–67 (the time it was under Jordanian rule). According to the first opinion, during that time the area was under a vacuum of sovereignty: Britain had abandoned the area, but Jordan could not fill this gap because it had occupied east Jerusalem by an illegal act of aggression (see E. Lauterpacht 1968, 46–48).

Under a second theory, similar to the parallel one concerning west Jerusalem, the Palestinian Arab people have had and continue to have title to "legal sovereignty" over the whole of Palestine, including east and west Jerusalem (see Cattan 1976, 1981, 1988; Quigley 1991, 1996; Van Dusen 1972).

A third opinion recognized Jordanian sovereignty over east Jerusalem, derived from the exercise of the right of self-determination by the inhabitants, in view of their wishes expressed by the resolutions that the notables adopted in Jericho in 1948 and 1949 (Dinstein 1981).[9]

9. For references on the Jericho meeting, see Lapidoth and Hirsch 1994b, 145–47. It is not known whether Dinstein has changed his opinion on the question of sovereignty owing to Jordan's disengagement from the West Bank (see Lapidoth and Hirsch 1994b, 339–43).

Finally, proponents of the fourth opinion have claimed that the *corpus separatum* solution still applies to both east and west Jerusalem (Cassese 1981; Mallison and Mallison 1981; United Nations 1979).

How did the changes that occurred in 1967 influence these opinions? Under the first opinion, the vacuum of sovereignty existed until Israel occupied east Jerusalem by a lawful act of self-defense and thus was entitled to fill the gap (see, e.g., Gruhin 1980; E. Lauterpacht 1968, 46–48; Schwebel 1970; Stone 1981). Under a slightly different interpretation, Israel has the strongest relative title to the area in the absence of a lawful "sovereign reversioner" because of Jordan's lack of valid sovereignty (Blum 1968, 1974).

The Six Day War did not have any effect on the opinion according to which the Palestinian Arab people have legal sovereignty over the whole of Palestine, irrespective of the factual situation (Cattan 1976, 1981, 1988; Quigley 1996).

If Jordan acquired sovereignty over east Jerusalem by virtue of the principle of self-determination, Israel has been a belligerent occupant in those sectors. If, as the Arab states claim, Israel was an aggressor in 1967, it has been an illegal occupant, but if Israel has occupied the area in an act of self-defense, it has been a lawful occupant (Dinstein 1981). The *corpus separatum* theory was not affected by the war (Cassese 1981; Mallison and Mallison 1981; United Nations 1979).

In practical terms, the international community has not recognized the sovereignty of either Jordan or Israel at any point. Moreover, since 1967, the UN, including the Security Council, has repeatedly stated that east Jerusalem is occupied territory subject to the 1949 Fourth Geneva Convention Relative to the Protection of Civilian Persons in Time of War (Lapidoth and Hirsch 1994b , 311, 351).

The attitude of the U.S. administration was expressed, inter alia, in the context of the 1978 Camp David Accords in a letter President Carter sent to both Egypt and Israel (Lapidoth and Hirsch 1994b, 300). The president wrote that the position of the United States remained as stated by Ambassador Arthur Goldberg at the UN General Assembly in 1967 and subsequently by Ambassador Charles Yost in the Security Council in 1969. There is, however, a difference between the speeches of the two ambassadors. Although they both emphasized that the actions of Israel in Jerusalem were merely provisional and that the problem of the city's future should be settled by negotiations, Ambassador Yost added that east Jerusalem was occupied territory to which the 1949 Fourth Geneva Convention applied (Lapidoth and Hirsch 1994b, 174–77, 236–38). This position, however, did not prevent the United States from asking Israel to extradite a person who lived in the eastern sector of the city (Lapidoth and Hirsch 1994b, 535–39).

The U.S. Congress has adopted an attitude quite different from that of the administration. Already in 1990, it had adopted a concurrent resolution in favor of recognizing Jerusalem as Israel's capital (Resolution of March 22, 1990). This, however, was not a binding text. But in 1995, Congress adopted the *Jerusalem Embassy Act,* a binding statute that provides, inter alia:

Sec. 2. Findings
The Congress makes the following findings:
(1) Each sovereign nation, under international law and custom, may designate its own capital.
(2) Since 1950, the city of Jerusalem has been the capital of the State of Israel.
(3) The city of Jerusalem is the seat of Israel's President, Parliament, and Supreme Court, and the site of numerous government ministries and social and cultural institutions.
(4) The city of Jerusalem is the spiritual center of Judaism, and is also considered a holy city by the members of other religious faiths. . . .
(16) The United States conducts official meetings and other business in the city of Jerusalem in *de facto* recognition of its status as the capital of Israel. . . .
Sec. 3. Timetable
(a)Statement of the Policy of the United States
(1) Jerusalem should remain an undivided city in which the rights of every ethnic and religious group are protected;
(2) Jerusalem should be recognized as the capital of the State of Israel; and
(3) The United States Embassy in Israel should be established in

Jerusalem no later than May 31, 1999. (U.S. Congress 1995; see also Halberstam 1996 and Watson 1996)[10]

The attitude of the European Community can be inferred from a 1980 declaration on the Middle East, which includes a paragraph on Jerusalem:

The Nine [member states] recognize the special importance of the role played by the question of Jerusalem for all the parties concerned. The Nine stress that they will not accept any unilateral initiative designed to change the status of Jerusalem and that any agreement on the City's status should guarantee freedom of access for everyone to the Holy Places. (qtd. in Lapidoth and Hirsch 1994b, 315)[11]

Moreover, in March 1999, the embassy of Germany in Israel sent, in the name of the European Union, a Note Verbale to Israel's Ministry of Foreign Affairs, saying that "The European Union reaffirms its known position concerning the specific status of Jerusalem as a corpus separatum" (qtd. in Eldar 1999).

The Israeli courts, on the other hand, have held, at first somewhat hesitantly, that the eastern sectors of Jerusalem had become part of the State of Israel. One of the earlier cases on this question is H. Ct. 283/69 *Ruidi and Maches v. Military Court of Hebron* (see Lapidoth and Hirsch 1994b, 502–6).[12] This case involved antiquities dealers from Hebron who transferred antiquities from Hebron to east Jerusalem without first obtaining an export license, as required by the Jordanian antiquities law that applied on the West Bank (including Hebron). One of the questions dealt with in the hearings in the Supreme Court concerned the status of east Jerusalem—namely, whether it is "abroad" vis-à-vis the West Bank. The majority of the Court—Justices A.

10. For a comprehensive review of the activities of Congress with regard to Jerusalem, see Levush 1995.

11. For an analysis of the Venice Declaration and its follow-up, see Ferrari and Margiotta-Broglio 1988, 597–99; Greiesammer and Weiler 1987, 44–52.

12. The petitioners in this case actually agreed that east Jerusalem had become part of Israel, but they relied on the fact that the annexation had occurred after the application of Jordanian law to the West Bank had been decreed by the military governor.

Witkon and Y. Cohn—expressed the opinion that east Jerusalem had become part of Israel and hence is "abroad" with regard to Hebron.

Perhaps the most comprehensive discussion of the status of Jerusalem under Israel law as well as under Jewish law is included in Justice Menachem Elon's judgment in the case of H. Ct. 4185/90, *The Temple Mount Faithful Association et al. v. Attorney General et al.* (Elon 1996), decided in 1993. In this case, the petitioners requested the High Court of Justice to order the attorney general and various other Israeli authorities to prosecute the Waqf (Muslim religious trust) for having undertaken on the Temple Mount/al-Haram al-Sharif certain works without the necessary permit. The High Court decided not to interfere in the discretion of the relevant authorities. In reaching its conclusion, the Court emphasized that the Temple Mount is part of the territory of the State of Israel and that the sovereignty of the state extends over unified Jerusalem in general and over the Temple Mount in particular. Hence, all laws of Israel apply to the Temple Mount, including those laws guaranteeing freedom of religion, right of access to, and protection against desecration of the Holy Places. Nevertheless, despite this principle, the Supreme Court has abstained in several cases from the full application of Israeli law on the Temple Mount/al-Haram al-Sharif because of the religious and political sensitivities involved.

Jerusalem's turbulent legal history and the conflicting opinions on its status may explain the hard bargaining over the city in the peace process.

Jerusalem and the Recent Stages of the Peace Process

In 1993, the PLO and Israel conducted secret negotiations in Oslo, Norway. As a result, certain letters were exchanged, and the Declaration of Principles on Interim Self-Government Arrangements was initialed in Oslo and later signed in Washington, D.C., on September 13, 1993 ("Declaration" 1993; see also E. Benvenisti 1993; Calvo-Goller 1993; Cassese 1993; Cotran 1996; Malanczuk 1996; Meigham 1994; Shehadeh 1997, 11–30; Shehada 1993; Singer 1994b; Watson 2000). This text constituted a turning point in the attitude of the two parties on the question of Jerusalem. The parties agreed that Jerusalem would not be included in the interim self-government arrangements—a concession by the Palestinians. Israel, on the other hand, conceded that Jerusalem would be one of the subjects to be dealt with in the framework of the negotiations on the "permanent status" to start in 1996 ("Declaration" 1993, Articles 4, 5(3), and Agreed Minutes). In addition, it was agreed that "Palestinians of Jerusalem who live there will have the right to participate in the election process" for the Interim Self-Government Authority for the West Bank and Gaza ("Declaration" 1993, Annex I, para. 1).

These provisions have raised several legal issues. First and foremost, what is "Jerusalem"? Probably the parties had east Jerusalem in mind because it seems that the dispute concerns only that part. The Palestinians, however, may also have certain claims with regard to west Jerusalem, including, for example, the claims of refugees who left those areas. In addition, if the parties agree to change the status of east Jerusalem, the question of freedom of access between the two parts could also arise.

A more burning question concerns the confines of Jerusalem: Did the provision in the Declaration of Principles envision the city in the limits that existed under the British Mandate? Or within the lines recommended in 1947 by the UN General Assembly (see Lapidoth and Hirsch 1992, 53)? Or those established by Israel and Jordan in the wake of the 1949 Armistice Agreement (see Lapidoth and Hirsch 1992, 88–89; Bahat 1987, 77; Gilbert 1994a, 101)? Or those adopted by Israel after the unification of the city in 1967 (Gilbert 1994a, 18; Bahat 1987, 81)?[13] This overall question has no great bearing on the problem of the Holy Places because most of them are situated in or around the Old City, which, under any definition, falls within "Jerusalem." But the matter could be crucial with regard to the new Jewish neighborhoods established after 1967, most of which only fall within the town limits established in 1967. Will these neighborhoods be considered as part of the West Bank or of Jerusalem? When concluding the 1993 Declaration of Principles, Israel presumably intended that its terms carry the meaning accorded them under Israel's internal legislation and, therefore, the term *Jerusalem* related to the area included in the municipal confines of the city under Israeli law, as described earlier in the historical introduction to this chapter.

It is unknown how the PLO intended to define the contours of

13. See note 3.

Jerusalem when it signed the Declaration of Principles. A strong presumption exists, however, in favor of the borders that had been practically in place for the preceding twenty-six years, in particular because the PLO did not express a different opinion upon signing the declaration.

If the parties agree, however, negotiations on Jerusalem could also encompass a larger area. This enlargement could serve two purposes. First, the inclusion of part of the periphery of Jerusalem would be helpful for demographic, technical, and economic purposes, such as water supply and disposal of sewage, as well as for communications and transportation planning. Second, the enlargement could facilitate the achievement of a compromise with regard to the national aspirations of the parties and could, perhaps, accommodate claims for two capitals in Jerusalem—an Israeli one and a Palestinian one (al-Quds) (Albin, Amirav, and Seniora 1991–92; Hirsch 1996, 718–19; Beilin-Abu Mazen Proposal 1995, Article 6).

Another question concerns the possible substantive scope of negotiations on Jerusalem. The three principal areas of dispute have probably been national aspirations, Holy Places, and municipal government. Will Israeli negotiators be restricted by the 1980 Basic Law: Jerusalem, Capital of Israel (see Lapidoth and Hirsch 1994b, 322)? It seems likely that the provisions added to the law in 2000,[14] while not preventing negotiations, would subject a resolution of the government purporting to transfer any political or municipal powers to the need for parliamentary approval by a majority of the members. Similarly, a resolution in which the law, jurisdiction, and administration of Israel would cease to apply requires the approval of the same majority, according to a 1999 law (see note 6).

The second provision in the Declaration of Principles relating to Jerusalem concerned the elections for the "Council"—the Palestinian Self-Government Authority ("Declaration" 1993, Article 1; see also Ghanem 1996). As already mentioned, the declaration states that "Palestinians of Jerusalem who live there will have the right to participate in the election process, according to an agreement between the two sides" ("Declaration" 1993, Annex 1, para. 1). This provision has raised several legal questions.

14. In an unpublished 1993 paper, Dr. Moshe Hirsch has outlined some of the possible alternatives in this sphere.

The Israeli-Palestinian Interim Agreement on the West Bank and the Gaza Strip (1995; see also Giladi 1995; Shehada 1997, 31–72; Singer 1995),[15] signed on September 28, 1995; an additional agreement on the Initial Registration Canvass, signed on September 23, 1995;[16] and the Palestinian Election Law of December 7, 1995,[17] resolved most of these problems.

The first question that comes to mind is: Who are Palestinians? The agreements did not address this question, but the Palestinian Election Law of December 7, 1995, has dealt with it.

> For the purpose of this Law, a Palestinian is a person who:
>
> a) Was born in Palestine, as defined by the territory covered by the British Mandate, or had the right to Palestinian citizenship according to the laws in force during that period.
>
> b) Was born in the Gaza Strip or in the West Bank, including Jerusalem.
>
> c) Irrespective of place of birth, has one or more direct ancestors that meet the requirements of paragraph (a) above.
>
> d) Is the spouse of a Palestinian who meets the above-mentioned requirements.
>
> e) Has not the Israeli citizenship. (Article 7[2])

As for the question of defining Jerusalem: for the purpose of qualifying for participation in these elections, the existing municipal boundaries were in fact accepted. The expression "who lives there" begs another question: What were the criteria for "living there"? How long must a person have lived in Jerusalem to qualify to participate in the elections? The general principle laid down in the 1995 Interim Agreement for voters in the West Bank and the Gaza Strip was that a person had to be entered in the population register maintained by the Palestinian Authority or by Israel. Others

15. The full text has been published in the Israel Collection of Treaties: *Kitvei Amana,* no. 1071, vol. 33, 1.

16. The author wishes to express her thanks to Mr. Daniel Taub for having kindly given her a copy of this document.

17. The author wishes to thank Ms. Yael Ronen and Mr. Rotem Giladi, who have kindly given her a copy of this law.

were allowed to vote only if they could prove that they had lived in those areas for at least four years immediately prior to the signing of the Interim Agreement (Annex 2, Article 2). For people older than forty, the required period of residence was only three years. In accordance with these criteria, for all the relevant areas in the West Bank and the Gaza Strip, Polling Station Commissions, established by the Central Election Commission, and appointed by the Palestinian Authority, undertook a canvassing operation and compiled an Electoral Register. For the Palestinians of Jerusalem, however, no official Polling Station Commission was foreseen by the Interim Agreement, but it was stipulated that

> a. A canvass of Palestinians of Jerusalem will be undertaken, on a contractual basis, by the Ibrahimiya College, which will contract Palestinian teachers of Jerusalem possessing Jerusalem identity cards to conduct the canvass. The canvass documentation shall accordingly not bear any titles or emblems.
> b. The results of this canvass will be provided to the relevant DEO [District Election Offices] which will be responsible for their inclusion in the initial draft register (Initial Registration Canvass Agreement of September 23, 1995, Article 4).

The results of this canvass were submitted to a joint Palestinian-Israeli committee.

The inclusion of a person in the Electoral Register pursuant to canvassing did not confer the legal right to live in Jerusalem and to be included in the Israeli Population Register of the city: "The inclusion of any person on the Electoral Register at any address shall be without prejudice to the question of that person's legal abode at that address" ("Israeli-Palestinian Interim Agreement" 1995, Annex 2, Article 2[1][h]). The aim of this provision was to permit the numerous West Bankers who practically lived in Jerusalem to participate in the vote, without granting them a legal right to live there.

But the most difficult question concerned the expression "participate in the election process" ("Declaration" 1993, Annex 1). Did it refer only to the active right to vote, or did it also include the passive right to be elected? The parties probably had contradictory intentions with regard to the meaning of this provision when they signed the Declaration of Principles.

The distinction between active and passive voting is not merely technical because the granting of a passive right to be elected could be interpreted as incompatible with Israel's claim to sovereignty over united Jerusalem, whereas a mere right of active voting may more easily be reconciled with that sovereignty (Housen-Couriel and Hirsch 1992, 5–8). The 1995 Interim Agreement laid down that only a Jerusalemite who had an additional address in the West Bank could be elected, and he or she would represent the other area, not the city of Jerusalem: "Every candidate for the Council . . . must have a valid address in an area under the jurisdiction of the Council in the constituency for which he or she is a candidate. . . . Where a candidate has more than one valid address, he may enter all such addresses on his nomination paper" ("Israeli-Palestinian Interim Agreement" 1995, Annex 2, Article 3[1][b]). Because the Palestinian constituency of Jerusalem established by the Palestinian Election Law was much larger than the city of Jerusalem, a person could be a candidate if he or she had an additional address in that constituency, beyond the limits of the city.

The parties also reached a compromise concerning the location of the polling stations at which the east Jerusalem Arabs were to cast their votes. In the elections that took place on January 20, 1996, most Jerusalemites voted within the boundaries of the Jerusalem constituency, namely in Abu Dis, beyond the limits of the city of Jerusalem (*Haaretz,* Jan. 18, 1996, 4a).

The Interim Agreement, however, permitted a small number of Palestinians to vote in post offices within the boundaries of the municipality of Jerusalem proper ("Israeli-Palestinian Interim Agreement" 1995, Annex 2, Article 6[2][a]).[18] The number of those allowed to vote at the designated post offices depended on "the capacity of such post offices." In fact, approx-

18. This article states that "[a] number of Palestinians of Jerusalem will vote in the elections through services rendered in post offices in Jerusalem, in accordance with the capacity of such post offices." The legality of elections at the post offices was challenged in H. Ct. 298/96, *Elisha Peleg v. Government of Israel,* and in H. Ct. 317/96, *Zalman Shoval et al. v. the Chairman of the Joint Subcommittee, Hagai Merom, et al.* It was alleged that elections in the post offices violate Israeli sovereignty over Jerusalem and are contrary to Section 1 of the Basic

imately 4,500 people, including mainly old and sick people, voted at the post offices *(Haaretz,* Jan. 18, 1996, 4A). Voting at the post office was procedurally somewhat different from voting at a regular polling station. This procedural distinction was intended to emphasize that Jerusalem was not part of the areas under the jurisdiction of the Palestinian Council. In Jerusalem, election campaigning required permits from Israel ("Israeli-Palestinian Interim Agreement" 1995, Annex 2, Article 6[1]).

About a month after the signing of the 1993 Declaration of Principles, Foreign Minister Shimon Peres of Israel sent a letter concerning Palestinian institutions in east Jerusalem to the foreign minister of Norway, Johan Jürgen Holst.[19] The letter remained secret for some time, and its discovery aroused much criticism in Israel. According to this letter,

> I wish to confirm that the Palestinian institutions of East Jerusalem and the interests and well-being of the Palestinians of East Jerusalem are of great importance and will be preserved. Therefore, all the Palestinian institutions of East Jerusalem, including the economic, social, educational and cultural, and the holy Christian and Moslem places, are performing an essential task for the Palestinian population. Needless to say, we will not hamper this activity. On the contrary, the fulfillment of this important mission is to be encouraged. (Peres 1994)

The meaning of this text and its legal or political effect raise difficult questions of interpretation (see Lapidoth 1994, 428–30; Singer 1994b).[20]

Once the ice was broken between Israel and the Palestinians, progress became possible in the negotiations between Israel and Jordan. The parties agreed on a "common agenda" on September 14, 1993, adopted a joint declaration on July 25, 1994, and on October 26, 1994, signed a peace treaty. This treaty provides, inter alia, that "Israel respects the present special role of

Law: Jerusalem, Capital of Israel. The Supreme Court rejected the arguments and dismissed the petitions.

19. Apparently, the sending of the letter had already been secretly promised in September (see Savir 1988, 93–94, 97, 98).

20. On the developments that led to the sending of this letter, see Musallam 1996, 37–48, and M. Klein 1995, 26.

the Hashemite Kingdom of Jordan in Muslim Holy Shrines in Jerusalem. When negotiations on the permanent status take place, Israel will give high priority to the Jordanian historical role in these shrines" ("Israel–Jordan Treaty of Peace" 1995, Article 9).[21]

In light of Israel's improved relations with both the Palestinians and Jordan, several other countries established or reestablished diplomatic relations with Israel. The normalization of relations between Israel and the Holy See, as expressed in the Fundamental Agreement of December 30, 1993, is of particular interest.[22] Although this document does not deal expressly with Jerusalem, some of its provisions are relevant to the city. For example, the agreement includes a commitment to favor Christian pilgrimages to the Holy Land and the right of the Roman Catholic Church to establish schools and carry out its charitable functions. The agreement includes an interesting provision under which the parties affirmed their "continuing commitment to maintain and respect the 'status quo' at the Christian Holy Places to which it applies" ("Fundamental Agreement" 1993, Article 4, para. 1). A similar provision was included in the February 2000 agreement between the Holy See and the PLO—a reference to the status quo established in the eighteenth and nineteenth centuries by the Ottoman Empire that regulated the rights of various competing Christian churches at Holy Places in Jerusalem and in Bethlehem (see note 2).

As already mentioned, it was agreed that Jerusalem should be on the agenda of the negotiations on the permanent status of the West Bank and the Gaza Strip. A single opening meeting of these negotiations took place in May 1996, but the substantive discussions started at the end of 1999.

In July 2000, the parties met at the Camp David retreat under the aus-

21. For an analysis of this provision, see Merhav and Giladi 1999, 35–52; Lapidoth 1994, 430–32; M. Klein 1996, 745–63; and Reiter 1997, 18–20. For the background to this provision, see Zak 1996, 173–84, and Shragai 1995, 387. The inclusion of this provision in the Peace Treaty was resented by the Palestinians (see Musallam 1996, 75–117). On the rivalry between Jordan and the Palestinians, see Breger and Idinopulos 1998, 37–41.

22. "Fundamental Agreement Between the Holy See and the State of Israel" 1993. On November 10, 1997, another agreement was concluded between the Holy See and Israel; it deals with matters of legal personality.

pices of President Clinton in order to promote agreement on the permanent-status issues. It seems that one of the main stumbling blocks was the question of sovereignty over the various parts of Jerusalem, in particular over the Temple Mount. Similarly, no agreement was reached at additional negotiations, which took place at Taba in January 2001. As these lines are being revised, severe acts of terror and violence have replaced the peace process.

Some Reflections on the Future of Jerusalem

Hopefully, when the parties return to the negotiating table, the diplomatic battle over Jerusalem is likely to be fierce and protracted because feelings about the city are strong on all sides. Perhaps the parties might facilitate negotiations by dividing the discussion into at least four components: national aspirations, Holy Places, municipal government, and the relation between Jerusalem and its periphery. These four components are interrelated, but, for practical purposes, more or less separate negotiations on each may be advisable.

Management of the sovereignty issue may be facilitated owing to the changes that this concept underwent in the twentieth century, as discussed below (see, e.g., Lapidoth 1992b, 1995, and references therein). In defining sovereignty, a clear distinction exists between its internal and external aspects. The former denotes the highest original, as opposed to derived, power within a territorial jurisdiction. This power is not subject to the executive, legislative, or judicial jurisdiction of any foreign power or to any foreign law other than public international law. The external aspect of sovereignty underlines the independence and equality of all states. It emphasizes that the state is an immediate and full subject of international law; it is not under the control of any other state; and it is able and free to exercise a fair amount of state power subject to the limits of international law. Sovereignty also implicates the right to nonintervention in a state's affairs, in particular in its relations with its subjects, the exclusivity of a state's powers within its territory, the presumption in favor of a state's powers, the lack of any obligation to submit to binding third-party adjudication, the right to wage war, and the theory that all international law has its source in the states' will.

The concept of sovereignty, however, has undergone great changes. The establishment of federal states as well as the democratization and the recognition of the supremacy of international law have reduced its impact. Although some earlier scholars believed that sovereignty was indivisible, in fact it has been divided in a number of historical and contemporary instances, such as condominia and federal states. In the eighteenth and nineteenth centuries, the expression "half sovereign" was used to describe entities, such as protectorates, that were dependent on other states. Today, numerous conceptions of qualified sovereignty and of a variety of notions related to sovereignty have acknowledged its flexible nature. Residual or de jure sovereignty denotes a right to sovereignty that may be subject to certain limitations, whereas de facto sovereignty refers to the actual exercise of power over a territory. Others distinguish between *territoriale Souveraenitaet* (legitimate title to an area) and *Gebietshoheit* (physical control). Quebec politicians have used the expressions *souveraineté-association* and *souveraineté-partagée*. The notion of spiritual sovereignty, an attribute of the Holy See, is also of interest.

Functional sovereignty is a relatively new notion based on developments in the law of the sea. According to the 1982 UN Convention on the Law of the Sea, the power of littoral states vis-à-vis their continental shelves and exclusive economic zones have been defined as "sovereign rights for the purpose of exploring . . . and exploiting its natural resources."[23] Environmental needs have caused the development of the notion of cooperative sovereignty. Moreover, nowadays the element of responsibility involved in sovereignty is underlined.

These developments tend to confirm that sovereignty is not indivisible and that two or more authorities may have limited, relative, differential,[24] scattered, shared, or functional sovereignty over certain areas, groups, or resources.

The demise of the notion that the state has full, comprehensive, and exclusive sovereignty is warranted by developments in the international sys-

23. See "United Nations Convention on the Continental Shelf" 1958, Article 2, and "United Nations Convention on the Law of the Sea" 1982, Articles 77 (regarding the continental shelf) and 56(1) (regarding the exclusive economic zone); see also Riphagen 1975.

24. A term used by Amiram Gonen in a conversation with the author.

tem. Today's financial markets are interconnected worldwide by modern communication systems. People, ideas, and criminals move across borders in great numbers, while pollution and ballistic missiles reduce the relevance of those borders. The permeability of borders necessarily reduces the effectiveness and relevance of territorial sovereignty, while free trade agreements and common markets work to render notions of a state's self-contained economic system obsolete.

Finally, certain normative developments, such as the severe limitation on the right to wage war and the development of international protection of human rights, have reduced the scope of sovereignty.

Despite these developments, it seems that time is not yet ripe to dispense with sovereignty. Public opinion in most states—particularly new, small, or fledgling ones—clings to the concept of sovereignty.

It is hoped that the diminished concept of sovereignty may assist in the quest for a compromise on Jerusalem. The parties should avoid arid discussions about sovereignty—an abstract notion with strong emotional appeal that would hinder compromise. In order to avoid the zero-sum attitudes about sovereignty, certain solutions could be considered. First, the parties could agree to suspend claims to sovereignty, either indefinitely or for a long period, and negotiate on a division of powers and responsibilities. A similar result would be achieved by attributing de jure sovereignty to God. This solution would also be in conformity with King Hussein's idea that sovereignty, at least in the Old City, belongs to God. Second, the parties could agree on a partial territorial division of sovereignty while keeping the city open and preserving freedom of access. Third, territorial sovereignty could be replaced by functional or shared sovereignty,[25] joint or relative sovereignty, or any other "mixes of sovereignty" (an expression George P. Shultz used [1990, A23])—a solution made possible by recent developments in the notion of sovereignty described above. Fourth, if no compromise is found, each party could keep up its claim to sovereignty, even if it is not recognized by the other party, and they could nevertheless reach practical solutions.

25. Sari Nusseibeh proposed a shared sovereignty solution (Nusseibeh 1993, 49–53); however, this solution has been analyzed and rejected as impractical (Breger 1994).

This kind of device is sometimes called "without prejudice" arrangements—that is, an agreement not to agree on a sensitive preliminary question.

An interesting example of such an agreement not to agree on sovereignty is the Ems-Dollard case. Before entering the North Sea, the German river Ems flows through a shallow estuary separating the mainlands of Germany and the Netherlands. The Dollard is a bay within the estuary. Each of the two neighbors has a port on the banks of the estuary. The two countries disagree about the location of the international boundary in the estuary but have reached agreements on practical matters and cooperation, while maintaining conflicting claims to the location of the boundary (Nolte 1995). Similarly, Britain and Argentina have concluded several agreements on practical matters concerning the Falkland/Malvinas Islands while disagreeing on sovereignty over the islands.[26]

When looking for solutions for Jerusalem, one could envision a mixture of the above-mentioned alternatives. Moreover, different solutions could be applied to various parts of the city. Instead of bickering about sovereignty, the negotiating parties should emphasize the division or sharing of powers. This division should be based on territorial, personal, and functional considerations.

As to the Holy Places, they have been a source of severe friction. Moreover, religious feelings have been exploited for political aims. In the search for solutions, the parties may have to consult the representatives of the millions of Christians, Jews, and Muslims who do not live in Jerusalem. Israel's policy has been to entrust the administration of each Holy Place to the religious community for which it is sacred and to provide financial aid for maintenance and renovation. Moreover, the Holy Places enjoy certain fiscal privileges (Berkovitz 1978, 545–50). The representatives of a considerable number of religions are satisfied with Israel's policy in this matter (see, e.g., Papastathis 1996). Because, however, others prefer to have an international ingredient or guarantee (Ferrari 1996), a degree of functional internationalization may be warranted (on internationalization, see Wolfrum 1995). While excluding the obsolete notion of exterritoriality, the adoption of a

---

26. See, for instance, the Joint Declaration on Cooperation over Offshore Activities in the South West Atlantic 1995 (*International Legal Materials* 35 [1996]: 301–8).

special statute for the Holy Places, with some monitoring by an interreligious group or council, might be agreed upon.

An important question that will have to be dealt with is the definition of *Holy Places*. Whereas the number of Holy Places in Jerusalem included in a list compiled by the UN in 1949 was 30 (E. Lauterpacht 1968, 5, n. 1), a list prepared in 2000 by a Christian, a Jewish, and a Muslim expert includes 326 entries (Reiter, with Eordegian and Abu Khalaf 2000). In order to reduce the danger of friction, it is advisable that the parties should establish an agreed list of Holy Places, which may be changed only by agreement.

At the municipal level, Jerusalem can perhaps learn some lessons from other heterogeneous cities. A division into boroughs or arrondissements, with each borough in charge of its own local affairs, may provide a possible solution (Hasson, Schory, and Adiv 1995). Coordination would be achieved through a joint, overarching municipality. The division of powers between the various boroughs can be on a territorial basis in some spheres and on a personal one in other matters.

In addition, the future settlement should also assure cooperation and coordination in the Jerusalem metropolitan area, irrespective of any political boundaries, because severing the city from its surroundings would hamper its development and engender difficulties in communications and services.

Finally, there is the possibility of dealing with Jerusalem in stages.

Conclusion

Writers have offered very different opinions on the status of west and east Jerusalem. To date, foreign states have not recognized any sovereignty over Jerusalem, but they have acquiesced in de facto Israeli control over west Jerusalem, while claiming that east Jerusalem is occupied territory. For the Israel authorities, the whole of Jerusalem is part of the State of Israel.

This chapter has shown that there has always been a close link between Jerusalem and the Holy Places. Differences of opinion about Jerusalem have concerned sovereignty over the city, and disputes about the Holy Places have related to ownership or the right of possession, as well as the right of access and of worship. But in 2000, the dispute also concerned sovereignty at the Temple Mount/al-Haram al-Sharif and the Western Wall. The Palestinian delegation even denied that any Jewish temple had ever existed on the Temple Mount. Those Holy Places that are sacred to only one religion or one denomination have only rarely been the subject of disputes.

When negotiations hopefully resume, Jerusalem will be one of the core issues. The parties will have to deal with thorny issues such as sovereignty, jurisdiction and powers (in particular in the spheres of security, transportation and access roads, town planning), the Holy Places (primarily those that are holy to two or more denominations), municipal matters (such as water, sewage, roads, and education), the notion of "open city" recommended in previous negotiations, and the rights of individuals. Unfortunately, these are difficult situations, but with good intentions and creative thinking, they can be solved.

3

The Future Settlement
of the Dispute over Jerusalem

Strategical and Institutional Aspects

Moshe Hirsch

N umerous Middle Eastern analysts consider the long-standing dispute
over Jerusalem the most formidable stumbling block to the achievement of a genuine and durable peaceful solution to the Arab–Israeli conflict.
The gap between the positions of the two main rivals, Israel and the Palestinians, seemed so vast in the past that even the very initial arrangements the
parties reached in the 1993 Declaration of Principles on Interim Self-
Government Arrangements astonished most observers ("Declaration"
1993). Indeed, the declaration's provisions regarding Jerusalem demonstrate
that both parties have significantly deviated from their traditional positions,
setting the stage for a new phase in the long and disputed history of
Jerusalem. The declaration's provisions state that the future of Jerusalem will
be negotiated between Israel and "the Palestinian people representatives"
(the "Palestinians") in the permanent-status negotiations ("Declaration"
1993, Article 5, 1529).

This chapter uses some concepts of game theory as well as the institu-

An earlier version of this article appeared in 45 Catholic University Law Review 699
(1996) and is reprinted with permission.

tional approach in international relations theory for two principal aims: (1) to identify the factors standing at the base of the dispute over Jerusalem and to analyze their influence on the outcome of the future negotiations; and (2) to explore the possibilities of changing the structural features of the existing setting of Jerusalem and to establish some joint institutions as means to enhance the prospects of achieving an agreed and stable settlement to this long-standing dispute.

It should be noted here that though it is common to refer to the "Jerusalem question," the controversy over the future of Jerusalem generally is restricted to control over east Jerusalem. Almost all the involved parties agree that west Jerusalem should remain under Israeli control (see chapter 2 of this volume). This discussion, therefore, is limited to the future of east Jerusalem.

The Provisions of the Israeli–Palestinian
Agreements Regarding Jerusalem

Three principal issues regarding Jerusalem are regulated in the recent agreements between Israel and the Palestine Liberation Organization (PLO): the jurisdiction of the Palestinian Council, the elections to that council, and the negotiations on the permanent status. The parties to the 1993 Declaration of Principles and to the 1995 Israeli–Palestinian Interim Agreement on the West Bank and the Gaza Strip agree that a Palestinian Council will be established for a transitional period not exceeding five years. Both instruments provide that the Palestinian Council will not have jurisdiction in Jerusalem for the five-year interim period ("Declaration" 1993, Articles 4–5, 1528–29; "Israeli–Palestinian Interim Agreement" 1995, Article 17). This statement contradicts the traditional PLO position that Israel should completely withdraw from east Jerusalem, the intended capital of the Palestinian state.[1]

---

1. On October 11, 1993, Israel's minister of foreign affairs sent a letter to the foreign minister of Norway regarding the preservation of the Palestinian institutions in east Jerusalem. For a discussion of the possible legal effects of this letter, see Lapidoth 1994, 402, 428–30; Singer 1994a, 292–93; and M. Klein 1995, 26–27.

According to both agreements, the Palestinians of Jerusalem will have the right to participate in the election process for the Palestinian Council. The election arrangements in Jerusalem are elaborated in the Israeli-Palestinian Interim Agreement (1995, Annex 2, Article 6). These arrangements, implemented on January 24, 1996, reflect a shift in Israeli policy, resulting from a change in the government itself following the 1992 Israel elections. Prior to these agreements, Israel was reluctant to allow the Arabs of east Jerusalem to participate in the elections for the Palestinian Council (see Lapidoth and Hirsch 1992, 357–65; Housen-Couriel and Hirsch 1992).

As to the more distant future, beyond the interim period, both the 1993 and the 1995 instruments state that the issue of Jerusalem's future will be one of the subjects on the agenda for the permanent-status negotiations to commence not later than May 4, 1996 ("Declaration" 1993, Article 5, 1528–29, and Agreed Minutes, 1542; "Israeli-Palestinian Interim Agreement" 1995, Article 31[5]). Unquestionably, this arrangement represents a clear deviation of both parties from their long-standing policies. Israel's leaders formerly asserted that the status of Jerusalem was not open for negotiations (see, e.g., Rabin 1996), and their Palestinian counterparts insisted that any solution affecting the West Bank also should apply to east Jerusalem (al-Husseini 1996; Klein 1999, 74, 97).

The emerging situation from these developments is somewhat mixed. The prominent fact is that Israel will continue to exercise control over east Jerusalem in the transitional period. On the other hand, Israel did agree to apply the election arrangements to east Jerusalem; these arrangements are quite different from those applying to the other areas under its sovereignty. As to the future, it seems that the parties' consent to negotiate the issue of Jerusalem in the permanent-status negotiations indicates that the current arrangements in east Jerusalem are modifiable to a certain degree.

Game Theory and the Controversy over Jerusalem

Basic Elements of Game Theory

This section explains some basic elements of game theory. The aim here is not to present a general introduction to game theory but rather to expose briefly its most basic notions, which will enable us to analyze the problems relating to the future of Jerusalem.[2]

Game theory is a discipline "designed to treat rigorously the question of optimal behavior" of decision makers in strategical situations (Morgenstern 1968, 62). The term *strategical* refers to situations in which the outcomes depend not only on the decision maker's conduct alone, or solely on those of nature, but also on the conduct of other participants (the latter fact led some scholars to label the theory "interactive decision theory") (Aumann 1987, 2). The participants are assumed to be rational in the sense that they have certain goals that they strive to attain through their actions; they have a consistent preference ordering of the goals; they know the rules of the game; and they know that the other players are also rational. The attainment of these goals does not necessarily direct the actors to beat each other, and not infrequently they are required to help the others as a condition to realize their own aims. In its formative years, game theory was developed chiefly by mathematicians and then rigorously applied to economics. The theory also was applied in other disciplines such as political science, international relations, law, sociology, and biology (see Aumann 1987, 2; Binmore 1990, 15; Fudenberg and Tirole 1991, 4; Morgenstern 1968, 62; Von Neumann and Morgenstern 1953, 1–29).

Game theory models the interactions between the participants in two principal forms of representation: the normal (or strategic) form and the extensive (or tree) form. A matrix showing each player's payoff for each combination of strategies often represents a normal game. The normal representation is more appropriate for simultaneous decision making, whereas the extensive form is more convenient for sequential-move games. The extensive-form representation also displays the information each player knows when making his or her decisions (see Baird, Gertner, and Picker 1994, 50; Fudenberg and Tirole 1991, 67; Gibbons 1992, 115–16). A game is defined as "any interaction between [players] that is governed by a set of rules specifying the possible moves for each participant and a set of out-

---

2. For a general introduction to game theory, see Fudenberg and Tirole 1991; Gibbons 1992; Heap and Varoufakis 1995; Luce and Raiffa 1957; Von Neumann and Morgenstern 1953.

comes for each possible combination of moves" (Heap and Varoufakis 1995, 1–2, 4).

The basic elements of the normal form game are (1) *the players*—the actors who make the decisions (either individuals or collective decision-making units such as firms or states); (2) *the strategy space*—the range of moves available to a player in a given situation (e.g., to cooperate or to defect); and (3) *the payoffs* (utilities)—the outcome generated for the players from a chosen move or strategy (see Baird, Gertner, and Picker 1994, 7–9; Fudenberg and Tirole 1991, 4–5; Gibbons 1992, 2–4; Von Neumann and Morgenstern 1953, 15–16, 48–54).

Reducing some set of interactions to a normal or extensive game, the next step is to determine the game's solution. Finding the solution of a game may serve two major purposes: first, a normative goal because it may guide us to the best strategy a rational player may adopt; and second, a predictive aim because it may indicate how rational players are likely to behave in such situations. A simple example is the notion of dominant strategy. A strategy is considered strictly dominant to any other when it is the best choice for a player regardless of what the other players will do (see Baird, Gertner, and Picker 1994, 11–12). When it is possible to identify a single dominant strategy, we can safely assume that a rational player will adopt the dominant strategy and reject the subordinate ones. Whereas a strict dominance strategy will not solve many games, the Nash-equilibrium solution applies to a much broader spectrum of games. A Nash-equilibrium is the combination of strategies, representing each player's best response to the predicted strategies of the other players. Such a prediction may be called strategically stable or self-enforcing because no single player is interested in deviating from his or her predicted strategy (Fudenberg and Tirole 1991, 11; see also Baird, Gertner, and Picker 1994, 19–25; Gibbons 1992, 8–9; Lyons 1992, 93, 101).

This description is only a limited exposition of the most basic elements of game theory; some others are presented in the following sections.

Is It Possible to Apply Concepts of Game Theory
to the Jerusalem Question?

Now having some knowledge of the basic concepts of game theory, the reader might wonder whether it is possible to apply such concepts to the question of the future of Jerusalem. The major difficulties to game-theoretic analysis of this problem relate to three principal factors: (1) the assumption regarding the rationality of the players; (2) the possibility of assigning accurate payoffs to the players' moves; (3) the role of elements that game theory does not take into account.

As explained above, one of the most basic assumptions of game theory is that the players are rational. The rationality assumption is the most notable obstacle for the application of the theory to the question of Jerusalem because there is considerable doubt that the national decision making with respect to this issue proceeds in a rational way. Indeed, one of the central factors explaining why it is so difficult to find an appropriate solution for the question of Jerusalem is located on the symbolic or psychological level rather than on the rational one.

One of the principal reasons underlying the dispute over Jerusalem is that the controversy exceeds the city's boundaries. In contrast to almost all other cities in the world, the future of Jerusalem is important not only to those who inhabit the city. During the last few decades, Jerusalem has become a major national and religious symbol for Jews, Muslims, and Christians all over the world. Thus, the main struggle is not for territorial, strategical, or economic gains, but rather for symbols.

Given the symbolic character of the dispute, is it rational to analyze it in a rational framework such as game theory? A distinction should be made here between the process of choosing an appropriate aim and the process of its attainment. The players in game-theoretic models are assumed to be rational in the sense that they strive to maximize their interests. It is not a precondition to the application of the theory that the chosen interest be selected in a rational process. The focus here is on the instrumental sense of rationality (see Heap 1992, 4–5)—that is, on the manner in which the selected interest will be maximized.

As to the dispute over east Jerusalem, the principal interest of the main contending parties, Israel and the Palestinians, is to exercise sovereignty or control over Jerusalem. Although it is true that the factors motivating the decision makers to adopt this interest as a desirable one are not wholly rational, we safely can assume that the actors do strive to maximize this interest. Thus, the symbolic (or irrational) factors standing behind the aim of exercising sovereignty or control over east Jerusalem do not bar us from applying concepts of game theory to the process of attaining this aim.

The second difficulty the tools of game theory encounter in the analysis of the question of Jerusalem is how to allocate accurate payoffs to expected outcomes. The knowledge that both parties are interested in exercising sovereignty or control over east Jerusalem does not enable us to assign a numerical payoff to this outcome. The problem is further complicated if an attempt is made to allocate accurate payoffs to some intermediate outcome, such as partial control over east Jerusalem or certain sections of it. In fact, this problem recurs in numerous situations in which concepts of game theory are used to analyze social phenomena.

In some cases, it is possible to assign *ordinal payoffs* to expected outcomes (i.e., to organize the various outcomes in accordance with the order of priorities for the relevant player) and then to allocate a respective ordinal number to each outcome. The use of this method may assist us in arriving at interesting inferences in numerous situations,[3] but without knowing the distance between payoffs on an interval scale, it is impossible to calculate accurately the probabilities with which each party would choose each outcome (Brams 1975, 20). Furthermore, in some cases, it is impossible to attribute even ordinal payoffs to the different results and, as a consequence, to calculate the accurate probability that a certain decision will be made. Even in such situations, as we shall see below, game-theoretic analysis may well be a valuable tool to provide us with significant indications regarding the expected trends of decision makers and the pattern of decisions likely to be adopted in particular settings.

The third difficulty of analyzing the question of Jerusalem in light of

3. For a discussion of this method of assigning payoffs, see Heap and Varoufakis 1995, 5–11, and Snidal 1985, 46–48. See also Brams 1975, 13–16, on the use of the ordinal method of assigning payoffs to analyze a specific case.

game theory lies in the fact that such an analysis does not take into account various personal and social factors. It is undeniable that factors external to game theory frequently influence the behavior of states and other political entities. Such factors relate, for example, to the psychological characteristics of the decision makers and to social values prevailing in the decision makers' environments. Indeed, this basic fact should be kept in mind whenever one attempts to analyze social phenomena with the aid of concepts of game theory. Although game theory may shed light on one of the more central aspects of the dispute over Jerusalem's future, it certainly is not the only methodology to be used in a comprehensive study of that question.

In summary, the two principal difficulties accompanying a game-theoretic analysis of the question of Jerusalem's future are the impossibility of assigning numerical payoffs to specific outcomes and the influence of external factors that game theory does not take into account. These difficulties do not exclude the importance of such an analysis but rather restrict its ramifications. Although the first difficulty bars us from arriving at precise conclusions, game-theoretic analysis nevertheless provides a valuable tool to detect important indications regarding the expected trends of decision makers and the pattern of decisions in particular settings. The second difficulty demonstrates one of the limits of game-theoretic analysis but certainly does not deprive such an analysis of any significance.

The Elements of the "Game" of Jerusalem

The first phase in a game theoretic analysis of a particular situation is to define the basic elements of the situation in terms of game theory.[4] Here, we must define who the players are, the moves available to them, and the payoffs in the game of Jerusalem.

The Players. The players in the game of Jerusalem may be divided into three circles in accordance with the level of their involvement and interests in the game.

1. External Circle: In the external circle we find the players that have

4. The term *game* is used here and throughout this chapter to refer only to an interactive situation within the framework of game theory.

some general but no direct interest in the future of Jerusalem. These players do not claim a significant position in the future regime of the city. The players in this circle are, for example, the United States, the European Union, and the United Nations.

2. Middle Circle: The players in the middle circle claim, explicitly or implicitly, some significant role or special rights in the future system to be established in east Jerusalem and particularly regarding the administration of the Holy Places. Here, we may find Jordan,[5] the Vatican,[6] and various churches and Christian denominations that possess religious buildings of sites in the city (e.g., the Greek Orthodox Church and the Armenian Church).

3. Inner Circle: The players in the inner circle expressly claim the legal right of sovereignty or control over east Jerusalem. The main players in the core of the game are Israel and the Palestinians.[7]

5. Jordan was considered a main player in the past. From 1967 to the early 1970s, Jordan demanded that Israel withdraw from east Jerusalem, as well as from the entire West Bank so that Jordanian sovereignty would be restored in this area (see Hirsch, Housen-Couriel, and Lapidoth 1995, 135). Since the early 1970s, however, this position has gradually changed, especially following the 1974 Arab Summit Conference at Rabat. The new Jordanian policy, which does not claim sovereignty over east Jerusalem, was formally expressed in a speech that King Hussein delivered on July 31, 1988. In this speech, the king announced, "the dismantling of the legal and administrative links between Jordan and the West Bank," including east Jerusalem (see Hirsch, Housen-Couriel, and Lapidoth 1995, 135). Despite the king's declaration, however, "Jordanian officials nevertheless indicated that Jordan would continue to play its historical role as the guardian of the Islamic Holy Places in Jerusalem" (see Hirsch, Housen-Couriel, and Lapidoth 1995, 135; Bin Talal 1979, 17–49; "Israel-Jordan" 1994, 43, 50). For a discussion of a more recent developments regarding Jordan's position, see M. Klein 1995, 43–56.

6. The Vatican's position regarding east Jerusalem has also changed over the years. In the past (at least until 1967), the Vatican supported the idea of internationalization (see Hirsch, Housen-Couriel, and Lapidoth 1995, 127–28). More recently, however, Vatican representatives have advocated the idea of a special status for the Old City, supported by international guarantees to ensure the rights of the three monotheistic faiths (see Hirsch, Housen-Couriel, and Lapidoth 1995, 128; Irani 1986, 75–81; Stevens 1981, 172).

7. For a survey of the main parties' legal claims to east Jerusalem, see Blum 1974, 1; Cattan 1981, 111–21; Dinstein 1971; Hirsch, Housen-Couriel, and Lapidoth 1995, 18–21; E. Lauterpacht 1968, 48–49; Mallison and Mallison 1986, 197–201, 206, 233; and Stevens 1981, 162–63.

Although the players in all circles have some influence over the future regime to be established in east Jerusalem, their levels of respective influence are different. It is quite clear especially since the conclusion of the 1993 Declaration of Principles that the players in the inner circle have the crucial role of shaping the future arrangements to be applied to the city, whereas the other players will have to accept the "deal" they strike. Some of the players in the other circles may have some objections to the agreement Israel and the Palestinians reach, but their ability to block its implementation seems quite modest. This observation does not exclude the possibility that certain players in the middle or outer circles will have some role in the negotiating process or in the future regime on which the main actors agree.

The Strategies. Three principle strategies are available to the main players in the negotiations over the future of Jerusalem:

1. To continue exercising (for Israel) or to gain (for the Palestinians) full sovereignty or control over all parts of east Jerusalem;

2. To relinquish the claim to full sovereignty or control over all parts of east Jerusalem; or

3. To negotiate partial arrangements, of which there exists an endless range of possible territorial and functional arrangements for sharing sovereignty or control over the whole or parts of the territory of east Jerusalem. Examples of possible partial arrangements are discussed below.

The Payoffs. The expected payoffs for each party from the exercise of full sovereignty or control over all parts of east Jerusalem are considerable. As explained above, Jerusalem has become a major national and religious symbol for both the Israeli and the Palestinian peoples (and much beyond them). The importance of the Jerusalem issue for both peoples prescribes very high negative payoffs for the party that would relinquish its claim to sovereignty or control over all parts of east Jerusalem. The price of the latter strategy seems so immense that it may well be insurmountable for national leaders on both sides. This fact practically rules out almost any possibility that the two main players will accept an agreement embodying one of the two extreme strategies.

This point directs us to the third strategy: reaching some partial arrangement. It is clear that the payoffs arising for the parties from some partial arrangement will correspond to the content of the specific agreement. Beyond this general observation, it is noteworthy to point out that some elements of partial arrangements may carry asymmetric payoffs for the players. An identification of all such elements is important and may narrow the practical range of possible partial arrangements that the main players are likely to accept. Such a comprehensive task, however, exceeds the limits of this discussion, which must be confined to the identification of the most principal elements that produce asymmetric payoffs.

For Israel, the negative payoffs expected from certain partial arrangements may be higher than those expected for the Palestinians. This expectation is particularly true with regard to the Western Wall and the new Jewish neighborhoods in east Jerusalem. The government of Israel might suffer considerable negative payoffs if it would relinquish control of or recognize Palestinian sovereignty over the Western Wall because the site is most sacred to Jews. The immense negative payoffs arising from such a concession practically rule out this possibility.

The issue of the new Jewish neighborhoods in east Jerusalem illustrates the technique of preemption, or irrevocable commitment, which is well known in game theory. The use of this technique enables a player to change the payoffs produced from some move by committing, at an early stage, certain resources, part of which must be sunk (i.e., unrecoverable in a later stage). Such action increases the negative payoffs arising for the investing party from a particular move, and if the commitment is unambiguously visible to the other player, it changes the other player's equilibrium strategies (Baird, Gertner, and Picker 1994, 57–63; Schelling [1960] 1980, 22–28). Since the Israeli seizure of east Jerusalem in 1967, Israeli governments have committed vast amounts of financial and personal resources to build new neighborhoods and to settle more than 150,000 Jews in this part of the city.[8] The negative payoffs expected for Israel from withdrawing from these areas or from relocating a significant number of Israeli inhabitants seem very high. This fact considerably reduces the likelihood that Israel will adopt such a move. In fact, it seems that the Palestinians are aware of these facts, and some

8. The approximately 160,000 Jews living in east Jerusalem constitute 38 percent of the city's total Jewish population and 48 percent of the overall population in this part of the city (Choshen 1998b, 38).

of their leaders already have indicated implicitly that they would be ready to recognize Israeli sovereignty and control over these new neighborhoods in the future (Klein 1995, 40).[9]

For the Palestinians, some elements of a partial arrangement may produce greater negative payoffs than for Israel. This fact is most prominent with regard to al-Aqsa Mosque and the Dome of the Rock on the Temple Mount. Because both sites are sacred to Islam, Palestinian recognition of Israeli sovereignty or control over these shrines would generate considerable negative payoffs for the Palestinians. Again, the expected negative payoffs from such a Palestinian move practically rule out this possibility.

Similarly, the Palestinians are likely to suffer significant negative payoffs if the new arrangement fails to establish or recognize a clear link between the Palestinians living in east Jerusalem and the Palestinian entity in the West Bank and the Gaza Strip. As noted above, the Palestinians previously asserted that east Jerusalem is an integral part of the West Bank and that the same legal regime should apply to both territories. The recent agreements between Israel and the Palestinians include some link between the Palestinians of east Jerusalem and the Palestinian Council. The election arrangements to which the parties agreed entitled these Palestinians to participate in the election process in the West Bank and Gaza Strip.

Structural Features of the "Game" of Jerusalem

Although numerous analysts agree that the question of Jerusalem's future is the most difficult issue on the agenda between Israel and the Palestinians, different reasons have been presented to explain this difficulty. In this sec-

9. The legal actions Israel took at the municipal level in July 1967 also may be perceived, to some extent, as a preemption act. Shortly after the Israeli seizure of east Jerusalem, the Israeli Parliament and government enacted a series of legislative measures resulting in the application of Israeli law, jurisdiction, and administration to east Jerusalem (see Lapidoth and Hirsch 1992, 167). The legal significance of these enactments has been examined in several decisions Israeli courts handed down, embodying the unequivocal conclusion that east Jerusalem had become part of Israel (see Lapidoth and Hirsch 1992, 489–90, 502–6, 535–39). Although these legislative and judicial actions are not irreversible, they certainly increase the negative payoffs Israel can expect if it relinquishes some of its sovereignty over east Jerusalem.

tion, I discuss some structural features that shape the problematic interaction in the game of Jerusalem. The identification of the structural stumbling blocks and the comprehension of their content lead to a consideration, in the next section, of possible changes that may influence future negotiations between the parties.

Zero-sum Games. The zero-sum game (or constant-sum game) is unquestionably one of the most famous concepts of game theory that served, especially in the early stages of the theory's development, as a polar case and historical point of departure. The key feature of a zero-sum game is that the sum of payoffs is constant: "[i]n a two-player zero-sum game, whatever one player wins the other loses" (Fudenberg and Tirole 1991, 4; see also Von Neumann and Morgenstern 1953, 46–47, 98–100). Two-player zero-sum games represent strictly competitive situations; the players have opposed preferences and are considered rivals. Players are in conflict and not inclined to cooperate. Thus, as long as the structure of a given situation is that of a zero-sum game, the likelihood of a compromise is significantly reduced.

The basic structure of a dispute between Israel and the Palestinians over Jerusalem has strong features of a zero-sum game. The parties perceive the conflict over east Jerusalem chiefly as a territorial dispute. Each party is interested in gaining full and exclusive sovereignty or control over all parts of the eastern city. Needless to say, these preferences are bitterly opposed because any gain for one party directly entails a loss for the other.[10] As long as the situation has the basic features of a zero-sum game, the prospects for a compromise between Israel and the Palestinians is significantly reduced.

Exit Options. One of the central factors influencing the outcomes of a bargaining process is the exit option available to each player in case of bargaining failure. Exit options influence the readiness of the respective parties to leave the negotiation table, and as Frederik Zeuthen observes in his celebrated article "Economic Warfare," the parties' readiness "to fight the matter out" determines the course of the negotiations (1975, 145, 151, 162). The principal question arising here is: What is the alternative for each party if an agreement is not reached? In the game of Jerusalem, two

10. The game of Jerusalem is not a pure zero-sum game. Although each gain for one player entails a loss for the other, the value of such payoffs is not always symmetrical.

kinds of exit options may be relevant: legal exit options and factual exit options.

Legal Exit Options. The legal system relevant to the question of sovereignty or control over Jerusalem is international law. International law, like municipal systems of law, provides default rules applicable to the relationship between the parties, as long as the parties do not reach an agreement embodying different rules.[11] The content of these default rules has considerable bearing on the outcome of the bargaining process; therefore, it is commonly said that negotiations are conducted "in the shadow of law." Generally, the content of alternative legal rules narrows the range of possible arrangements to which the parties can agree.

One of the principal factors explaining the difficulty in resolving the dispute over Jerusalem is that international law does not provide the parties with clear default rules, if any, to the question "Whose Jerusalem?" States and scholars have presented numerous legal positions on this question, but neither the international community nor any authoritative institution has accepted them. As in other legal spheres, where law does not give clear answers to existing problems, its influence on the behavior of the actors diminishes, which is clearly the case with the extent of the influence of international law on the course of the game of Jerusalem. Thus, the absence of legal exit options enhances the role of factual alternatives available to the parties.

Factual Exit Options. The factual alternatives to bargaining failure between Israel and the Palestinians over the issue of east Jerusalem are asymmetric. In the absence of an agreement between the parties, the current situation is likely to proceed into the future, and this exit option is in Israel's favor. Israel currently maintains control over east Jerusalem,[12] and this situation is expected to continue unless Israel unilaterally decides to relinquish such control or an outside power forces it to do so; both developments, however, seem very remote. Israeli insistence on preserving the present sta-

11. Important (though not frequent) exceptions to this observation are mandatory rules of any legal system that the parties to an agreement cannot modify.

12. Since 1967, Israel has allowed the Waqf to administer al-Aqsa Mosque and the Dome of the Rock.

tus quo, however, would not satisfy minimal Palestinian demands and expectations (following the provisions of the Declaration of Principles), and such a situation may lead to a deadlock in the permanent-status negotiations. Cessation of or considerable delay in the negotiations may result in violent clashes between Palestinians and Israelis.

Thus, the exit option to bargaining failure in the game of Jerusalem is a certain continuation of Israeli control over all of Jerusalem, with the possibility of an impasse in the negotiations and some violent activities on the part of the Palestinians. Although this alternative might produce negative payoffs for both sides, it is clearly more favorable to Israel than to the Palestinians. The existence of such a favorable exit option for Israel indicates that Israel's readiness to face a bargaining failure in the game of Jerusalem is greater than the Palestinians'. Moreover, this feature explains Israel's past policy of refusing to enter into negotiations over the future of Jerusalem.

Embedded Games. The above analysis of the structure of the game of Jerusalem may explain why the main parties have not reached a final compromise thus far, but the initial compromise achieved in the 1993 Declaration of Principles can hardly be explained. Furthermore, as to future prospects for any agreed upon settlement, given the above factors, Israel does not seem to have a considerable incentive to relinquish even part of its control over east Jerusalem and to bear the ensuing negative payoffs. Indeed, if the game of Jerusalem had been an isolated one, the pre-1993 deadlock likely would have proceeded into the future. The concept of embedded games may explain the dramatic change in the 1993 Declaration of Principles and possible changes in the future.

Frequently the failure to analyze a social phenomenon properly by game-theoretic models stems from misidentification of a particular situation as the game itself, although, in reality, the situation is embedded in a larger game. The characterization of a given game as a subgame within a larger one and the identification of the larger game itself have important implications for the analysis of that characterization.[13] Particularly, as in other cases, focusing on only the interactions between Israel and the Palestinians in the

13. The meaning of the term *subgame* in this context is not identical with its meaning in game theory.

game of Jerusalem may hinder our ability to properly understand the whole game and its likely course of play.

The game of Jerusalem is of great importance to both Israel and the Palestinians, but it certainly is not the only one and not even the most crucial one between them. Rather, the game of Jerusalem is embedded in a larger framework, in which the master game is the regime to be established in the West Bank and the Gaza Strip, and the degree of independence Israel will accord to the Palestinian self-governing authorities. The linkage between these two issues was formed in the negotiations between the two parties that concluded the 1993 Declaration of Principles. The Palestinians were not ready to sign the agreement stipulating the principles for Palestinian self-government in the West Bank and Gaza Strip unless Israel included some compromise regarding Jerusalem in the agreement. The parties reached only an initial compromise, but without this linkage between the two subgames, the likelihood of such an agreement would have been slight.

Domestic Win-Sets. The significant factors influencing the outcomes of the negotiations over Jerusalem are located not only on an international level, but on a domestic level as well. As Robert Putnam has analyzed, the dynamics of many international negotiations can be conceived usefully as a two-level game. At "the national level, domestic groups pursue their interests by pressuring the government to adopt favorable policies and politicians seek power by constructing coalitions among those groups. At the international level, governments seek to maximize their own ability to satisfy domestic pressures, while minimizing the adverse consequences of foreign developments" (1988, 436–37). Each national leader appears at both game boards. The underlying fact is that the domestic constituents must endorse[14] any agreement concluded on the international level.[15]

14. Putnam labels the process of endorsement by domestic constituents as "ratification." This ratification may take several forms such as voting procedure or any other decision process at the domestic level that is required to endorse or to implement the agreement, whether formally or informally (Putnam 1988, 438).

15. This is particularly true for democracies, but it applies to nondemocratic regimes as well because the actors at the domestic level may represent bureaucratic agencies, interest

Putnam defined a win-set for a given domestic constituency as the set of all possible international agreements that would win the endorsement among the domestic constituents (Putnam 1988, 439–40). Thus, by definition, any successful international agreement must fall within the domestic win-set of each of the parties to the agreement; in other words, the agreement is possible only if those win-sets overlap. The clear result is that the larger the win-set of each player, the more likely they are to overlap; or, the opposite, the smaller the win-sets, the greater risk that the negotiations will break down. One factor influencing the win-sets of the parties is the extent of homogeneity of the domestic constituents with respect to the issue at the negotiation table. It is not rare that some segment of one party's domestic population supports the contention of the other party (e.g., regarding trade liberalization). Generally, the more diffuse the positions are within the domestic constituents of the parties, the easier it might be to achieve an agreement on the international level (Putnam 1988, 443–45; see also Raiffa 1982, 12).

The relative size of the respective domestic win-sets affects not only the likelihood of successful negotiations, but also the distribution of the payoffs between the players. Generally, the larger the win-set of a party, the more amenable that party is to granting concessions in the other party's favor; or, conversely, the player with the narrower win-set is in a better position to compel the other player to make greater concessions. Thus, quite paradoxically, a narrower win-set might be considered an advantage during international negotiations (Putnam 1988, 440).

The size of the respective win-sets of Israel and the Palestinians provides one significant reason why it has been so difficult to achieve an agreement in the game of Jerusalem. As stated above, Jerusalem has become a major national and religious symbol for peoples on both sides, thus significantly reducing the win-sets of both players and the likelihood of an overlap. An examination of the level of homogeneity within the domestic constituents of the parties reinforces the conclusion. The domestic constituents of both parties are quite unified in that regard (i.e., the majority of the domestic

---

groups, social classes, or even public opinion (Putnam 1998, 438–39).

populations of both Israel and the Palestinians is very much interested in having its respective government exercise sovereignty and control over east Jerusalem), which increases the likelihood of a bargaining failure.

Possible Structural Changes and the
Future Negotiations over Jerusalem

The above analysis of the basic structure of the game of Jerusalem raises two principal questions: Are the structural factors static or amenable to changes? And what are the effects of some possible changes on the outcomes of future negotiations? As shown below, the main parties in the middle and external circles certainly may modify some structural features. This section analyzes possible changes and their likely implications.

One factor that has a major influence on the outcome of future negotiations is the structure of the game of Jerusalem as a zero-sum game. As explained previously, the key feature of a zero-sum game is that whatever one player wins the other loses. Players in such situations are considered to be in conflict and are not inclined to cooperate or compromise. So far, the game of Jerusalem has had strong features of a zero-sum game, and as long as this situation prevails, the likelihood for a compromise is significantly reduced. Three principal techniques may transform the structure of the game into a non-zero-sum game: (1) changing the payoffs for some moves, (2) expanding the scope of the game, or (3) combining several subgames into one game.

The first technique to change the structure of a zero-sum game is to provide the players (either one or both) with some additional payoffs if an agreement is reached, but without a correlative loss to the other party. The players in the external and middle circles (e.g., the United States or the European Union) primarily may supply the new payoffs. The players in these circles may provide the main players with various kinds of assistance, the most notable (but not necessarily the most important) being economic assistance. Thus, for instance, the United States or the European Union may channel significant financial resources into east Jerusalem to raise the standard of living of the Palestinians residing in that area or to establish new medical or academic institutions in the Jewish neighborhoods. Economic assistance also may take the form of trade preferences, whereby the United States or the European Union may grant privileged trade concessions to products manufactured in east Jerusalem (by either Jews or Palestinians) and imported into their territories.

Economic payoffs are not the only payoffs in game theory, however, and the game of Jerusalem illustrates well a game in which social, religious, and symbolic gains outweigh economic ones. One noneconomic payoff that players outside the inner circle provide may be international recognition. States in the middle and the external circles, such as the United States and European Union, may decide to recognize Jerusalem as the capital of Israel and transfer their embassies to the city. To Israel, such a move might be considered a significant payoff.[16] As for the Palestinians, the United States and European Union may assist the Palestinian Authority to become a regular member of some intergovernmental organization or recognize it as a sovereign state.

The second possible technique to change the structure of the game is to have the main players themselves expand its scope. An expansion of the game into new domains that do not have a zero-sum character may transform the structure of the game into a non-zero one. The game of Jerusalem may be enlarged to include either new territories or new symbols or both. On the geographical level, the city boundaries may be expanded to include areas that currently are not within Jerusalem.[17] The enlarged Jerusalem may include adjoining territories in the West Bank. Though there is a controversy over the final status of the West Bank, the dispute over its status does not have the strong zero-sum features of the game of Jerusalem.[18]

16. Although Israel has declared Jerusalem to be its capital, most states have declined to recognize, at least de jure, this fact. The states' reactions have resulted in a variety of measures, the most prominent being the location of all embassies (except two) outside Jerusalem. For a discussion of the possibilities and significance of trade privileges to enhance the prospects of peace in the Middle East, see Hirsch 1998.

17. Press reports indicate that possible expansion of the city's boundaries may constitute an important element of the future agreement between Israel and the Palestinians (see "Israel Hints at Jerusalem Compromise" 2000).

18. Although under Israeli law, east Jerusalem is considered a part of Israel, this is not the case with the West Bank and the Gaza Strip.

On the symbolic level, the game of Jerusalem may be expanded to include new symbols. As noted above, the main struggle in Jerusalem is for symbols, and the main parties may create some new symbols, mainly religious and cultural in nature. Thus, for instance, new symbols may take the form of recognizing new title roles such as the guardian of the Muslim Holy Places in Jerusalem or the chairman of the Consultative Committee on the Muslim Holy Places in Jerusalem, or of raising a religious Muslim flag over some Muslim holy shrines. Symbolic functions in the Muslim Holy Places may well play a significant role in the game of Jerusalem, and their allocation should not necessarily be limited to the main players. In fact, granting such roles to some Arab states may encourage them to provide significant payoffs (either financial or nonfinancial) to the main players.

Last, but not least, the possibility of establishing new religious buildings or monuments in Jerusalem should not be discarded lightly. The importance of such new sites certainly will be on a much lower scale than the Western Wall or al-Aqsa Mosque, but this does not mean that they will be of no significant symbolic importance at all for the parties. The establishment of new religious buildings or monuments may assist the main parties to allocate symbols, both among themselves and with players in the other circles.

The third possible method to change the structure of the game of Jerusalem is to embed it in some other subgame. Here, it may be desirable to embed the subgame of Jerusalem with other subgames that do not have inherent zero-sum features. The difference between the heretofore described method of expanding the game and the method of embedding it within some other subgame lies in the nexus between the relevant game and the new element. Whereas the technique of expansion assimilates the new element into the existing game, the method of embedding creates a link between the two subgames, yet preserves their independence.

The front-runner subgame to be embedded within the game of Jerusalem is the permanent status of the West Bank and Gaza Strip. The linkage between these two issues was already formed in the negotiations leading to the 1993 Declaration of Principles, and this pattern may recur in the next round of negotiations. For instance, it is possible that Israel might be ready to relinquish its opposition to the establishment of a Palestinian state in exchange for Palestinian recognition that part of east Jerusalem is under Israeli lawful sovereignty. Beyond the possibility of embedding the Jerusalem subgame within that of the permanent status of the West Bank and Gaza Strip, the parties also may consider other subgames, such as those involving security arrangements and economic relations.

The win-sets of the respective parties also may undergo some changes and modify the likelihood that the parties will reach an agreement. As explained above, the greater the domestic win-sets of the players, the more likely they are to overlap and lead to an agreement. The win-sets of the parties may be enlarged or narrowed in accordance with changes in the payoffs to the parties or in line with a combination of the game of Jerusalem with other subgames. These possible changes are enumerated above and need not be repeated here. If changes to the game of Jerusalem modify the preferences of only some segments of the domestic population (as expected in our case), it will lessen the current level of homogeneity within the domestic constituents and increase the likelihood of an agreement. Again, the more diffuse the domestic positions are, the easier it might be to achieve an agreement on the international level.

The larger the win-set of a party on the domestic level, the more amenable the party will be to concessions on the international level. This fact may lead the parties to seek to enlarge the win-set of the other side during the negotiations (e.g., by communicating directly with the other side's domestic constituents), and, likewise, because the player with the narrower win-set is in a better position to compel the other player to greater concessions, the negotiators may attempt to portray their respective sides as having very narrow win-sets.

The Institutional Theory and the Settlement of the Dispute over Jerusalem

The Institutional Approach in International Relations Theory

The institutional approach in international relations literature focuses on the role of international institutions in world politics in general and on their contribution to the development of international cooperation in particular. Theoretically, international cooperation may also occur outside of international institutions, but in most cases such cooperation is sporadic and short term.

There are several streams in institutionalist theory, both within the international relations discipline and in other disciplines (such as sociology, economy, political science). The difference between these streams is sometimes considerable. As clarified below, the institutional theory may well complement game theory and other strands of rational choice theory (Abell 1995, 3). Most of this section is focused on the rational choice variant of institutionalism.

Institutions may constitute an important instrument that shape the payoff structure or other unique properties of a particular setting. Consequently, the establishment of new institutions or the introduction of some alterations to existing ones may serve as a valuable tool to alter the structure of settings susceptible to collective-action failure.

International institutions may enhance the prospects of eliciting and maintaining cooperation between states. This aim may be achieved by various methods. International institutions may establish a prominent focal point in settings with multiple equilibria (see Garrett and Weingast 1993, 173, 181–85; Keohane and Martin 1995, 39, 43). Game theoretic analysis of many international settings does not lead to a unique equilibrium, and international institutions may be helpful to shape the needed focal points.

International institutions frequently administer retaliatory mechanisms (see Axelrod and Keohane 1985; Garrett and Weingast 1993, 176; Keohane and Martin 1995, 49), which are crucial to obtain cooperation in numerous settings (see Patchen 1987, 164). Effective sanctioning machinery may reshape the payoff structure by increasing the cost of noncooperative strategies and enhance the likelihood of cooperation. An efficient retaliatory mechanism frequently presupposes an effective monitoring system to detect defections,[19] and numerous international institutions establish comprehensive monitoring procedures.

Linkage between several spheres is expected to play a major role in the

19. In some spheres, such as tariffs and use of force, noncooperative moves are visible and need not necessarily be detected by monitoring mechanisms.

future negotiations on Jerusalem. As noted above, linkage arrangements may change the payoff structure of the competitive game of Jerusalem. Linkage may broaden the scope of issues available for tradeoffs between the parties and may widen the space available for contingent strategies that are important to elicit cooperation in numerous settings. A party that cannot adopt retaliatory measures within a particular sphere may find new opportunities in the expanded regime.[20] One of the major contributions of international institutions to the enhancement of cooperation is the creation of institutionalized linkages. These linkages establish a long-term nexus between several issues areas and, in this way, significantly raise the price of disassociation for a party who considers the option of departing from the path of cooperation.

International institutions frequently provide accessible communication channels that facilitate improved cooperation and may be of special importance to reduce tensions during periods of crises.

The various institutions established by the 1998 Good Friday Agreement in the United Kingdom well exemplify several important methods through which international institutions alleviate conflicts over disputed territories. Some institutional arrangements of this agreement may provide us some guidance regarding the future settlement of the dispute over Jerusalem.

The Northern Ireland Conflict: Brief Background

Approximately three thousand people have been killed because of the political violence in Northern Ireland since 1969, and many more have been injured.[21] The core of the conflict is related to the future status of this territory: since the partition of Ireland into two political units in 1920 (Ireland and Northern Ireland), the Unionists (mostly Protestants) insist that Northern Ireland must remain part of the United Kingdom, whereas the Irish Nation-

20. For a discussion of linkage arrangements as an instrument to enhance the prospect of future environmental cooperation in the Middle East, see Hirsch 1999.

21. This section is based on the following sources: Hoppen 1989, 173–203; Hughes 1994, 6–88; Johnson 1992, 173–93; Lee 1989, 410–57; McGarry and O'Leary 1995; O'Leary and McGarry 1997.

alists (mostly Catholics) have argued that this region should be united with the Republic of Ireland.

Northern Ireland has an area of 13,483 square kilometers. According to a population census conducted in 1991, it has approximately 1.6 million inhabitants, 56 percent of whom are Protestants and 41 percent Catholics. The birthrate of the Catholics is greater than that of the Protestants. In the period between 1920 and 1972, Northern Ireland had a special status under the British law, and special institutions had autonomous powers in various spheres. In this period, supreme authority for Northern Ireland rested with the British Parliament. The Protestant majority was larger than it is today, and the Protestant community wielded political power. Following the wave of intercommunal violence and complaints of severe discrimination against the Catholics, the home-rule arrangements were abolished and direct control of the region reverted to the British Parliament (to which the residents of Northern Ireland may vote and stand for election).

The 1998 Good Friday Agreement

The Good Friday Agreement (or the Belfast Agreement), signed on April 10, 1998, is the culmination a long and turbulent peace process in Northern Ireland (see Greenspan 1986, 585; McKittrick 1996; O'Leary and McGarry 1997, 220–239; Walker and Weaver 1994, 817). The agreement contains several documents (declarations, annexes), and its major principles are as follows:

(1) commitment to democratic and peaceful means of resolving the differences, and opposition to any use or threat of force;

(2) recognition of the legitimacy of the choice exercised by the majority of the people of Northern Ireland with regard to its status;

(3) affirmation that the power of the sovereign government in Northern Ireland shall be exercised with rigorous impartiality and full respect of civil rights and religious liberties of everyone;

(4) commitment to human rights protection;

(5) decommissioning process under the auspices of the Independent International Commission on Decommissioning;[22] and

(6) establishment of several kinds of institutions.

In our context, the most important institutions are autonomous institutions in Northern Ireland (mainly the assembly), cooperative institutions to operate among the various parties, and supervisory human rights institutions. These institutions are examined in more detail in the sections that follow.

The Assembly. The United Kingdom government will transfer to this autonomous body some of its current powers (mainly in the economic and social fields) regarding the administration of Northern Ireland. Under the Good Friday Agreement, a democratically elected assembly will exercise some legislative and executive powers. There will be safeguards to ensure that key decisions are taken on a cross-community basis. The Assembly will have authority to pass primary legislation for Northern Ireland in the devolved areas. The British secretary of state will remain responsible for Northern Ireland matters not devolved to the Assembly and the Westminster Parliament will legislate for the nondevolved issues ("Good Friday Agreement" 1998, Strand One: Democratic Institutions in Northern Ireland).

North-South Ministerial Council. This body was the most contentious subject during the negotiations leading to the Good Friday Agreement. It was established at the demand of the Catholics, and it highlights the link between Northern Ireland and the Republic of Ireland. Under the agreement, the council consists of executive officers from Northern Ireland and the Irish government, and its aim is to develop consultation and cooperation within the island of Ireland on matters of mutual interest (e.g., strategic transport planning, environmental protection, inland waterways, and tourism). All council decisions will be made by agreement of the two parties and within the competence of the respective administrations. The council may establish new implementation bodies to execute its decisions on a cross-

---

22. The decommission process is the most difficult issue in the implementation of the agreement (see "I.R.A. and the Arms Principle" 2000).

border or all-island level. The agreement also establishes a linkage between the North-South Council and the Assembly: they are mutually interdependent, and one cannot successfully function without the other ("Good Friday Agreement" 1998, Strand Two: North-South Ministerial Committee).

British-Irish Council (Council of the Isles). This body, which was established following the Protestants' demand, represents the link between the various peoples in the Irish and British Islands, and its aim is to promote cooperation between these peoples. It will consist of the representatives of the British and Irish governments; the devolved institutions in Northern Ireland, Scotland, and Wales (when established); and possibly also the representatives of the Isle of Man and the Channel Islands. The institution will exchange information and consult in order to reach agreement on cooperation on matters of mutual interest within the competence of the relevant administrations (e.g., agricultural, cultural, and health issues). The council may agree (normally by consensus) on common policies or common actions, but each individual member may opt not to participate in such common programs ("Good Friday Agreement" 1998, Strand Three: British-Irish Council).

British-Irish Intergovernmental Conference. This conference represents the link between the governments of Britain and Ireland, and acknowledges the legitimate interest of the Irish government in Northern Ireland. The stated aim of this institution is to promote bilateral cooperation on all matters of mutual interests within the competence of both governments. The government of Britain recognizes "the Irish Government's special interest in Northern Ireland," and there will be regular meetings of the conference to discuss nondevolved Northern-Ireland matters. Cooperation within the framework of the conference will include facilitation of cooperation on security matters, and it will address also other issues such as human rights, prisons, and policing in Northern Ireland ("Good Friday Agreement" 1998, Articles 1 and 2: British-Irish Intergovernmental Conference).

Northern Ireland Human Rights Commission. This body was established as a response to Catholics' complaints regarding human rights violations against the Catholic community in Northern Ireland. As to the substantive rules on human rights protection, the parties employ here the existing rules of the Council of Europe. Under the agreement, the British government undertook to incorporate the provisions of the European Convention on Human Rights into the Northern Ireland legislation; it is also bound to allow the inhabitants of Northern Ireland direct access to the courts and to provide remedies for breach of the European Convention ("Good Friday Agreement" 1998, Article 2: Rights, Safeguards, and Equality of Opportunity: Human Rights).

In addition, an independent Northern Ireland Human Rights Commission will be established, with membership from Northern Ireland (reflecting the community balance). Among the commission's functions are reviewing the adequacy and effectiveness of laws and practices, making recommendations to government, providing information and promoting awareness of human rights, and, where necessary, bringing court proceedings or providing assistance to individuals to do so ("Good Friday Agreement" 1998, Article 5: Rights, Safeguards, and Equality of Opportunity: Human Rights).

Institutional Analysis of the Good Friday Agreement

The institutions established by the Good Friday Agreement fulfill several classical functions of institutions in promoting peace and international cooperation. In-depth examination of these institutional arrangements, however, provides us with insights regarding additional roles of institutions in such disputed settings. The typical functions of the institutions established by the Good Friday Agreement are creating institutional linkage (between the functioning of the North-South Council and the Assembly), monitoring functions (which are prominent regarding human rights protection), and facilitating improved communication through the various mixed institutions (e.g., in the British-Irish Conference). These functions are indeed valuable to the promotion of international cooperation between the disputed parties, but the new institutions fulfill additional and no less important functions in the strife-ridden setting of Ireland.

A quick examination of the agreement's provisions reveals that the new institutions, and especially the disputed ones, are not entrusted with significant powers. The Assembly will have powers in the economic and social fields, but not within the important spheres of security, police, trade policy, custom, and taxation. The celebrated North-South Council does have the power to develop cooperation between Ireland and Northern Ireland (as the Catholic community aspires), but the representatives of Northern Ireland in the council are bound to act in accordance with the mandate given to them by the Assembly (which is still controlled by Protestant majority). In addition, these cooperative programs must fall within the powers of the Assembly (i.e., only in the economic and the social spheres).

Similarly, the Council of the Isles may develop joint programs, but the latter must be within the competence of each administration, and, more important, each individual member may opt not to participate in the common programs.

In light of these relatively weak powers, a hasty conclusion may be reached that the new institutions are not likely to play an important role in future Northern Ireland politics. Such a conclusion, it is submitted, may well overlook the underlying substance of the controversy over the future of Northern Ireland, however.

As discussed above, the main thrust of the controversy over Northern Ireland is the conflicting aspirations of the Nationalists and Unionists. The underlying motive of intercommunal struggle, particularly since 1972, is a struggle over the national identity of this land, whether it is British or Irish. National identity may take many forms, and national symbols are of considerable importance in that respect.

The paramount importance of the North-South Council does not stem from its (very limited) legal powers but rather from the link it represents between Northern Ireland and the Republic of Ireland. The main significance of the British-Irish Conference derives from the acknowledgment of Ireland's legitimate interest regarding the future of Northern Ireland. Thus, the new institutions, in addition to their classical functions in accordance with the rational choice theory, constitute significant national symbols for the parties. These institutions represent mixed links with various parties and dilute the zero-sum tension regarding exclusive sovereignty in Northern Ireland. The Council of the Isles serves in that respect to obscure somewhat the dichotomous nature of the struggle between the two camps.

Thus, it is apparent that one of the principal functions of the new institutions established in the agreement is symbolic. This observation somewhat deviates from the classical rational choice approach to the study of international institutions. Indeed, the functions of these institutions in Northern Ireland direct us to the counterpart approach to international institutions, the reflective approach. Very briefly, the reflective approach stresses the role of impersonal social forces, such as values, norms, and cultural practices that have important effects on the international institutions (Keohane 1988, 389–93). Such factors, as it is noted above, are important to the understanding of the role of the institutions in Northern Ireland and in other places.

Application of Institutional Principles of the Good Friday Agreement to a Future Settlement of the Dispute in Jerusalem

Although the situation in Northern Ireland is very different from that in Jerusalem, certain areas of similarities can be discerned. In both places, the population consists of two polarized communities bearing radically different characteristics. The communities differ in religion and national affiliation, and the economic disparity between them is significant. Most important in our context, the two communities that reside in Northern Ireland and in Jerusalem have conflicting political aspirations with respect to the future status of their locale. Most of the Catholics in Northern Ireland want to unite with Ireland, whereas most of the Protestants want unification with Britain. Most of the Jewish inhabitants in Jerusalem want the city to remain under Israeli sovereignty, whereas the majority of the city's Arabs would prefer to be under the jurisdiction of the Palestinian Authority. Not less important, the dispute in both places involves significant symbolic features.

In light of the conflicting political aspirations of the communities in Northern Ireland, the Good Friday Agreement establishes a number of institutions with links to different political entities. The establishment of a number of institutions with mixed affinities in the Jerusalem area could meet, if only in part, the different aspirations of the communities in and around the city and help to lessen the dispute over the sovereignty question.

Consideration could be given to establishing an institution parallel to the North-South Council that would include representatives of the Jerusalem municipality and the Palestinian Authority. In such a case, the Jerusalem delegation would be formed according to the relative size of the two communities within the city. This body would discuss the development of cooperation between the parties in various spheres, such as environmental protection, transportation, public health, and the like. Each delegation to the joint institution would act on the basis of the decisions taken by its respective administration.

An institution analogous to the Council of the Isles might be a metropolitan body consisting of representatives of the Israeli and Palestinian municipalities in the Jerusalem area (e.g., Jerusalem, Bethlehem, Ramallah). The representatives attending the meetings would be chosen by each municipality according to the specific function subject on the agenda (e.g., transportation, tourism, pilgrimage to Holy Places). This body would hold consultations to promote cooperation among the municipalities involved. Decisions would be made by unanimous agreement, with each side entitled to decide whether to participate in the joint programs.

Consideration should be given to the creation of an institution parallel to the British-Irish Intergovernmental Conference, consisting of representatives of Israel and the Palestinian Authority, who would hold discussions on various subjects relating to Jerusalem. Each side would be entitled to raise for discussion issues related to the exercise of powers that lie with other side (e.g., Israeli officials' implementation of police powers in east Jerusalem).

Finally, a human rights commission might be established to supervise the protection of human rights in Jerusalem. Such a body would be composed of Israeli and Palestinians living in Jerusalem, and its main function would be to supervise human rights protection for Jerusalem's inhabitants by the Israeli government and the Palestinian Authority. As with the Good Friday Agreement, the substantive standards might be incorporated into the bilateral agreement from some multilateral human rights convention, such as the 1966 International Covenant on Civil and Political Rights.

Conclusion

This chapter uses two distinct (but related) theories to analyze the controversy over Jerusalem and to suggest some proposals to enhance the prospects of achieving an agreed solution to this long-standing dispute. Both theories are valuable tools for these purposes, but their modes of assistance are not identical. Game-theoretic analysis enables us to identify some important structural features standing at the base of the conflict over Jerusalem and to understand the course of the game up to the present time. Furthermore, the comprehension of these factors provides an instrument to modify the competitive structure of the setting. Such modifications, if adopted by the parties, may improve the likelihood of successful negotiations. In contrast, the institutionalist approach does not aim to provide systematic tools to analyze the particular properties of a given setting. Generally, it is more oriented toward suggesting the means to enhance the prospects of establishing and maintaining a long-range cooperative regime.

Game theory and institutional theory are not mutually contradictory; in fact, the two theories complement and supplement each other. This fact is noticeable when we deal with the rational choice variant of the institutional theory. As analyzed above, however, the complementary character is maintained also with respect to the reflective stream of institutional theory.

The structural features of the game of Jerusalem, especially its character as a zero-sum game with small domestic win-sets, explain why it is so difficult to negotiate a solution to the issue. An examination of the exit options available to the parties reveals the asymmetric bargaining positions of the parties, with a clear preference for Israel. Moreover, the existence of viable exit options explains Israel's past policy regarding negotiations over Jerusalem. These structural features alone indicate the low probability that a compromise between Israel and the Palestinians will be achieved in the future.

The probability of a successful compromise will increase, however, if the structure of the game of Jerusalem is changed either by increasing the payoffs generated to the parties in the event of agreement or by expanding the game's functional scope (through the technique of embedment or enlargement). Such moves, if the contending parties adopt them, may enhance their ability to exchange payoffs in a broader domain, and make it easier for them to reach some compromise. If an agreement is not achieved in the next round of negotiations, Israel will continue to exercise control over all parts of east Jerusalem, with the Palestinians possibly terminating the negotiations in all tracks and initiating violent activities. Israel's current preferred exit option seems so solid that it would be very difficult, even with the employment of the above methods, to balance completely the competing bargaining positions of the parties. This factor leads to the conclusion that certain structural changes may increase significantly the probability of a compromise between the parties, but Israel's preferred position likely will continue to overshadow the future course of the game of Jerusalem.

In light of the preceding analysis, we may examine the contributions of game theory to the research on the question of Jerusalem and its resolution. Game theory is focused on one set of factors (i.e., strategical factors) in the interaction between the players in the game of Jerusalem. Game-theoretic analysis does not take into account external factors, such as the personal characteristics of the decision makers or the social values prevailing in their communities. The significance of the latter factors in numerous interactive situations indicates that game theory should not be the only instrument used to analyze social phenomena such as the controversy over the future of Jerusalem. The limitation to only interactive factors, however, enables us to concentrate on one set of variables and to explore in depth their effects on the behavior of the players and the interplay between these variables.

A game-theoretic analysis of the controversy over Jerusalem enables us to bring forward some proposals to modify the competitive features of this setting. It should be noted, however, that although theoretically it is always possible to change the structure of an interactive situation, such changes are not possible in all cases. This is true, for example, with regard to a change in the exit options of the game of Jerusalem because it is doubtful whether customary international law or future agreements between the parties will modify the legal exit options in the coming years. Similarly, the main players or the players in the middle or external circles may theoretically change the factual exit options in the game of Jerusalem, but the likelihood of a significant development in that respect is quite remote.

Institutional theory is focused on the role of international institutions in world politics, particularly on their contribution to facilitate and enhance international cooperation. An analysis of the institutional arrangements established by the Good Friday Agreement in Northern Ireland reveals that the new institutions fulfill some of the classical functions of international institutions in accordance with the rational choice theory (i.e., institutional linkage, monitoring, and communication). These functions are valuable to the promotion of international cooperation between the contending parties in Northern Ireland and may be valuable in other places (such as Jerusalem).

In-depth examination of the institutional arrangements in the Good Friday Agreement reveals that the new institutions have limited powers and their center of gravity is located on the reflective-symbolic level.

The new institutions represent distinctive links between Northern Ireland and other states. These links are of great value to the rival parties in Northern Ireland and may similarly be of value in Jerusalem. Consequently, this chapter suggests that some parallel institutions be established in the framework of the future regime in Jerusalem. The proposed institutions may create mixed links between the city of Jerusalem and Israel, the Palestinian National Council, and other parties. Such mixed links may somewhat weaken the current zero-sum nature of the dispute over Jerusalem.

The institutional part of this discussion is based largely on the rational choice stream of the institutional theory, but as the analysis of the functions of the institutions in Northern Ireland indicates, that stream cannot always provide a comprehensive account of the role of international institutions in international settings. Factors stressed by the reflective approach (such as values, norms, and cultural practices) should also be considered when analyzing the functions of international institutions in a particular international setting.

The proposals elaborated throughout this chapter, both the game-theoretic and the institutional ones, could be integrated into a variety of regimes to be agreed upon by the parties to the controversy over Jerusalem. They are not designed to predetermine the outcome of the negotiations; rather, they may provide the decision makers on both sides with building blocks to shape a wide range of possible solutions. The common denominator to most of the above proposals is the attempt to diffuse the zero-sum nature of the dispute. Such a structural change is imperative for any agreed solution on the future of Jerusalem.

4

Jerusalem and the U.S. Congress

Geoffrey R. Watson

For three decades, the U.S. Congress has jousted with the president over U.S. policy on Jerusalem. Since 1967, Congress has repeatedly asserted that the United States should unequivocally recognize Israel's claim to all of Jerusalem, whereas every president, Democrat and Republican, has taken the position that the final status of Jerusalem should be determined by negotiations (cf. U.S. Congress 1995, *Jerusalem Embassy Act,* Section 3[a][2]; Leich and Watson 1993, 478; McDowell 1977, 634; Vance 1986, 103). Likewise, Congress has repeatedly called on the president to move the U.S. embassy from Tel Aviv to Jerusalem, whereas every U.S. president since 1967 has asserted that the U.S. embassy to Israel should remain in Tel Aviv pending a negotiated settlement (cf. Christopher 1995a; U.S. Congress 1995, *Jerusalem Embassy Act,* Section 3[a][3]; Leich and Watson 1993, 479).

These presidents have argued that moving the embassy to Jerusalem would needlessly antagonize the Arab states and the Palestinians, who claim that al-Quds is their capital (see Palestine National Council 1988, Annex 3, Agenda Item 37, 13; see also Quigley 1996, 765–80). Congressional supporters of Israel reply that the United States should drop any fiction that the status of Jerusalem is open to question; they also claim that failing to main-

This chapter is a revised version of an article that first appeared in 45 *Catholic University Law Review* 837 (1996) and is reprinted with permission.

tain an embassy in Jerusalem undermines U.S. support for Israel and that Israel is one of the few countries in the world in which the United States does not maintain its embassy in the host state's capital.[1] They dismiss suggestions that moving the embassy would damage the peace process, arguing that no one can realistically expect Israel to move its capital away from Jerusalem and that pretending otherwise unnecessarily raises Palestinian hopes to the contrary (see, e.g., D'Amato 1995). In any event, they add, the embassy can be located in west Jerusalem, where Israel's claim to sovereignty is generally acknowledged (see, e.g., Boxer 1995).

The struggle over Jerusalem policy intensified during the Clinton administration. In 1995, Congress enacted the *Jerusalem Embassy Act,* which

---

1. Supporters of the act sometimes say there are no other cases in which a U.S. embassy is not located in the host's capital city (see, e.g., Letter from 92 U.S. Senators 1995). In fact, there are several other cases in which the United States maintains an embassy in a place other than the capital city. The U.S. embassy in Belize is in Belize City, not in the capital city of Belmopan. The U.S. embassy in Benin is in Cotonou, not the capital city of Porto Novo. The U.S. embassy in Cote d'Ivoire is in Abidjan, not the capital, Yamoussoukro. (See U.S. Dept. of State, *Country List Organized by Geographic Area/Bureau,* and U.S. Dept. of State, Office of the Geographer, *Independent States in the World* [both documents are available through the State Department's Web site at http://dosfan.lib.uic.edu/index.html]; see also Rajewski 2000, 157, 163, 181.)

In many (perhaps most) cases, the situation appears to be temporary. For example, Nigeria recently moved its capital to Abuja, in the north part of that country, but the U.S. embassy in Nigeria is still in Lagos. A branch office of the U.S. embassy has been opened in the new capital (see Rajewksi 2000, 183–84).

In a few cases, location of the embassy is a matter of choosing between different seats of government, so it is not possible to locate the embassy in one "capital" city. For example, the United States maintains its embassy to Bolivia in La Paz, the executive capital, not in Sucre, the legislative and judicial capital (see Rajewski 2000, 157). Likewise, the U.S. embassy to the Netherlands is in The Hague, the seat of government, rather than in Amsterdam (see Rajewski 2000, 182). Similarly, the U.S. embassy in South Africa shuttles between Pretoria and Cape Town because the South African government itself changes seats depending on the season.

Of course, there are a number of countries in which the United States maintains no embassy at all, even though it does maintain diplomatic relations with them. Indeed, even the lack of diplomatic relations with a country (e.g., Cuba) does not necessarily imply nonrecognition.

purports to require the president to move the U.S. embassy from Tel Aviv to Jerusalem (U.S. Congress 1995). President Clinton took no action on the act, allowing it to enter into force on November 8, 1995. The act states that a U.S. embassy in Israel was to be established in Jerusalem by May 31, 1999, and it provided for a 50 percent cut in the State Department's building budget if the embassy were not opened by that time. It permitted the president to waive the budget cut for successive six-month periods if necessary to protect the "national security interests of the United States" (§7[a][1]).[2] Citing this waiver authority and his constitutional authority as chief executive, President Clinton waived the budget-cutting provision. On June 18, 1999, he determined that it was "necessary to protect the national security interests of the United States" to suspend the budget limitation in the act for six months (Clinton 1999).[3] The president made a similar determination six months later, on December 17, 1999.

The president's decision to waive the act's provisions provoked angry responses from influential members of Congress, some of whom introduced new bills to induce the president to comply. One bill, for example, conditioned funding for construction of a new U.S. chancery in Berlin on "comparable" progress in constructing a U.S. embassy in Jerusalem.[4] Some members also proposed bills to require U.S. maps to show Jerusalem as being part of Israel and to require U.S. government publications to list Jerusalem as part of the State of Israel. Other proposals would require U.S. passports to list

2. The act also requires regular reporting on progress toward establishment of an embassy in Jerusalem.

3. The full text of President Clinton's memorandum to the secretary of state reads: "Pursuant to the authority vested in me as President by the Constitution and laws of the United States, including section 7(a) of the Jerusalem Embassy Act of 1995 (Public Law 104–45) (the "Act"), I hereby determine that it is necessary to protect the national security interests of the United States to suspend for a period of 6 months the limitation set forth in section 3(b) of the Act. You are hereby authorized and directed to transmit this determination to the Congress, accompanied by a report in accordance with section 7(a) of the Act, and to publish the determination in the Federal Register. This suspension shall take effect after transmission of this determination and report to the Congress" (Clinton 1999).

4. H.R. 4181, 105th Cong., 2d Sess., Section 4 (introduced June 25, 1998).

"Israel" as the place of birth of U.S. nationals born in Jerusalem if the holder of the passport so requests.[5]

The most salient legal challenge to President Clinton's Jerusalem policy, however, was the contention that he had only limited authority to waive the requirements of the *Jerusalem Embassy Act*. Influential sponsors of the act, including Senators Robert Dole and Jon Kyl, suggested that the president did not have unfettered discretion to waive the act and that he could not string together a succession of six-month waivers. These arguments implicitly raise important questions of constitutional law. In whom does the Constitution vest the authority to formulate U.S. policy on Jerusalem: Congress or the president?

In this chapter, I argue that the Constitution vests this power primarily (if not exclusively) with the president and that the *Jerusalem Embassy Act* (and similar statutes) must be interpreted in accordance with the commands of the Constitution. In the first part of this chapter, I briefly sketch the legislative history of the *Jerusalem Embassy Act*. In the second part, I consider the scope of the president's waiver authority under the act and more generally how this statute and others should be interpreted in light of the separation of powers mandated by the Constitution.

Adoption of the *Jerusalem Embassy Act*

The United States immediately recognized Israel upon Israel's independence in 1948 and shortly thereafter opened its embassy in Tel Aviv, then the seat of Israeli government.[6] At that time, Israel had control of west Jerusalem, and Jordan had control of east Jerusalem. After the Six Day War in 1967, east Jerusalem came under Israeli control, as did the West Bank, Gaza, and the Golan Heights.

The *Jerusalem Embassy Act* of 1995, then, is just the latest shot in a long-

5. H.R. 2832, 105th Cong., 1st Sess., Section 1(d) (introduced Nov. 6, 1997).

6. See testimony of Lawrence S. Eagleberger, undersecretary of state for political affairs, before the Senate Committee on Foreign Relations, Feb. 23, 1984, excerpted in Leich and Watson 1993, 483.

standing battle between Congress and the president over the location of the U.S. embassy to Israel. The act's immediate precursor was S. 770, introduced by Senator Kyl in May 1995.[7] That bill was different from the final act in two ways: first, it mandated the commencement of construction of a Jerusalem embassy in 1996, and, second, it had no provision for a presidential waiver. The Clinton administration opposed the bill on policy grounds and on the grounds that it was unconstitutional (see Christopher 1995b; see also Dellinger 1995). S. 770 had sixty-two cosponsors in the Senate, not quite enough to override a presidential veto. Accordingly, Senator Dole introduced a new bill, S. 1322, that eliminated the requirement that construction begin in 1996. Thereafter, Senator Dole and his cosponsors reluctantly added the presidential waiver in order to allay concerns about the bill's constitutionality and to preserve some flexibility for the president as a policy matter. Overwhelming majorities in both Houses adopted the bill in this form.[8]

On the same day, the White House announced that the president would neither sign nor veto the bill, allowing it to go into effect by default.[9] Press Secretary Mike McCurry released a statement reiterating the president's opposition to the legislation. The statement acknowledged the near-unanimous votes in Congress and concluded that a veto "would only prolong a divisive debate and risk further damage to the peace process" (McCurry 1995, 1). The statement added:

> The President will not, however, sign this legislation. To do so would be inconsistent with his pledge to take no action which would undermine a peace process that shows so much promise of creating a better future for Is-

7. S. 770, 104th Cong., 1st Sess. (May 9, 1995).

8. 93–5 in the Senate, with one not voting; 374–37 in the House, with 5 voting "present" and 17 not voting. The sponsors of the bill were also anxious to speed its passage through Congress before Prime Minister Rabin arrived at the U.S. Capitol rotunda for a ceremony honoring the 3,000-year anniversary of Jerusalem. However, several House members complained that no hearings had been held on the bill.

9. The U.S. Constitution provides that when Congress is in session, a bill becomes law if it is not acted on by the president within ten days of its presentation to the president.

rael and its neighbors. Therefore, when the bills passed this week become law, the President will use their waiver provisions to prevent the legislation from adversely affecting the Middle East peace process. (1)

Unlike some of the administration's earlier statements on the bill, McCurry's statement did not directly charge that the act is unconstitutional.

After that point, the administration filed reports with Congress, as is required by the act. The first report, dated December 8, 1995, set forth various options for the establishment of an embassy, ranging from construction of a new building to lease of an existing one. The second report, dated March 1, 1996, elaborated on possible time lines for opening an embassy. But it added that the president "would take no action which would undermine the peace process. Thus, as we consider how best to respond to the provisions of the Act, we should do so in a way that avoids damage to the peace process." [10] Finally, in June 1999, the president formally invoked the waiver provisions of the act, suspending its operative terms for a six-month period. The president's exercise of this waiver authority raises important statutory and constitutional questions.

Interpretation of the *Jerusalem Embassy Act:*
Statutory and Constitutional Considerations

The waiver authority in the *Jerusalem Embassy Act* raises two questions of interpretation. First, is there any limit to the number of successive waivers a president may invoke? A few congressional proponents of the act have suggested that some such limit exists. Second, how broad is a president's discretion to invoke the waiver? The administration's statements, particularly McCurry's statement, imply that President Clinton had broad discretion to invoke the waiver. During floor debate on the bill, many supporters of the legislation suggested otherwise. These interpretive questions are, of course,

10. *Report Pursuant to Section 6 of Public Law 104–45 [*Jerusalem Embassy Act], *at 4, attached to letter from Wendy R. Sherman, assistant secretary for legislative affairs, to Newt Gingrich, Speaker of the House, Mar. 1, 1996.*

related to the question of the constitutionality of the statute. Where possible, statutes are construed consistently with the Constitution, but interpretation of the act begins with its text.

The first interpretive question, relating to successive waivers, is readily answered by the plain language of the waiver provision. Section 7(b) provides for additional suspensions "at the end of any period" during which a suspension is already in effect (U.S. Congress 1995). The provision must mean that the president can issue an indefinite string of six-month waivers. It says quite plainly that the president may tack a new waiver at the end of "any" existing period in which a waiver is in effect.

In a colloquy on the Senate floor in 1995, Senators Dole and Kyl tried to suggest otherwise. Senator Kyl asked whether the intent of the drafters was to give the president the "right to invoke the waiver in perpetuity" (Kyl 1995b). Senator Dole replied, "The waiver authority should not be interpreted to mean that the President may infinitely push off the establishment of the American Embassy in Jerusalem" (Dole 1995b).[11] But Dole undermined his own position by adding, "If a waiver were to be repeatedly and routinely exercised by a President, I would expect Congress to act by removing the waiver authority" (Dole 1995b). This statement implies that the act does not prevent a president from waiving it in perpetuity—that a further act of Congress would be required to prevent him or her from doing so. In any event, insofar as the colloquy contradicts the plain language of the statute, the latter must prevail. The current president can link together an infinite series of waivers.

The second interpretive question is more difficult. Does the act permit the president to waive its provisions for any reason at all, or is the president's discretion constrained, and, if so, to what extent? Section 7(a) of the act provides that the president "may suspend" the 50 percent cut in the State Department's building budget for a period of six months if "necessary to protect the national security interests of the United States" (U.S. Congress 1995). By its terms, of course, the provision does constrain the president, who must base the waiver on the "national security interests" of the United

11. Earlier, when speculating about the possibility of adding waiver language to the bill, Senator Kyl also stressed that it would be a "temporary waiver only" (Kyl 1995a).

States. Still, the Clinton administration's statements about the act implied that the president would be free to invoke the waiver because potential damage to the peace process always threatens U.S. national security interests. Following the practice of prior administrations, the Clinton administration took the position that it had unfettered discretion to determine whether moving the embassy jeopardizes U.S. national security interests.

Again, Senators Dole and Kyl sought to make legislative history to narrow the president's discretion. Senator Dole said that the president could not invoke the waiver "simply because he thinks it would be better not to move our Embassy to Jerusalem" or simply because he thinks it would be better to "move it at a later time" (Dole 1995a). Dole added that the phrase *national security interests* is "much narrower" than the term *national interest.* "No President should or could make a decision to exercise this waiver lightly." Other legislators echoed the view that the authority should be construed narrowly (see, e.g., Feinstein 1995; Robb 1995).[12] On the other hand, at least one or two legislators seemed to believe that the waiver provision permitted the president to waive the act's provisions fairly freely (W. Cohen 1995; cf. Daschle 1995).

The use of the term *national security interests* in other statutes may support the conclusion that a president has broad discretion to interpret the waiver provisions of the *Jerusalem Embassy Act.* Over the years, the executive branch has grudgingly abided by a whole panoply of statutes requiring certain actions unless the president certifies that they are not in the country's "vital national interests" or "national security interests" (see, generally, Meyer 1988, 69). The statutes regulating international narcotics trafficking, for example, require the president to certify that certain foreign states are cooperating on the war on drugs as a condition of their continued receipt of foreign aid, but the law permits the president to permit continued aid to a decertified country if he or she determines it to be in the "vital national interests" (U.S. Congress 1986, *Anti-Drug Abuse Act*). In practice, the president has enjoyed discretion to determine those "vital national interests"—a higher standard than the "national security interests" the president must cite to waive the

---

12. Even some opponents of the legislation thought the waiver authority restricted the president's discretion to waive the act (see, e.g., Rahall 1995; cf. Chafee 1995).

Jerusalem Embassy Act (cf. Meyer 1988, 74).[13] Similarly, statutes on human rights supposedly condition foreign assistance on human rights considerations, subject to presidential waivers. Again, presidents have asserted broad discretion to interpret these statutes. They have been reluctant to find, for example, that any state actually engages in a "consistent pattern of gross violations of human rights" (U.S. Congress 1974, *Foreign Assistance Act,* Section 502B)—a statutory finding that would curtail foreign assistance to the state in question—even though many states seem to do so (see Carleton and Stohl 1985, 211–27; Saul Cohen 1982, 256–74). If past practice is any guide, then, the president will enjoy discretion to interpret whether moving the U.S. embassy to Jerusalem implicates "national security interests."

In principle, the scope of the waiver authority should also be construed in light of international law. Statutes are presumed to be consistent with treaty obligations unless they "clearly and unequivocally" evince intent to the contrary (see *United States v. Palestine Liberation Organization* 1988). In this case, however, international law probably does not demand any particular reading for at least two reasons. First, international law does not regulate which branch of government dictates the placement of its embassies. It speaks only of mutual consent of the "states" involved (cf. Vienna Convention on Diplomatic Relations 1961, Article 2). Second, regardless of what international law requires, the *Embassy Act* evinces a "clear and unequivocal" intent to recognize Jerusalem as the undivided capital of Israel and to move the U.S. embassy there. It appears, then, that international law does not mandate a broad or narrow reading of the act's waiver provision.

The U.S. Constitution, however, probably does require a broad reading of the waiver provision. Statutes must be construed to avoid constitutional infirmity, and a narrow construction of the waiver provision could impermissibly constrain the president's powers in foreign affairs. The Constitution vests the president with the "executive power" and, subject to the advice and consent of the Senate, with the more specific powers to make treaties and to

13. More recent waiver provisions have sought to limit the president's discretion by imposing numerical standards, reporting and consulting requirements, shortened authorization periods, and even "shadow fact-finding" (see Meyer 1988, 83–85). But the president still has the "executive" authority to interpret the law.

receive and appoint ambassadors. It may be going too far to suggest, as the Justice Department has, that the president has the "exclusive" authority to conduct the nation's diplomatic relations with other states (see Dellinger 1995). The president's power to appoint ambassadors, for example, is shared, not exclusive, and that power certainly affects the "conduct" of diplomatic relations. But it is true, as the Justice Department asserts, that the president has the power to recognize foreign states and governments (see Dellinger 1995). That power is exclusive and apparently extends not just to states and governments, but also to claims of territorial sovereignty, such as claims to sovereignty over disputed cities such as Jerusalem.[14] The president's exclusive recognition power implies that he or she has broad discretion to interpret the waiver provisions of the *Jerusalem Embassy Act*. Recognition power implies that the president has broad latitude to determine whether moving the embassy undermines the "national security interests" of the United States.[15]

Dole and others who prefer a narrower reading of the waiver authority may acknowledge that the president has a power of recognition, but they will argue that this power, even if exclusive, does not include an exclusive power to decide on the location of a U.S. embassy. They will point out that the location of an embassy does not necessarily imply recognition of that city as a state's capital. They will conclude that moving the embassy to Jerusalem does not usurp the president's recognition power because the president can always clarify that the move does not change U.S. recognition policy—that Jerusalem's status should be resolved through negotiations. Indeed, the United States has done so in other circumstances. It maintained an embassy in East Berlin but made clear that it did not regard East Berlin as the capital of Germany. Even today the United States maintains a few embassies

14. Cf. S.C. Res. 662, U.N. SCOR, 45th sess., 2934th mtg., at 20, U.N. Doc. S/INF/46 (1990), calling on states to refrain from "indirect recognition" of Iraq's annexation of Kuwait.

15. Because the president is relying on an exclusive power, it is not dispositive that this case arguably falls into "category 3" of Justice Jackson's famous three-part analysis in the Steel Seizure case (see *Youngstown Sheet and Tube Co. v. Sawyer*, 343 U.S. 579, 635–37 [1952] [J. Jackson, concurring], cited in Halberstam 1995). Even at its "lowest ebb," an exclusive power is still exclusive.

in cities other than the host state's capital city. In such cases, the executive branch is perfectly capable of clarifying what it regards as the actual capital of the host state. Therefore, this argument runs, Congress can influence the location of an embassy without intruding on the president's recognition power, and the president's waiver authority can be invoked only in "dire" circumstances (see Robb 1995).

But acts speak louder than words, even (or perhaps especially) in diplomacy. Changing the location of the embassy will inevitably create a changed perception of U.S. recognition policy, no matter what a president says to the contrary. Indeed, international law recognizes that acts can themselves amount to indirect recognition (see note 14). And indirect recognition is, after all, the main point of the *Jerusalem Embassy Act*. Its sponsors seek to move the embassy not because it would be more convenient for the ambassador and staff to work in Jerusalem, though this might account for some support for the measure, but because it would demonstrate that the United States recognizes a united Jerusalem that is the capital of Israel.[16] Senator Dole's narrow interpretation of the waiver authority could undermine the president's recognition policy in a region of the world in which the tea leaves of recognition are read very closely. As the Supreme Court has said, the recognition power "is not limited to a determination of the government to be recognized. It includes the power to determine the policy which is to govern the question of recognition" *(United States v. Pink* 1942). Put in terms of the act's waiver provision, the president has broad discretion to determine whether moving the embassy is in the "national security interests" of the United States.[17]

Supporters of the act stress that it does not require the president to open an embassy in Jerusalem but instead merely creates financial incentive for the president to do so (see Charnoff, Cooper, and Carvin 1995). That is, it merely cuts certain State Department appropriations if the president fails to

16. Thus, the three-part statement of policy in the act provides that Jerusalem should remain an undivided city in which the rights of ethnic and religious groups are protected, that Jerusalem should be recognized as the capital of Jerusalem, and that the U.S. embassy should be established in Jerusalem by May 31, 1999 (see U.S. Congress 1995, Section 3[a]).

17. This conclusion is consistent with the practice of past administrations.

move the embassy; it does not eliminate them altogether. But Congress cannot use unconstitutional conditions to achieve indirectly what it cannot achieve directly.[18] Proponents of the *Jerusalem Embassy Act* rely heavily on *South Dakota v. Dole* (cited in Charnoff, Cooper, and Carvin 1995), in which the Supreme Court upheld a federal statute withholding 5 percent of highway funds from any state whose drinking age is less than twenty-one. The *Dole* Court stressed, however, that the condition involved only a "relatively small percentage" of the funds in question, and it reaffirmed warnings in earlier Supreme Court cases that a more coercive condition—one in which "pressure turns into compulsion"—might be unconstitutional. The *Jerusalem Embassy Act,* by contrast, involves a 50 percent cut in funding—well past the point at which incentive becomes coercion and pressure becomes compulsion.

In any event, the Supreme Court has since suggested that the rationale of *Dole* does not extend to separation-of-powers cases (see, e.g., *Metropolitan Washington Airports Authority v. Citizens for the Abatement of Aircraft Noise* 1991). This suggestion makes sense. The powers of the federal government are not just separate; in some cases, they are inalienable. Unlike highway funds, these powers cannot be bargained away. The president cannot give up the president's power to recognize any more than the Congress can give up its power to declare war.

This reasoning suggests that other recent congressional proposals on Jerusalem would also impair the president's exclusive power of recognition. The president, not Congress, has the primary responsibility for enunciating the nation's policy on Jerusalem in maps, government publications, and passports. Congress can perhaps insist that its view also be reflected in such fora but not in such a way as to confuse a statement of congressional preference with a statement of the president's policy. Responsibility for recognition policy resides in the White House, not on Capitol Hill.

A final objection to these conclusions is the view that in a democracy, foreign affairs should be shared. Indeed, in the United States, most foreign-affairs powers are shared. Shared powers serve democracy, perhaps at the ex-

18. See, e.g., *United States v. Butler* 1936 (where Congress lacks power to legislate, it "may not indirectly accomplish those ends by taxing and spending to purchase compliance").

pense of efficiency. But exclusive powers serve democracy, too. When exclusive powers are exercised poorly, there is no doubt about whom to blame. The president, like Congress, is elected. If the president's recognition policy is bad, the president (or his vice president or his political party) will pay for it at the polls.

Conclusion

The president has broad authority to interpret the waiver provisions of the *Jerusalem Embassy Act*. This construction of the act is supported by its text and by practice under similar "national security interest" provisions in other statutes. It is also probably required by the Constitution, which treats recognition as the exclusive province of the executive branch. The president, not Congress, has the power of recognition, and the location of the U.S. embassy to Israel has inescapable implications for U.S. recognition policy. The president, not Congress, is entrusted with the responsibility to determine what that policy should be.

5

Rule and Role in Jerusalem

Israel, Jordan, and the PLO in a Peace-Building Process

Menachem Klein

M uch has been written about the Israeli–Arab conflict in Jerusalem, but little has been written about peacemaking efforts in the city. This chapter deals with different arrangements made about Jerusalem since 1948, whether formal and public accords or secret ad hoc understandings and arrangements on various issues.

I deal with two groups of questions in this chapter. First, I try to discover the partners directly involved with Israel in these arrangements. Was there more than one Arab partner, and, if so, what was the relative weight of each? Second, I look at the partition lines of Jerusalem on which Israel and its Arab partner agreed, and whether they were discussing a geographic or a functional partition.

In attempting to answer these questions, I found both the historical method and a chronological discussion useful and illuminating. In such a historical analysis, one can hardly avoid the conclusion that although during the years 1948–93 Jordan was Israel's only Arab partner to various arrangements about Jerusalem, since 1994 the Palestinian Authority has completely taken over the district of Jerusalem and has restricted the functions Jordan

An earlier version of this article appeared in 45 Catholic University Law Review 745 (1996) and is reprinted with permission.

fulfilled in the city itself and in the Islamic Holy Places (al-Haram al-Sharif/the Temple Mount). Yasir Arafat has in fact become the main Arab partner in negotiations about an arrangement in Jerusalem. Analysis of the negotiations between Israel and the Palestine Liberation Organization (PLO) about Jerusalem and the agreements reached between them are beyond the scope of this chapter, however (see M. Klein 1999). Instead, I focus on Jordan's role in peacemaking efforts in Jerusalem: how Jordan built up its partnership with Israel and how it was disenfranchised from that partnership and by whom.

The 1948 War and the Partition of Jerusalem Between Israel and Jordan

The leadership of the emerging Jewish state and the Emirate of Transjordan already began discussing Jerusalem before the 1948 war. The issue of Jerusalem was raised during the years 1947–48 in contacts between King Abdallah and the head of the State Department of the Jewish Agency, Golda Meyerson (Meir). Evaluation of these negotiations has been a bitter and fascinating issue among historians studying this period, but it is generally agreed that nothing had been achieved concerning Jerusalem until the beginning of the 1948 war. Although the Jewish Agency and the Jordanian emir arrived at some sort of understanding about nonbelligerency and a quiet partition of Palestine between them, they did not come to an agreement regarding Jerusalem. When the fighting began, the Jordanian Legion sought—for political reasons—to refrain from military involvement in the city itself (in contrast to its northern and eastern approaches and the Arab quarters surrounding it), assuming that the Israeli army would also abstain from occupying the city. This assumption was realistic as far as the Old City of Jerusalem was concerned, but not about the western city.

The leadership of the Jewish Agency, and later of the Israeli government, decided to mold the future of west Jerusalem as the capital of Israel by force of arms. In winter-spring of 1948, the Haganah and the Israeli Defense Forces (IDF) fought several battles for control of the road leading into Jerusalem from the west—from Tel Aviv and the coastal area—and conducted several military operations in order to lift the Arab blockade imposed on the city from April 20 to June 2, 1948. The lifting of the blockade was meant not only to allow the transport of food and supplies to the besieged Jews of the city but also to establish Israeli sovereignty in west Jerusalem. However, Israel did not invest the same effort toward the conquest of the Old City as it directed toward west Jerusalem. It assumed that a conquest of the eastern part of Jerusalem, with its Christian and Islamic Holy Places, would eventually lead to the ousting of Israel from the western city as well. Israel therefore conducted only two military operations in the eastern city, both directed at the Jewish Quarter of Old Jerusalem. The first attempt was made May 17–19, 1948—when the IDF entered the Jewish Quarter but left it a few hours later. The Jordanian Legion immediately entered the Old City on May 19 and conquered the Jewish Quarter on May 28. The Israeli attack thus gave Abdullah the legitimization he had been seeking to conquer the Old City and to turn it into the religious-spiritual capital of his kingdom. Incidentally, he acted against the military advice of John Glubb, commander of his army, and of Alek Kirkbride, the senior British representative in Jordan. By conquering the Old City, Abdullah wished to expand the understanding reached on the eve of the war between himself and the Jewish Agency to include Jerusalem proper and to bring about its partition. The Israeli leadership was not bound to such an agreement, and in July 1948 it made a second attempt to free the Jewish Quarter. This attempt also failed, and following the first cease-fire agreement on June 11, 1948, a borderline was drawn, dividing the city: west Jerusalem—including the Arab quarters of Baqa, Talbiyeh, Qatamon, and part of Abu-Tor—came under Israeli control, whereas the whole of the Old City in the east became Jordanian. The borderline resulted from the fighting and not from a prior agreement between the leaders of the two warring parties (Morris 1996, 13–17; Pundik 1994, 105–10; Rabinovich 1991; Sela 1990; Shlaim 1988, 217–18).

Israel's foremost aim directly after the fighting ceased was to be accepted as a member of the United Nations (UN), thereby bolstering the political status of the newborn state. Israel's leaders faced a dilemma: its acceptance to the UN required that it agree to some form of internationalization of the whole of Jerusalem, in keeping with the decision of the UN General Assembly. However, the Israeli leaders wished to preserve the achievements of the war: to establish the partition of the city between Israel and Jordan and to declare west Jerusalem the capital of Israel. Israel therefore repelled Abdullah's attempts at the end of 1948 to reach a partition of Jerusalem; it offered instead a functional internationalization: international rule over the Holy Places only. However, because the Holy Places are situated mostly in a small area of the Old City, Israel's proposal was just another way to distinguish west Jerusalem from east Jerusalem. Because Israel's offer naturally did not gain international support (Bialer 1985; Golani 1994; Karpel 1995), Israel then turned to Jordan in order to reach a quick understanding that would block the internationalization of Jerusalem—an understanding that suited the intentions of King Abdullah, whose primary aim was to maintain his sovereignty over the areas he had occupied during the war: the West Bank and east Jerusalem (Pundik 1994, 156–57, 170, 242).

Israel presented the partition of Jerusalem as a common interest of both itself and Jordan: Abdullah could gain legitimization of his rule and justify annexation of the West Bank through his control over the Islamic Holy Places in Jerusalem; and Ben-Gurion could declare west Jerusalem the capital of Israel. The joint interest in blocking the internationalization plan brought about Israel's surprising and radical offer to Jordan in January 1949, in talks conducted by Moshe Dayan, the military commander of Jerusalem, with his Jordanian colleague Abdallah al-Tal. Dayan offered to reach a quick agreement over Jerusalem, which would form part of an overall agreement between the two countries. Dayan openly admitted that Israel's wish to arrive at a quick agreement was the reason for its significant concessions. Israel offered to concede the Arab quarters it had conquered in 1948—Qatamon, the German Colony, Baqa, and Malha; its military posts in Mount Zion and Abu-Tor; the Israeli kibbutz Ramat Rachel; and the two Jewish quarters Talpiot and Mekor Haim. Thus, Jordan would achieve a territorial continuity from east to west and south to west. Jerusalem, as a broad strip of land, connected the Arab city of Jerusalem with Bethlehem. Israel asked in return for control over the Ofel Hill, in order to gain a narrow corridor to the Jewish cemetery on Mount Olives, and to be granted rule of the Jewish Quarter in the Old City, which connects with the Ofel Hill on the east and with Mount Zion and west Jerusalem on the west. Mount Scopus, according to Dayan, would stay under Israeli rule, as would the road leading to it. In contrast to the sites in the Old City with which there was territorial continuity, Mount

Scopus was a completely surrounded Jewish enclave. Israel suggested connecting it to the Jewish city via a new road that would circumvent the Arab quarters (American Consul 1949a).

The Jordanian king could not reject outright such a generous offer, which would hand him through political means much more than his army had achieved by military means. However, he was in no hurry and raised his demands. In addition to the Arab quarters, he demanded full Jordanian sovereignty over the Jewish Quarter in the Old City. He was also unsatisfied with control of the military posts in Abu-Tor and Mount Zion, and demanded full sovereignty over both. These demands, although made for the sake of bargaining only, caused the loss of the time element inherent in the Israeli offer. Talks conducted later with Abdallah al-Tal also led nowhere (Amman to Washington 1949).

The consuls of the United States, France, and Great Britain in Tel Aviv and Amman discussed Dayan's offer informally among themselves and with the Jordanian king. The U.S. position at the end of January 1949 was that partition of the city by mutual agreement was better than coerced internationalization. The United States supported partition of Jerusalem according to the lines Dayan had drawn, without, however, granting either Israel or Jordan sovereignty over their parts of Jerusalem. In order to appease the UN, Washington stated that any bilateral agreement would need the ratification of the UN General Council. The U.S. position was acceptable to Jordan because it enhanced its gains. Jordan did not intend to transfer its capital from Amman to Jerusalem, and it stood to lose less than Israel from not gaining sovereignty over the city. Jordan even went one step further than the U.S. proposal to suggest the enlargement of the city's international zone. In direct talks with Israeli delegates at the end of January 1949, Jordan suggested partitioning the city according to the U.S. proposal, allowing loose international supervision. This suggestion did not appeal to Israel at all, and two weeks after Dayan's generous proposal, Israel again demanded sovereignty over west Jerusalem and the internationalization of east Jerusalem—the site of the Holy Places (American Consul 1949b; First Secretary McDonald 1949). The Americans received the impression that Israel's foreign minister, Moshe Shertok, was ready for a UN stamp of approval on an Israeli-Jordanian agreement for the partition of the city (Meeting of Dean Rusk

1949). At the same time, Israel barred the way to the realization of Dayan's offer by starting to settle the southern Arab quarters it had conquered (American Consulate 1949c; Krystall 1998).

Aside from the international position, Jordan had two other reasons for rejecting Dayan's offer, as well as all other Israeli offers about Jerusalem. First, Jordan noticed Israel's eagerness to come to an agreement on the partition of Jerusalem and wanted to capitalize on the Jerusalem question by pressuring Israel regarding concessions in other areas on its agenda with Israel—such as solution of the refugee problem and the future of the Negev (between Jordan and Israel). The Negev was a bone of contention between Abdullah and the British rule, their priorities being different. Britain saw the Negev as a strategic asset, whereas Abdullah placed a higher priority on the West Bank and Jerusalem than on using the Negev as a corridor to the Gaza Strip and the Mediterranean. He did not view territorial demands in the Negev as a "must" because he could find an alternate Jordanian corridor to the Mediterranean (Pundik 1994, 156, 173–74, 194, 197, 278–79). Second, Israel's insistence on establishing its capital in Jerusalem raised Jordan's apprehensions that Israel would not long tolerate a divided capital, with Jordanian rule in the Old City and the Jewish Holy Places. It also feared that Mount Scopus would serve as a base for an Israeli attack on east Jerusalem, whereby the Jordanians would be caught in a vice crushing east Jerusalem from the west and northeast. Jordan saw a hint to that effect in Israel's demand for sovereignty over the road to Mount Scopus. Abdullah therefore linked the solution of the Jerusalem question with a solution to all other outstanding questions between the two countries. He made a proposal similar to that of the United States: autonomy to both Israel and Jordan in Jerusalem without sovereignty to either one, as well as minimal internationalization (American Consul 1949d).

Meanwhile, the need created by the fighting remained: a silent, practical agreement between Israel and Jordan on the partition of Jerusalem according to the alignment of the Israeli and Jordanian armies at the end of the war.

The next attempt to anchor the partition of Jerusalem in a written agreement between the two countries, including territorial alterations in their sovereignty in the city, was made at the end of 1949 and the beginning of 1950. It was again the proposal for internationalization of Jerusalem that brought Israel and Jordan to the negotiating table. In November 1949, the UN General Council decided to ratify once more the internationalization proposal it had ratified two years previously (Golani 1994), and it was time to renew vigorous political contacts in order to reach an overall agreement between Israel and the Hashemite Kingdom of Jordan. Israel had territorial demands in Jerusalem. On the eve of the talks between the two countries in November 1949, Prime Minister David Ben-Gurion's aim was to achieve territorial continuity to the Western Wall through the Jewish Quarter in the Old City, as well as to Mount Scopus. In exchange, he was willing to cede to Jordan a certain area in the southern part of the city, whose size was not clearly stated.

On December 13, 1949, a joint Israeli-Jordanian document was drawn up, defining an outline of the agreement between them. The document promised Israel sovereignty over the Jewish Quarter in the Old City and over the Western Wall next to it; however, Israel did not gain territorial continuity to Mount Scopus. In order to allay Jordanian apprehensions that Israel would use the territorial continuity to Mount Scopus in order to attack the Jordanian city, Israel had to accept a jointly agreed passage to Mount Scopus through Jordanian territory. In return, Jordan would receive, following Ben-Gurion's original idea, territorial continuity from the eastern side of the city to its south (Rabinovich 1991, 119–24; Shlaim 1988, 233–34, 440).

It was not the issue of Jerusalem that caused the failure of this agreement, but the lack of consent on other territorial issues, such as the Negev and the Latrun area. Thus, between December 1949 and February 1950, the two sides strove to reach an agreement at least about Jerusalem—a less-controversial issue. However, negotiations began now at a much lower level, and the former understanding seemed to have dissipated. Israel proposed partitioning the city into a northern district that would belong to Jordan and a southern district—including the Old City—belonging to Israel. Of course, Jordan rejected this proposal outright. Alternately, Israel reiterated its demand for sovereignty over the area from the Western Wall through the Jewish Quarter and up to the western city, as well as territorial continuity from west Jerusalem to Mount Scopus. The Jordanians retaliated with a demand to receive the Arab quarters Israel held in the western city, and it was Israel's turn to refuse outright. Instead, Israel agreed to negotiate about the exchange of territories in Jerusalem and about financial compensation for the Arab neighborhoods that would stay under its rule, but these negotiations also reached a dead end.

The failure of the negotiations about Jerusalem has been a cause of much discussion among historians, who have tried to determine the reasons for the failure and who was to blame for it. Rabinovich (1991, 111–67)and Pundik (1994, 280–81) believe that the king of Jordan was guilty of the failure. The steps he took toward annexation of the West Bank immediately after the end of the fighting required him to include in the negotiation members of his government, among whom were West Bank Palestinians. The government thus took a negative stand toward any territorial concession to Israel on the issue of Jerusalem. These historians also believe that King Abdullah's maneuverability within his government had weakened since he had begun the process of annexation and that he lacked energy and dynamism at that time. The weakness of the king vis-à-vis his government and the sociopolitical reality in the West Bank were responsible for the failure of the agreement. Shlaim, on the other hand, believes that the blame must be laid on Israel, who raised excessive demands in order to stall the agreement (1988, 111–67). The Israelis did not want a firm and agreed borderline in Jerusalem so that they could change it by force later on. Shlaim claims that Israel preferred to wait for an opportune time to conquer the whole of Jerusalem. However, on July 20, 1951, a radical Palestinian and follower of the mufti murdered King Abdullah, and the option of reaching an Israeli-Jordanian agreement—whether comprehensive or partial—became but another historical chapter.

For lack of a broader agreement, the de facto partition of the city remained, as well as the cease-fire agreement signed at the end of the war. On July 7, 1948, Israel and Jordan agreed, among other things, to "resume the regular work of the cultural and humanitarian institutions on Mount Scopus [i.e., the Hebrew University of Jerusalem and the Hadassah Hospital], with free access to them; free access to the Holy Places and the Jewish cultural institutions in the Old City [e.g. synagogues], and use of the cemetery on Mount Olives" (Hirsch, Housen-Couriel, and Lapidoth 1995, 4). However, Jordan did not honor this part of the agreement. The agreement also stipulated that Mount Scopus would be demilitarized, that a small force of police officers and civilian workers would be present there, and that the UN would ensure provision of water and scientific equipment and would regulate a bi-weekly replacement of the Israeli police officers. In effect, Israel sent to Mount Scopus soldiers dressed as police officers, smuggled arms and military equipment, and turned the mountain into an observation post and a main stronghold for its planned conquest of east Jerusalem (Narkiss 1975, 1991).

During the nineteen years between 1948 and 1967, Jerusalem was divided between Israel and Jordan, both of which grew to accept this partition. The areas bordering between the two grew into neglected no-man lands, not into springboards for an eastward or westward expansion. On December 5, 1948, Prime Minister Ben-Gurion claimed Jerusalem as part of Israel and eight days later the Israeli Knesset declared it the capital of Israel. Annexation of east Jerusalem to the Kingdom of Jordan occurred about one week later, on December 13, 1948, with the annexation to Jordan of the entire West Bank. It was a de jure annexation, which became de facto in May 1950. Only Pakistan and Great Britain recognized the annexation, the latter declaring that it did not recognize Jordan's sovereignty over Jerusalem, only its practical governing of it. International recognition of the reality of a divided Jerusalem was granted in 1952, when the UN General Council decided that Israel and Jordan would be responsible for an arrangement about Jerusalem in accordance with the UN resolution. Thus, the UN recognized Israel and Jordan's joint authority to decide on the future of the city and directed them to do so according to the UN resolution on internationalization, without stating how the two would implement a decision that both opposed. In other words, the UN recognized Israel and Jordan as the governing authorities in Jerusalem and tacitly accepted the demise of the idea of internationalization. The Arab League recognized Jordan's annexation on May 15, 1950, the latter having confirmed its commitment that the annexation of the West Bank would not damage in any way the final settlement of the Palestine problem. From that time until the Six Day War, Jordan was recognized as controlling the West Bank (Hirsch, Hausen-Couriel, and Lapidoth 1995, 3–6).

On July 13, 1951, elections were held to the municipality of Jordanian Jerusalem, and on April 1, 1952, the borders of the Jordanian city were extended to include adjacent areas (e.g., Silwan and Ras al-Amud). The area of the Jordanian city was thus 6.5 square kilometers, whereas the built-up area was only 3 square kilometers. In February 1958, the Jordanian municipality of Jerusalem initiated extension of the city's area northward toward the airport of Kalandia. This plan was not implemented, nor was the 1963 plan to extend the city's area to 75 square kilometers. Discussions concerning these plans ceased in 1967 with the outbreak of the war (al-Tafukji 1996, 363). On the other side, west Jerusalem occupied at that time an area of 38 square kilometers, after extension of its area westward—reflecting the difference in status between the capital of Israel and Jordanian Jerusalem, which remained an outlying town with symbolic-religious importance only. west Jerusalem's status in Israel was higher than east Jerusalem's in Jordan, although the center of Israeli economical, cultural, and social life and of its political parties, trade unions, and main newspapers was Tel Aviv.

The Six Day War: Israeli Rule
and Extensive Sharing of Authority with Jordan

The Six Day War of 1967 was not premeditated, and the involved parties—other than the PLO and the radical wing of the Syrian government—entered it against their will. On the day the fighting began, Israel sent a message to Jordan asking it not to enter the war, stating that it would accept Jordan's token participation in the fighting—such as diffuse firing of light weapons on the borders of Jerusalem. However, Jordan did not respond to this request. This was after communication between the two heads of state was totally disrupted as a result of the extensive Israeli military action in Samo'a in November 1966, in which the Jordanian army suffered heavy losses.

In accordance with accepted Israeli strategic-military thinking prior to the establishment of the State of Israel, the military scenarios of Israel in the 1960s did not include conquering the Old City of Jerusalem, but only taking possession of the road to the Israeli outpost on Mount Scopus. Israel's first step during the war was in this direction; at the same time, the high commissioner's headquarters in the south and the area surrounding it were occupied in order to keep Jordanian fire away from adjacent Jewish neighborhoods and to prevent Jordan's occupation of the high commissioner's headquarters. The next step was to surround the Old City, and only when this maneuver had been completed, causing no political outcry, was the command given to attack the Old City (Zak 1996, 106, 115). Zak recounts that Israel's anger with Jordan's King Hussein for opening fire was so intense that Israeli warplanes bombed the king's palace on the first day of the war in an attempt to kill him (1996, 116).[1]

Immediately after the war, Israel annexed east Jerusalem and extended all the municipal boundaries of the city. The Jordanian city was annexed, as well as some 64,000 dunams of villages in the West Bank and some of the area of towns of Bethlehem and Beit Jala. Thus, Israel turned Jerusalem into the largest city in Israel in area, total population, and the number of both Jewish and non-Jewish inhabitants (Choshen and Shahar 1998). At that time, the government considered the possibility of establishing Palestinian self-rule in parts of the West Bank outside Jerusalem, but this idea was shelved in September 1968 (Pedahzur 1995). After the Palestinian option had been dormant for twenty years, the Jordanian option surfaced. On September 27, 1968, Foreign Minister Abba Eban of Israel met with King Hussein, specifying the Israeli principles for negotiation. In contrast to its position before the war, Israel was not ready now to share with Jordan the sovereignty over Jerusalem. It demanded that Jerusalem stay united and under its own political sovereignty—under which it was ready to grant a Jordanian-Muslim status to the Arab section of Jerusalem, including the Temple Mount. Abba Eban also mentioned the possibility of providing Jordan with a territorial corridor connecting this part of Jerusalem to the other parts of the West Bank, which would be returned to Jordanian sovereignty. In other words, Israel intended to retain its sovereignty over the city but was willing to grant Jordan a foothold in east Jerusalem provided its structure and authority be religious only.

Jordan sent a polite refusal: at most, it would agree to Israeli sovereignty over the Jewish Holy Places in east Jerusalem—excluding al-Haram al-Sharif, which was viewed as holy to the Muslims but not to the Jews. Jordan agreed with Israel that the city must stay open and free to all traffic, trade, and passage between its two parts, but it would not agree that the city that was united de facto would remain so de jure under Israeli sovereignty.

1. On the events leading to the Six Day War, see M. Klein 2000.

At most, it would agree to a special status for east Jerusalem (Zak 1996, 157–59). King Hussein consistently maintained this policy throughout his consequent secret negotiations with Israel.

In 1972, to the Palestinians, King Hussein offered to establish an equal-status federation of the east and west banks of the Jordan River, after their liberation from Israeli occupation. East Jerusalem would be the capital of the Palestinian region of this federation. Prime Minister Golda Meir gave the Israeli reaction to this proposal in a secret meeting with King Hussein: she would be ready to recognize the king as custodian of the Islamic Holy Places in Jerusalem but would not under any circumstance relinquish Israeli sovereignty over east Jerusalem. Hussein insisted on gaining sovereignty over east Jerusalem or at least on extricating the city from Israeli sovereignty and establishing a special rule. Hussein's longing for the city he had lost in the Six Day War was so strong that on March 7, 1974, he refused the offer of Defense Minister Moshe Dayan to hand back to him the government of all of the West Bank except east Jerusalem. Hussein was willing to leave negotiations on Jerusalem to the last, as Dayan suggested, but demanded a prior Israeli commitment to give back to Jordan the sovereignty over Jerusalem (Zak 1996, 161–66, 180).

The broad gap between Israel and Jordan from the beginning of the secret dialogue between them diverted their efforts from finding an overall agreement to a number of limited understandings and ad hoc arrangements (Garfinkle 1992). Israel allowed Jordan to consolidate its hold on east Jerusalem by means of the religious structures. Until it repealed the annexation of the West Bank in 1988, Jordan appointed the chief of the Supreme Muslim Council and the mufti of Jerusalem, controlled the Waqf (Muslim religious trust) and its assets, and paid the salaries of the officials (e.g., teachers, doctors, and municipal and government employees) who were officially employed by the Hashemite Kingdom. Via the various properties of the Waqf and state appropriations, Jordan financed schools, colleges, graveyards, mosques, and social and welfare services; supplied employment to its supporters; and developed patronage networks and political influence in the West Bank and in Jerusalem. With a budget of $17 million—$5 million for Jerusalem alone—the Jordanian Waqf managed some 950 mosques in the West Bank (180 in Jerusalem and environs), and paid the salaries of 2,500 employees (1,000 in Jerusalem and environs). Over the years 1953 to 1994, Jordan invested in the West Bank through the Waqf about $485 million and from 1967 to 1989 another $250 million. In addition, King Hussein donated in the summer of 1998 more than $8 million for the renewal of the golden dome on the Dome of the Rock. In response, the Saudi king donated a similar sum to the Holy Places on the Temple Mount. The Jordanian donation was handled through official channels of the Hashemite Kingdom, and the Saudi donation was handled by UNESCO in coordination with the PLO (Friedland and Hecht 1996, 286–88; Merhav and Giladi 1999; Musallam 1996, 97–98, 107; Reiter 1997; Zak 1996, 175–78).

Israel approved the Jordanian steps because they were in accordance with the Israeli policy of granting Jordan a religious status in Jerusalem. They also bolstered Hussein's political control over other parts of the West Bank, limiting the influence of the PLO and suppressing all signs of local Palestinian autonomy. When on July 24, 1967, an Israeli official asked a Muslim preacher to let him review his Friday sermon for the services in the Dome of the Rock, the Supreme Muslim Council declared that Muslims would not allow non-Muslims to supervise Muslim affairs. In retaliation, Israel expelled some of the signers of this declaration, including Shaykh Abd al-Hamid Saikh, head of the Supreme Muslim Council (and from 1983 to 1993 president of the Palestinian National Council) (M. Benvenisti 1996, 101–2; Zak 1996, 175–78).

Despite Jordan's extensive investments, its status and influence decreased steadily, for several reasons: its inability to reach an overall agreement with Israel or to uproot Israel even partially from the West Bank; Israel's growing hold over the West Bank by means of its settlements; the advancement of the PLO to a major role in the political scene; and the Intifada (Palestinian uprising) that began in December 1987. Since the mid-1970s, and especially after the mid-1980s, the Palestinian identity of the West Bank inhabitants grew steadily. They established civil institutions and allowed PLO organizations "outside" (i.e., outside Palestine) to gain a foothold in the local institutions. This trend was true also for east Jerusalem, albeit at a different pace and scope (M. Klein 1999). The September 1993 agreement between Israel and the PLO and the establishment of the Palestinian Authority in mid-1994 regulated the Palestinization of the inhabitants of the West Bank, Gaza Strip, and east Jerusalem. In the wake of these agreements, Jordan decided the time had come to sign a peace agreement with Israel.

The Peace Treaty:
Israeli Rule and Jordanian Religious Authority

The Israeli-Jordanian peace talks culminated in the Washington Declaration, signed on July 25, 1994, by Prime Minister Yitzhak Rabin of Israel and King Hussein of the Hashemite Kingdom of Jordan (Jehl 1994). One of the declaration's clauses relates to the Holy Places in Jerusalem. This clause, later copied in substantially similar language into the Israeli-Jordanian peace treaty of September 1994, confirmed Palestinian apprehensions about Israeli activities in Jerusalem and rekindled discord between the PLO and Jordan. The Washington Declaration states that

> Israel respects the present special role of the Hashemite Kingdom of Jordan in Muslim Holy shrines in Jerusalem. When negotiations on the perma-nent status will take place, Israel will give high priority to the Jordanian historic role in these shrines. In addition the two sides have agreed to act together to promote interfaith relations among the three monotheistic re-ligions. *(Haaretz,* July 26, 1994; *FBIS Daily Report,* July 26, 1994; see "Washington Declaration" 1994; Ibrahim 1994, 1)

Curiously, this clause did not appear in the Agreement of Principles that King Hussein and Foreign Minister Shimon Peres of Israel were about to sign on November 2, 1993, although that agreement is generally similar to the Washington Declaration *(Haaretz,* Nov. 23, 1994). Rabin and Hussein formulated this clause in person (Kokhanovski 1995), with the purpose of separating the discussion of the political sovereignty over Jerusalem from the issue of the religious status of the Holy Places. In effect, until the signing of the Washington Declaration, there were deliberations within the Israeli es-tablishment among the heads of the Foreign Ministry, the Ministry of De-fense, and the prime minister as to whether Israel needed a stronger Jordan for the formulation of the permanent agreements. The Foreign Office saw in the proposed clause a needless provocation and an insult to the Palestinians. They believed in the inevitability of turning the Palestinian Authority into a state, and therefore Israel should not try to prevent this process by placing a Jordanian protectorate over the Authority, or should at least assist it in becoming the dominant partner in a Jordanian-Palestinian Confederation. In any case, asked the Foreign Ministry, will the Hashemite Kingdom not disappear after Hussein is gone? Why arouse the Saudis, Moroccans, and Egyptians—who would not relish Israel's preference of Jordan over themselves and would foil such a process? On the other hand, the Ministry of Defense and the prime minister believed that it would be possible to overcome Arab opposition to the preference of Jordan. Hashemite Jordan will not disappear, and it is in Israel's interest to supply it with the means of later supervision over the Palestinian neighbor whom both suspect and whom both would like to see remain small and weak. They also claimed that such a process was acceptable to Jordan, who would agree at the time of the permanent agreement to establish an alliance with Israel (Galilee 1996).

In reality, Jordan went along with the new trend set by Prime Minister Rabin, who forced his opinion on the Foreign Office and Peres. In his speech before the U.S. Congress in 1994, King Hussein stated:

> My religious faith demands that sovereignty over the Holy Places in Jerusalem resides with God and God alone. Dialogue between the faiths should be strengthened; religious sovereignty should be accorded to all believers of the three Abrahamic faiths, in accordance with their religions.
>
> In this way, Jerusalem will become the symbol of peace and its embodiment, as it must be for both Palestinians and Israelis when their negotiations determine the final status of Arab Eastern Jerusalem. (Hussein I 1994)

Crown Prince Hassan of Jordan was more open and direct. He stated that Jordan had never and would never relinquish its responsibility over the Islamic Holy Places in east Jerusalem. In his view, one must do everything to separate the religious and political issues of east Jerusalem, not only in the interim period but also in the permanent agreement—including even separate divisions of Jerusalem for religious and political purposes. In the permanent agreement, political sovereignty would be held by the Palestinians when they attain it, but religious sovereignty would be in the hands of a pan-

Islamic council in which both Palestinians and Jordanians would participate (*Davar* Nov. 2, 1994, 3; *Haaretz* July 20, 1994, 2).

Thus, with the Washington Declaration, Israel undertook an initial commitment about the permanent status of Jerusalem. The terms of the Washington Declaration suggest that Israel has relinquished any claim to actualize sovereignty over the Islamic Holy Places in Jerusalem and has surrendered the Temple Mount as a religious site. Israel claims that its paramount interest is to guarantee its political sovereignty over the eastern city and that management of the Islamic Holy Places and their religious status is not part of their political sovereignty.

Furthermore, in the Washington Declaration, Israel officially recognized for the first time Jordan's special status with regard to the Islamic holy shrines in Jerusalem. Historically and traditionally, the Waqf administration has been responsible for these holy shrines. The Waqf of Jerusalem remained subordinate to Jordan even after the Israeli conquest of 1967, and even the severance of Jordan's legal and administrative ties to the West Bank in July 1988 did not alter this subordination. The Hashemites have developed a special attachment to the Islamic Holy Places in Jerusalem and have derived from the shrines much of the legitimacy for their rule and political survival.[2] Until the Israeli-Jordanian treaty, Jordan maintained this role by virtue of continuation of the past state of affairs, not by choice or conscious preference about the future. Finally, the Washington Declaration established the possibility for future application of the option for the expropriation of the Holy Places in Jerusalem from any religious sovereignty.

Adnan Abu Odeh, the former Jordanian prime minister as well as King Hussein's confidant, suggested—possibly with the king's knowledge—that the Old City of Jerusalem (inside the walls) should be expropriated from political sovereignty and regarded as a Holy Place. A joint Jewish-Muslim-Christian council would administer the site, and each religion would have custody of its own shrines (Abu Odeh 1992, 183, 185; see also *Haaretz* Apr. 23, 1992, B3).

One must emphasize that in the Washington Declaration, Israel and Jor-

---

2. In the framework of this commitment, King Hussein refurbished the golden dome of the Dome of the Rock in 1994 (Hoffman 1994).

dan did not adopt Abu Odeh's position but merely one of his guiding principles: the separation of political from religious sovereignty. The Washington Declaration went further than his plan. Abu Odeh did not advocate a preferential position for Jordan in the administration of the Holy Places, nor did he intend to accord even indirect legitimacy to Israel's political hold over east Jerusalem, but rather to oust Israel from its political hold. This position also guided his reference to the new quarters that Israel had built in east Jerusalem outside the walls as settlements.

Abu Odeh's statement did not elicit any response from Israel at the time. After the Oslo Accords, Israel adopted the Jordanian tendency to separate the political future of Jerusalem from the future of the Holy Places. Since 1967, Israel has aspired to retain political sovereignty over east Jerusalem and to accord its actions a pan-Arab, pan-Islamic, and international legitimacy. In return for Jordan's agreement to separate political and religious questions regarding Jerusalem, Rabin was willing to endorse Jordan's special religious status over the Islamic Holy Places in Jerusalem—although he stated informally that he wished to discuss with more than one partner the future of the Islamic Holy Places in Jerusalem *(Haaretz,* July 27, 1994). Jordan claimed to have received from Israel a foothold in the Islamic Holy Places in Jerusalem by excluding Israel from them and that Israel thus came closer to acceptance of expropriating the Holy Places from all political sovereignty, including its own. Israel claimed to have bolstered its view that the mere existence of Islamic Holy Places in east Jerusalem did not in itself eviscerate Israel's political sovereignty over the city. The Washington Declaration embodied Jordanian-Israeli cooperation, which would clearly weaken the Palestinians' position in their struggle to establish east Jerusalem as their capital.

As expected, the Palestinians did not accept the Washington Declaration. The Palestinian Authority organized a popular campaign against it and protested to the president of the Conference of Islamic Countries and the secretariat of the Arab League (Musallam 1996, 93–103). In response to Israel's invitation to King Hussein to come and pray in Jerusalem and the rumors in the West Bank that this invitation would soon be acted on, Arafat declared that he alone had the right to issue invitations to pray in Jerusalem. He mobilized the Supreme Muslim Council headed by Hassan Tahbub, who declared that the council was the sole body responsible for the Islamic

Holy Places in Jerusalem. Arafat also accused Israel of violating the Israeli-Palestinian Declaration of Principles and added that the Palestinians therefore demanded the accelerated commencement of negotiations over the future of Jerusalem (Musallam 1996, 93–104; see also *Haaretz,* July 27, 1994, 6).

Did Israel really violate the agreement with the PLO? Two Israeli jurists argued that Israel did not violate the agreement on four grounds. First, Jordan was not named as partner to the negotiations over the permanent agreement, and the agreement with Jordan cannot substantially influence the results of the negotiations over the permanent status of Jerusalem. Israel merely resolved that, in future negotiations, Jordan's present role in the Holy Places would be given a priority. Second, the agreement with Jordan does not bind the PLO and does not violate Palestinian rights but indicates Israeli priorities in its negotiations with the PLO. Third, the agreement with Jordan refers to the permanent status, whereas the commitment to the PLO assures observance of the status quo. Fourth, Israel's agreement with the PLO determines only the timetable for discussions about Jerusalem and nothing else. At most, the agreement with Jordan deviates from Palestinian expectations (Immanuel and Hutman 1994, 1; see also *Haaretz,* Aug. 4, 1994, 1). Rabin and Hussein carefully worded the paragraph about Jerusalem in the Washington Declaration so that the Palestinians could not legally claim that it violates any Israeli commitment toward them. Yet the declaration suggests Jordan's indirect acceptance of Israel's political sovereignty over east Jerusalem *(Haaretz,* Nov. 23, 1994, 3). Even if Israel did not violate its agreement with the PLO from a legal or literal point of view, a political breach unmistakably occurred. Israel wanted to exploit its contacts with Jordan to influence the permanent status of Jerusalem, while at the same time weakening the Palestinian claim to sovereignty over east Jerusalem.

The Washington Declaration, which the Palestinians interpreted as an Israeli attempt to marginalize the Palestinian Authority, naturally incensed the PLO. Moreover, according to the PLO, Palestinians must have political sovereignty; they must be the ones to decide the future of the Islamic Holy Places in Jerusalem. The Palestinians cannot contemplate a separation of political and religious sovereignty over the Islamic Holy Places, especially because Palestinian claims to political sovereignty in east Jerusalem are based largely on the religious status of al-Haram al-Sharif in Islam. Therefore, the PLO viewed the treaty between Israel and Jordan as an attempt to cut the ground from under its feet in Jerusalem. It interpreted this treaty as a deal under which Jordan was willing to accept Israel's political sovereignty in east Jerusalem in return for placing the Islamic Holy Places dominantly in Jordanian hands, after being exclusively under Israeli rule in the interim agreement. Arafat remarked that "no Arab or Israeli leader controls the holy shrines in Eastern Jerusalem. This right is the Palestinians' alone" *(Haaretz,* July 27, 1994, 1).

In response, King Hussein stated that the PLO's emphasis on the Holy Places was motivated by its need to cover up its inability to extract sovereignty over al-Haram al-Sharif from Israel or to establish a Palestinian state with Jerusalem as its capital. Hussein assured the PLO that he had no wish to challenge its role as political representative of the Palestinians. Although Jordan had surprised the PLO by signing a treaty with Israel, Hussein claimed that the PLO had failed to consult Jordan over its secret negotiations with Israel that led to the Oslo Accords *(Haaretz,* Aug. 22, 1994, 3). Hussein tried to appease the PLO by stating that separation between the political and the religious questions of the future of Jerusalem could not harm political negotiations between the PLO and Israel or threaten the PLO's political status as sole and legitimate representative of the Palestinians.

The controversy between Jordan and the PLO over the preferred status of Jordan in the Temple Mount resulted from continued mistrust between Arafat and Hussein as well as between the two political entities. Thus, on August 23, 1994—the eve of the signing of the Israeli-Palestinian Declaration of Principles—Arafat visited Amman and told King Hussein of secret negotiations with Israel during which a draft of a declaration of principles had been drawn up, which was still incomplete. He did not elaborate further and refrained from showing the draft to the Jordanian king, although he had shown it to Egypt's president Husni Mubarak. Despite his advisors' efforts, Arafat was not convinced that the signing of the Oslo Accords had completely done away with the Jordanian option—which might still be implemented, thus preventing Palestinian independence. Because of these apprehensions, Arafat demanded that Israel redeploy its forces not only in the Gaza Strip, but also in Jericho—the town through which Jordan had entered the West Bank in 1948. The "Jericho Congress" had been convened here, in which Palestinian notables had asked King Abdullah to extend his protectorate over the West Bank. Jericho had been discussed in 1974, in the Israeli-Jordanian talks about political negotiations over the West Bank. Israel had offered Jordan the "Jericho corridor plan," according to which Jordan would receive a corridor connecting Jericho with the mountain region around Ramallah—a first step toward the realization of the "Allon plan." Jordan had demanded Israel's full retreat from the West Bank, the first step of which would be a separation of forces along the Jordan Valley, such as had been carried out along the borders with Egypt and Syria (Zak 1996, 163–66). The signing of the Declaration of Principles just a few days after Arafat's visit to him angered Hussein, who saw in Arafat's concealment of information a sign of mistrust and a denial of Jordan's massive aid to the PLO, mainly after the contacts about the Madrid Conference (Nuofal 1995, 143–44).

The Hamas also criticized the Washington Declaration, although this movement tended from its inception to seek support in Jordan against the Palestinian Authority and the PLO. The agreement laid a foundation for peace and normalization between the two countries, to which the Hamas objected strongly. It claimed that Jordan's agreement with Israel facilitated the latter's negotiations with the Palestinians about a permanent agreement, and that Jordan thus relinquished to Israel its political sovereignty over Jerusalem. The Hamas also claimed that the Jordanian step increased friction between Jordan and Saudi Arabia, which—like the rift between the PLO and Jordan—plays into Israel's hands. However, the Hamas refrained from attacking the Washington Declaration with the same vehemence with which it attacked the Oslo Accords—which it regarded as a complete surrender and a betrayal of all that is holy. Wishing to detract from Arafat's worth, the Hamas agreed with the idea of religious sovereignty in Jerusalem. At the same time, it attacked the Washington Declaration for what seemed the granting to Israel political sovereignty over al-Haram al-Sharif and Jerusalem (*al-Byyan,* July 22, 1994, and July 29, 1994; *al-Istiqlal,* Oct. 28, 1994; *Filastin al-Musalima,* Sept. and Nov. 1994, 5; al-Maqadme n.d.; Shabbat 1997, 187).

Since the signing of the Washington Declaration, several attempts have been made to reconcile Jordan and the PLO. Crown Prince Hassan tried to convince the Palestinians that Jordan, by extracting the Islamic Holy Places from Israel's hold, was acting as an envoy of the Arab and Islamic world, thereby serving the Palestinian interest *(FBIS Daily Report* 1994, 6; see also *Jordan Times,* Nov. 2, 1994; Walker 1994).

A month earlier, Prime Minister Abd al-Salam al-Majali of Jordan was even more outspoken *(FBIS Daily Report,* Oct. 31, 1994, 8). His condition for relinquishing the rights over the Holy Places to the Palestinians was the achievement of Palestinian political sovereignty. Al-Majali thus established a higher threshold than had Crown Prince Hassan, whose condition was that Israeli acquiescence to transfer of religious rights. Al-Majali's approach reflected his doubt as to whether the Palestinians would be able to oust Israel from east Jerusalem.

In early December 1994, Faisal al-Husseini, who handled Jerusalem affairs for the Palestinian Authority, visited Jordan to settle differences concerning Jerusalem and to prepare the ground for an official visit by Arafat to Jordan. At the end of his visit, he said, "Jordan considers the Holy Places a trust that will be turned over to the Palestinians when they become capable of shouldering this responsibility. We agreed to maintain the situation as it is and to hold further coordination so we will not make any wrong moves" *(Haaretz,* Dec. 5, 1994, 3; *FBIS Daily Report,* Dec. 5, 1994, 7).

Thus, both sides agreed that the Palestinian Authority shall recognize the status quo existing in Jerusalem since 1967, including Jordanian guardianship of the Islamic Holy Places in the city. In return, the Jordanian authorities will undertake to regard guardianship over these places as a trust that transfers to the Palestinians when the latter is in a position to accept it. It is not clear whether al-Husseini received a mandate from Arafat to reach this agreement, which seems nearer to the Jordanian position than the Palestinian position. Arafat did not ratify this agreement, and his visit to Jordan did not take place in early December 1994, as planned. Instead, Arafat relocated arbitration between himself and Hussein to a new arena, the Organization of the Islamic Conference.

The PLO Forces the Acceptance of Different Principles for Partition

The seventh meeting of the Organization of the Islamic Conference (OIC) was held in Casablanca, Morocco, in December 1994.[3] An open discussion between Jordan and the Palestinian Authority over the Holy Places in Jerusalem ultimately disintegrated. Jordan—supported by Qatar, Oman, and Yemen—demanded that the closing statement of the OIC extol Jordan's role as guardian of the Holy Places and praise King Hussein for his interest in the Holy Places in Jerusalem. In his effort to mobilize the leaders of Islamic countries, King Hussein claimed that as soon as Israel and the Palestinians reach a final agreement on the permanent status of Jerusalem, Jordan would relinquish to the Palestinians guardianship of the Holy Places in the city. But the PLO—supported by Saudi Arabia, Egypt, and Morocco—recognized Jordan's political intent and refused. The Palestinians claimed that the clause dealing with this issue in the Jordan-Israel treaty is a stumbling block to their achieving sovereignty in east Jerusalem and Israel's withdrawal. Morocco, Saudi Arabia, Egypt, and the PLO even tried to convince the assembly to form a committee on behalf of the OIC that would replace Jordan as guardian of the Holy Places until such time as the Palestinian Authority has full responsibility over Jerusalem. When King Hussein could not achieve a majority among the assembly for recognizing Jordan's role in guarding the Holy Places until the permanent agreement is reached, he left the OIC meeting before it ended. For the first time since the founding of the OIC in 1972, the conference lacked consensus over its resolutions, which were adopted over Jordanian opposition *(al-Quds,* Dec. 15, 1994, 1; *al-Wassat,* Dec. 19, 1994, 10).

In the closing statement, the OIC "emphasizes again that the problem of Palestine and of Honorable Jerusalem is the fundamental problem for all

3. The first Islamic Summit was held in Rabat, Morocco, in 1969, in response to the al-Aqsa fire. This meeting was followed in 1970 by the first Islamic Foreign Ministers' Conference in Jeddah, Saudi Arabia, which resulted in the formation of the OIC in 1972. The OIC gathered together all Muslim states, headed by King Hassan II of Morocco (Esposito 1984). For a discussion of the prestatehood period, see Kramer 1986.

Muslims, and they identify with the PLO in its just struggle for the removal of every vestige of Israeli occupation and building Palestinian institutions on Palestinian land" (al-Quds, Dec. 16, 1994, 1; Haaretz, Dec. 22, 1994, 1, and Jan. 2, 1995, 1). Furthermore, it states that members of the OIC "must assist the PLO in its future negotiations, until all authority and sovereignty in the occupied territories—including Honorable Jerusalem—will be transferred to the hands of the Palestinian sovereignty" (al-Quds, Dec. 16, 1994, 1; Haaretz, Dec. 22, 1994, 1, and Jan. 2, 1995, 1). Moreover, the statement stipulates that responsibility for Jerusalem in the interim period must be handed over to the Palestinian Authority, thus completely disregarding Jordan's role in the Holy Places.

This statement emphasizes the political aspect of the situation. The ire of the strongest Muslim countries in the Middle East was aroused not so much by the preferential religious status accorded to Jordan, but by the political implications of the Washington Declaration, through which Jordan indirectly recognized the annexation of east Jerusalem to Israel. The debate among Muslim countries over the Holy Places was held not over the religious issue, but over political sovereignty. Saudi Arabia, Egypt, Morocco, and the PLO believed that the status of the Holy Places in Jerusalem derives from political sovereignty over it. Therefore, if political sovereignty remains with Israel, the Holy Places remain occupied. Saudi Arabia even suggested that King Hussein's separation of religion and politics in Jerusalem is foreign to Islam. On January 16, 1995, the Jerusalem Committee of the OIC convened in Morocco. In its new composition—as initiated by Morocco, Saudi Arabia, Egypt, and the PLO—the controlling members of the conference finalized what they had begun in the plenary session one month earlier. The Jerusalem Committee refused to acknowledge the preferred position Jordan was to be given by Israel and disagreed with the latter's claims in favor of taking the Jordanian move (al-Quds, Jan. 18, 1995, 1).

If Israel had thought it could outflank the PLO politically by using the religious card, the Islamic states laid such ideas to rest. In 1974, an Arab summit meeting had removed Jordan from its position as the legitimate representative of the Palestinian people alongside the PLO; twenty years later the Islamic countries removed Amman from its preferential position in the places holy to Islam in Jerusalem.

Fundamentally, the debate among the Islamic states was between two political alternatives. Jordan was extremely skeptical about the Palestinian prospects of extracting an agreement from Israel to turn the Palestinian Authority into a state and thought it even less likely that Israel would agree to forego sovereignty in east Jerusalem. Therefore, the Jordanians reasoned, at the very least Israel should be deprived of its religious hold on the Islamic Holy Places in the city by separating political from religious sovereignty, which naturally would entail strengthening Jordan's religious status in Jerusalem. But most of the Arab and Islamic states thought that this approach would be tantamount to implicit recognition of Israel's political annexation of east Jerusalem. They insisted that the termination of Israel's religious hold on the sanctuaries of Islam in Jerusalem was inseparably bound with the termination of the occupation itself. It followed that the optimal course of action would be to strengthen the Palestinians and not assent to preferential religious status for Jordan. The Arab and Islamic states are certain that they will be able to obtain Israel's agreement to the transformation of the Palestinian Authority into a state—hence their decision to oust Jordan from its Israel-conferred preferential status.

After the issue of the Holy Places was settled in favor of the Palestinians, it was possible for Arafat to visit Jordan. On January 25, 1995, Arafat arrived in Jordan to sign a memorandum of understanding and cooperation between the Palestinian Authority and the Hashemite Kingdom of Jordan in the areas of communications, passage of goods and people, banking, post, culture, education, and local administration. The signing of these agreements was postponed until the establishment of the Palestinian Authority and the signing of separate, detailed agreements with Israel by Jordan and the Palestinian Authority. The agreement between Jordan and the Palestinian Authority was intended to regulate bilateral relations between the Palestinian Authority and the kingdom to its east. Following the signing of the agreement, Jordan decided to establish a liaison office in Gaza. As an introduction to the agreement signed, a political document was drawn up (al-Shark al-Awssat, Jan. 27, 1995, 1; al-Haiat, Jan. 24, 1995, 1; see also Haaretz, Jan. 27, 1995, 1; FBIS Daily Report, Jan. 25, 1995, 7).

This document neither indicates Jordan's special status in Jerusalem nor deals directly with the Islamic Holy Places in the city. It states clearly, however, the political sovereignty of the Palestinian people over Jerusalem. The spirit of this document reflects an agreement between two political entities of equal national status. The Palestinian side views favorably the peace treaty between Jordan and Israel, and states that this treaty does not harm the other tracks of negotiations between Israel and its neighbors. Other such tracks include Syria's efforts to regain sovereignty over the whole of the Golan Heights. This document portrays the Jordan–Israel peace treaty as ensuring Jordan's rights "on its land, water and borders, and toward securing the rights of the refugees" and does not contradict the rights of the Palestinians. Jordan pledges, therefore, to assist the Palestinian people and the PLO to realize their right of self-determination and to establish a state, with Jerusalem as its capital. The document implies that Jordan may not deter the Palestinians by separating political sovereignty over Jerusalem from religious sovereignty over the Holy Places within it. Specifically, the document contains a clause in which Jordan pledges to cooperate with the Palestinian Authority and to assist in establishing its national institutions. Therefore, nothing in the Jordanian–Palestinian agreement confirms Jordan's preferential status over the Holy Places in Jerusalem *(al-Shark al-Awssat,* Jan. 27, 1995, 1; *al-Haiat,* Jan. 24, 1995, 1; see also *Haaretz,* Jan. 27, 1995, 1). Thus, one of the prominent clauses in the Jordan–Israel peace treaty disappeared completely in the agreement between the Palestinian Authority and Jordan.

The new situation, created by the OIC and later by the agreement with the Palestinian Authority, was forced on King Hussein, making it difficult for him to come to terms with it. Because the issue of Jerusalem remained unresolved and would be discussed fully before establishing the permanent peace accord between Israel and the Palestinians, Hussein hoped to reverse this situation in time. In the signing ceremony of the agreement with the Palestinian Authority, Hussein said that his country would continue to fulfill its duty and give its auspices to the Holy Places in Jerusalem "as it did in the past" *(al-Haiat,* Jan. 27, 1995, 1; *al-Shark al-Awssat,* Jan. 27, 1995, 1; see also *FBIS Daily Report,* Jan. 26, 1995, 4). It would do so "out of its diligence to cherish these Holy Places and as a fulfillment of its obligation to guard Jerusalem and preserve its Arab and Muslim identity" *(al-Haiat,* Jan. 27, 1995, 1; *al-Shark al-Awssat,* Jan. 27, 1995, 1; see also *FBIS Daily Report,* Jan. 26, 1995, 1). We may judge the complexity and convolution of the

Jerusalem issue to King Hussein from an interview he gave to Ibrahim Nafa, editor of the Egyptian daily *al-Ahram,* about one month after signing the agreement with the Palestinian Authority early in 1995 *(FBIS Daily Report,* Feb. 21, 1995, 16).

If anything, King Hussein's statements obscure Jordanian policy. The contradictions and confusion are apparent in every section of the interview. The king stated that Jordan is responsible for east Jerusalem yet insisted that the Hashemite Kingdom had at that time no aim or aspiration in Jerusalem; the negotiations about the permanent agreement between Israel and the Palestinians will determine sovereignty over Jerusalem, yet at the time of the interview Jordan believed that national-political sovereignty over the Holy City should not be given to any of the contesting parties. The king hoped that Jordan will be a party to the permanent agreements but stated that the Palestinians must come to an agreement with Israel. In addition, the purpose of the peace process is to establish Palestinian sovereignty over Palestinian soil. In spite of Hussein's statement that Jordan had no aim of its own in Jerusalem, he also claimed the kingdom would continue to supervise the Holy Places during the interim period, as its solemn duty. Although his words indicated a retreat from the Washington Declaration toward Abu Odeh's plan (Abu Odeh 1992), Hussein did not clearly state this. In effect, the OIC toppled his entire strategy. He wrestled with the reality forced on him and had difficulty in accepting it; also, because Jerusalem's permanent status had not yet been decided in the debate between Israel and the Palestinians, he still had hopes of convincing the Islamic countries in the future.

The fact that the disagreement between Jordan and the Islamic states was fundamentally political is significant with regard to future administration of the Islamic Holy Places. It is far from certain that the Islamic states will agree to exclusive Palestinian administration. The Islamic states want to end Israeli occupation of east Jerusalem and therefore have supported the Palestinian demand; yet they still have to decide who will administer the Holy Places after Israel transfers east Jerusalem to Palestinian sovereignty. The option of joint religious administration of the Islamic Holy Places in Jerusalem under the political auspices of the Palestinian regime remains viable.

The PLO: Control of Jerusalem District and Shared
Authority with Jordan over al-Haram al-Sharif

The alignment of the Muslim states with Arafat strengthened him in his confrontation with King Hussein. The establishment of the Palestinian Authority in mid-1994 raised the question of control over the Waqf in Jerusalem: Would the Palestinian Waqf, which was in charge of the Waqf in the West Bank, also control Jerusalem—or would the Jordanian Waqf continue as in the past because the Palestinian office was prevented from acting in Jerusalem? Arafat decided in August 1994 to establish a Palestinian Waqf administration to replace the Jordanian one, but he failed to establish Jordan's agreement to this step *(Haaretz,* Aug. 8, 1994, 3). According to this decision, Palestinian Waqf employees would take over control of the Waqf in the West Bank and in Jerusalem as of October 1994.

Jordan, fearing that its ousting from Waqf administration would put an end to its senior status in al-Haram al-Sharif, immediately appointed its followers to the directorate of the Jerusalem Waqf and increased its financial aid to the Jerusalem institutions that it and the Waqf supported (e.g., the Maqassed Hospital). It utilized the ban on the Palestinian Authority to act within Jerusalem to claim that the ousting of Jordan from the city would leave a vacuum into which Israel would readily step. At the same time, Jordan could not ignore the full legitimization and authority of the Palestinian Authority in the territories under its control. It therefore decided, on September 29, 1994, to disassociate itself from the Waqf in the West Bank and to hand it to the Palestinian minister for the Waqf, Hassan Tahbub (who also presided over the Supreme Muslim Council sitting in al-Haram al-Sharif). Jordan relinquished to the Palestinian Waqf the documents pertaining to administration of Waqf affairs in the West Bank but not those pertaining to Jerusalem (Musallam 1996, 105–9).

The controversy between Jordan and the Palestinian Authority now narrowed down to Jerusalem, regarding three issues in parallel. The first was the right to appoint the mufti of Jerusalem. In mid-October 1994, after the death of Mufti Sulayman al-Ja'bari of Jerusalem (scion of a renowned and respected pro-Jordanian family), Jordan—as was its wont since 1948—hurried to appoint as his successor Shaykh Abd al-Qader Abidin. On the very same day, Arafat, as chairman of the Palestinian Authority, appointed his own candidate to this office—no other than Shaykh Ikrima Said Sabri, who had been dismissed by Jordan in June 1987 as chief *immam* at al-Aqsa Mosque for his support of the PLO (in a controversy with Jordan over the Amman Agreement of 1985 and over the appropriate way to convene the International Conference for Peace in the Middle East). The position of mufti of Jerusalem has been highly esteemed in the Palestinian religious-political hierarchy since the time of Hajj Amin al-Husseini, head of the Palestinian national movement under the British Mandate. The controversy therefore also concerned the status of the chairman of the Palestinian Authority: Does Arafat's authority extend over Jerusalem and its religious staff, which had formerly been controlled by Jordan? It also reflected an attempt on the part of both competing sides to tighten their hold on the Islamic Holy Places in Jerusalem. This controversy was eventually settled in favor of Shaykh Sabri because of the Palestinian Authority's superior control and supervision: the Security Services of the Authority directed to Shaykh Sabri's office all who came to honor the mufti of Jerusalem. Thus, Shaykh Abidin was left with his title only, and when he retired in 1998, Jordan did not appoint a successor, but placed a young *shaykh,* Abd al-Azim Salhab, in charge of the Sharai courts (religious courts) in Jerusalem, which had been under the jurisdiction of Shaykh Abidin *(Kol Hair,* Feb. 27, 1998, 10).

The second Jordanian-Palestinian issue had to do with the talks about the permanent agreement. In May 1996, on the eve of elections in Israel, Hussein, Mubarak, and Arafat met in Cairo to coordinate their actions. The talks that had begun that month about the permanent agreement—during which the Jerusalem question might arise—increased Arafat's apprehensions that Israeli-Jordanian cooperation would weaken his own hold on Jerusalem in general and on al-Haram al-Sharif in particular. Arafat saw this fear as realistic because under the Labor government the peace agreement with Jordan had been signed, granting the Hashemite Kingdom a preferred status in Jerusalem. Such cooperation might continue if Shimon Peres won the elections. Public-opinion polls indicated that Peres and Benjamin Netanyahu of the conservative Likud Party were running very close, and the members of the Cairo summit were anxious. Arafat was more apprehensive than Hus-

sein, who had refrained from making any negative statements against Netanyahu and had even met with him during the election campaign. Arafat
mobilized Mubarak in order to tie Jordan's hands under any eventuality.

Hussein promised not to conduct negotiations behind Arafat's back
about a permanent agreement in Jerusalem. At Arafat's request, he also
agreed to prohibit Hamas chiefs in Jordan from acting against the Palestinian
Authority or from conducting campaigns of agitation against Arafat. Arafat
saw a connection between these two topics, claiming that Jordan had permitted the Hamas to act in its territory and to attack him personally in order
to supplant him in Jerusalem eventually with the aid of Hamas support.

Arafat on his part agreed to coordinate his positions and actions with
Jordan, accepting the argument that Jordan would be affected by any agreement between Israel and the Palestinians about refugees, permanent borders,
and Jerusalem. He agreed to leave the Islamic Holy Places in Jerusalem
under Jordanian jurisdiction, accepting the view that Jordan's stepping out at
this time would play into Israel's hands. Jordan reiterated its commitment to
be the first to recognize Palestinian sovereignty over east Jerusalem, as soon
as the Palestinians would achieve it *(al-Quds,* May 13–15, 1996, 1). "Arab
Jerusalem is an occupied area, and God willing our brothers [the Palestini-
ans] will succeed in returning it to their jurisdiction, so that it will be a symbol of Israeli-Palestinian peace, followed by an Arab–Palestinian peace," said
King Hussein at the end of the summit *(al-Quds,* May 13, 1996, 1). He stated
at the opening of the Jordanian Parliament: "We declared very clearly to the
Arabs and the Muslims our commitment to the Holy Places. . . . We shall
hand them over to the Palestinians at the conclusion of the talks about the
permanent settlement and the founding of the Palestinian State whose capital will be al-Quds" *(al-Quds,* Nov. 20, 1996, 1).

During this 1996 minisummit, Arafat reiterated the 1984 suggestion
that in order to arrive at the negotiating table with Israel in a stronger position, a Jordanian-Palestinian confederation should be declared. He believed
that an implicit Jordanian recognition of the Palestinian state would prevent
an Israeli-Jordanian accord against Palestine. In making this suggestion,
Arafat reversed his political tactics, for between 1986 and 1996 he had been
wary of establishing a confederation between the veteran, strong kingdom
and the weak Palestinian entity, and therefore had intended to establish it

only after having achieved independence for Palestine. However, he now wished to use the idea of a confederation as a tactical and political step, a voucher for achieving full Palestinian independence. His plan was that the confederation would assume full meaning after Palestinian independence was achieved. Jordan rejected this proposal—as Jordan's position was at the end of 1995 and the beginning of 1996—on the grounds that the time was not yet ripe: the Palestinians must first reach an agreement with Israel in which their legal and political status would be clarified (whether they have won statehood and in which boundaries), and only then would it be possible to agree on a Palestinian-Jordanian confederation. Jordan didn't believe that the Palestinians could extract from Israel recognition of their own independent state. A failure of negotiations carried out under the banner of a Jordanian-Palestinian confederation in which the Jordanian side was stronger than its partner would be blamed on Jordan—a situation from which it meant to protect itself (*al-Quds,* Feb. 7, 1996, 1, and May 14, 1996; *al-Wassat,* Dec. 25, 1995, 1).

The idea of a Jordanian-Palestinian confederation had first surfaced in 1984, at the talks about the Amman Agreement (M. Klein 1988), Jordanian policy on the Palestinian issue swung between cooperating with Israel (or at least waiting on the sideline for the results of Palestinian negotiations with Israel) and backing the Palestinian Authority and lending a helping hand to its achievement of independence. Jordan took the first stance during the Labor rule in Israel and the second during the rule of the Likud coalition. Jordan considered that the traditional policy of the Likud—massive settlement in the West Bank—endangered the very existence of the Hashemite Kingdom on the East Bank and undermined the demographic balance in the kingdom between Jordanians of West Bank descent and those of East Bank descent. The Hashemite character of the East Bank was hard won, gained by a process in which citizens of Palestinian descent—those accepted into Jordan after the annexation of the West Bank in 1948 and the 1967 refugees—became supporters of the Hashemite Kingdom. Many of the businessmen, relatives of government employees, central figures in the middle classes, and a major part of the financial and economic sector are Palestinian in origin. They have made a crucial contribution to the shaping and development of the state, and the economic life of the country is highly dependent on them. Jordanians of Palestinian origin have made an unofficial political pact with the palace and have supported the king in identifying the kingdom with his own Hashemite descent. They have encouraged the king to aid the PLO and to establish relations with the organization, thus helping to oust those in the Jordanian establishment who opposed it—the intelligence services, senior government officials, and the bourgeoisie, who advocate a separate Transjordanian identity and close cooperation with Israel (al-Tal 1996; Susser 1995).

The Likud policy in Israel bolstered the position of the former. During the 1980s, the Jordanians cooperated with the PLO in helping the Palestinians hold on to their land; on the eve of the Madrid Conference, they gave the PLO the necessary backing to form a joint delegation to the conference, in accordance with Likud demands, and upon Netanyahu's ascent as prime minister they supported Arafat in his negotiations with Israel. It was King Hussein who brought before Netanyahu in January 1997 a Palestinian-Jordanian-Egyptian compromise proposal for an agreement for redeployment in Hebron and the rest of the West Bank. Moreover, King Hussein was the first Arab head of state who, in October 1996, visited the Palestinian Authority in Jericho following the "al-Aqsa battle" (clashes between Israel and the Palestinians over Netanyahu's opening of the Western Wall tunnel). The king thus expressed Jordan's complete withdrawal from negotiations over the West Bank and its stance together with the Palestinians against the government of Israel (Mu'asher 1996).

The third issue between the Jordanians and the Palestinians dealt with control of the Waqf in the city itself and in al-Haram al-Sharif. In October 1996, a conflict erupted between the Jordanian Waqf employees and their Palestinian counterparts. Following rumors of financial corruption, both the Palestinian minister for the Waqf and the governor of the Jerusalem District demanded that the Waqf treasurer, whom Jordan had appointed, relinquish his authority to a PLO man whom Arafat would appoint. This demand was accompanied by a presidential security—"Force 17"—show of force. The Jordanian directorate of the Waqf turned for help to its offices in Amman, and the chiefs of the Jordanian Waqf Ministry invited their western colleagues for a meeting, in which it was decided that the Jordanian protectorate over the Waqf in al-Haram al-Sharif would continue, and the Jordanian treasurer would remain in office. Until the establishment of the permanent agreement, "the Palestinian Authority appreciates the role of Jordan and its protectorate over the Holy Places and the Islamic Waqf in Jerusalem," stated Tayeb Abd al-Rahim, secretary of the presidential office of the Palestinian Authority (*al-Quds,* Nov. 5, 1996, 1). However, outside the municipal boundaries—i.e., in the Jerusalem district of the Palestinian Authority (identical with the Jordanian Jerusalem district)—the responsibility for Waqf possessions and its offices would be turned over to the Palestinian Authority. These offices comprised about 150 employees out of the 700 who were active in the city and in the district—administering schools, mosques, and other Waqf possessions in the environs of Jerusalem (e.g., Azariya and Abu Dis), ruled by the Palestinian Authority (*al-Quds* Nov. 5, 1996; Arafat 1996).

Jordan thus recognized in 1996 the status of the Palestinian Authority in the urban region of Jerusalem—which it had refrained from doing until then. The Jordanian interest in the Waqf now narrowed to al-Haram al-Sharif—the only site in which Jordan wished to keep a foothold in the framework of a permanent agreement. Two token expressions were given to the new situation: the announcement of the Jordanian Waqf Ministry delegation to the talks with the Palestinians that King Hussein would refurbish al-Aqsa Mosque, as he had done with the Dome of the Rock in 1994, and that on that very same day the pro-Jordanian daily newspaper *al-Nahar* would be closed down. In 1986, as a result of the controversy between Jordan and the PLO over the Amman Agreement, *al-Quds,* the most widely read newspaper in the west Bank, had changed not only in ownership but from a pro-Jordanian policy to a pro-PLO policy. Pro-Jordanians had then founded *al-Nahar,* but ten years later this paper had no readers and no political or financial backing. The interests of Jordan in al-Haram al-Sharif no longer warranted a separate daily paper (D. Rubinstein 1997).

Since the beginning of 1997, Jordan's effective authority in al-Haram al-Sharif has shrunk considerably. Its guardianship of the Islamic Holy Places is a front behind which stand mainly Palestinian political bodies. A change in the Supreme Muslim Council illustrates the process of Palestinization of al-Haram al-Sharif. The Supreme Muslim Council was founded during the British Mandate and renewed its activities after 1967. Neither Jordan (in the 1948–67 period) nor Israel (after 1967) recognized the council, and the latter even deported its 1967 chairman, Shaykh Abd al-Hamid Saikh, who later became chairman of the Palestinian National Council. The council's main aim was to observe events in al-Haram al-Sharif and in the Waqf authorities. On the eve of the founding of the Palestinian Authority in 1994, Hassan Tahbub was appointed head of the Waqf (later to be appointed minister of the Waqf on behalf of the Authority), and Faisal al-Husseini—the member of the PLO Executive Committee responsible for Jerusalem—was appointed as his deputy. The council thus became a body whose heads are national and local political leaders, which was of help to the council and to the Palestinian Authority in their struggles for control over al-Haram al-Sharif.

The next step in the Jordanian-Palestinian Authority struggle took place in January 1997, when Arafat decided to include in the Supreme Muslim Council eighteen dignitaries from the West Bank and Gaza Strip (among them a former minister of the Palestinian Authority's Executive Council, Dr. Abd al-Aziz al-Haj Ahmed, as well as the governor of the district of Jerusalem of the Palestinian Authority, Jamil Othman Nasser, whose office is located in Abu Dis) (D. Rubinstein 1997). Thus, the council as a whole, and not only its leaders, turned into a body whose main members are Palestinian political leaders and that is able to conduct the affairs of al-Haram al-Sharif and supervise Waqf personnel still under Jordan's jurisdiction.

Summary:
The Road to Jerusalem Passes Through the West Bank

The first attempt to reach peace in Jerusalem took place immediately after the 1948 war but led nowhere. Negotiations were conducted between Israel and Jordan only, and the most interesting element was their joint assumption that whatever the structure of the agreement, Jerusalem must be divided between them. A complete partition was considered: a physical and geographical division, as well as a division of authority and sovereignty, together with exchange of territories in the city between the two countries. The negotiated Israeli-Palestinian agreement should give a formal status to the positions at the termination of fighting, regulate the interests of each partner in the partition, and express the national ideology and priorities of Israel and Jor-

dan. Being engaged in state and nation building, Israel and Jordan each preferred to consolidate its share—west and east Jerusalem accordingly—rather
than to lay claim to control over the other's part (although each was interested to some extent in the other's part and did not wish to relinquish it entirely). However, between 1948 and 1967, neither intended to invade the
other's territory in Jerusalem. Jerusalem was an outlying city of limited,
mostly symbolic importance. west Jerusalem became the capital of Israel and
a national symbol, and east Jerusalem served as a religious symbol giving legitimization to the Hashemite rule. Eventually, the formal peace building of
1949–51 failed—not over the Jerusalem question, but over other unsolved
problems. For lack of an agreement, the cease-fire regime and the de facto
partition of the city were perpetuated.

Israel's conquest of east Jerusalem in the Six Day War destroyed the former partition lines of the city. At the end of the 1960s and beginning of the
1970s, Israel proposed to Jordan new partition lines: Israeli sovereignty over
east Jerusalem and full religious authority to Jordan over the Islamic Holy
Places in Jerusalem. Through its control of the religious apparatus, Jordan
was to gain informal influence and political status in Jerusalem.

Jordan rejected the Israeli proposal and made a counterproposal: its own
sovereignty over the eastern city with a religious status for the Jews or for Israel
in the Western Wall and other Jewish holy sites in the eastern city, excluding
al-Haram al-Sharif. Alternately, Jordan was willing to agree to a special
regime for Jerusalem. This proposal would cause a full or partial revocation of
Israeli sovereignty over east Jerusalem—which Israel refused, along with
Hussein's demand to return to his sovereignty all of the West Bank through a
gradual process. As in the past, because there was no overall agreement, Israel
and Jordan drew up a series of ad hoc understandings, whose gist was application de facto of the Israeli proposal. Sovereignty over east Jerusalem remained
in Israeli hands without legitimization from Jordan; and without a formal declaration, Jordan controlled the Islamic institutions and bolstered its political
status in the West Bank as a whole and in Jerusalem in particular.

This arrangement was upset with the entry of the Palestinians into the
picture. The politicization of the PLO, which began in 1974 and accelerated
in the 1980s; the hold of the PLO organizations over the West Bank since the
end of the 1970s; the Intifada; and the stands taken by the governments of Is-

rael, which since 1967 were far from those of Jordan—all served to oust Jordan from the West Bank, enhancing the Palestinian identity of its inhabitants and anchoring it within the PLO. In the summer of 1988, Jordan had no choice but to annul officially its annexation of the West Bank and to conduct a losing battle with the PLO for control of the Jerusalem District. The wheel of history had turned back. In 1948, Jordan had entered Jerusalem through the West Bank. During and after the war, Jordan used military and diplomatic means to increase its understanding (if not more) with Israel about division of the mandate territory between the two countries—an understanding also covering Jerusalem. When Jordan lost its hold on the West Bank between the late 1970s and middle 1980s, its status in Jerusalem weakened accordingly.

The PLO trod a similar path. Its entrenchment in the West Bank and Gaza Strip gave it a foothold in Jerusalem. The establishment of the Palestinian Authority in mid-1994 enhanced this process, and in 1996 the Authority received from Jordan control of the Waqf administration in the district of Jerusalem—excluding Jerusalem itself, where the Oslo Accords prevented it from acting. The competition between Jordan and the Palestinian Authority has concerned control of the Islamic Holy Places in Jerusalem, and since 1994 the Authority has won on this issue as well.

The conflict between Jordan and the Palestinian Authority has also concerned the lines of partition of the city to be included in the final peace agreement. The peace agreement between Israel and Jordan (1994) states that in the future there will be a division of authority in al-Haram al-Sharif: Israel did not give up its sovereignty but only religious control over the site and in fact has made a commitment to grant Jordan a preferred status in this site with the signing of a permanent agreement. Jordan claimed that by this commitment, Israel has also been ousted politically from the site and is approaching the principle of evisceration of all political sovereignty over the Holy Places. Israel did not accept this interpretation, and at the Conference of Islamic Countries at the end of 1994, neither did the PLO, Egypt, Saudi Arabia, Syria, and Morocco. They all claimed that it is impossible to separate political sovereignty from religious status, and the Palestinian Authority must be supported in achieving political sovereignty in east Jerusalem. Thus, the Islamic countries permitted the PLO to oust Jordan from the district of Jerusalem, limiting its influence to al-Haram al-Sharif and to the city proper.

In other words, in preparation for discussions about a permanent agreement—which, according to the Oslo Accords, were to be concluded by mid-1999—the PLO has succeeded in forcing on Israel and Jordan different lines of partition and in establishing itself as the main negotiator with Israel on the issue of Jerusalem.

Conclusion

It seems that King Abdullah's policy about Jerusalem and al-Haram al-Sharif is different from that of his father, King Hussein. Abdullah was a child when his father lost Jerusalem and has never ruled over the West Bank. He is not fettered by the heavy load of suspicions, disappointments, and bitter memories toward the PLO and Arafat, which culminated in Black September in 1970. When he ascended the throne in 1999, the Palestinian Authority was an established fact, and the ambivalence that had characterized King Hussein's position on the Palestinian issue changed into an unequivocal attitude. When King Abdullah listed the topics of the permanent agreement between Israel and the Palestinian Authority, in which Jordan is a partner, he did not mention the Jerusalem question, only the refugees and the water issue. "Jerusalem from our point of view is occupied Palestinian territory, to be treated as the other occupied Palestinian territories" *(al-Ayyam,* Sept. 16, 1999, 1). Prime Minister Rowabda of Jordan, talking about al-Haram al-Sharif, said, "At this moment we are involved [with it,] and we administer the Waqf in [occupied] Jerusalem through the Jordan government and in conjunction with our Palestinian brothers. If our Palestinian brothers wish to take this role upon themselves, Jordan is quite willing to hand it over to them. We are part of our Arab and Islamic nation. Our involvement in Jerusalem derives from our being sons of this nation, and we do not mean to take the place of our Palestinian brothers" *(al-Ayyam,* Aug. 31, 1999, 1).

On the eve of renewal of negotiations about the permanent agreement, the starting points are clearer than ever before. Israel will conduct the negotiations over Jerusalem, including the Temple Mount, with a Palestinian factor. The PLO, the OIC, Egypt, and Jordan are out of the picture on this issue, although they may gain some sort of status in al-Haram al-Sharif. However, this status will not be granted them by Israel but in the framework of an internal arrangement inside the Arab or Islamic world. For the Arab and Islamic countries, al-Haram al-Sharif is not merely a holy site, devoid of any political affiliation or significance. The same may be said for Israel, which since 1967 has attached great importance to being the supreme sovereign over the site. At the end of 1994, Jordan and Israel failed in separating the religious and political aspects—that is, in convincing the Arab world of their honest intention to avoid political contamination of the holy site. The heads of the Arab states had the impression that behind Israeli and Jordanian leaders' declarations about separating the religious from the political lay a political intention: to weaken the Palestinian hold on al-Haram al-Sharif and to forge a preferred status for Jordan under Israeli patronage.

The way things look now, negotiations over Jerusalem will not be separated from other issues outstanding between Israel and the Palestinians, which means that negotiations over al-Haram al-Sharif will be affected by the way negotiations about other issues develop, especially those concerning Jerusalem or the holy sites in and outside it.

Israel did not wish at first to have the Palestinians as a partner in negotiations about al-Haram al-Sharif; as stated, it preferred Jordan. Yet its ability to determine its partner was limited. The PLO forced its presence by means of action in two parallel tracks. The first was within the political framework, in the Arab Islamic arena, where the PLO was recognized as the political-religious landlord of both Jerusalem and al-Haram al-Sharif. The second was through activity on the ground, gaining key positions in the religious establishment residing in al-Haram al-Sharif and managing it. Thus, while Israel was trying to bolster Jordan's position by a top-down action, the PLO acted "bottom up" and secured both its flanks—the Arab and the Muslim. On both these tracks, the PLO had an advantage over Jordan. Its hold over the establishment and the public was greater, and its international standing had strengthened since the Declaration of Principles with Israel in 1993 and the establishment of the Palestinian Authority in 1994.

Keeping the peace and ensuring freedom of worship in al-Haram al-Sharif are of the highest interest to Israel, as it has thus succeeded in ensuring its rule over east Jerusalem even though the international community did not recognize its right to do so. In order to preserve public order, security, and freedom of Islamic worship, Israel negotiated with the Islamic establishment administering the site. It did not speak with the national or municipal Palestinian leadership about the future of the site, but with its local administrators. When the PLO entered from the "outside," outside Palestine, and then from the West Bank into Jerusalem and al-Haram al-Sharif, the religious establishment on the site became the last link in the chain leading to national leadership. Control of the functional space is not in the hands of a religious authority devoid of connection to the Palestinian political establishment. It seems that the PLO is the winner in the competition over control of the functional space, and Jordan is conducting a losing battle for some sort of foothold on the site. The ongoing talks and the agreements reached have taken on a new meaning as the Palestinian chain of action has led to a political factor, the Palestinian Authority.

Israel's Labor government offered King Hussein status in the religious administration of the Temple Mount in the framework of a peace treaty between Israel and Jordan. Similarly, Prime Minister Menachem Begin considered incorporating representatives of Arab states along with religious leaders in the Islamic council that was, according to his plans, to administer al-Haram al-Sharif. In both cases, the implementation of these ideas would give a status in the site to political factors other than Israel, whose own authority over the site would shrink to a token sovereignty only, for Israel was not to be a part of the religious council administering the site. Moreover, Begin also considered implementing here the Vatican model, which would mean relinquishing Israel's sovereignty and establishing a special legal status for the Temple Mount and for the officials functioning in it.

A combination of all these considerations points to the fact that Israel and the PLO have the necessary means to begin crystallizing agreements over the Temple Mount (al-Haram al-Sharif). Negotiations between them will not begin from scratch, but from ordering, institutionalizing, and officially ratifying former understandings between them.[4]

4. Points of contest and consent regarding the Temple Mount were discussed between Israel and the Palestinian Authority during the final status talks in Camp David and in Taba. The Hashemite Kingdom of Jordan did not participate. The author summed up and analyzed these talks in his forthcoming book, *Shattering a Taboo—the Contacts Toward a Permanent Status Agreement in Jerusalem 1994–2001.*

6

The Role of the Hashemite Kingdom of Jordan in a Future Permanent-Status Settlement in Jerusalem

Legal, Political, and Practical Aspects

Reuven Merhav and Rotem M. Giladi

In the Washington Declaration and again in the Israel-Jordan Treaty of Peace, Israel declared that it respects the present special role of the Hashemite Kingdom of Jordan in Muslim holy shrines in Jerusalem. Moreover, it undertook to give high priority to the Jordanian historic role in these shrines when negotiations on the permanent status will take place. These provisions deal with two different matters that require inquiry and elucidation: Jordan's present special role and its historic role in holy shrines in Jerusalem. Moreover, the extent of the legal obligation assumed by Israel has to be investigated, and the political aspects of the situation must also be examined: Is it desirable, from Israel's perspective, that Jordan fulfill any role in these shrines in a future settlement and, if so, what form does the Jordanian role have to take in order to fulfill its functions?

The aim of this essay is to explore Israel's options with respect to a future Jordanian role in the Muslim Holy Places in Jerusalem from legal, political,

This essay is a short version of policy research we conducted during 1998 at the Jerusalem Institute for Israel Studies.

and practical perspectives. We first describe the dynamics taking place in east Jerusalem between Jordan and both the autonomous Palestinian Authority established under the Oslo peace process in mid-1994 and its successor elected in 1996, the Palestinian Council. Especially, we focus on the dynamics in the al-Haram al-Sharif/Temple Mount compound. This description may reveal what Jordan's "present special role" in the Holy Places was at the relevant time, what it is today, and what its prospects are, as well as the limits of those prospects.

This essay presents a legal analysis of the obligations undertaken by Israel in the Washington Declaration and again in the Israel-Jordan Treaty of Peace concerning a future Jordanian role in the Muslim Holy Places in Jerusalem. This discussion sheds light on the restrictions that international law imposes on future Israeli policy concerning the Jordanian role.

After briefly introducing several political factors relevant to the establishment of a future Jordanian role in Muslim Holy Places in Jerusalem, we discuss the merits and demerits—from a Israeli point of view—of that future Jordanian role. On this basis, we present the problems and prospects of the Jordanian role and the ramifications for future Israeli policy.

Historical Background and Jordanian–Palestinian Dynamics in Jerusalem Since 1994

Zionist-Hashemite relations began before either Jordan or Israel were established (see Dann 1994, 15; Garfinkle 1992; Pundik 1994; Satloff 1994; Schueftan 1986; Sela 1992, 623).[1] Jordan, as ruler of the West Bank and east Jerusalem between 1948 and 1967 (Nevo 1996), has maintained close ties with these territories since it lost them to Israel, including administering both the Holy Places in Jerusalem and Waqf (Muslim religious trust) activities in the city and the West Bank. In 1988, Jordan announced its disengage-

---

1. On the establishment of the Transjordan Emirate, see Dann 1982 and Kleiman 1970. Note that the first Hashemite-Zionist agreement touched on the question of the Holy Places: "The Mohammedan Holy Places shall be under Mohammedan control" (Agreement between the Emir Feisal of Hedjaz and Dr. Chaim Weizmann of the Zionist Organization, Jan. 3, 1919, Article 6, reproduced in Lapidoth and Hirsch 1992, 21).

ment from the West Bank *(International Legal Materials* 27 [1988], 1637; *Palestine Yearbook of International Law* 4 [1987–88], 30), but continued fulfilling its religious functions in the West Bank and Jerusalem (Reiter 1997).

The Gulf War, the Madrid Conference, and the Oslo Peace Process

The late King Hussein's siding with Iraq during the Gulf War was a nadir in Jordan's relations with the West. Jordan had to absorb many of the Palestinians deported from the Gulf states at a huge cost to its economy (Dann 1990). The Madrid Peace Conference of October 1991 provided Jordan with the opportunity to resume its strategic partnership with Israel and to use Israel's U.S. connections to save its economy and improve its military.

The Palestine Liberation Organization (PLO) was not represented directly at the conference because of Israel's objections. For this reason, a joint Jordanian-Palestinian delegation was constituted and took part in the conference (E. Rubinstein 1998, 524). Parallel to the official bilateral talks conducted in Washington between Israel and the two segments of the joint Jordanian-Palestinian delegation, however, Israel and the PLO conducted clandestine negotiations in Oslo. It appears that King Hussein did not know about these talks,[2] which produced the September 13, 1993, Declaration of Principles on Interim Self-Government Arrangements.

Article 5(3) of the Declaration of Principles listed Jerusalem as one of the issues to be negotiated between Israel and the Palestinians in the permanent-status negotiations. It did not prescribe the nature of the permanent status—that is, it did not require the establishment of a Palestinian state, nor did it preclude, for example, the creation of a Jordanian-Palestinian confederation. Indeed, another issue for the permanent-status negotiations is "relations with other neighbors." Although the Palestinian Council was not to have jurisdiction in Jerusalem (or in any other permanent-status issue) (Agreed Minutes, "Declaration" 1993; Agreed Minutes to Article 4; see also "Israeli-Palestinian Interim Agreement" 1995, Articles 11(2) and 17(1))[3];

2. On August 23, Arafat notified the king of the negotiations but did not show him the draft he showed President Mubarak of Egypt (M. Klein 1999, 123).

Giladi 1995, 506; Singer 1995, 1),[3] the Declaration of Principles constitutes a clear preference for a Palestinian rather than a Jordanian option.

The Washington Declaration and the Israel–Jordan Treaty of Peace

King Hussein now had to reduce the harm to Jordanian interests. Through the bilateral Washington talks, Israel and Jordan signed on September 14, 1993, a Common Agenda to peace negotiations.[4] This document, which was completed prior to the Declaration of Principles (E. Rubinstein 1998, 524), did not refer to the issue of Jerusalem. On November 2, 1993, King Hussein and Foreign Minister Shimon Peres of Israel were to sign an agreement specifying agreed principles, which did not mention Jordan's role in the Holy Places in Jerusalem (M. Klein 1999, 119; cf. Zak 1996, 294). By contrast, the Washington Declaration included a provision drafted by the late king and the late Prime Minister Rabin,[5] which was eventually incorporated, with slight variations, in Article 9 of the Treaty of Peace between the State of Israel and the Hashemite Kingdom of Jordan (1994).

The Aftermath of the Washington Declaration: Palestinian–Jordanian Competitive Dynamics

The Palestinians were outraged by the Washington Declaration (Musallam 1996, 113; Shragai 1995, 389),[6] arguing that it contradicted Israel's undertaking in the Declaration of Principles to conduct negotiations on the Jerusalem issue with only them, to the exclusion of other parties (M. Klein 1995, 45). Since the establishment of the Palestinian Authority in May 1994

3. Article 1(7) of the Interim Agreement prohibits the council from locating its offices in Jerusalem.

4. It seems that the Common Agenda was agreed on as early as October 1992 (see Satloff 1995, 55).

5. Article B(3) of the Washington Declaration. On the debate that arose between the Prime Minister's Office and the Ministry of Foreign Affairs concerning the strengthening of Jordan toward the permanent-status settlement, see Klein 1999, 119.

6. Palestinian popular response was strong. Morocco and Saudi Arabia refused to accept the Israeli-Jordanian understanding.

(see "Agreement on the Gaza Strip" 1994), it began struggling with Israel over control of east Jerusalem and over its status (see chapter 5 of this volume). Now the Palestinians initiated another front aimed at minimizing Jordanian physical and political control of east Jerusalem, especially al-Haram al-Sharif/Temple Mount (see chapter 5 of this volume).

This front resulted in a dynamic process of Palestinian strengthening and consolidation and a corollary Jordanian withdrawal. At the same time, both parties exercised mutual restraint, stemming from many codependent relationships existing between them. These codependencies also led them, from time to time, to reach temporary agreements that reflected their relative power positions[7] and that postponed the settlement of their disputes. Examples of these dynamics follow.

The struggle over political status in Jerusalem and the Holy Places. With the signing of the Washington Declaration, Israel formally invited King Hussein to pray in al-Aqsa Mosque in al-Haram al-Sharif/Temple Mount; in return, Chairman Yasir Arafat argued that it was his exclusive privilege to invite King Hussein, demonstrating the Palestinian interpretation of the Washington Declaration: first, the declaration impairs the Palestinian Authority's powers (by allegedly transferring powers to Jordan); second and worse, in Palestinian eyes, it amounts to a Jordanian recognition of Israel's sovereignty in east Jerusalem and so harms the chances of the future Palestinian state to establish its capital in the city under the permanent-status arrangements.

In an interview in *Der Spiegel (Haaretz,* Aug. 22, 1994), King Hussein argued that Jordan in fact saved the Holy Places from Israel's hands, which the PLO could not accomplish. According to the late king, Jordan was not competing with the PLO on the representation of the Palestinian people, nor did it seek to damage the conduct of the permanent-status negotiations. The king distinguished between political sovereignty in Jerusalem and the resolution of the problem of the Holy Places, which is going to be based on "god's sovereignty" (M. Klein 1999, 120).

7. These relationships stem from, for example, the Palestinian component in Jordan's population; the Palestinian real property and bank accounts in Jordan; and the West Bank population's constant dependence on Jordan for the exercise of freedom of movement of persons, goods, and capital.

In an attempt to appease the Palestinians, Crown Prince Hassan declared in November 1994 that in the permanent settlement, when full responsibility will be transferred to the Palestinians, Jordan will transfer the responsibility for the Holy Places to the Palestinian Authority (see note 50 for an analysis; see also M. Klein 1995, 47). Although aimed at achieving a comprehensive understanding of principles, attempts at mediating between Jordan and the Palestinian Authority failed.

The Palestinian Authority protested to the Secretariat of the Arab League, the presidency of the Organization of the Islamic Conference (OIC), and the United Nations (UN) secretary-general. The OIC meeting held in Casablanca in December 1994 rejected Jordan's proposal that the conference's concluding statement back up Jordan's custodianship of Jerusalem's Holy Places. In order for this initiative to succeed, Hussein was willing to transfer the authority of this custodianship to the Palestinians upon an Israeli-Palestinian agreement on the permanent status.

Egypt, Saudi Arabia, and Morocco (the hosting country) supported the PLO, but the PLO failed to have the conference establish a committee to take from Jordan the responsibility for the Holy Places until the Palestinian Authority will have secured jurisdiction in Jerusalem. The concluding statement of the conference, nevertheless, reflected PLO achievements with regard to Jordan; it did not mention Jordan's role at all.[8] Although decisions of the conference have to be made by consensus (so that Jordan could have at least put the motion to vote), King Hussein left the conference before its conclusion.

An agreement signed between the Palestinian Authority and Jordan at

---

8. The statement recognized the Palestinian identity of Jerusalem and the right of the Palestinians to establish their capital in Jerusalem. It called on the members of the conference to assist the PLO in the future negotiations so that Jerusalem is returned to Palestinian sovereignty and that all authorities in Jerusalem are transferred to the Palestinian Authority. Furthermore, the PLO succeeded in changing the composition of the conference's Jerusalem Committee, which was then headed by King Hassan II of Morocco. With regard to the Holy Places, however, the conference's concluding statement viewed Jerusalem as an all Islamic problem; it did not identify the Palestinians as the party to take charge of the responsibility for the Holy Places in Jerusalem. It is therefore a basis of future Egyptian, Saudi, or Moroccan intervention in the negotiations using all-Islamic pretexts.

the end of January 1995 emphasizes the Hashemite Kingdom's support of the Palestinian people as represented by the PLO, Jordan's support of the implementation of Palestinian self-determination, and Palestinians' right to establish an independent state with Jerusalem as its capital. It determines, on the other hand, that the Israel-Jordan Treaty of Peace assists the other tracks of the peace process.[9] The agreement does not address the question of the Holy Places, although it recognizes the Palestinian claim for political sovereignty in the city. In the signature ceremony, the late King Hussein said that Jordan would continue to extend its custody over the Holy Places in order to preserve the city and its Arab and Islamic identity.

On the eve of the May 1996 elections in Israel, a tripartite summit consisting of King Hussein, President Husni Mubarak of Egypt, and Chairman Arafat convened in Cairo. The agreement achieved included a Jordanian commitment not to conduct negotiations with Israel behind the Palestinians' back; a Palestinian agreement to coordinate its moves with Jordan; a Palestinian agreement that Jordan would temporarily retain responsibility in the Holy Places (accepting that Jordan's abandoning Jerusalem would serve only Israel's interests); and a Jordanian pledge to recognize Palestinian sovereignty in east Jerusalem, when achieved, and to transfer the Holy Places to the Palestinians after the establishment of a Palestinian state with Jerusalem as its capital.

The struggle for physical control in al-Haram al-Sharif/Temple Mount. In August 1994, Chairman Arafat sought to replace Waqf administration officials, traditionally appointed by Jordan, with officials nominated by the Palestinian Authority. Failing to secure Jordan's consent, he decided unilaterally that the Palestinian Ministry of Awqaf would be in charge of the Waqf administration in both the West Bank and Jerusalem. Jordan responded by enlarging Waqf budgets and appointing more of its trusted loyalists to key positions, arguing that because the Palestinian Authority was legally barred from acting in Jerusalem, its own departure from Jerusalem would serve only Israeli interests.

9. Agreement for Cooperation and Coordination between Jordan and the Palestinian Authority of January 25, 1995 (see Klein 1999, 125), a framework agreement for an array of cooperation agreements in different spheres.

Since then, the status of Jordan in the Waqf administration has been diminishing. At the end of September 1994, Jordan transferred control of the Waqf administration in the West Bank to Hassan Tahbub, director of the Palestinian Authority's Awqaf portfolio, president of the Supreme Muslim Authority, and a past senior Jordanian official (M. Klein 1999, 128).

In October 1994, the Jerusalem Mufti Sulayman al-Ja'bari passed away. Jordan appointed the successor, Abd al-Qadir Abidin, as it had done since 1948. Chairman Arafat challenged this appointment by appointing Ikrima Said Sabri as mufti, thereby asserting that the Palestinian Authority had the responsibility for the Holy Places in Jerusalem. Palestinian Authority security personnel "redirected" to Sabri's office any public going to Abidin's office . Abidin was left with no work to do, and upon his recent retirement, Jordan bowed to the inevitable and appointed Abd al-Azim Salhab to the lesser post of Qadi al-Qudat (chief Qadi), whose office is located in Amman (Reiter 1997, 6–7).[10] Talks between the Palestinian Authority and Jordan resulted in agreement that Jordan would continue to pay the salaries of Waqf functionaries in Jerusalem, whereas the Palestinian Authority would be responsible for religious affairs in the West Bank. Since 1995, the Palestinian Authority has indeed financed the activities of most religious institutions in the West Bank.[11]

The struggle over control of al-Haram al-Sharif/Temple Mount compound and the Waqf administration continued. Many of Jordan's loyalists joined the Palestinian Authority's side. The Authority also took over the Waqf-operated educational and social institutions in east Jerusalem.

In October 1996, the Palestinian Council demanded the treasurer of the

10. After the death of Tahbub on April 1998, Ikrima Said Sabri was appointed by the Supreme Muslim Authority to replace him in July 1998. Sabri now bears both posts (H. Cohen 1998).

11. According to Jordanian data, in 1994 the Jordanian Ministry of Awqaf was supporting 180 Mosques in Jerusalem and its surroundings, and was paying the salaries of one thousand employees. The budget for these activities was U.S.$5 million of $17 million Jordan was spending on religious matters in the West Bank as a whole (Musallam 1996, 97). Since 1953, Jordan spent about $485 million on the activities of the Ministry of Awqaf in the West Bank and Jerusalem (Musallam 1996, 107).

Waqf (appointed by Jordan) to step down in favor of an appointee of Chairman Arafat, a demand backed by the presence of the Palestinian "Task Force 17." Talks held between the two sides determined that Jordanian custody over al-Haram al-Sharif/Temple Mount would continue and that the treasurer's position would remain Jordanian pending the permanent-status agreement. Jordan, however, would hand over control of the Waqf in the Jerusalem district (comprising east Jerusalem and parts of the West Bank). In practice, this agreement does not stop the Palestinians from further undermining Jordan's role in al-Haram al-Sharif. The two significant positions held by Jordan loyalists are the Waqf treasurer and the director of Waqf property, but Jordan's continued long-term control of these positions should not be taken for granted.

Current Jordanian Assets and Interests in Jerusalem

Jordan's position in the Holy Places of Jerusalem derives from both physical control of al-Haram al-Sharif/Temple Mount compound and the degree of political and religious legitimacy to its custodianship over the Holy Places themselves. Its position, however, also depends on the kingdom's involvement in other spheres and aspects of life in east Jerusalem.[12]

Symbolic assets. The Hashemites, descendants of the Prophet, rulers of Hedjaz, and guardians of its Holy Places, were ousted from their role and control of Mecca and Medina by Abd al-Aziz Aal Saud after World War I. It is no coincidence that they have established a connection with Jerusalem Holy Places. For them, Jerusalem is a symbol of their exalted descent and status, and, as such, an important source of legitimacy. It is the last remnant of past Hashemites' glory after different family members were deposed from Arabia, Syria, and Iraq, and after Abdallah's Pan-Arab scheme came to

12. This review of Jordanian present-day assets and interest in Jerusalem is not based on a methodological field research and does not purport to substitute such research. Rather, it is the accumulation of personal impressions of personalities whom we interviewed. The purpose of this review is to present current trends rather than an exhaustive survey.

naught. It is a primary Hashemite asset. The Hashemite interests and assets in Jerusalem are the result of this relation rather than its cause.[13]

The focus of the Hashemite concern is al-Haram al-Sharif/Temple Mount, which gives Jerusalem its religious and political importance. Sharif Hussein Ibn Ali of Hedjaz is buried in the compound near al-Aqsa Mosque. His son Abdallah, Jordan's founder and its first king, was assassinated by an agent of his archenemy Hajj Amin al-Husseini, the grand mufti, outside the same mosque on July 20, 1951, when he came to pray there with his grandson Hussein. King Hussein's personal and emotional commitment to Jerusalem's Holy Places was very strong; that he also bore the burden of losing the Holy Places to Israel in 1967 served only to deepen this commitment.

Official political status. Except for Jordan's status in Jerusalem stemming from Article 9 of the Israel-Jordan Treaty of Peace and especially after the 1988 disengagement from the West Bank, Jordan has no claim for an official political or sovereign status in east Jerusalem. Its history in the city and the interim and autonomous nature of the Palestinian Council,[14] however, leave Jordan with a residual political status in Jerusalem,[15] which stems also from the fact that the territorial jurisdiction of certain ecclesiastical bodies includes both Jordan and Israel. Thus, the Latins in Israel, Jordan, and Cyprus are all subordinate to the spiritual authority of the Latin patriarch of

13. A prominent Jordanian journalist told late Prime Minister Rabin that without Jerusalem, the king's role is comparable to that of "the Mayor of Irbid" (authors' files; see also Schueftan 1986, 39, 102).

14. As well as the fact that the Palestinian Council is legally precluded from operating in Jerusalem.

15. This was demonstrated by the Waqf annexation of two rooms adjacent to the building of the Basilica of the Holy Sepulcher, formerly occupied by Greek Orthodox monks, to the nearby al-Hanaka Mosque. The heads of the three major Christian rites in Jerusalem—the Greek Orthodox, the Latin, and the Armenian Orthodox—asked the Israeli prime minister, the late King Hussein of Jordan, and Chairman Arafat, in three different letters, to restore the status quo. The two rooms remain with the mosque; according to one source, it was King Hussein who was successful in reaching a compromise, according to which the Greek Orthodox rite received possession of a mosque building in Jordan that had been a church in the past. Another source maintains that this compromise was not effected, but that the heads of the rites no longer seek restoration of the status quo, not wanting to confront the Palestinian Council (authors' files).

Jerusalem, whereas the Greek Orthodox autocephalic Patriarchate extends to the respective territories of Jordan and Israel.

Realty. In 1967, Jordanian government property was vested in the government of Israel by law ("State Property Law" 1951, 52;"Legal and Administrative Matters Law" 1970, Section 26, 138). In practice, this property was not transferred to the government en bloc; the Israel Land Administration registers in the name of the government any estate that it comes across. It is not clear how many such estates exist, registered or unregistered because this data is not open to the public. It is also not clear whether there are in Jerusalem any estates registered in the name of any of the Hashemites personally.[16]

Jordanian nationals who are east Jerusalem Palestinians may own private property in Jerusalem.[17] Nonresident Jordanian nationals who owned property in Jerusalem prior to the Israel-Jordan Treaty of Peace are, however, absentees; their property is absentee property (see "Absentees' Property Law" 1951, 86),[18] vested in the Custodian of Absentee Property in 1967 and managed by the custodian. Data as to these estates are also not available.[19]

16. There may be, however, Hashemite-owned estates registered in the name of nominal owners, the most famous of which is the unfinished building commonly known as the Palace in Tel al-Ful.

17. Section 4 of the Legal and Administrative Matters (Regulation) Law (Consolidated Version, 1970) provides that residents of east Jerusalem will not be regarded as "enemy" or "enemy subjects" under Israeli law, and Section 3 provides that they will not be regarded as "absentees" in relation to property in east Jerusalem. They remain, however, absentees in relation to property in the rest of Israel's pre-1967 territory (see Benvenisti and Zamir 1993, 1998).

18. This is also true for West Bankers who own property in east Jerusalem *(Levi v. the Estate of Mahmoud Mahmoud)*.

19. It turns out that no preparatory work in this respect was prepared in Israel prior to the Israeli-Jordanian negotiations owing to a lack of time and lack of desire to open Pandora's box. Jordan raised the question of absentee property (in Israel in general) during the negotiations, but late Prime Minister Rabin and the king eventually agreed to leave the question open. That is why the Treaty of Peace makes only vague provisions on the question of the 1948 refugees and the 1967 displaced persons. As to future relations, Section 6 of the Law Implementing the Treaty of Peace between the State of Israel and the Hashemite of Jordan (1995, 109) amends the Absentee Property Law, so that property in Israel shall not become absentee property subsequent to November 10, 1994:"Only by reason that a holder of a right

Nationality and civil status. The civil status of West Bank Palestinians always served as a yardstick for Jordanian policy toward them as both individuals and a collective. As early as 1949—even prior to the unification of the
two banks—Jordan considered it necessary to grant Jordanian nationality to
all Palestinians on both banks. Jordan treated the 1967 displaced persons in a
similar manner. The geography, demography, and history of the two banks
compel the kingdom to maintain a close link between the concept of "Jordanian people," along with its legal definition, and that of "Palestinians," despite the constant need to consolidate Jordanian national identity.[20]

Most east Jerusalem Palestinians who came under Israel's rule in 1967
were Jordanian nationals and remained so after 1967: few chose to substitute
their Israeli residence status *(Mubarak Awad v. Itzhak Shamir et al.* 1988) with
Israeli nationality, which would have required waiving their Jordanian nationality.[21] As part of the 1988 disengagement from the West Bank, Jordan
revoked West Bank Palestinians' nationality but kept operating the population registry services.[22] West Bank Palestinians, however, were issued temporary Jordanian "passports," which differ from national Jordanian passports
in that they do not attest the nationality of their bearers. They constitute, in
fact, no more than laissez-passer (travel documents). Jordan has issued these

---

therein was a national or subject of Jordan, or was in Jordan after that date." Jordanians may
now legally own property in east Jerusalem without it becoming absentee property, but this
law does not affect the status of property that became absentee property prior to the date
mentioned.

20. Hence Jordan's enormous interest in participating in future arrangements dealing
with monetary compensation to refugees—and to the countries absorbing them.

21. Israeli nationality legislation requires that nonautomatic acquisition of Israeli nationality (such as by neutralization) will be accompanied by waiver of the former nationality. Jordanian law contains similar provision. The Arab League also forbids dual Arab nationality
(Agreement of 5 April 1954 on Rules Relating to Citizenship among the Member Countries
of the League of Arab States).

22. These services consist of registration of birth, death, marriage and divorce, and the
like. After 1967, they were given by a Jordanian official located at the offices of the Jordanian
Chamber of Commerce in east Jerusalem. Since 1992, the Jordanian official is located in the
Sharia courts in east Jerusalem.

documents during the interim agreement, pending the permanent-status negotiations.

Business interests, banking, and monetary law. It seems that the activity of Jordanian firms in east Jerusalem is very limited. The Jordanian Chamber of Commerce, which in the past performed governmental functions on behalf of Jordan, is now ruled by the Palestinian Council, like many other institutions and organizations in east Jerusalem.

With regard to banking, one has to note that until 1967, foreign banks were operating in the West Bank and east Jerusalem. When these areas came under Israeli Defense Forces control, their branches were closed down, and the cash forfeited. Their premises—usually leased property—are managed by Israel as absentee property.[23]

The legal tender in east Jerusalem is the Israeli shekel.[24] In practice, however, Israel refrains from enforcing its monetary laws on dinar transactions. It has also allowed the activity of exchange bureaus, which were part of the Jordanian banking system. The Israeli-Palestinian Interim Agreement of September 28, 1995, transferred to the Palestinian Council authority in monetary matters in parts of West Bank and Gaza Strip territory. In practice, the introduction of a Palestinian currency is prohibited ("Israeli-Palestinian Interim Agreement" 1995, Article 4, Annex 5). The Palestinian Council, established under the Interim Agreement, is interested in issuing a Palestinian currency as a manifestation of sovereignty, despite professional advice to the contrary. The Interim Agreement prohibition also serves Jordanian concerns that a Palestinian currency will destabilize the dinar (Zak 1996, 294).[25]

Officials and dignitaries. As a result of the Palestinian Council actions, Abd al-Qadir Abidin, nominated by Jordan on October 6, 1994, as successor to the deceased mufti, had in fact no work to do and no power to exercise until his retirement. Jordan did not appoint a successor to Abidin; rather, it nom-

23. These estates are managed by the Bank of Israel, acting under empowerment of the Custodian of Absentee Property. Israeli-Jordanian clandestine agreements of the 1980s and the early 1990s on the reopening of banks in the West Bank did not cover Jerusalem.

24. In the West Bank, both the shekel and the dinar are legal tender.

25. Note that great sums of Palestinian capital are deposited in Amman.

inated Abd al-Azim Salhab to the lesser post of Qadi al-Qudat, whose office is in Jordan. Today, the Palestinian Council appoints almost all Waqf posts in Jerusalem. The council also exerts influence on the appointments of the east Jerusalem Sharai courts (religious courts). Council appointees now control various east Jerusalem organizations and institutions run previously by Jordan loyalists.

Apparently, Jordan still pays the salary of the Interior Ministry official employed in east Jerusalem. Also, a network of several dozens persons are loyal to the king because of either clan alliances or personal and business interests. These men are viewed generally as the king's representatives, and harm caused to them is harm caused to the king. The royal succession and the strengthening of the Palestinian Council in east Jerusalem at Jordan's expense have undermined the size and weight of this group, which will continue to decrease.

Society, public opinion, and the media. The first Palestinian uprising (Intifada) enhanced the national identity of many east Jerusalem Palestinians, especially the younger generations that have never been King Hussein's subjects. Popular support for Jordan—or Jordanian sentiments—in east Jerusalem is very low. Jordan lost an important asset when the Jordan-funded east Jerusalem daily newspaper submitted to the pressure of the council's Preventative Security Service and became pro-Palestinian. Similar developments took place in the field of education. Waqf educational institutions controlled by the council are using a new Palestinian curriculum, which seems to be in use also in municipal schools in east Jerusalem.[26]

The kingdom's policy in Jerusalem focuses on the Holy Places at the expense of social, institutional, and other matters. This focus should be viewed as both a cause and a result of Jordan losing its popular support base. It may be that in the long run, after immediate Palestinian national aspirations are met and depending on the measure of public dissatisfaction regarding the rule of the Palestinian Council, its lack of respect for basic human rights, and the corruption attributed to some of its officials, pro-Jordanian sentiments will resume, but this outcome is not very likely.

26. Where the new Palestinian curriculum is not yet in existence, a Palestinian Council sticker replaces the Jordanian emblems.

Jordanian assets and interests: conclusions. Despite the admitted partiality of the review presented here, a clear pattern emerges. Commensurate with the Jordanian policy focusing on preserving its status in Jerusalem's Holy Places, the kingdom abandoned any involvement in the life of the population in east Jerusalem. Thus, Jordan demonstrates only a residual and minor interest in the economy, local politics, and society in east Jerusalem. In other words, it does not view the population in Jerusalem as a tactical or strategic goal.

Legal Perspective:
Article 9 of the Israel-Jordan Treaty of Peace

History of the Article

Article 9 of the Treaty of Peace reads:[27]

Places of Historical and Religious Significance

1. Each party will provide freedom of access to places of religious and historical significance.
2. In this regard, in accordance with the Washington Declaration, Israel respects the present special role of the Hashemite Kingdom of Jordan in Muslim holy shrines in Jerusalem. When negotiations on the permanent status will take place, Israel will give high priority to the Jordanian historic role in these shrines.
3. The Parties will act together to promote interfaith relations among the three monotheistic religions, with the aim of working towards religious understanding, moral commitment, freedom of religious worship, and tolerance and peace.

On the history of Article 9, Shragai writes:

27. The English, Arabic, and Hebrew texts are equally authentic. In case of divergence of interpretation, however, the English text prevails. See the concluding paragraph of the Treaty of Peace. For a legal analysis of the Treaty of Peace, see Reisner 1995 and E. Rubinstein 1998.

Hussein demanded symbols of sovereignty on the [Temple] Mount within a few months. Israel refused. According to a concept developed in the office of the Foreign Minister, Shimon Peres, the principles of which were accepted by Prime Minister Rabin, the Holy Places in Jerusalem were to be governed in the future by a multinational administration comprised of representatives of Jordan, Morocco, Saudi Arabia, the Palestinians and the Vatican. According to the same plan, the administration was to be invested with ex-territorial authorities and exercise religious control over the areas which will be defined as Holy Places. Halevy [the prime minister's envoy to the talks in Amman] proposed to Hussein, on behalf of the Prime Minister, that Israel will recognize the preferential status of Jordan in the Muslim Holy Places in Jerusalem, i.e. within the framework of the multinational religious administration that will be established for the Temple Mount in the future. Hussein accepted the principle. Detailed negotiations on the definition of the preferential status started intensely. (1995, 387, footnotes omitted)[28]

Zak (1996) writes that the initiative for including a clause dealing with the Jordanian role in Jerusalem came from the Jordanians, who proposed it in an early draft. According to this account, on November 2, 1993, Foreign Minister Peres handed King Hussein a draft recognizing the Jordanian role in the Holy Places in Jerusalem (cf. M. Klein 1999, 120), but the king insisted on a preferential status. Its seems that Peres was concerned that such language would contradict the contents of a letter he sent to Foreign Minister Johan Jürgen Holst of Norway.[29] The lack of agreement over the Jerusalem

28. Contrary to the last sentence in this citation, it seems that negotiations on the contents of the "special role" did not take place. Parks (1994) makes similar observations, referring to an Israeli proposal that authorities will be transferred to an interreligious committee comprising of representatives of Jordan, Saudi Arabia, Morocco, the Palestinian Authority, the Vatican, and Israel.

29. This letter reads: "I wish to confirm that the Palestinian institutions of east Jerusalem and the interests and well-being of the Palestinians of east Jerusalem are of great importance and will be preserved. Therefore, all the Palestinian institutions of east Jerusalem, including the economic, social, educational, cultural and the holy Christian and Moslem places are performing an essential task for the Palestinian population. Needless to say, we will not hamper their activity; on the contrary, the fulfillment of this important mission is to be encouraged."

issue and others delayed the completion of a joint declaration. Prime Minister Rabin sought to achieve a compromise on the Jerusalem issue and so agreed with King Hussein in their May 28, 1994, meeting that the text also state that priority is to be given to the historic role of Jordan in Muslim Holy Places in Jerusalem (Zak 1996, 292–94). Rabin thought that the final text clarified that Israel would accord the Jordanian role high priority; this implied recognition of Israel's authority to do so. It appears that Peres indeed regarded the wording of the final text as problematic in light of his letter to Holst (Zak 1996, 307, note 11).

As mentioned earlier, the text of the Washington Declaration dealing with the Jordanian role in Muslim Holy Places in Jerusalem was later transformed into Article 9(2) of the Treaty of Peace. In fact, this paragraph contains two distinct provisions regulating Israeli conduct toward Jordan in relation to Muslim Holy Places in Jerusalem.

Obligation to Respect the Present Special Role of Jordan

The first part of Article 9(2) states that "Israel respects the present special role of the Hashemite Kingdom of Jordan in Muslim holy shrines in Jerusalem."

"Muslim holy shrines in Jerusalem." The subject matter of the first part of Article 9(2) is not clearly defined. A list of Holy Places compiled by the UN Trusteeship Council Secretariat in 1950 enumerates as Muslim Holy Places in Jerusalem proper al-Haram al-Sharif itself; other sites inside it (al-Aqsa Mosque and the Dome of the Rock); and al-Buraq al-Sharif, which forms the western boundary of al-Haram al-Sharif (the Western Wall). It also includes sites located outside al-Haram al-Sharif: the Mosque of Ascension on Mount Olives and the Tomb of David *(Ad Coenaculum)* on Mount Zion.[30]

Article 9, however, refers to Muslim *holy shrines* rather than to Muslim *Holy Places.* Should there be a distinction—at least for the purposes of Arti-

---

The *Jerusalem Post* daily published the letter on June 7, 1994. See note 47 for an analysis of the letter.

30. This list, however, includes "the most important Muslim sites in the Jerusalem area" and does not purport to be exhaustive (United Nations Trusteeship Council 1950, 27–28).

cle 9—between these two terms? Lapidoth argues that the term *holy shrine* is indeed narrower than *Holy Place* (1994, 431).[31] If so, Article 9(2) must be construed as referring, at most, to sites enumerated in the Trusteeship Council list. Other Muslim sites in Jerusalem are excluded from its purview. These other sites, in any case, seem not to be recognized as Holy Places in Muslim Orthodoxy (Reiter 1997, 92); their political significance is certainly lesser than that of sites that do appear in the list. But it seems that Article 9(2) has to be interpreted as referring only to al-Haram al-Sharif compound and the sites inside it. True, it refers to holy shrines in Jerusalem in general rather than to *the* holy shrines specifically. Nevertheless, it is doubtful whether any other Muslim sites in Jerusalem will qualify as holy shrines. According to Webster's dictionary, a *shrine* is, among other things, "an object, structure or place that is considered sacred by a religious group and that serves as the focus of the performance of some ritual."[32]

At the signing ceremony of the Washington Declaration, President Bill Clinton of the United States addressed King Hussein in the following terms: "In the declaration . . . your role as guardian of Jerusalem's Muslim holy sites, al-Aqsa among them, has been preserved" (Mussalem 1996, 48).[33] We know of no single conflictual incident in any Muslim Holy Place situated outside al-Haram al-Sharif ever taking place throughout the period of Palestinian-Jordanian struggle for physical control and recognition of political predominance in the Holy Places of Jerusalem.

31. An even broader term is used in the Heading of Article 9 and in paragraph 9(1) (in relation to ensuring freedom of access): "Places of Historical and Religious Significance." Compare to Article 6 of the Feisal-Weizmann Agreement (see note 1).

32. *Webster's Third New International Dictionary of the English Language Unabridged.* It is submitted that the last part of this definition distinguishes al-Haram al-Sharif and the sites within it from other sites in Jerusalem that may meet the criteria of a "Holy Place" (see also Lapidoth 1994).

33. We will not address the question whether the whole al-Haram al-Sharif compound constitutes a Holy Place or a holy shrine. It is sufficient for our purposes to note that all those concerned—including Israel (in granting de facto autonomy in the compound)—act as if the whole compound meets the legal definition of a Holy Place or a holy shrine. For another view, see Berkovitz 1997, 23, and the authorities cited there. On Muslim Holy Places in Jerusalem situated outside the al-Haram al-Sharif compound, see Reiter 1997, 91.

"The present special role." The first and second parts of Article 9(2) deal with two distinct matters. Whereas the former is concerned with the present special role of Jordan in Muslim holy shrines in Jerusalem, the latter deals with the Jordanian historic role in these shrines—that is, a certain role it fulfilled some time in the past. Neither role is defined in the Treaty of Peace. Other than the text itself, little indication of the drafters' intentions in this matter is available to us. Note that the two parts regulate Israeli conduct in different times: the former regulates the present ("Israel *respects*"), whereas the latter provides for the future ("Israel *will give* high priority") (cf. Lapidoth 1994, 431).

This conclusion is supported not only by the ordinary meaning of the words of Article 9(2) but also by the historical context. A comparison of Jordan's role in the Muslim Holy Places in Jerusalem prior to the establishment of the Palestinian self-government institutions and its present-day role reveals a sharp contrast. Jordan's current role in these sites is much diminished. If the drafters intended to discuss a single role, they would have chosen to describe it in identical terms in both parts of Article 9(2)—or to do so by reference.[34]

The present role of Jordan is the role it held at the time of the signing of the Washington Declaration and of the Treaty of Peace. These dates constitute the "critical period" for the purposes of the first part of Article 9(2): Israel respects the special role of Jordan as it stood at that time, which affirms that there is no duty incumbent on Israel to restore the special role of Jordan if its scope in the past (i.e., the historic role) surpasses its present scope.

"The special role." Ambiguity surrounds the use of this expression. From an international law perspective, it is indeed unique for a state to invoke a status in the sovereign territory of another state, but such an invocation does not in itself create legal rights and duties. It seems therefore that this phrase is used symbolically, in that it is meant to express Israeli recognition of the actual and historical context of the linkage between the Hashemite Kingdom and the Muslim holy shrines in Jerusalem. The term *special* does not indicate Jordanian supremacy in any hierarchy (of interested parties) in relation

---

34. For example, by phrasing the second part as follows: "When negotiations . . . will take place, Israel will give high priority to *this* Jordanian historic role in these shrines."

to the holy shrines. Reading Article 9(2) as a whole, as will be demonstrated below, supports this conclusion.

The declaratory nature of the provision. The most significant feature of the first part of Article 9(2) is the use of the present simple tense,[35] which denotes recurrence of events and continuity but does not in itself make an explicit stipulation as to the future. This choice of tense is why this provision appears to be a mere declaration of existing policy ("Israel respects") rather than a regulation of future conduct. The implication is, therefore, that Israel undertook no concrete obligation with regard to Jordan's present special role. By contrast, the second part of Article 9(2), dealing with Jordan's historic role, clearly imposes on Israel a specific legal obligation ("Israel *will*"). The parties chose to employ seemingly nonbinding language where binding language could have been used (e.g., "Israel shall respect"). It may be argued, on the other hand, that the use of the verb *respect*—whatever the tense—denotes an intention to create legally binding obligations.[36] Finally, one has to cite the legal principle prescribing the interpretation ("Vienna Convention on the Law of Treaties" 1969, Article 31[1])[37] and observance of treaty obligations in good faith ("Vienna Convention" 1969, Article 26).[38] In consequence, even if the language of Article 9(2) does not create a legal obligation, per se, Israel will not be permitted to cease respecting the Jordanian role in Muslim holy shrines in Jerusalem unilaterally prior to, in the least, holding consultations with Jordan.

"Respects the present special role." It is not altogether clear what exactly the obligation to "respect the present special role" of Jordan entails. One interpretation may be that Israel is obliged to preserve the status of Jordan in the

35. Arabic does not recognize a present tense, which raises doubts as to the intentions of the Jordanian drafters. Nevertheless, the English text prevails.

36. It may be that this denotation can be explained by fact that statespersons, rather than lawyers, formulated this article.

37. Article 31(1) provides:"A treaty shall be interpreted in good faith in accordance with the ordinary meaning to be given to the terms of the treaty in their context and in the light of its object and purpose." Note that under Article 25(2) of the Treaty of Peace, the parties undertake to fulfill in good faith their obligations under the treaty.

38. Article 26 provides:"Every treaty in force is binding upon the parties to it and must be performed by them in good faith."

Muslim holy shrines, which involves, in fact, the maintenance of the status quo in these sites. The status quo is a well-known technique for managing religious disputes in Holy Places in and around Jerusalem; still, it is not clear what status quo has to be maintained. The application of the status quo in Christian Holy Places, extrapolated to Muslim Holy Places, may mean maintaining the balance of power in al-Haram al-Sharif/Temple Mount compound between functionaries appointed by Jordan and those selected by the Palestinian Council. Respecting the Jordanian role in this sense means guarding the Jordanian position against Palestinian encroachments.[39]

By contrast, the status quo to be maintained by Israel may be the status established by Israel's government in 1967. Under these arrangements, Israel does not interfere with the Waqf administration's religious management of al-Haram al-Sharif/Temple Mount, but it retains overall responsibility for security in and around the compound. If this is the case, a passive duty not to change these autonomous arrangements is incumbent upon Israel, together with an active duty to prevent such changes, whatever their cause, from taking place. It may even be that Israel's duty is to maintain both the existing autonomous arrangements and Jordan's dominance in al-Haram al-Sharif/Temple Mount vis-à-vis the Palestinian Council.

The vagueness of the provision suggests that Israel's obligation is to do neither. All Israel is obliged to do is refrain from acting in a manner that will affect in any way the present Jordanian role in al-Haram al-Sharif/Temple Mount, whatever this role may be, either de facto (by pursuing a policy) or de jure (by passing Knesset legislation or by judicial ruling). Changes in the Jordanian role—as it was at the critical period—that are not the result of Israel's actions should not concern Israel. Respecting the Jordanian role, ac-

39. At the signing ceremony of the Washington Declaration, President Bill Clinton told the late King Hussein: "In the declaration . . . your role as guardian of Jerusalem's Muslim holy sites, al-Aqsa among them, has been preserved. And Israel has agreed to accord a high priority to Jordan's historic role regarding these holy sites in final-status negotiations" (Mussalem 1996, 48). It is improbable that this statement was coincidental and not agreed upon by all three parties in advance. In any case, it lends some support to the interpretation presented above. Since 1994, Jordan passed on several occasions messages requesting Israeli assistance against Palestinian encroachments into its diminishing control over al-Haram al-Sharif and the religious apparatus operating therefrom.

cording to this interpretation, does not impose on Israel any active obligations (see also Lapidoth 1994, 430–31). The provision has, nonetheless, declaratory value in that it expresses Israel's recognition that Jordan is an interested party in al-Haram al-Sharif/Temple Mount and that its past role in the shrines gives rise to a future role, albeit more limited in scope. The concrete articulation of this recognition is contained in the second part of Article 9(2), whereby Israel undertook a specific, active obligation vis-à-vis Jordan and its future role in al-Haram al-Sharif.

Obligation to Give High Priority to the Jordanian Historic Role

The second part of Article 9(2) provides that "Israel will give high priority to the Jordanian historic role" in Muslim holy shrines when negotiations on the permanent status will take place.

"Muslim holy shrines in Jerusalem." It is clear that the shrines referred to in the second part of the article are those mentioned in its first part. The above discussion of the identity of these sites applies equally here: the Haram al-Sharif compound and the sites it encompasses are, in most probability, the subject matter of the article.

"The Jordanian historic role." As noted above, the Israel-Jordan Treaty of Peace does not define this term. The distinction between the present special role and the historic role drawn previously does not serve to clarify the meaning of the latter phrase. In the past (i.e., at the "critical period"), Jordan indeed fulfilled several specific roles in the Muslim holy shrines in Jerusalem. Between 1950 and 1967, it asserted sovereignty over the parts of Jerusalem east of the armistice lines, which included the Old City.[40] Since 1967 and until the establishment of the Palestinian Council, Jordan was the beneficiary of de facto religious administrative autonomy in al-Haram al-Sharif/ Temple Mount.

It may be, however, that the Jordanian historic role is not a specific function (or an amalgam of several), but a general manifestation of the special at-

40. Neither Israel nor the international community recognized Jordan's sovereignty in Jerusalem. King Hussein, moreover, proclaimed that the meaning of this provision is not the reinstatement of Jordanian sovereignty over the city (Zak 1996, 292).

tachment of the Hashemites to Jerusalem's Holy Places that led them to rule the city in the past. Recall President Clinton assuring King Hussein that the Washington Declaration preserved his role "as guardian of Jerusalem's Muslim holy sites."[41] The title Clinton used ("guardian of . . . Muslim holy sites") is an example of such a general manifestation of the Hashemite attachment to Jerusalem's Holy Places.

Apparently, the vague expression "Jordanian historic role" was included in the article because no agreement on the precise future role of Jordan could be reached. According to Shragai, there was a general understanding, however, between Prime Minister Rabin and King Hussein that Jordan would enjoy a preferential status within a future multipartite framework for the religious administration of the Holy Places (1995, 387; personal communication, May 3, 1998). Nevertheless, this understanding does not form part of the Washington Declaration or of the Treaty of Peace.

The obligatory nature of the provision. Unlike the first part of Article 9(2), its second part is clearly meant to impose a legally binding obligation. The language is clearly mandatory: "Israel will give high priority"; moreover, the article establishes a time frame for performance: "When negotiations on the permanent status will take place." Note, however, that the content of this obligation—giving high priority to the Jordanian historic role—is rather vague.

"High priority." One possible meaning of the high priority Israel is to give to the Jordanian historic role is that Israel has to bring into account the Jordanian historic role, among other considerations it may have, when it conducts the permanent-status negotiations with the Palestinians.[42] In a

---

41. In this sense, the historic role consists of preserving the Holy Places, funding the activities of the Waqf apparatus and of the Sharia courts, making the appointments to these institutions and determining their policy, controlling the content of religious addresses and the relations with the Israeli authorities, and the like. Note that Musallam views the Jordanian role, in the context of Article 9, as concerning "religious supervision" (1996, 75–76).

42. It is clear that the negotiations referred to are those to be held between Israel and the Palestinians pursuant to Article 5 of the Declaration of Principles, which is evident from the use of the definite article: "When negotiations on *the* permanent status will take place" (emphasis added). Moreover, Article 8 of the Treaty of Peace, dealing with refugees and displaced persons, includes in paragraph 2.b(2) an express reference to "the permanent status negotiations pertaining to the territories [that came under Israeli military government control in

sense, Israel will serve (but not in a legal sense) as a trustee or an agent of the Jordanian interest. Giving the Jordanian historic role high priority also means that Israel will not discharge its duty by merely taking it into account, but will have to give this duty a significant weight in relation to its other considerations. This does not mean, however, that the Jordanian consideration will have to be given an overriding weight in relation to Israel's other considerations.

It is very difficult, however, to quantify weight given to different considerations in the course of diplomatic negotiations. In practice, Israel will be carrying out its obligations if it gives the Jordanian historic role significant weight and does so in good faith. Legally, then, Israel will not be able to present claims or positions that take into account the Jordanian historic role for the protocol alone and then withdraw these claims or positions at the first available opportunity, or to bring them up as bargaining chips used to advance its other objectives. It will be observing its obligations to Jordan in good faith if it makes an honest and serious attempt to include Jordan's interest in the negotiated settlement.

Israel will not be required to frustrate the negotiations only because its honest and serious efforts to make Jordan's interests part of the settlement fail. "High priority" and negotiating "in good faith" do not mean that Israel is bound as to the result of the negotiations (Lapidoth 1994, 431).[43] These phrases do mean, however, that Israel has to conduct the negotiations subject to several limitations described above.[44]

A second possible meaning of "high priority" is that in a future settlement in al-Haram al-Sharif, Jordan will enjoy a status preferential to that of

---

1967]." Any other interpretation runs contrary to the intentions of the parties and leads to absurd results (see "Vienna Convention" 1969, Articles 31(4) and 32(b); see also Lapidoth 1994, 431, and the section "Article 9 and the Identity of the Parties to the Permanent-Status Negotiations," later in this chapter.

43. Note that Israel has to give high priority to the historic Jordanian role in the negotiations and not in the settlement.

44. Lapidoth opines that "Israel only committed herself to adopt a certain attitude in the negotiation" (1994, 432). We respectfully submit that Israel has also committed itself procedurally—that is, to act in certain manner.

the Palestinians or of any other actor. To a certain extent, the legislative history of Article 9 supports such an interpretation. A general understanding existed to that effect between Prime Minister Rabin and King Hussein in connection with a future multipartite framework for the religious administration of the Holy Places. This understanding, however, does not form part of the Treaty of Peace. Moreover, it is incompatible with the language of Article 9. This language dictates that in the negotiations Israel will give high priority to the Jordanian historic role rather than that the settlement itself will give high priority to the Jordanian role. In addition, the interpretation that suggests Israeli commitment to Jordanian supremacy in a settlement would make both the Washington Declaration and the Treaty of Peace incompatible with the Declaration of Principles.

When two different treaties regulate the same subject matter and one state is a party to both (but the other party to each treaty differs), the treaty between the party to both treaties and the other party will apply in their mutual relationship (see "Vienna Convention" 1969, Article 30[4][b]; see also next section). This provision, however, does not annul or suspend the other treaty or exempt the party to both treaties from liability for having concluded treaties creating conflicting obligations. If that party chooses to rely on Article 30 of the Vienna Convention on the Law of Treaties and carry out its obligations toward one party that are in conflict with its obligations toward the other party under the other treaty, its liability will extend to its actions undertaken under the one treaty that conflict with its obligations under the other treaty (see "Vienna Convention" 1969, Article 30[5]; see also Lapidoth 1994, 432).

It should also be noted that Article 25(6) of the Treaty of Peace requires that its provisions shall prevail in the case of conflict between them and other obligations of the parties (e.g., Israel's Declaration of Principles obligations vis-à-vis the Palestinians)—subject to the supremacy of the United Nations Charter.

Article 9 and the Identity of the Parties
to the Permanent-Status Negotiations

Article 9(2) contains an Israeli recognition that Jordan has a certain status in al-Haram al-Sharif/Temple Mount. Based on this recognition, Israel undertook to act for the promotion of the Jordanian interest in the context of the future Israeli-Palestinian negotiations. Doubts arose over whether this provision affects the identity of the parties that are to participate in the permanent-status negotiations.[45] There can be little doubt that, politically, Article 9 gives Jordan a certain standing in the permanent-status negotiations. Legally, however, this is not the case. There could be conflict between the Declaration of Principles and the Treaty of Peace if the former establishes that permanent-status negotiations will be conducted between Israel and the Palestinians, whereas the latter provides that Jordan will participate in these talks.[46]

Article 5(3) of the Declaration of Principles provides that the permanent-status negotiations will cover, among other things, Jerusalem. It is implicit in the overall context of the declaration that these negotiations will be conducted between Israel and the Palestinians, which, nevertheless, does not mean that either party may not aspire to have third parties participate in these talks or, for that matter, agree with those third parties on their participation. The other party, however, will not be bound to agree to the involvement of the third party. The law of treaties does not recognize the imposition of a treaty obligation on a third party without its consent (see "Vienna Convention" 1969, Articles 34 and 35; see also Lapidoth 1994, 431–32). Just as the Declaration of Principles does not prohibit Israel from conducting negotiations concerning Jerusalem with Christian representatives or the PLO from conducting negotiations concerning Jerusalem with Arab states or Islamic representatives, it should not be construed as allowing Israel—or, indeed, the PLO—to conduct negotiations with Jordan on the future of Jerusalem. There may be, however, circumstances under which agreement with a third party on its involvement in negotiations that are to be held with

45. Lapidoth, for example, raises the question whether the fact that Article 9 does not mention the parties to the future negotiations indicates that there may be a valid Jordanian claim for participation in the negotiations (1994, 431). Likewise, Musallam refers implicitly to Palestinian concerns that Article 9 may mean "exclusion" of the Palestinian side from the negotiations (1996, 76).

46. Our assumption is that the Declaration of Principles and the Israeli-Palestinian agreements made pursuant to it are all agreements governed by international law.

another party will constitute a breach of good faith. Such a breach will take place when negotiating with the third party will adversely affect the negotiations with the other party to such an extent so as to nullify them.

Moreover, it may be argued that there cannot be an incompatibility between the Declaration of Principles and the Treaty of Peace because they deal with different subject matters. This view relies on the fact that the Declaration of Principles does not specify which matters make up the Jerusalem issue, whereas Article 9 of the Treaty of Peace deals only with the Muslim holy shrines and not with the Jerusalem issue as a whole. The Jerusalem issue under the Declaration of Principles, in other words, does not necessarily cover every aspect of the Jerusalem question.[47] Thus, Israel negotiated with the Holy See to the effect that it will maintain the status quo in Christian Holy Places. Similarly, nothing in Article 5 of the Declaration of Principles prevents the Palestinian side from holding negotiations with Arab or Muslim partners.[48]

This argument, however, cannot be substantiated: the Treaty of Peace itself assumes that the matter of the Holy Places in Jerusalem will be discussed in the permanent-status negotiations. In addition, an Israeli position according to which the matter of Muslim Holy Places in Jerusalem is not included

47. Such as, for example, the status of the western parts of the city. Note, however, that there is a very strong indication that the parties viewed the matter of the Holy Places—Christian and Muslim alike—as covered by the Jerusalem issue. On October 11, 1993, Foreign Minister Peres wrote his Norwegian counterpart Johan Jürgen Holst the letter cited in note 29. For a description of the circumstances surrounding the letter and analysis of its contents, see M. Klein 1999, 26. Lapidoth doubts the binding nature of the letter and opines, after analyzing its contents and context, that it "probably does not contain any meaningful political commitments concerning Jerusalem" (1994, 428–30). Joel Singer—one of the drafters of the Declaration of Principles and later the Israeli Foreign Ministry legal advisor—wrote that the letter attests that the declaration did not seek to prohibit the operation of existing Palestinian institutions in Jerusalem, but rather to forbid the Palestinian Authority from operating in the city or extending the scope of operations of these institutes and transforming them into a part of its apparatus (1994a, 292–93).

48. Note, however, that limitations on the territorial jurisdiction as well as on the authority of the Palestinian Council foreign relations may serve to prohibit it from conducting such negotiations (see Singer 1994a, 292–93).

in the Jerusalem issue seems to be incompatible with its own traditional position regarding a settlement in Jerusalem. Nor can this position be raised in
good faith—with or without reference to the Peres–Holst letter.

In any case, Israel did not undertake to involve Jordan in the permanent-
settlement talks, nor did it commit itself as to the results of the negotiations.
The Vienna Convention on the Law of Treaties does not allow it to impose
a legal obligation on the Palestinian side without its consent. For these reasons, the interpretation of Article 9 presented here does not affect the question of the parties to the permanent-status negotiations and does not conflict
with the Declaration of Principles. A different interpretation of Article 9—
one allowing, for example, Israeli refusal to negotiate without Jordanian participation—contradicts the Declaration of Principles and leads Israel to
breach either of its two obligations.

Politically, however, it may well be that Jordan, as well as other Arab and
Muslim sides, will be able to secure a place at the negotiating table.

Conclusions: Legal Limitations on a Future Jordanian Role in Muslim Holy Shrines in Jerusalem

Our analysis of Article 9(2) is based on a distinction between its two parts,
each dealing with a different Israeli commitment applicable in a different
time. The first part deals with the "present special role" of Jordan in the
Muslim holy shrines in Jerusalem. There may be several interpretations to
this provision, which is particularly vague. Our conclusion is that this part
of the article appears to impose no active duty on the part of Israel. Israel's
duty to respect the Jordanian role should be interpreted as a passive duty not
to initiate changes in Jordan's role, whatever its scope and meaning. This
part of the article, however, also constitutes Israeli recognition of Jordan's
interests in the future settlement in the Muslim holy shrines, recognition
that is the background for the concrete duty Israel assumed in the second
part of Article 9(2).

Despite the vagueness of the expression "Jordan's historic role" and the
ambiguity of the duty to give it high priority, the second part of the article
imposes on Israel active duties with regard to Israel's positions and the man-

ner in which it conducts the permanent-status negotiations. Amman and Jerusalem had a certain general understanding on a possible settlement in the Holy Places and Jordan's role in it, but this understanding was not included in the agreed text. Israel's active duties do not require anything with regard to the outcome of the talks. Had this been the case, the inevitable conclusion would have been that Israel has undertaken conflicting commitments. Article 9(2) can and should be interpreted in such a way so that it does not conflict Israel's commitments with regard to the Palestinian side.

Jordan's Role in a Permanent Settlement in Jerusalem: Problems and Prospects

An essay of this scope cannot, for obvious reasons, describe all considerations that will have to be taken into account in the making of an Israeli policy decision concerning Jordan's role in the Muslim holy shrines in Jerusalem in the context of the pending permanent-status settlement. Thus, we briefly present the major considerations by way of demonstration.

There is the internal Israeli arena. Despite the practical demise of the "Greater Israel" ideology and the general public support of the Oslo process, there remains consensus in Israeli public opinion that Jerusalem must remain within Israeli sovereignty. The May 1999 elections focused on the Jerusalem issue, with Likud and Labor accusing each other of willingness to divide Jerusalem. Nevertheless, concessions made "in Jerusalem" and perceived as benefiting Hashemite Jordan (conceived as a true partner) rather than the Palestinians (conceived, at best, as an enemy to make peace with) may attract less public opposition, especially if they are viewed as formalizing the existing state of affairs in al-Haram al-Sharif/Temple Mount.

The most predominant domestic Jordanian consideration is Jordan's demography, which has a significant role to play in the making of Jordan's Palestinian policy. A large portion of the population of the Hashemite Kingdom is Palestinian, but it does not comprise a single, homogenous group. Some of Jordan's Palestinians, especially those who went east of the river prior to 1947–48, are well integrated into the political, economic, and social systems. Others, especially the 1967 displaced persons, are less integrated into the kingdom and form a constant burden on Jordan's economic and political stability.

Public opinion in Jordan about Jordanian-Palestinian relations is divided into two main viewpoints (see Altel 1996; Pappé 1994, 61; Susser 1994, 211). The less-dominant Transjordan view advocates a separate and exclusive Jordanian political identity, which Jordanian Palestinians will be able to choose (thereby exercising political return). The other viewpoint postulates a binational Jordan. It argues that demographic, historic, economic, and geostrategic considerations dictate that the two banks maintain the closest possible ties. Official Jordan is interested in a future partnership, and this interest/policy will affect its ultimate perception of its role in Jerusalem. This perception in turn will be affected by Jordanian public opinion, which is sensitive to Jordanian policy on Jerusalem and the role of the kingdom in the Holy Places.

Another internal Jordanian factor is the royal succession. At the time of his death, King Hussein was the longest-surviving ruler of the region (a few months before his death, forty-five years of his rule were celebrated). The policy of his son and successor, King Abdallah, so far has been to follow the path his father demarcated. There is little doubt that it will continue to be his policy. True, King Abdallah did not rule the city in the past, nor does he bare the burden of losing the city. His primary concern will be to consolidate his reign, but because Jerusalem is an asset for any Hashemite ruler, he might adopt the Jerusalem issue—and the permanent-status negotiations at large—so as to give effect to his father's political testament, a source of legitimacy or an opportunity to delineate his relations with the Palestinians. The Hashemite succession in Jordan thus does not announce a change of policy with regard to Jerusalem, nor does it change the basic assumptions of Israeli policy in this regard.[49]

49. In an interview with ABC's Peter Jennings on May 19, 1999, King Abdallah expressed his hope that "when we reach final status discussions . . . Jordan will have a voice on the future of Jerusalem" and that the city "should be an open city for Christians, Jews, and Muslims to be able to live in harmony." Since this interview, King Abdallah and high-ranking Jordanian officials have maintained a moderate position toward Palestinian concerns regarding the future of the Holy Places in Jerusalem. Until there is unequivocal evidence to the

Internal Palestinian politics are also relevant. The "Jerusalemite" and other oppositions to Chairman Arafat will make Palestinian concessions in Jerusalem very difficult to effect. Succession is a major factor also in the internal Palestinian arena. Arafat's potential successors are already building their power bases and seeking the patronage of Arab states. Chairman Arafat's own desire to enter the promised land—that is, to be the first president of Palestine—may make a settlement in Jerusalem more negotiable than it may seem to be.

Past Israeli-Jordanian relations, the strategic position of Jordan as an eastern buffer for Israel, Jordan's moderate ideology, and the two countries' mutual concerns regarding the prospective Palestinian state all give rise to a strong case for Jordanian participation in a Jerusalem settlement. Jordanian participation may also help the Palestinian state to counterweigh radical Islamic factions in al-Haram al-Sharif/Temple Mount.

The Palestinian side may not welcome Jordanian participation in the permanent-status negotiations and in the settlement itself, however, especially if brought about by Israeli pressure. Although the Palestinians succeeded in taking over physical control of the holy shrines and of the Waqf administration operating in Jerusalem, they have refrained from removing the last remnants of Jordan's presence in al-Haram al-Sharif/Temple Mount because the codependence that exists between Jordan and the Palestinians in many spheres dictates that competition between them remain only limited in scope. This codependence also leads to coordination, negotiations, and the attainment of formal and informal understandings and agreements—as well as a considerable amount of rhetoric and lip service. It will determine the nature of future Jordanian-Palestinian relations in general and in Jerusalem in particular.

The need to cooperate in Jerusalem is made even greater for the Palestinians and the Jordanians by the fact that other Arab and Muslim parties are interested in taking part in a settlement in Jerusalem holy shrines. These parties recognized the predominance of the Palestinian political claim to

---

contrary, this moderation should be viewed as a tactical means to defer an overt confrontation rather than as a waiver of the Jordanian interest in the Holy Places.

Jerusalem, thereby rejecting Jordan's claims, but at the same time rejected Palestinian exclusivity in the Muslim holy shrines (see Nevo 1994, 103).

Jordan's Perspective

For the Hashemites, a role in Jerusalem means religious and political legitimacy: in Jordan, vis-à-vis the Palestinians and the rest of the Arab world. The Oslo process led Jordan's having to abandon many of the functions it had previously carried out in Jerusalem. With the establishment of the Palestinian Council, Jordan had to focus on preserving its status in the Holy Places. Thus, the kingdom obtained Israel's recognition of a future Jordanian role, but it did not succeed in preserving its status in the holy shrines and in the religious establishment with regard to the Palestinians. Jordanian loyalists still hold several important administrative positions, however, and they mark the kingdom's ongoing, albeit residual, connection to the holy shrines pending the final-status negotiations. In a sense, Jordan succeeded in precluding the deterioration of its conflict with the Palestinian side.

To the best of our knowledge, Jordan has only begun preparations for the negotiations on future arrangements in the holy shrines. Since its treaty of peace with Israel, its Jerusalem policy has been passive and reactive. The initiative—both in the political inter-Arab and inter-Muslim arenas and in terms of physical control—has become Palestinian.[50] Despite the limitations

50. Compare several Jordanian political speeches and statements dating 1993–97. In a speech in Parliament dated November 23, 1993, the late King Hussein said that Jordan will not recognize any sovereignty over Jerusalem except that of God (Palestinian Academic Society 1996, 159–60). He also advocated the establishment of an apolitical Arab-Muslim body charged with caring for the Muslim Holy Places and overseeing them. The king, however, clarified that although Jordan will support such a body, it will not relinquish its religious and historic responsibility toward Jerusalem, the Waqf, and Muslim Holy Places in Palestine.

In a statement of policy made right after the Washington Declaration (July 28, 1994), Jordan maintained that there was no inconsistency between returning political sovereignty over Arab Jerusalem through Israeli-Palestinian negotiations and Jordan's continued role in executing its religious custody over the Holy Places in Jerusalem (Palestinian Academic Society 1996, 159–60). The statement further noted that the Washington Declaration did not establish the Jordanian right to take care of the Holy Places but, rather, declared that which has

on Jordan's capabilities, it might have taken several actions that would have emphasized the connections between al-Haram al-Sharif/Temple Mount and the Hashemites, if only symbolically. Thus, for example, the date marking the death of the Sharif Hussein, who is buried in the al-Haram al-Sharif compound, is not commemorated in Jordan, nor is the date of his son Abdallah's assassination, which took place in al-Haram al-Sharif itself.

At the inception of the interim period, Jordan assumed that its good relations with Israel, on the one hand, and the competitive relations between Israel and the Palestinians, on the other, would serve its interest pending the permanent settlement. Today, after its formal conclusion but before any agreement has been reached between the parties, Amman feels that Israel let it down (authors' files). When Jordan quietly sought Israel's assistance in preserving its physical control over al-Haram al-Sharif/Temple Mount, Israel did not respond. Israel was speaking in too many official voices and leaking too much for the Jordanian taste: Jordan trust of official Israel started wearing down. The tendency of the Peres government to focus on the Palestinian track, on the one hand, and the slowing of the peace process under the Netanyahu government, on the other, enhanced Jordan's disappointment. But Jordan's expectations, one has to admit, were exaggerated to start with.

---

already been in existence. This position, it was stated, stems from Jordan's commitment to support the PLO's efforts to achieve political and geographical in all Palestinian Arab territories, including Jerusalem, and from the continuance of Jordan's historic role in exercising religious custody over the Holy Places in Jerusalem.

Jordan had to moderate its position as early as November 1994. Former crown prince Hassan clarified then that in the permanent settlement, when full responsibility will be transferred to the Palestinians, Jordan will transfer the responsibility for the Holy Places to the Palestinian Authority. Since then, Jordanian policy statements emphasize, on the one hand, that Jordan does not stand in the way of either Palestinian sovereignty in east Jerusalem or of Palestinian responsibility to the Holy Places. On the other hand, these statements restate that the Jordanian role in these places will continue without explaining what this role may comprise or how it reconciles with transfer of responsibility to the Palestinians. In addition, the Jordanian policy statements stress that the Israeli-Palestinian Declaration of Principles, by deferring the Jerusalem issue to the permanent-status negotiations phase, has created a legal vacuum that may be filled by "others"—namely Israel. See the speech the late King Hussein made in Parliament on December 13, 1997 ("King Says Jordan Faces" 1997).

Jordan continues to rely on Israel concerning the permanent-status negotiations. It assumes that the Palestinians will find it very difficult to win from Israel real concessions in Jerusalem and the Holy Places. This assumption allows Jordan to use lenient rhetoric toward the Palestinians and thus, for example, in the permanent settlement, when full responsibility will be transferred to the Palestinians, Jordan "will transfer the responsibility for the Holy Places to the Palestinian Authority."[51]

Jordan is interested in having a central role in carrying out responsibility for the Muslim Holy Places and their management but is aware of its limited capabilities. Jordanian policy statements include, from time to time, basic outlines of a settlement (see note 50). The work of defining the role it seeks as well as how to achieve that role is in its embryonic stages in Amman.[52] It is not clear, therefore, whether Jordan will be content with a titular and symbolic role in the Holy Places in addition to maintaining the right to continue budgeting the Holy Places. Jordan may insist on carrying out an active,

51. This formula is taken from the statement the former crown prince made in November 1994. Note its obscure meaning: If full responsibility is to be transferred to the Palestinians in the framework of the permanent settlement, why would the Palestinians, who exercise physical control in the Holy Places, have to have the very same authority transferred to them by Jordan, who no longer exercises it anyway? There is an apparent discrepancy between Jordan's policy and its statements in this regard (some of which are referred to in note 50; see also the king's 1999 interview in *Der Spiegel*). Jordan's statements are aimed at help managing open conflicts between Jordan and the Palestinians over the Jerusalem question and minimizing Arab and Islamic pressure on Jordan. They cannot be regarded as reflecting Jordanian policy or evidencing a Jordanian abandonment of a future role in the Holy Places, even if they do attest the weakness of Jordan's position.

52. Note that King Hussein's initiative to create informal consultations between religious leaders on Jerusalem as a religious center. It seems that this initiative was intended, among other things, to establish a forum, which will manifest the Jordanian role in the Muslim holy shrines. See interview with Foreign Minister David Levy by Dalia Yairi, Israeli Radio, Dec. 29, 1996 (cited in Palestinian Academic Society 1996, 139). Note that Article 9(3) of the Treaty of Peace establishes a framework for interfaith dialogue: "The Parties will act together to promote interfaith relations among the three monotheistic religions, with the aim of working towards religious understanding, moral commitment, freedom of religious worship, and tolerance and peace."

albeit not exclusive part in the management of the Holy Places, despite its limited physical assets on the ground.

In addition to a role in the Holy Places, Jordan's role in a permanent settlement in Jerusalem could extend to other spheres. In certain spheres, for which Jordan was responsible in the past, the Palestinian Council does not exercise or is legally barred from exercising governmental authority. The result is a governmental vacuum. Israel is either uninterested in or incapable of filling this vacuum, and Jordan has done little to preserve its status in east Jerusalem in all matters except for the Holy Places.

Take, for example, the sphere of nationality. During the interim period, east Jerusalemites continue to enjoy the benefits of Jordanian nationality (mainly travel documents). Parallel to that, they enjoy the advantages of their Israeli residency rights (national insurance benefits). The Palestinian Council, however, cannot issue useable travel documents or compete with Israel's social security payments and is thus having trouble establishing a civil link between itself and east Jerusalem Palestinians.[53] Israel itself is ambivalent: on the one hand, it can use the residency status of east Jerusalem Palestinians as an important bargaining chip;[54] on the other hand, that status reduces the size of the Jewish population in the city.[55]

Jordan continues to operate the population registry with respect to Palestinians of east Jerusalem and to issue temporary travel documents during the interim period. In doing so, it preserves the existing state of affairs pending the outcome of the permanent-status negotiations. But the existing

53. The voting of east Jerusalem Palestinians to the Palestinian Council creates, of course, such a link, although legally it does not prejudice the outcome of the permanent-status negotiations. Consider also the census conducted by the Palestinian Council during December 1997.

54. Note the relatively low voting rate in Jerusalem in the January 1996 elections to the Palestinian Council.

55. Hence, the plan introduced in 1998 to enlarge the municipal boundaries of Jerusalem westward and the so-called quiet-transfer policy of recent years. Under this policy, the Israeli Interior Ministry confiscates Israeli resident cards from Palestinian residents of east Jerusalem who "moved the center of their lives" outside the municipal boundaries into the West Bank.

state of affairs may, in fact, give Jordan long-term holdings in Jerusalem. It may be assumed, for example, that in the course of the negotiations Israel may not accept that east Jerusalem Palestinians will be nationals of the Palestinian state. The solution might be to take advantage of the existing state of affairs: east Jerusalemites will be able, for example, to choose between Israeli or Jordanian nationality and between voting for the Jordanian Parliament, the Palestinian Parliament, or Israel's Knesset. This solution may integrate into a Palestinian-Jordanian confederate framework constituted after the establishment of the Palestinian state.

Israel's Perspective: A Competitive Premise

We examine Israel's possible policy on the future Jordanian role in the Holy Places based on three scenarios. The first assumes that the permanent settlement will be the result of Israeli-Palestinian negotiations. The second scenario assumes that such negotiations will fail, that the settlement will be based on unilateral acts of the parties, and that relations may deteriorate into violent conflict. The third scenario postulates that the parties will agree to postpone the permanent settlement in Jerusalem for a further interim period, during which the status quo will be generally preserved. We address the last two scenarios jointly.

A common premise in Israeli conception is that any arrangement in east Jerusalem benefiting Jordan comes at the expense of the Palestinians. The Palestinian-Jordanian relations are seen in Israel as a zero-sum game. The advantage in Jordanian participation, according to this premise, is that it reduces, by definition, the Palestinian part in whatever arrangement is applied in Jerusalem. Jordanian-Palestinian competition in al-Haram al-Sharif/Temple Mount is therefore viewed as a desired future development because it will reduce the measure of Palestinian control of al-Haram al-Sharif.

We believe that this premise is based on a misconception of east Jerusalem realities, a misunderstanding of Jordanian-Palestinian relations, and a misjudgment of long-term Israeli interests. Nevertheless, it is treated as a common wisdom. For this reason, we examine this premise in detail before presenting the readers with the grounds for its negation. At that stage, we also introduce our own alternative premise.

Scenario One: Successful permanent-status negotiations. Jordan's role in Jerusalem may take different forms, each of which has to be examined in order to reveal the overall value of Jordan's place. First, the kingdom may play a substantive role in the administration of the Holy Places, with or without sharing power with the Palestinians. Second, it may take on a symbolic and titular role not involving the exercise of substantive functions. Third, it may participate in a wider multipartite Arab or Islamic institutional arrangement, whatever the contents of its specific role.

(a) A substantive Jordanian role. The transfer of substantive responsibilities to Jordan, which will detract, in part or in whole, from the responsibilities of the Palestinian side, will require constant enforcement, including by force. That kind of an arrangement is bound to fail. Such an arrangement disregards the realities of the last seven years (1993–2000); Jordan itself will not take part in a settlement forced on the Palestinians. Even if Jordan would, there will be no guarantee that it will be able to exercise the functions effectively. The success of the Palestinian Council in eroding Jordan's control in al-Haram al-Sharif/Temple Mount would be repeated shortly after the conclusion of the permanent-status agreement. In order to preserve Jordan's role, Israel will have to change its policy radically to guard Jordanian interests actively. Israel will not have the time, the resources, or the institutional will to take an active side in a Palestinian-Jordanian competition. Its intervention will be perceived as interference in what is essentially an internal Muslim and Arab affair, and will portray Jordan as Israel's puppet. It will involve use of force, which public opinion in and outside Israel will not tolerate. The Jordanian role will be reduced, at best, to a symbol. A Jordanian-Palestinian agreement is the only way to achieve a viable substantive Jordanian role.

(b) A symbolic and titular Jordanian role. A symbolic role does not involve the transfer of responsibilities that can be eroded, nor does it require a Jordanian power base in Jerusalem or reliance on Israel. Indeed, one should ask, What is the Israeli interest in a role that does not make Jordan a competitor to the Palestinian side in Jerusalem? If the Palestinian Council is exercising control in al-Haram al-Sharif/Temple Mount, reason dictates that dealings be conducted with it alone.

There are, however, compelling reasons not to pursue this course of action. First, King Abdallah is an ally, and Jordan is a strategic asset for Israel, both as an eastern buffer and as a moderate Arab regime in Israel's immediate vicinity. Moreover, the Israel-Arab conflict cannot be fully resolved without Jordan's participation. Reconciliation and peaceful relations between the two peoples cannot be obtained without Jordan. It is an essential side in a subregional triangle, which is Israel's future reference point to the Arab world in the long run. This is the reason Jordan has to take part in long-term Israeli-Palestinian arrangements and hence the importance of a symbolic Jordanian role, even if it cannot satisfy concrete Israeli interests in Jerusalem.

Second, the Palestinian control in al-Haram al-Sharif/Temple Mount does not necessarily mean that the Palestinians can maintain exclusivity in the administration of the Holy Places. Saudi Arabia, Morocco, and Egypt, which see themselves as interested parties, will strive to take part in the arrangements. It is doubtful that the Palestinians will be able to negotiate an agreement that Jordan and these countries oppose. In addition, the strongholds of the fundamental Islamic movements in al-Haram al-Sharif also jeopardize Palestinian Council exclusivity.

The conclusion is that although a symbolic Jordanian role in al-Haram al-Sharif/Temple Mount does not serve narrow Israeli interests in connection with a settlement in the Holy Places, it nevertheless corresponds to broader Israeli interests.

(c) A Jordanian role within an institutional multipartite framework. Jordan's role may be more than merely symbolic yet still protected from erosion if it is part of an Islamic or Arab multipartite framework for the administration of the Holy Places in Jerusalem. Arguably the benefits of such an arrangement are that (1) it offers a wide legitimacy base; (2) only states and organizations maintaining normal relations with Israel will be able to participate; (3) Israel will be allowing freedom of religion and worship, and will rid itself of the need to intervene in internal Arab and Muslim affairs; and (4) Israel's partner in Jerusalem will be well defined and, more important, dependent on Israel in matters of day-to-day administration (e.g., transit right to personnel, visitors, and pilgrims; privileges and immunities of functionaries; and the like).

But Israel will not be able to guarantee the cooperation of a multipartite institution in crucial matters or to prevent that institution's transformation into an anti-Israeli platform. Even with an Israeli agreement to leave the establishment and composition of the institution for the Arab world to decide (without which no Arab state is likely to take part in such a decision), while explicitly retaining specific functions, it is not certain that agreement can be reached on the establishment of such a framework or on each state's part in the framework. In this case, the Palestinians will be left as sole actors in al-Haram al-Sharif/Temple Mount.

But even if this framework is constituted, Jordan's place in it cannot be guaranteed. Without Israeli intervention on Jordan's behalf—which will only be counterproductive—Jordan will have a difficult time competing with a coalition of other Arab states. The establishment of an Arab or Islamic multipartite body for the administration of the Holy Places in which Jordan's role is minute or nonexistent will constitute a personal affront to King Abdallah and will considerably damage both Israeli-Jordanian relations and, inevitably, Israel strategic political interests.

So far we have assumed that the main advantage to Israel in Jordanian participation in a settlement in the Holy Places is the positing of a competitor to the Palestinian Council. None of Jordan's possible roles can obtain this objective. A Jordanian-Palestinian competition in al-Haram al-Sharif/Temple Mount, therefore, cannot serve Israeli interests as defined by the premise according to which a settlement benefiting Jordan will weaken the Palestinians. We return later to this premise and its repudiation. The interim conclusions concerning the negotiated-solution scenario are reaffirmed when assessing Jordan's potential role in a unilateral action or agreed deferment scenarios.

Scenario Two: Unilateral actions. Following the signing of the Wye River Memorandum (between the government of the State of Israel and the PLO) and its nonimplementation, and after the formal conclusion of the interim period, it may be that a failure of the parties to reach an agreement on the permanent status will lead to a unilateral declaration of Palestinian independence. Israel may respond by annexing large portions of the West Bank. A violent conflict may ensue, including Jerusalem. Israel will then direct its resources toward protecting its own interests rather than those of Jordan. Moreover, the Palestinians may seize the opportunity and remove the remaining Jordanian presence in al-Haram al-Sharif/Temple Mount.

King Abdallah has every reason to be concerned with such developments. A violent conflict between Israel and a Palestinian state in the making (recognized by the international community) will force him to choose the Palestinian and Arab side. Armed Arab intervention, should it follow, would compel him to take action lest he be denounced and his rule imperiled. The absence of an Israeli-Palestinian political process also would deny Jordan its assisting and mediating role.

Scenario Three: Agreed deferment of a settlement in Jerusalem. This scenario may have similar consequences. Deferment of settlement of the Holy Places question will not give Jordan new instruments with which to enhance its position in al-Haram al-Sharif/Temple Mount. Israeli-Palestinian struggle in east Jerusalem will continue and drive the Palestinians to solidify further the Palestinian identity of the al-Haram al-Sharif compound against residual Jordanian presence.[56]

Israel's Perspective: An Alternative Premise

The competitive premise repudiated. The premise that a settlement in the Holy Places benefiting Jordan will necessarily come at the expense of the Palestinian side and that this fact serves Israeli interests is incorrect. It ignores the measure of control the Palestinian Council exercises in the Holy Places and the religious establishment as well as the consequent limitations on Jordan's freedom of action. At the same time, it disregards the restraint both sides have exercised in order to refrain from direct confrontation in Jerusalem. This restraint stems from different leverages each side has on the other. Thus, the Palestinians did not take advantage of their physical control in the al-Haram al-Sharif compound in order to end Jordanian influence therein.

In addition, the competitive premise does not take into account the respective goals of Jordan and the Palestinians with regard to the permanent settlement in Jerusalem. Jordan has no interest in weakening the Palestinian position that Jerusalem be the capital of the Palestinian state. Rather, it fo-

---

56. On the other hand, it may be argued that the need to consolidate Palestinian statehood will compel the Palestinians to seek Jordanian assistance—which will require mutual compromise, cooperation, and accord over the matter of the Holy Places, if only by way of formalizing the status quo.

cuses on the religious status in the Holy Places, which may have political consequences, but does not necessarily detract from the political status of a future Palestinian entity.

The paramount objective of the Palestinian Council is to establish a Palestinian state, the capital of which is east Jerusalem. The parties' respective power positions make the attainment of this objective conditional on Palestinian willingness to swap territorial sovereignty in east Jerusalem for a link between a Palestinian capital in municipal Jerusalem's periphery and east Jerusalem neighborhoods (or boroughs, councils, or the like).[57] The participation of Jordan in arrangements in the Holy Places does not jeopardize this objective. Had Jordan jeopardized this objective, the council would have effected Jordan's total exclusion from al-Haram al-Sharif/Temple Mount long ago, whatever the cost.

In addition, the competitive premise does not reflect the nature of the relationship between Jordan and the Palestinian Council. Geographical proximity; the Middle Eastern geostrategic layout; and the demographic, political, religious, historic, and economic ties between the two banks of the river all dictate the establishment of a partnership of some confederate nature between Jordan and a Palestinian state. Thus, all competition for resources, including religious and political resources, will be limited to and aimed at improving relative positions within the partnership rather than at obtaining a total victory over the other. Both Jordan and the Palestinians act on the dictates of this relationship. Israel should not and cannot aggravate the competition between the Palestinians and Jordan because they both will compete only up to a limit. Furthermore, such Israeli action will impair its own credibility.

The future of Jordan and the Palestinian state is in long-term partnership. Both attach great importance to their respective status in the Jerusalem Muslim Holy Places. Neither one will let this issue, however, jeopardize the greater importance of the mutual interests in long-term partnership. Encouraging acute competitive patterns between Jordan and the Palestinians will undermine the Israeli geostrategic goals: the resolution of the Israeli-Palestinian conflict while achieving regional stability.

57. The Beilin-Abu Mazen understandings demonstrate that this willingness exists.

The alternative: The partnership premise. The attainment of Israel's strategic goals in connection with the peace process necessitates the establishment of a Jordanian-Palestinian long-term partnership. The aim of Jordan's role in Jerusalem's Holy Places, according to this alternative premise, is to consolidate this partnership in connection with the permanent-status settlement and to strengthen the Jordanian pillar in the partnership. The two banks are inseparable; the political weight of a Palestinian-Jordanian partnership will surpass the two countries' individual powers. In the long run, the geographical reference point for ensuring Israel's continued political, strategic, economic, and human existence is the territory on both banks of the Jordan River. This territory is the heart of the conflict with the Arabs, the key to its solution and to Israel's future integration in the region. Establishing a stable Jordanian-Palestinian partnership in the permanent-status settlement (or soon after), and beyond, and having it complemented by a correlating partnership with Israel are (and should be) primary Israeli interests. An Israeli policy aimed at a separate arrangement with either party as a substitute rather than as a catalyst to an arrangement with the other is predestined to fail. Full Israeli-Palestinian reconciliation cannot be achieved without coordination with Jordan and its participation in the settlement of the conflict. Israel will not be able to attain regional stability and security through Jordan or through the Palestinians alone. We believe that the Jordanian option is no option at all: it is an imperative.

Israel's interest in a Jordanian role. Apart from the general Israeli interest in Jordanian participation in arrangements to apply in the Holy Places in Jerusalem, Jordan—Israel's strategic partner—can and should contribute to the stability and moderation of the Muslim religious establishment in Jerusalem. Thus, it can form a coalition with the Palestinian Council against the fundamental Islamic movements operating in al-Haram al-Sharif/Temple Mount. It can also provide the Palestinian state with experienced human resources, administrative experience, funds, pilgrims, and important religious legitimacy.

The desired scope of the Jordan's role. The natural question to ask at this stage is: What should the scope of Jordan's role in the Jerusalem Muslim Holy Places be in order for it to obtain the objectives derived from Israel's strategic interests as presented in this essay? We submit that the answer to this question is relatively unimportant and that the scope of Jordan's role need not be defined in advance. If the objective of Jordan's role is to cement a Jordanian-Palestinian partnership, then any arrangement that satisfies Israel's security needs (and other essential interests), does not undermine Israel's overarching sovereignty, and is acceptable to both Palestinians and Jordan serves this objective effectively. Therefore, the main question to ask is: How can such an arrangement be achieved?

Nevertheless, it is possible to describe the prospective scope of the Jordanian role in the Holy Places that furthers the interests of all three parties. Israel's security needs will be met by its control of the surroundings of the Temple Mount by formalizing the existing entry and policing arrangements, which will, however, be the subject of coordination mechanisms with the religious authorities in al-Haram al-Sharif.

The Palestinian interest in enjoying the political and religious status resulting from control of the Holy Places will be met by Israeli and Jordanian recognition of that status as a consequence of the national rights of the Palestinian people. The Palestinian state will thus be responsible for the day-to-day administration of the compound. This responsibility will be exercised on the basis of a Hashemite empowerment. Jordan—which contributed significantly to the preservation of the Holy Places and is ruled by the Prophet's descendants—will accord permanent and ongoing empowerment to the Palestinian state to administer the Holy Places. Israel and the Palestinian state will recognize the Hashemite ruler of Jordan as Guardian of the Holy Places in Jerusalem. Jordan may also take part in particular symbolic or substantive arrangements to apply in al-Haram al-Sharif. These arrangements may include formalization of the existing state of affairs (i.e., funding and certain appointments) or novel arrangements (i.e., formal approval of religious nominations, the conduct of certain ceremonies, and the like)—as agreed between Jordan and the Palestinians. The institutional Jordanian-Palestinian relationship will integrate into bilateral arrangements to apply between the two states after the permanent-status settlement. Coordination and cooperation with Israel will take place in both bilateral and trilateral forums. An inter-Arab or inter-Islamic body operating alongside the bilateral or trilateral institutions in al–Haram al–Sharif—in other words, a body that will not derogate from Jordanian, Palestinian, or Israeli authority—can be established by agreement of all parties concerned.

How to accomplish the Jordanian role. We have demonstrated above that a Jordanian role in the Holy Places that does not impair Israel's essential interests and is the result of Palestinian–Jordan agreement serves Israel's objective. The main issue of concern is the way to accomplish an agreed trilateral arrangement in Muslim Holy Places in Jerusalem. Allegedly, the simplest course of action would be to conduct trilateral negotiations. However, the lack of trust inherent in tripartite negotiations, aggravated by the current distrust among all three parties, will reduce the chances of direct trilateral negotiations. Public opinion, a major constraining factor in any negotiations over the Jerusalem issue, will add another dimension: each party will face the argument that it has maneuvered itself into a minority position.

A series of three parallel bilateral tracks of negotiations may thus prove more efficacious. The Jordanian-Palestinian track will be concerned with arrangements in the Holy Places. The Israeli-Palestinian track will deal with ensuring essential Israeli interests and harmonizing the understandings of the former track into a permanent-status agreement (e.g., the status of al-Haram al-Sharif/Temple Mount territory and administration; freedom of movement, access, and worship; prohibition on incitement). Similarly, the Israeli-Jordanian track will focus on coordinating Jordan's role (as agreed between Jordan and the Palestinians) with an Israeli-Palestinian permanent-status agreement. Above all, Israel will use the two tracks in which it will participate to guard its "red lines."

Any track of negotiations concerning Jerusalem will be subject to both internal and external criticism. An official track of negotiations cannot always satisfy the need for secrecy, indirect tripartite coordination, and flexibility. We therefore recommend the establishment of additional tracks: from academic exchange through unofficial talks to official negotiations.

Conclusion

The historic role of Jordan, which Israel recognized in the Treaty of Peace, is guaranteed by an array of religious, political, and economic ties Jordan maintains with the Arab population of western Palestine and by its connection with the Muslim Holy Places in Jerusalem. An Israeli-Palestinian permanent settlement depends on obtaining an agreement regarding Jerusalem. This agreement will have to address the problem of Muslim Holy Places in Jerusalem by reflecting the tripartite interests in the Holy Places—including their administration and the supervision of their surroundings—and by guaranteeing freedom of access and worship. In order to establish a Jordanian role consistent with Israel's goals—the establishment of trilateral cooperative patterns—a measure of willingness, readiness, and preparedness is required of all three parties. Each will have to recognize the bounds of its capabilities. Israel and the Palestinians will have to refrain from implementing policies based on unilateral actions in Jerusalem.

Jordan's role in the Holy Places of Jerusalem is the result of the Hashemites' struggle for predominance in the Arab world—and, to a great extent, of their lack of capability to accomplish their ambitions. After the Hashemites were ousted from Arabia and the failure of King Abdallah's Pan-Arab aspirations, they were established as rulers of the East Bank of the Jordan. Later, they obtained, for a short nineteen years, control of the West Bank, including east Jerusalem, the third holiest site in Islam. During those years, the Hashemites developed a practical and symbolic connection to Jerusalem's Holy Places. Today, this connection is mostly residual. Jordan invests substantial economic and political capital in the preservation of this connection. Israeli-Jordanian relations in the past fifty years demonstrate that Jordan will not make a separate arrangement with Israel over the Holy Places in Jerusalem or over any other issue. Jordan doe˜ not want and cannot agree to an arrangement imposed on the Palestinians. It follows that Israel may be an important Jordanian bargaining chip and insurance policy with regard to the Palestinians, but one of limited use. A bilateral Israeli-Jordanian arrangement excluding the Palestinians is not possible.

Furthermore, a bilateral arrangement is not desirable. Israel's interests in permanent-status negotiations—the attainment of a long-term reconciliation with the Palestinians—will have to be based on permanent peace and stability within a trilateral Israeli-Palestinian-Jordanian framework. Israel cannot benefit from Palestinian-Jordanian conflict in al-Haram al-Sharif/Temple Mount. Its long-term strategic interests necessitate tripartite exchange and the attainment of arrangements acceptable to Jordan and the Palestinians alike.[58]

Since this paper was sent for publication, the attempt to reach a permanent status agreement in the July 2000 Camp David Summit and its following deliberations have failed, leading to—together with other causes—the resumption of violence between Israelis and Palestinians. This is neither the place nor the time to evaluate the impact of these developments on the position of the Hashemite Kingdom or on the situation in Jerusalem. Nevertheless, it may be said that these developments altered neither the premises of our research nor its conclusions. The resumed violence may have further complicated Israeli-Palestinian relations and delayed the attainment of an agreed solution, but as long as the geopolitical arena and the parties concerned remain the same, so will the tripartite nature of the solution of the question of the Muslim holy places in Jerusalem, even if the exact role of each of the three may vary.

58. Rotem M. Giladi serves as legal adviser to the Tel Aviv delegation of the International Committee of the Red Cross (ICRC). This article reflects the views of the author alone and not of the ICRC.

PART TWO

Issues of Law and Religion

7

The Religious Significance of Jerusalem in the Middle East Peace Process

Some Legal Implications

Silvio Ferrari

C ertain cities are identified as having a specific value and become a symbol of that value throughout the world. Florence, for example, is synonymous with art; Zurich evokes thoughts of business; and Oxford reminds
us of culture. In a sense, each of these cities has universal significance because
each expresses one of the many dimensions of human life.

Jerusalem is identified with religion. The destiny of the Holy City is to
be the City of God and to manifest this grandiose (and tragic) attachment
throughout human existence. This identification is the only true significance of Jerusalem in humankind's history. *"Haec est Jerusalem, Ego eam in
medio gentium posui et in circuitu eius terras"* (Ezek. 5:5).

From the time of the prophets until the present day, the theme of the
centrality of Jerusalem in human history recurs with an intensity and fre-
quency clearly not in keeping with the modest political and economic significance of the city. The maps of antiquity presented Jerusalem as the center
of the earth, the point where Europe, Asia, and Africa meet; scholars de-

An earlier version of this article appeared in 45 Catholic University Law Review 733
(1996) and is reprinted with permission.

223

scribed it as the *umbilicus mundi;* theologians used its name to indicate the kingdom of heaven ("celestial Jerusalem"); and, even today, people of culture throughout the world unite to speak of *"Jerusalem, l'unique et l'universel."*[1]

The sole reason this city continues to exercise a singular attraction on humankind's conscience is that, in the words of Pope John Paul II, "Jerusalem represents the geographical point of tangency between God and man, between the eternal and history" (quoted in Farhat 1987, 187). For the Jewish, Christian, and Islamic religions alike, Jerusalem is by definition the Holy City—the place where, as an old legend explains, the sky bends down to touch the earth.

Yet this definition remains insufficient to capture the peculiarities of Jerusalem, the distinctive elements that make it a unique, inimitable place. Certainly there are other cities of God in the world, such as Rome and Mecca, but none possess the distinctive characteristics of Jerusalem—the historical meeting point of various religions, the place that marks the crossroads where their paths meet.

Of course, we cannot deny the historical priority of Jewish interests in Jerusalem, but how can we forget the unique meaning of this city for Christians or the very important place it occupies in Islamic religion? From this standpoint, it must be stressed that Jerusalem is different from all other holy cities that attest to the strong links between a place and a religion. Specifically, the historical vocation of Jerusalem is to be the meeting place of three religions and continually to relaunch the challenge of their peaceful coexistence within the same physical space.

As a result of the events that took place in Jerusalem and of the city's identification with the destiny of a people, it has a special character that we may define as holy, for the faithful of the Jewish, Christian, and Islamic religions. Unfortunately, this character has turned Jerusalem into a divided city, the object of bloody conflicts between peoples and sovereigns who want to control it, but it also provides hope that through a change in history to which every person of good will is called on to make a contribution, peace finally may come to Jerusalem based on a different and more sound concept

1. This is the title of the nineteenth Colloque d'Intellectuels Juifs de Langue Francaise, which was held in Paris in 1979.

of peace, rather than on the imposition of force or on the inventions of diplomacy.

In this sense, the idea that the city belongs to a single religion, to the exclusion or limitation of all others, constitutes an impoverishment and betrayal of the universal destiny that has befallen Jerusalem—a destiny that makes it, more than any other holy city, the spiritual heritage of all humankind. Even those who do not belong to the "religions of the book" cannot fail to be interested and involved in the "sacred experiment" that is designed to transform the difference in religious affiliation—which for centuries has opposed Christians, Jews, and Muslims against each other in bloody conflict—into a factor working for peace.

For Jerusalem to become, as Giorgio La Pira hoped, "the city of universal peace" (1979, 563), there must be a complete upheaval of history that can no longer find its roots in law or in political compromises, but must go much deeper, touching the hearts of all humans. This claim does not mean however, that law and politics do not have, in this more complex context, their own roles in achieving the most favorable institutional conditions for Jerusalem to become the meeting point and place of reconciliation between believers.

For many years, the universal meaning of Jerusalem was associated with its internationalization: the belief that internationalization was the natural and necessary outlet at the institutional level for the peculiar character of the city. The United Nations (UN) resolutions of the 1946–47 period expressed this policy (United Nations General Assembly 1947), as did the Vatican, which for a long time defended this proposal. In recent years, mistrust of plans for the internationalization of the city has grown, and both the government of Israel and Arab countries have firmly rejected such plans.

Other ideas suggest a new division of the city into two parts (i.e., a return to the geographic division of the 1948–67 period) or joint sovereignty over Jerusalem, whereby the city would remain physically undivided, yet serve as the capital of two states at the same time (see, generally, Hirsch 1996; Hirsch, Housen-Couriel, and Lapidoth 1995; Lapidoth and Hirsch 1994b).

Although the choice of one or the other solution is far from irrelevant, in this chapter I intentionally avoid addressing the issue of sovereignty over Jerusalem. Of course, the political and religious dimensions of the Jerusalem question cannot be separated totally, but it is not impossible to distinguish the former from the latter. The Jerusalem question presents many facets, and politics and religion do not share the same importance when dealing with each facet.

The political dimension is concerned primarily with the adjudication of sovereignty over Jerusalem. It is a debate over boundaries, territorial control, armed forces, and so on. The political stage is dominated by two actors: the Israelis and the Palestinians.

The religious dimension, in contrast, focuses on the significance of Jerusalem for believers in God. The cast is different: the main actors are not Israelis and Palestinians, but Jews, Christians, and Muslims, whose faith is inseparable from Jerusalem. From a religious point of view, sovereignty over the city is not the main issue. Rather, its place is taken by the search for a way to harmonize the different significances Jerusalem has for Jews, Christians, and Muslims with the common significances shared by Jews, Christians, and Muslims.

This search involves both the land (i.e., the places, buildings, sites, and so on) and the people. The two factors cannot be separated. Each factor, taken alone, is not enough. A holy land or a holy place, if deprived of a community of the faithful living around it, has little religious significance. The great mosque of Cordoba, for example, is a jewel of Muslim architecture and a recollection of the Muslim past of Spain, but its mere existence does not confer Cordoba with any particular religious importance for today's Muslims. Similarly, the fact that many Christians, Jews, and Muslims live in London does not give London any religious prominence because it lacks the religious events or landmarks at the root of such a coexistence.

Preserving Jerusalem's Religious Significance

The greatness—in a sense the "uniqueness"—of Jerusalem is the land and the people together. More precisely, it is the fact that Jews, Christians, and Muslims have been and are living there because of the holiness of the land called Jerusalem. Therefore, preserving Jerusalem's religious significance means preserving both the city and its Holy Places, on one hand, and the communities residing in the city, on the other hand.

My remarks here are designed to give legal and institutional consistency to the religious significance of Jerusalem. This goal may be achieved more easily by envisaging three different degrees of protection, corresponding to three different geographical areas of Jerusalem (i.e., the Holy Places, the Old City, and the area surrounding the Old City), and the different needs they present.

Holy Places

First, there are the Holy Places, not only in Jerusalem but everywhere in the Holy Land. They require the highest and most specific degree of protection. The Holy Places must be precisely identified because not every mosque, church, or synagogue is a Holy Place in the technical sense used here. As a starting point, one may refer to the list of Holy Places prepared by Lionel G. A. Cust during the British Mandate (1980 [1929], 12, 13) and to the list prepared by the UN Conciliation Commission in 1950 (see Collin 1974, 54–56).

The granting of an extraterritorial status is the simplest way to protect the Holy Places. That means the Holy Places are areas included within the territory of a state, but areas over which the state cannot exercise (or at least cannot exercise fully) its sovereignty.

Both in Italy and (to some extent) in Greece, there are Holy Places with extraterritorial status. In Rome, three Catholic basilicas enjoy such a status. Article 15 of the Lateran Treaty between Italy and the Holy See grants the basilicas the same immunities conferred on the embassies of foreign states in Italy ("Italy—the Holy See" 1985). In particular, it is stated that the basilicas are property of the Holy See, cannot be expropriated by the state, are exempted from taxes, and can be repaired and renovated without authorization of or permits from the Italian authorities. In addition, Article 15 of the treaty declares the Italian police cannot enter the basilicas without first being invited by the religious authorities.

A second and more complex example of a Holy Place with a special status is Mount Athos, a Greek peninsula where a large community of monks, clergy, and laymen live (see Papastathis 1993). Mount Athos's special status provides for, among other things, a system of self-administration, which applies not only to the internal organization and activity of the religious communities but also to some aspects of the secular life of the people (laymen included) living in the Mount Athos area (Papastathis 1993, 56). Therefore, Mount Athos has autonomous institutions that exercise legislative, administrative, and judicial powers (ibid., 56). For example, it has an autonomous police force in charge of maintaining the religious order, as well as autonomous courts that judge civil disputes and minor criminal offenses (ibid. 1993, 64–65).

Although this administrative system concerns primarily the people and not the places, two other features of the Mount Athos legal regime deserve attention. First, the special status of Mount Athos is granted by a law called the Mount Athos Charter (Papastathis 1993, 59). The charter enjoys a formal force that is superior to all other laws of the Greek state (ibid., 60). Consequently, the state cannot unilaterally modify its provisions. Rather, first the representatives of the Mount Athos monasteries and then the Ecumenical Patriarchate and the Greek Parliament must approve any change to the charter (ibid., 60). In this way, the religious authorities of Mount Athos are assured that the existing legal regime cannot be altered against their will.

Second, the European Union has accorded indirect international recognition to the autonomous status of Mount Athos. In the Final Act concerning the accession of the Hellenic Republic of Greece to the European Community, Joint Declaration No. 4 states that the special status of Mount Athos will be taken into account in the application and preparation of provisions of European Union law ("Documents" 1979).

It is obvious that not each and every provision contained in the Lateran Treaty and in the Mount Athos Charter can be transplanted to the Holy Land and applied to the Holy Places of Jerusalem, but the treaty and the charter provide good examples of systems working to ensure the protection, conservation, and administration of Holy Places by the religious communities to which they belong. There are some critical differences, however, between the Holy Places that the Lateran Treaty and the Mount Athos Charter protect, and the situation involving the Holy Land of Jerusalem.

First, both the basilicas in Rome and Mount Athos are Holy Places to a single religion, whereas the Holy Land includes places holy to different religions. In fact, some of the Holy Places in Jerusalem are in the undivided possession of a number of religious communities. Such a situation raises complicated problems. In dealing with these problems, some guidance may be found by examining the status quo that governs the relations of the various Christian communities attending the Church of the Holy Sepulcher. Although this system is far from perfect, it nevertheless has been in place for more than four centuries and provides proof that the sharing of the same Holy Place among a number of different religious communities is possible. Particular attention should be paid to the provisions excluding modifications of the status quo that the religious communities do not agree on and preventing any interference from external powers (see Sayegh 1971; "Fundamental Agreement" 1993, Article 4; "Basic Agreement" 2000, Article 4).

Another critical difference between the Jerusalem situation and the Holy Places protected by the Lateran Treaty and the Mount Athos Charter lies in the fact that both the basilicas in Rome and Mount Athos in Greece are located in states where the Catholic and Orthodox religions, respectively, are the majority religions. Conversely, the Holy Land includes places that are holy to one religion but located in a territory where a different religion is professed by the majority of the population. This geographical situation raises the problem of guaranteeing (eventually through an international provision) freedom of access to and freedom of worship in the Holy Places of Jerusalem.

Although the need to give complete security to the Holy Places is the point of departure for any discussion of the sacred character of Jerusalem, their mere protection is not enough to express the universal vocation of the Holy City, nor does it seem capable of properly soliciting interreligious dialogue and collaboration. The limitation implicit in the mere protection of the Holy Places would not be overcome even if that protection were to be extended to include free access. Even once free access is granted, there nevertheless remains insufficient consideration of the fact that the universal dimension of Jerusalem and its Holy Places transcends the rights of those who travel there as pilgrims. It affects the interests of all the faithful of the three monotheistic religions, so that Jerusalem, translating the indications of its history into concrete reality, can become a tangible sign of understanding and reconciliation between different religious experiences.

To achieve this objective requires Jews, Christians, and Muslims' involvement in a process of joint participation. Such joint participation would present a much larger base than the essential—but still preliminary—conservation of the Holy Places and, in some way, would involve the whole of historical Jerusalem as well as its basic life and activities. Only in this way will the faithful of various religions be able to go beyond a mere, but sterile physical coexistence and to take the road full of risks, but also promises, to the possibility of some form of agreement.

These considerations introduce the need to identify a geographical area that can act as a support to a reconciliation movement of this kind—a reconciliation movement that would not acquire the solidity necessary to have a profound effect on the relationship between the three religions, if it were so "disincarnated" as not to imply some territorial extension. Of course, this geographical area need not coincide with the confines of the whole of Jerusalem. As a matter of fact, given modern Jerusalem's expansion, the dynamic nature of its commercial and tourist activities, as well as the development of secular characteristics proper to any modern city, a solution that required this geographical area to equal all of Jerusalem, besides creating dangerous tensions, would express poorly those unique spiritual features of Jerusalem that need to be protected.

It is, therefore, simpler and more opportune to concentrate our attention on the historical city of Jerusalem (the part of the city inside the city walls), where an urban fabric sufficient to exalt the community values of human existence has remained intact, where the main Holy Places of the three religions are located, and where large groups of Christians, Jews, and Muslims live together elbow to elbow.

The Old City

The UN Education, Scientific, and Cultural Organization (UNESCO) already has recognized "the exceptional importance of the cultural property in the old city of Jerusalem, particularly the Holy Places . . . not only to the States directly concerned but to all humanity, on account of their artistic, historical, and religious value" (UNESCO 1968, 53).[2] This heritage would

---

2. This theme frequently was discussed in subsequent UNESCO resolutions and decisions.

be lost if the Old City were divided. Hence, whatever the final decision may be regarding sovereignty over Jerusalem, it would appear to be absolutely vital that this area be considered an indivisible unit that cannot be broken up by any boundary running inside it.

Limited to the Old City of Jerusalem and with reference to only those aspects that appear to be more strictly connected to the objective of protecting the religious character, it seems appropriate to examine some legal measures that give expression to the universal meaning of the historical city of Jerusalem and that might ensure the creation of an administrative regime that offers the most propitious guarantees for dialogue and understanding between the various expressions of faith.

One group of legal provisions is designed to protect the historic city of Jerusalem against any transformation that is incompatible with its holy character. Such protection is an interest and an obligation both of the state (or states) exercising sovereignty over this part of the city and of the world community. The Old City of Jerusalem and its walls already have been included in the World Heritage List, which specifies the monuments, buildings, and sites that "are of outstanding universal value" and constitute "a world heritage for whose protection it is the duty of the international community as a whole to co-operate" (see UNESCO 1985, Article 1 of 1979 Convention Concerning the Protection of the World Cultural and Natural Heritage). Thus, the obligation—both from a national and an international standpoint—is to avoid any urban or architectural transformation that might damage or destroy the historical, cultural, or religious character of the old Jerusalem. To this end, it is useful to recall some of the provisions of the 1954 Hague Convention for the Protection of Cultural Property in the Event of Armed Conflict ("United Nations Convention" 1954). The provisions protect historical buildings and historical centers, including those of a religious nature, against damage they might suffer as a result of military operations ("United Nations Convention" 1954, Article 3). The provisions also guarantee access to places and buildings for worship, even in the event of war.

Setting aside the event of war, it is possible to consider the hypothesis that the state (or states) exercising sovereignty over Jerusalem could subscribe to the commitments contained in the 1972 UNESCO Convention Concerning the Protection of the World Cultural and National Heritage (see UNESCO 1985), further specified in the 1976 UNESCO recommendation on the protection of the historic and traditional areas (see UNESCO 1985). These commitments explicitly consider historic cities and extend protection not only to buildings, but to spatial structures, environmental areas, and human activities and settlements in the area as well. Should the state (or the states) exercising sovereignty over the Old City promise to respect the provisions contained in those international documents, a first set of legal norms offering a minimum of protection to the religious heritage of Jerusalem would take shape.

The protection of the Holy Places is strictly connected with the protection of the communities of the faithful living around the Holy Places. After all, the religious significance of Jerusalem would be diminished greatly if the Holy Places became like museums, witnessing a past and not a living present. Therefore, a second set of legal provisions should consider the communities living in the Old City and guarantee their continued presence there.

In this respect, models and guidelines are not lacking. It would be possible, for example, to look at the provisions governing multilanguage cities, such as Brussels or Montreal, and to combine them with the system of districts and boroughs existing in other cities, such as London; or to bring attention to the treaties concerning the German-speaking minority living in some regions of Northern Italy, where that minority is provided with special rights in the field of employment, housing, and the like; or to consider the arrangements already in force in the Mount Athos area, adapting them to the multireligious reality of Jerusalem.

But maybe it is better to start from the suggestions put forward some years ago by the former mayor of Jerusalem, Teddy Kollek, who, speaking of the whole city, proposed legislative measures designed to guarantee each community the right to administrative autonomy in matters of education and health care; the power to levy taxes for public services; the jurisdictional power to hold its own courts; and, most important, the security of geographic boundaries for each quarter of the historic city and the respect for religious homogeneity (Kollek 1988–89, 156, 165, 168). Of course, the regime envisaged for the Old City is strictly dependent on the regime that will be applied to the whole of Jerusalem, but some of Kollek's suggestions (in particular those regarding the geographic borders and religious homogeneity of the quarters) could be adapted quite well to the Old City and to the Jewish, Christian, and Muslim Quarters existing there.

A different proposal has been more recently put forward by Jordan's former permanent representative at the United Nations, Adnan Abu Odeh: that a council comprising representatives of the Christian, Jewish, and Muslim communities run the Old City of Jerusalem, whose sovereignty should be left to God (Odeh 1996, 694).

Although Kollek's and Odeh's proposals envisage two different scenarios, they have the common purpose to preserve the multicultural and multireligious character of the Old City. Both of them could provide a good framework to safeguard the different communities living there.

Outside the Old City

Finally, the area surrounding the Old City must be considered—not only the remaining part of Jerusalem but also the territory of the state (or states) within whose borders the Old City of Jerusalem will be included. The need to consider this wider area is easily explained, for even the best system of guarantees of the Holy Places and religious communities in the Old City could be disrupted easily by provisions applying to the area outside Suleiman's walls. It would be possible, for example, to limit the freedom of access to Jerusalem, to prevent the faithful of a religion from getting there, or to deny residence permits to the clergy of another religion.

There is no need to invent special guarantees in order to avoid these dangers. Rather, it is enough to apply the general provisions already existing in the field of religious liberty. From this point of view, it should be emphasized that Israel already has signed the International Covenant on Civil and Political Rights, under which Article 18 grants to every person the "freedom, either individually or in community with others and in public or in private, to manifest his religion or belief in worship, observance, practice and teaching" ("International Covenant" 1967; see also "Fundamental Agreement" 1993, Articles 1, 3, 5; "Basic Agreement" 2000, Article 1). Interpreted according to the UN Declaration on the Elimination of All Forms of Intolerance and of Discrimination Based on Religion or Belief (United Nations General Assembly 1981), Article 18 (once signed by any other state that also might exercise sovereignty over the region) could provide a sound base for creating and maintaining a favorable legal environment in the area surrounding the Old City of Jerusalem.

Conclusion

Provisions of an international nature *lato sensu* may be useful to manifest the universal character of Jerusalem and to supply an institutional support for interreligious dialogue in three primary areas: (1) the protection of the Holy Places; (2) the protection of the cultural heritage of the historical city of Jerusalem, through measures designed to prevent amendments that might change the Holy City's religious meaning or historical configuration (including the protection of the pluralism that characterizes that part of Jerusalem by means of guarantees directed to ensuring the stable presence of the faithful of the three religions); and (3) the guarantee of religious freedom in the area surrounding the Old City of Jerusalem.

None of these measures implies any form of physical separation between the historic city and the remaining part of Jerusalem or precludes the possibility that Jerusalem may be the capital of one or more states in the region. The attempt to "match the historical and temporal dimension with the dimension of the eternity" (Dubois 1976, 175) inherent in Jerusalem might run along the lines suggested above, transforming the Holy City from a symbol of struggle into a sign of reconciliation.

8

Haredim and Palestinians in Jerusalem

Menachem Friedman

The so-called Arab Revolt in Palestine (1936–39) reached its peak in the summer of 1938. The leadership of the Yishuv (the organized Jewish community in Palestine) had levied a voluntary defense tax, known as Kofer Ha'Yishuv, to finance the mobilization of young men to protect settlements and Jewish neighborhoods. When the tax collectors reached the market in Jerusalem's Meah Shearim neighborhood, they came face to face with a group of extreme *haredi* (ultraorthodox) Jews led by Amram Blau (1894–1974) and Aharon Katzenellenbogen (d. 1978), who opposed the tax in principle. In the scuffle that broke out, the *haredim* were severely trounced, but this did not dampen their opposition to paying the tax or stop them from encouraging others to refuse to do so.

Shortly after that episode, they published a placard listing the reasons for their opposition to Kofer Ha'Yishuv, which they signed using the appellation Neturei Karta. This is an Aramaic term, literally meaning "the Guardians of the City," that appears in a midrash (a homiletical interpretation of a biblical passage) of great relevance to the subject of this chapter. The midrash relates that Rabbi Judah Ha'Nasi, the religious leader of the Jewish community in Eretz Israel in the third century, sent three sages, Rabbi Hiyya, Rabbi Yose, and Rabbi Ami, on an itinerant tour of the cities and towns of the country. In one place, they demanded that the guardians of the city be brought to them. When armed guards appeared before them, the sages said: "These are not the guardians of the city; these are the destroyers of

235

the city." When asked who were the real guardians of the city, they pointed to the sages, those who studied the Law. This is a tale that seems to reflect antimilitarist tendencies among the Pharisees, as a consequence of the "Great Revolt" of the Jews against the Romans, that led to the destruction of the Second Temple in 70 C.E. However, this saying became a fundamental principle throughout the long centuries of exile of a Jewish entity no longer independent. Applying it in relation to the historical context of the summer of 1938 seemed only natural.

The overwhelming majority of the Jewish community that had developed in Palestine after the Balfour Declaration (November 2, 1917) and the country's conquest by the British was secular and Zionist oriented. A very small minority, mostly concentrated in Jerusalem, was *haredi* and anti-Zionist. From their point of view, there could be no greater contradiction than the establishment of a secular Jewish national home in the Holy Land. However, the 1929 riots, in which Arabs murdered dozens of *haredi* Jews in Hebron and Safed, together with the Nazi rise to power in Germany that turned Palestine into the almost sole haven for Europe's depressed Jews, led to a crisis within the *haredi* anti-Zionist group. Many of its members, led by Moshe Blau (1885–1946) and with the encouragement of the ultraorthodox World Agudat Israel movement, believed that it was necessary to seek a modus vivendi with the Zionist institutions and that criticism of the Zionist leadership should be toned down. A minority of radical younger persons, led by Amram Blau (Moshe's brother) and Aharon Katzenellenbogen, became even more extremist. For them, Kofer Ha'Yishuv was an example par excellence of the ideology and practice of secular Zionism and should be forcefully opposed. First of all, the tax was meant to finance the special Jewish police force mobilized to guard the Jewish settlements. At the bases of this force, Jewish dietary laws were not observed, and the Sabbath was openly desecrated. In other words, money donated by Orthodox Jews would be expended, at least in part, on acts that are prohibited by the Jewish religious law, making the donors accomplices to transgressions of the Jewish law. But what was most evident in the stand those radicals adopted was their opposition to the very principle that Kofer Ha'Yishuv represented, to which they gave explicit expression in the broadsheet they published.

Their major argument was that an armed force would not guarantee the existence of the Jewish settlement. The very opposite was true: it would lead to its destruction. Only the sages, the Torah scholars—the group to which Amram Blau and his colleagues ascribed themselves and claimed to represent—were the true "Guardians of the City," i.e., of the Jewish community in Palestine. "The very idea," they wrote on their poster, "of defending the Jewish settlement *by the force of hands and the power of the fist is a heresy,* God forbid, and on the contrary, it will bring only desolation and destruction" (author's personal archives, emphasis added). Kofer Ha'Yishuv, from their point of view, was an exemplary aspect of the secular Zionist concept of the Jews as a nation like all other nations that will redeem itself just as other peoples fought for their political freedom. The situation of the Jews in Palestine owing to the Arab Revolt as well as the condition of the Jews in Europe after the Nazi rise to power were punishment from heaven because of their "rebellion" against the Lord and the denial of the uniqueness of the Jewish people, two acts that found expression in Zionist ideology and in the establishment of a secular Jewish community in Eretz Israel, the Holy Land.

These arguments were not new. They formed a central, if not primary, part of the Orthodox anti-Zionist view. Rabbis and leading Jewish religious authorities who opposed Zionism repeatedly based their arguments on the "three oaths" mentioned in tractate *Ketubbot* (111:a) of the Babylonian Talmud, that the Lord imposed on the people of Israel: that they should not return to the Holy Land en masse. This is interpreted to mean that Israel should not try to influence its historical development by leaving the lands of its exile, immigrating to the Holy Land, and attempting to establish Jewish rule there before the coming of the Messiah. Rabbis who supported Zionism, too, could not overlook this talmudic injunction. The Balfour Declaration played an important role in the polemic between pro-Zionist and anti-Zionist rabbis, for it seemingly provided the former with proof that Zionism was not an infringement of that prohibition.

The more Arab opposition increased to the implementation of the Balfour Declaration and the greater the tension between the Zionist majority in the Yishuv and the *haredi* anti-Zionist minority that saw itself threatened by a process of rapid secularization of the new Jewish settlement in Palestine, so, seemingly, was there a greater common interest between Palestinian nationalism and the *haredi* minority.

The man who more than anyone else recognized the political potential of an alliance between these two anti-Zionist elements and tried to implement that alliance was Dr. Jacob Israel de Haan (1881–1824). A Dutch-Jewish poet, de Haan arrived in Jerusalem not long after it was taken by the British and quickly became the spokesman for the extremist anti-Zionist group of *haredim*. With the encouragement of anti-Zionist personalities in the British administration in Palestine, he tried to reach an agreement with the Arab nationalist leadership by which no restrictions would be placed on Jewish settlement in Palestine and the neighboring Arab countries, in return for which the Jews would forego the Balfour Declaration—i.e., Jewish political aspirations in Palestine. In June 1924, not long after he sent a memorandum to that effect to Sharif Hussein and his two sons, Feisal (later king of Iraq) and Abdullah (later the emir of Transjordan), de Haan was murdered in Jerusalem by members of the Haganah, the Jewish underground military organization of the Yishuv (see Friedman 1977, 230–52).

It was not the murder, however, that thwarted the plans of de Haan and other members of the anti-Zionist *haredi* group. Though on the surface an alliance between Arab nationalists and anti-Zionist *haredim* seemed to be a realistic, if not an almost natural option, in reality it was impossible to put it into practice for three reasons:

1. Jewish ethics and the deep sense of solidarity that had developed throughout two thousand years of exile and oppression ruled out any possible alliance of a Jewish minority with Arab nationalism against the majority of the Jews in Palestine and abroad, a step that would be considered a gross infringement of the age-old prohibition against handing Jews over to the Gentiles *(Moser* means "informer"). Agudat Israel, a religious movement with deep roots among Orthodox Jewry, could not initiate an act that was so opposed to Jewish solidarity.

2. Even though the Zionist movement was on the whole secular, it took great pains to cooperate with religious Zionism and to maintain an attachment to the central symbols of the Jewish heritage. The radical anti-Zionist group was, therefore, a minority among the Jews in Palestine and even among its Orthodox community.

3. The anti-Zionist *haredi* community was historically and socially an integral part of the "Old Yishuv" (the traditional pre-Zionist settlement in

Palestine), a nonproductive society supported by the financial donations of Diaspora Jewry, and this without fulfilling its objective of serving as a spiritual center. Thus, for much of the Jewish people, this group had lost the legitimization of its existence.

Yet the idea of an alliance between the *haredi* anti-Zionists and Arab nationalists did not die out. In fact, as the security situation of the Yishuv deteriorated, it surfaced again and again. The 1929 Arab riots proved a shock for the Yishuv and the Zionist leadership. Many people sensed that the Arabs would not allow the Jews to fulfill their dream of establishing a national home. In this seeming ebbtide of Zionism, the extreme anti-Zionists among the Agudat Israel leadership felt secure enough to broach once more the idea of reaching a Jewish-Arab modus vivendi in which the Jewish side would give up its political aspirations in Palestine. At the same time, the brutal murder of dozens of Jewish men, women, and children in Hebron and Safed, most of them belonging to the non-Zionist Old Yishuv, led Agudat Israel leaders in Palestine to believe that the members of their society were paying most of the price for what they believed to be a "Zionist adventure." They drew a direct connection between the riots and the blatant secularization of public life in the Jewish rural and urban centers of the Land of Israel, for which they held Zionism responsible. Reacting to a proposal that a day of fasting and prayer at the Western Wall, where the rioting began, be set to commemorate the events of 1929, Rabbi Yosef Haim Sonnenfeld, the spiritual leader of the anti-Zionist *haredim* in Jerusalem, wrote that a fast should be set not because of what happened at the Western Wall but because of what "really" caused the riots: desecration of the Sabbath and other Jewish holidays, the licentious dress of the women, the opening of the Hebrew University (in which heretical studies were conducted), and so forth. In other words, according to Sonnenfeld, it was secular Zionism, which was causing the secularization of the Holy Land and undermining the security of the Jews in Palestine.

It was this theological principle that brought some World Agudat Israel leaders to propose openly that an alliance be contracted with the Palestinian nationalists in which the Jews would forego what had been promised in the Balfour Declaration. With razor-sharp irony, one of them wrote: "Why are we afraid to openly declare that we want no part of the Balfour Declaration?

Would that be tantamount to denying one of the Thirteen Principles [of Faith, formulated by Maimonides], or is the Balfour Declaration more sacred than our Holy Scriptures?" (qtd. in Friedman 1977, 220–22). They seemed to believe that in the present state of affairs in Palestine Zionism had lost its ability to play a meaningful political role and that Agudat Israel could more easily reach an agreement with the Arab extremists. Thus, Agudat Israel could save the Jewish community in Palestine from the destruction brought on it by secularization of the Holy Land and the political short-sightedness of the Zionists.

More moderate Agudat Israel leaders, however, were not tempted to adopt such a policy. Yitzhak Meir Levin (1894–1971), the leader of Agudat Israel in Poland, well understood where the sentiments of the masses of *haredi* Jews in pre-World War II Poland and in other countries lay, and what would be their reaction should Agudat Israel initiate an alliance with Arab nationalism against Zionism. He and Jacob Rosenheim (1870–1965), president of World Agudat Israel, wrote in a joint letter that should Agudat Israel support an alliance with the Arabs in return for giving up the Balfour Declaration "Agudat Israel will be left without members and there will be mass defection from its ranks" (qtd. in Friedman 1977, 322). Moshe Blau, whose anti-Zionism was no secret, staunchly apprised his anti-Zionist colleagues among Agudat Israel leadership of the complex situation that the radical anti-Zionists faced. "I tell you from the depth of my heart," he wrote, "that no matter how much the haredi hates the non-religious, heretical, apostate Zionists, he hates the despicable Arab a hundred times over" (ibid., 321). Thus, even anti-Zionists such as Moshe Blau, though convinced that the Zionists were responsible for the Yishuv's wretched state of affairs, could not shut their eyes to the solidarity so deeply embedded in Jewish hearts. For Blau, the brutality of the Arab rioters who had slaughtered *haredi* Jews in Hebron and Safed closed the door to the "option" of an alliance with Palestinian nationalism. In another letter to one of the harsh anti-Zionists, Blau gave an excellent description of how he conceived this tragic situation. "Your Honor *is mistaken in thinking that peace with the Arabs is possible. The Arabs hate [us] bitterly. We [the anti-Zionist* haredim*] do not want to cast off the shackles of the Diaspora [like the Zionists], but neither do we want to be killed and slaughtered, to be like dung in the field.* We, who with the grace of God will live here and die here, we are at the front, for better or for worse" (ibid., 316, emphasis added). No one could have better described the insoluble dilemma in which the adherents of Agudat Israel in Palestine found themselves.

Mass immigration to Palestine from Poland and especially the wave of immigrants from Nazi Germany, together known in Zionist historiography as the Fifth Aliya (1929–39), greatly influenced the social and economic condition of the Yishuv during the thirties. Because of these significant changes, the British Royal Commission (better known as the Peel Commission), charged with investigating the causes of the "Arab Revolt" and with suggesting ways to solve the conflict in Palestine, could propose the partition of the country and the establishment of a Jewish state in part of it (July 1937). Zionist efforts had borne fruit, and the Yishuv seemed strong enough to cope with the challenges posed by statehood. The masses of Jews from Poland and Germany, among them many *haredim* who adhered to Agudat Israel, found in Zionist Eretz Israel a safe haven and economic opportunity. If Agudat Israel had at any time held an option for contracting an alliance with Palestinian nationalists, this was no longer possible in view of the great changes in the status of Zionist Palestine, which became a refuge for masses of persecuted Jews in Europe. This situation led to a split in the ranks of Agudat Israel in Palestine, for the extremist Neturei Karta could not resign themselves to seeing their movement become involved—in practice, if not in theory—in Zionist politics. It is very characteristic of the split that when Neturei Karta so sharply opposed Kofer Ha'Yishuv—which, as noted, symbolized for its members the very essence of secular Zionism—Agudat Israel remained almost completely silent. Neturei Karta was but a small, marginal group that did not even raise much support among its former colleagues in Agudat Israel and whose protests provided no alternative to Zionist policy.

It is not as if Neturei Karta's ideology was pacifist from the very outset. What they argued was that had the Zionists not striven to become "like all the nations," the Arabs would not have mounted attacks on Jews in Palestine, just as the Germans would not have become radical anti-Semites. Had the Jews been faithful to their ancestral traditions, masses of their brethren in Europe and in Palestine would not be in such a great danger, one that obligated them to take up arms. However, as Neturei Karta's struggle against the Zionists unfolded, and perhaps under the influence of popular pacifist ideas that were current on the eve of World War II, its members raised nonviolence to the level of a Jewish matter of principle. Such concepts took shape during World War II and later against the backdrop of Israel's War of Independence in 1948. With this in mind, we should read what Amram Blau wrote on the eve of the War of Independence in 1947:

> And after the destruction of the Temple and the exile of the People of Israel from its land, and after the Lord, Blessed be He, charged Israel not to rebel against the nations, there was no longer any possibility that Israel would have resort to the sword, to cruelty and to bloodshed, God forbid. And it is two thousand years since Israel has returned its sword to the scabbard and has passed all the years of its exile in a different manner, one of submission and peace. Pliantly it has faced all troubles and difficulties, and has greatly distanced itself from any sense of cruelty, not to mention murder and bloodshed. It has displayed a good and gentle spirit in its relations with the nations in whose lands it lives in exile. This pureness and innocence has been the glory of Israel in the eyes of the nations. And now there are some, who take the name of Israel, that have begun to resort to bloody hands, to turn the name of Israel known for its measure of compassion into one associated with murder and bloodshed, God forbid, to garb the People of Israel in clothing stained with blood. Even from the blood of their brethren they do not abstain, God forbid. (*Ha'Homa* [The Wall], Neturei Karta journal, Kislev, December 1947)

At the same time and for the same reasons, Rabbi Joseph Eliahu Henkin, the director of a Jewish charitable organization by the name of Ezrat Torah, was making similar statements in the United States. Henkin was an outstanding Torah scholar who was wont to express his views on current events in Jewish periodicals. He presented the principles that lay behind his religious historiographical outlook:

> The Lord, Blessed be He, has found no instrument more fortuitous for Israel than peace, not just among themselves but also with the nations of the world, even though they oppress Israel. Blessed be He who has made us different from those who are mistaken, and for the Jew who observes the

Law, war is abhorrent and hated;"lest he kill" bothers him more than "lest he be killed." *It is preferable that they be oppressed and place their trust in God, they should not war against, nor oppress, nor even rejoice in the fall of the wicked. That is the behavior that brings blessing to Israel and should Israel stray from it, they will be punished.* Thus was it in the days of Zedekiah, and also in the time of the second destruction [of the Temple] and the other generations, ours included. *And every Jew who is imbued with the true spirit of Judaism, as we were taught by the sages of blessed memory, let him flee from those who wage war, from them and their masses and thus will we rescue the surviving remnant* [of European Jewry]. (Henkin 1981, 93–94, emphasis added)

Though Henkin was not a religious authority of the first rank, it is almost certain that members of Neturei Karta read what he wrote. It may very well be that Henkin influenced Neturei Karta, and the opposite may also be true. What is important for the present discussion is to stress the logic common to radical anti-Zionism and to Jewish *haredi* pacifism.

When Great Britain referred the Palestine question to the United Nations (UN), both Agudat Israel and Neturei Karta became steadfast opponents of the idea of establishing a Jewish state. For both, such a solution posed "a great danger"—not the peril of Arab opposition, but the danger of a state controlled by the socialist, secular Zionists, a condition, like in the Soviet Union, that would not enable the *haredim* to preserve their religious traditionalist lifestyle. But whereas Agudat Israel could not afford to come out publicly against the United Nations Special Committee on Palestine (UNSCOP) recommendations to partition Palestine and to establish a Jewish state in part of the country, members of Neturei Karta had no compunctions about saying what was on their minds.

After the UN General Assembly resolution on partition, adopted on November 29, 1947, some among the Agudat Israel leadership referred to that event using the phrase *et-pekida* (meaning that the resolution is a clear "sign of remembrance"), language that is intimately connected to the coming of the Messiah, although the overwhelming majority of that movement's adherents were almost in full sympathy with the majority of the Yishuv. After the declaration of independence (May 1948), Agudat Israel completely abandoned its policy of isolating itself from the Zionists and the Yishuv institutions. It joined the Provisional State Council, and two of its leaders, Yitzhak Meir Levin and David Loewenstein, signed the Declaration of Independence. Furthermore, most members of Agudat Israel's youth movement, Zeirei Agudat Israel, joined the armed forces. For one of the youth movement's ideologues, Moshe Sheinfeld, service in the army was an indispensable condition that would enable young *haredim* to face up to the coming struggle over the character of the young state. In the very midst of the fighting in the War of Independence, he wrote:

> We acquired our right to the Land of Israel by the agony of our love for it, by our bond to the land through the observance of those commandments that can only be executed in the Land of Israel, *and through the pact sealed in blood that the hundreds of our members at the front are contracting anew with it every day.* God willing, our members will return from the war *standing upright, having ridden themselves of the inferiority complex that haredi Jews often suffer from.* [*They shall return*] *conscious of the fact that they have sacrificed everything for the country and the Yishuv,* and even after the physical conflict ends, they shall remain on duty as brigades fighting the war of the spirit, the war of our God and his Torah. (Sheinfeld 1948, emphasis added)

As for members of Neturei Karta, they viewed the outcome of the war as the victory of Satan. "We believe," wrote Amram Blau in reaction to the atmosphere of religious exuberance among the adherents of Agudat Israel, "that Redemption will not come to the People of Israel through might and force, and not by the good will of the nations. The People of Israel has [*sic*]no need of Redemption that stems from the secular claim that the House of Israel is a nation like all the nations" (Blau 1948). On April 8, 1948, during the war and when Jewish Jerusalem was still under siege, members of Neturei Karta mounted a demonstration that staunchly voiced its opposition to the call for the establishment of a Jewish state and demanded of the British Mandate authorities—then still in Jerusalem—that they not be subordinated to a Zionist government. They openly preferred an Arab regime to a Jewish Zionist one. "We do not recognize the rule of uprooters of the Torah and heretics, we are not bound by their authority, we do not obey their government, and their laws and ordinances do not obligate us," they sang in their anthem (printed on the first page of their periodical *Ha'Homa*).

The declaration of Israel's independence on May 14, 1948, involved both a conceptual and a practical transformation for the anti-Zionist *haredim,* those who for theological reasons had opposed the establishment of a Jewish state as a matter of principle. From the very outset, Agudat Israel, fearing that Israel would adopt a worse attitude toward religion and observant Jews than the Soviet Union, tried to reach an agreement with Prime Minister David Ben-Gurion and his colleagues that would guarantee their minimal rights to their own way of life. Even more, as already noted, they joined the Provisional State Council and later became part of the first government coalition.

It would seem, however, that the great fear of secular Zionism among many Agudat Israel leaders—especially the Torah sages, who believed that the real objective of Zionism was to uproot religious belief—was not characteristic of the rank-and-file members of this movement. At this point, the overwhelming majority of them were partner to the Zionist hope that the vision of a Jewish state would become a reality and received the establishment of the state with joy and enthusiasm. Agudat Israel's leaders were well aware of this state of affairs. They realized that their intention to oppose the establishment of a state and even to do so publicly was largely an empty threat. Members of Agudat Israel's Council of Torah Sages refused to convene and express their opinion on the establishment of a Jewish state. Even the most extreme among them cautioned the movement's political leaders against publicly opposing the establishment of a Jewish-Zionist state. The political leaders, for their part, well knew that should they oppose the establishment of the state and boycott its institutions, there would be a mass defection of members from the movement, which would then become an insignificant factor in Jewish society in Israel and in the Diaspora as well. Difficult as it was for them to admit, their fate was intimately bound up with Zionism and their future with the State of Israel. They had no other option (Friedman 1995, 51–82).

Within a few years, the *haredi* leadership of Agudat Israel realized not only that the Zionist State of Israel did not persecute observant Jews but that, on the contrary, it was providing them with the best opportunity to undo the destruction the Holocaust had wreaked on them, though they found it difficult to admit as much in public. After the firm establishment of the welfare state, once the status quo in religious matters and state funding of the independent *haredi* educational system were ensured, and with the exemption of yeshiva students from military service, the *haredim* could now turn all their efforts to reshaping themselves into a society of scholars that would not only ensure their existence but open the way to the flowering of a *haredi* society to an extent and level unprecedented in Jewish history. All this was happening precisely in a Zionist, Western, and to a large extent secular state (Friedman 1991). We shall return to the significance of this development.

But from the viewpoint of Neturei Karta, this story was completely different. There was no justification whatsoever for the establishment of a Jewish state, and the fact that they were living within that framework was a painful contradiction for which a priori it would be difficult to provide a remedy. The members of Neturei Karta were certain that the "heretic Zionist regime" would not allow people to live their lives as religious Jews. The fact that not only did their catastrophic vision not come true but that, to a large degree, the very opposite happened was for Neturei Karta a dilemma to which it could find no solution.

When the War of Independence came to an end, the division of Jerusalem into a western part under Israeli rule and an eastern sector under Jordanian control seemed to present Neturei Karta with a so-called Arab option—to move to east Jerusalem. Such a step would not only relieve them of the onus of having to live under a heretic Zionist regime, but also lend support to the *haredi* claim that the Zionists were guilty of undermining relations with the Arab world and responsible for the death of thousands of Jews and for endangering the lives of others. Moving to east Jerusalem would have another advantage as well: proximity to the Western Wall, Rachel's Tomb in Bethlehem, and Hebron, the city of the patriarchs.

And indeed, during the early years of the state, which were also years of sharp conflict between the state and Neturei Karta, and against the backdrop of attempts to conscript its members for military service, the idea of moving to east Jerusalem was broached from time to time. One of Neturei Karta's leading members, Arieh (Leibale) Weisfish (then referred to as its "foreign minister"), visited the UN General Assembly in New York and also traveled to Amman to try to implement the idea. Some time later, during one of the clashes with the police, Amram Blau openly raised the possibility of requesting permission from the Jordanian authorities to settle down in east Jerusalem.

In the final count, this idea remained a dream toward whose implementation no real effort was made. Perhaps it was the Jordanians who were not interested. At any rate, from the point of view of the Arabs, such a step could have provided them with advantageous propaganda whose far-reaching implications are even difficult to imagine. It is our opinion, however, that even had there been a real opportunity for the Neturei Karta to cross over into Jordanian territory, the overwhelming majority of its members would not have taken advantage of it. An analysis of the reasons for this can show us why the Arab option was so weak in anti-Zionist *haredi* policy, particularly after the establishment of Israel:

1. Like the majority of the *haredim,* most members of Neturei Karta spend their time primarily in Torah study and are financially supported by Jews living in the Diaspora. Many of the donors are religious Jews who hold Torah study in esteem, but are not necessarily supporters of militant anti-Zionism, especially that which could well serve Arab propaganda. Such a blunt violation of Jewish solidarity, especially so soon after the Holocaust, would have given rise to extreme opposition to Neturei Karta, even—perhaps primarily—among other *haredim,* and would also have been censured by Torah sages.

2. Although Neturei Karta members were quite well known, they were not a group completely isolated from *haredi* society, to which they were connected by many and complex ties, from economic relations to family connections. Moving to east Jerusalem would of necessity have severed these connections, a condition that Neturei Karta would have been unable to bear.

3. Although Neturei Karta members try to convince outsiders that they completely segregate themselves from Israeli society and its economy, they are linked to them in one way or another (e.g., through medical services on a high, Western level or through a standard of living higher than that of east Jerusalem). Furthermore, in Israel, the Neturei Karta live on the fringe of *haredi* society and thus can avail themselves, for instance, of high-level *haredi*

educational systems and of high-level Kosher food services financed by the developing economy of the State of Israel.

4. Despite ideal descriptions of life among the Arabs before the advent of Zionist settlement to Palestine, even Neturei Karta members would have found it difficult to place absolute trust in their Arab neighbors. The massacres in Hebron and Safed of 1929 were still fresh in their minds. Most of the residents of those two cities had not been Zionists and were murdered simply because they were Jewish.

It did not take long for the Israeli authorities to understand that it made little sense to clash heads-on continuously with the Neturei Karta and that on matters of principle it was best to leave them alone and not turn them into martyrs. Thus, they exempted Neturei Karta members, practically if not formally, from military service and refrained from other acts that could be construed as deliberate provocation. Though clashes between the Neturei Karta and the police and other government agencies continued, they never reached the level that would have made life for the Neturei Karta insufferable. On the contrary, they lived and continue to live quite comfortably in their own neighborhoods, especially Meah Shearim in Jerusalem. In sum, not only did they not have the opportunity to move to Jordanian-controlled Jerusalem, they also had no reason to do so.

The Six Day War of June 1967 fundamentally changed the geopolitical status of Israel. It also added another dimension to the relations between *haredi* society and the state. The sense of isolation that preceded the war, the seemingly miraculous victory over Egypt, Jordan, and Syria, and the return to the historical borders of the Land of Israel, to the Western Wall, Rachel's Tomb, and the Tombs of the Patriarchs in Hebron—all these were for *haredi* society events having more religious than political significance. The majority of *haredim* could only explain these developments as miraculous divine intervention in the course of history. Some among them believed the victory to be one stage in the process of messianic redemption, but even those who did not go so far were now forced to view the Jewish state in a different light. For them, the fact that Israel stood alone "facing the entire world," when it seemed that even "friends" par excellence, such as France and the United States, had abandoned it, was no less significant than the great victory itself. This sense of isolation seemingly pushed the Jewish state, which had wanted to be like all the nations, back toward Jewish history, in which the Jewish people had always stood alone and only the Lord "saved us from their [the enemies'] hands" (Passover ritual recitation). From the *haredi* point of view, then, the victorious outcome of the Six Day War was not a victory of the Zionist state, but of the Jewish people, "a people that shall dwell alone" (see Friedman 1989).

The political turnover of May 1977, when Menachem Begin became prime minister, is an even more important milestone for the present discussion. The *haredim* have always considered the left—as personified in Israeli politics by Mapai, later the Israel Labor Party—as the utmost expression of secular Zionism, of "Israelism" as compared to historic "Judaism." They have always conceived of Begin, on the other hand, as being more a Jew than an Israeli, or, as I was once told by one *haredi* leader, as the first "Jewish" prime minister of the "Jewish" state. No doubt, such sentiments influenced Agudat Israel's decision to join Begin's cabinet, something that they had refrained from doing since the early 1950s. The euphoria that captivated *haredi* society after Begin's election victory was a source of concern to some important rabbinical authorities, who feared that yeshiva students would identify with the "Zionist state." Rabbi Eliezer Menachem Schach, head of the most important yeshiva in Israel, the Panevezys Yeshiva, warned against such a transformation of *haredi* values:

And know you, my friend, *you should not think that now that there has been a changing of the guard and there is a new regime, that things have changed.* It is not so, my brother. The foundation is the same. The state is secular, with laws that are foreign to us, and based on "my power and the might of my hand" (Deut. 8:17). Most of the elected representatives of the people are far from observance of the Torah and fulfillment of its commandments. "And thou trustest in the staff of this broken reed" (Isa. 36:6), which is today the United States, or any other state that looks upon the State of Israel with a smiling face. But deep within their souls, they all are foes of Jacob, for it is a rule that "Esau is a foe of Jacob" . . . and the smile of any specific president is meaningless, for tomorrow he will smile at others, and we have no one to fall back upon except for our Father in Heaven and Redemption will not come by means of this state or another and not by means of this prime minister or another. . . .

Of course, we should lend more support to those who at least seem to
be more agreeable towards us, even though the danger still lurks there.
This is my considered opinion and that of my colleagues. (Schach 1988,
Letter 13 Av 5737 [August 1977], 6–8)

In these sentences, one meets with all the complexity of the official
Agudat Israel position, which is at one and the same time anti-Zionist, yet
can be termed patriotically Jewish, and which contains a dominant "anti-
Gentile" element. To fill in the picture, it should be noted that at the beginning of the letter quoted above, Rabbi Schach expresses his apprehension of
peace between Israel and the neighboring Arab states. He is very worried
lest such peace lead to a rapprochement between Arabs and Jews, and that
Arab students would enroll in Israeli universities (or the opposite, that Jews
would enroll in Arab universities), and as a result assimilation between Jews
and Gentiles would increase.

But the warning sounded by Rabbi Schach went unheeded. In the wake
of Agudat Israel's joining the coalition government came momentous trans-
formations in the political structure of *haredi* society and in the involvement
of its members in Israeli politics. As mentioned above, until the 1980s, Agudat Israel represented the major political stance of *haredi* society, one that was
willing to recognize—at least de facto, if not de jure—the State of Israel and
to participate in its political life. Membership in Menachem Begin's coalition government substantially increased government allocations for the
haredi Society of Scholars. Controversy over how to divide these allocations
led to the splitting up of Agudat Israel into three competing parties (Agudat
Israel, Degel ha-Torah, and Shas), which represent the various particularistic
tendencies that have developed in traditional Jewish society. As a result, the
power of the central institution of rabbinical leadership, the Council of
Torah Sages, has declined, which has in turn left its mark on the balance of
power within *haredi* society. The rabbinical and political leadership is increasingly finding it difficult to challenge trends in *haredi* public opinion.

Of the three parties, Agudat Israel is comprised primarily of various Hasidic groups who perpetuate Hasidic traditions that had their origins in
Poland and the Ukraine in the second half of the eighteenth century. Degel
ha-Torah represents the Jewish cultural milieu that opposed early Hasidim

(which explains the appellation *mitnagdim*—"opponent of Hasidim"—that was applied to its adherents). The third sector of *haredi* society—traditional Oriental Jewry that came to Israel from Islamic countries after the establishment of the state—is represented by the Shas Party (see Friedman 1991, 175–85).

The relevant question for our discussion is whether the analysis conducted above applies also to Shas, today the third largest party in the Israeli Parliament (Knesset)—17 out of a total 120 members—and a senior partner in the coalition government.

Shas emerged when Oriental Jews who identified with the Agudat Israel movement sensed that they were being discriminated against by the traditional Ashkenazi leadership that controlled the movement. In the 1984 elections, the first in which Shas ran for the Knesset, it managed to have four members elected, almost as many as the number of seats previously held by Agudat Israel when it represented all *haredi* groups, including some Oriental Jews who identified with it. Obviously, Shas had received the votes of many Oriental Jews who in the past had not voted for Agudat Israel, and it was the first time that a *haredi* political party broke out of the narrow confines of *haredi* society and succeeded in gaining the support of persons who in the past had voted for non*haredi* parties, including some nonreligious parties. This tendency has been growing constantly. Today, when Shas's parliamentary representation has increased more than fourfold since 1984, it is obvious that the vast majority of its supporters are not *haredim* in the accepted connotation of that term. It is very difficult to draw a religious profile of Shas voters. What we can say with certainty is that the majority of them are more traditionalist than *haredi*. Shas is a movement whose leadership is *haredi* and most of whose supporters are Oriental Jews who sense that the dominant element in Israeli society to some extent or another rejects their particularistic, Oriental identity.

Because the cultural-religious roots of Shas's voting public lie in the Jewish culture that developed in Muslim countries within a relatively tolerant Arab cultural milieu, especially when compared with a Christian society, it would be reasonable to assume that Shas would adopt a stance totally different from that of the other *haredi* parties (Agudat Israel and Degel ha-Torah) and that Shas's voters would be more enthusiastic supporters of the efforts to achieve peace between Israel and the Palestinians and the Arab states. But that is not the case. They clearly tend to support hawkish, right-wing opinions, and the majority vote for Likud candidates for prime minister.

There are those who claim that the Shas voters' support for the Likud candidates is not a result of their agreement with the Likud's hawkish stance, but is rather related to the fact that the vast majority of them belong to the lower classes, whereas the Labor Party—the Likud's opponent—is generally identified with the upper classes, most of whom are of Ashkenazi origin. I disagree. Undoubtedly, the equation of the Labor Party with the well-to-do, Ashkenazi social classes did influence and continues to influence the voting patterns of Shas supporters. However, most Shas voters hold hawkish, right-wing opinions because of their direct attachment to the Jewish ethnic tradition. In this aspect, their worldview does not greatly differ from that of the Ashkenazi *haredim,* who also are influenced by their direct relationship to the Jewish ethnic tradition as well as by the historic fate of the Jews who were destined to live as a religious minority under Gentile rule and under the yoke of a hostile religion.

The policy of Shas's spiritual leader, Rabbi Ovadiah Yosef, should be evaluated in this context. Although Rabbi Yosef—who during the early years of Israeli statehood was the spiritual leader of the Jewish community in Alexandria, Egypt—does at times adopt more dovish stances than do his followers, it would be a mistake to see in him a person who identifies with left-wing concepts. Some Ashkenazi *haredi* rabbis (the most outstanding among them being Rabbi Eliezer Menachem Schach) also adopted seemingly dovish stances. However, as I have noted elsewhere (Friedman 1989, 165–215), these stances are the result of what I term a Jewish patriotism that has a religious-ethnic point of departure and that embodies hatred of and lack of confidence in Gentiles—whether they be Muslims or Christians.

The *haredi* rank and file have exhibited a growing tendency to identify with right-wing parties, at times even with extreme rightist opinions that reject the Oslo Accord and absolutely oppose any policy of compromise with the Palestinian Arabs. This tendency could be clearly observed in the 1996 elections to the Knesset and to the office of prime minister. The rightist stance of the *haredi* public, in fact, forced the Council of Torah Sages (including Rabbi Schach) to abandon their neutral stance and to support openly Benjamin Netanyahu, leader of the right-wing Likud Party. Many polls showed that the *haredi* public holds extreme rightist opinions (see Ilan 1998). As a whole, it has no confidence in the Arabs: 86 percent do not believe that the Arabs truly seek peace, as compared with 54 percent of national-religious Jews. Furthermore, 70 percent of the *haredim* think that Arab Knesset members should not be allowed to vote in the Knesset on motions concerning the future of the "liberated areas" in the West Bank and Gaza, whereas only 9 percent expressed their support of the Oslo Accords.

Because of these developments, Neturei Karta has become a minute minority, estranged from *haredi* society as a whole. True, some of its members openly support the demands of the Palestinian Authority, and Rabbi Moshe Hirsch, the contemporary so-called foreign minister of Neturei Karta, was appointed by Yasir Arafat as a minister in the Palestinian Authority's cabinet. Not only is there no support for this policy in wider *haredi* society, but it meets with open hostility. Neturei Karta posters pasted on billboards and walls in *haredi* neighborhoods are quickly ripped off. There is no better indication than this of the lack of *haredi* support for such anti-Zionist and pro-Palestinian policy.

Furthermore, economic distress and the growing dependence of *haredim* on government welfare allocations have led many younger *haredi* families to move to the new *haredi* cities being built across the so-called Green Line, in the territories conquered in 1967 (Emmanuel, Upper Betar, and Upper Modi'in), because housing is much less expensive there. Thus, in addition to ideological-patriotic sentiments, the *haredim* now have an economic interest in supporting a policy that rejects making any concessions to the Palestinian Arabs and for a common front with the extreme national-religious movement Gush Emunim.

Taking all of this into account, it is not surprising that there was no contact whatsoever between *haredi* rabbis and the mufti of Jerusalem or other Arab leaders before 1948. After 1967, too, there was no contact between *haredi* rabbis and Muslim religious leaders over the question of modest dress and other issues. To this day, it is very difficult to bring together *haredi* rabbis and Muslim religious personalities. Both sides are not willing and not interested. The reason lies more in the sphere of religion than in that of nationalism.

If the Muslims participate in municipal elections, would they cooperate with the *haredim?* There are some who claim that they would, but I do not agree. The only group of *haredim* willing to cooperate with Muslim religious leaders is the small faction of Neturei Karta, but they are today—as indicated—an insignificant minority even among the *haredi* society.

Conclusion

Jewish-Zionist settlement in Palestine was from the outset opposed by both Arab nationalist and anti-Zionist *haredi* circles, but an alliance between Arab nationalism and *haredi* anti-Zionism did not stand a chance. As the Zionist-Jewish "national home" gained in strength and the status of the Jewish Diaspora in Europe was simultaneously declining, and as Palestine became almost the sole haven for those Jews, the anti-Zionist *haredim* turned into a small minority that had to change its policy to suit that of the Zionists. Neturei Karta, a group within *haredi* society that developed in the 1930s was no more than a protest group that public opinion increasingly viewed as being completely irrelevant in light of the Holocaust and the establishment of the State of Israel (1948). The Six Day War (1967) and Menachem Begin's election victory (1977) brought in their wake fundamental changes in the structure of political power within *haredi* society, which was now divided among three political parties—Agudat Israel, Degel ha-Torah, and Shas. The status of the Council of Torah Sages was weakened as the *haredi* rank and file increasingly and more openly expressed Jewish nationalist sentiments. In the 1990s, the *haredim* were already on the far right of Israeli politics. Neturei Karta positions were now held only by small fringe groups of *haredim* lacking almost any influence in Israeli *haredi* society. Even if the *haredim* have not been converted into Zionists, they have become ever more nationalist in outlook, placing themselves firmly in the right wing of Israeli politics in all that concerns a peace accord with the Arabs entailing concession of parts of the historical territory of the Land of Israel.

Only if and after an agreement with the Palestinians is reached and ratified by the Knesset can we expect some cooperation between the *haredim* and Muslim religious leaders on mutual problems. But as the situation appears now, the mutual animosity is even increasing. In February 2000, huge posters were pasted on the walls of the *haredi* ghetto in Jerusalem opposing the transfer of areas that border on *haredi* housing projects to the Palestinian Authority. The remembrance of the 1929 massacre in Hebron and Safed and the ethnic-religious fear of Gentiles are still very much alive among the *haredim*, more than in any other faction in Israeli society.

9

A New Status for Jerusalem?

An Eastern Orthodox Viewpoint

Charalambos K. Papastathis

The religious aspect of the status of Jerusalem is directly connected with the status of the Holy Land, although these two questions appear on the face to differ in nature. In this chapter, I examine these questions from an Eastern Orthodox viewpoint.

Status of Jerusalem

The status of Jerusalem was established de jure by the General Assembly of the United Nations (UN). Resolutions 181(II) (1947), 194(III) (1948), and 303 (1949) determine that the city of Jerusalem and its vicinity will constitute a *corpus separatum* under a special international regime and shall be administered by the UN (see Lapidoth and Hirsch 1994b, 6–10, 30–32, 85–86; see also Zander 1971). Today's de facto situation was established after the Israeli troops entered the city in 1967 and by the July 30, 1980, unilateral proclamation of Jerusalem as capital of the State of Israel (see Quigley 1991, 145, 150–53; Keegan 1992, 1; see also Lapidoth and Hirsch 1994b, 322–23). This de facto situation has not yet been officially recognized by the interna-

An earlier version of this article appeared in 45 Catholic Law Review 723 (1996) and is reprinted with permission.

tional community; thus, de jure, it still remains that of the *corpus separatum,* which is precisely why the heads of foreign diplomatic delegations to Israel are in Tel Aviv, not in Jerusalem. The *corpus separatum* (i.e., the international status of Jerusalem) is not acceptable to either party, Arab or Israeli alike.

The Palestinian party considers Jerusalem as part of the Occupied Territories (at present self-governed), with a view to making it the future capital of the Palestinians. The Israeli-Palestinian Declaration of Principles, of September 13, 1993, mentions that discussions on the status of Jerusalem were to start no later than May 1996 ("Declaration" 1993, 1525, 1529; see also "Israeli-Palestinian Interim Agreement" 1995). Reality shows that Jerusalem's status is a bilateral question, whose solution belongs to the Israelis and the Palestinians.

Status of the Holy Land

On the contrary, the status of the Holy Places is not connected to the exercise of territorial sovereignty, but to the exercise of certain religious rights on the territory of the Holy Land by certain religions—more precisely, as far as the Christian faith is concerned, by the Eastern Orthodox, Roman Catholic, and Armenian Churches. The exercise of these rights is independent of state sovereignty and is called the status quo. More specifically, it refers (1) to a determined territory, (2) to precise rights, and (3) to certain persons to whom these rights belong.

These concrete rights are determined by written and unwritten legal sources. They may be divided into three categories: rights related to the foundation of religious institutions in the Holy Land, rights referring to the cult, and rights connected to the shrines. On the other hand, the specific contents of these rights are determined in relation to the historical conditions, to the various religions and cults in the area, and to the local state authority. In these rights, all Christian Orthodox peoples focus their interest in the Holy Land and, by extension, in the regime of Jerusalem.

Historical Perspective

In early antiquity, Palestine had attracted the interest of the Greeks, who founded several colonies on its coast. The Philistines, a people of Cretan origin—according to the prevailing view—had settled there, Palestine being named after them. Alexander the Great conquered Palestine in 332 B.C.E. and after his death it came under the rule of the Greek dynasty of the Seleucids. Thus, Greek culture and language had been largely received and diffused all over the coast of the eastern Mediterranean and its extended hinterland. Greek rule lasted through the following three centuries, until the Roman conquest, in 63 B.C.E. Nevertheless, Greek civilization outlived the conquest; moreover, from 312 C.E. to 634, Palestine was attributed to the new Roman Empire of the Greek nation, commonly known as Byzantium, as it was named by Western scholars in modern times (in the sixteenth and seventeenth centuries).

In the year 451 C.E., the Fourth Ecumenical Council of the one and only Christian Church promoted, with its seventh canon, the then-autocephalous Church of Jerusalem into a Patriarchate (see Mansi 1980). It was the fifth in chronological order and precedence, after the churches-Patriarchates of Rome, Constantinople, Alexandria, and Antioch. The Patriarchate of Jerusalem, as the other three of the East, has since its foundation followed the Greek typicon and language, before and after the great schism of 1054. This same Patriarchate participated in the pentarchy of the Patriarchates—that is, it was the only canonical church in Palestine, as concerns both doctrine and administration, and together with the other churches mentioned above constituted the One Holy Catholic and Apostolic Church of the Universe. In spite of the great schism between Rome and the East in 1054 and in spite of the presence of other churches in Jordan and Israel, the Orthodox Patriarchate of Jerusalem has uninterruptedly remained in the area as the canonical church par excellence, a fact evidenced also by its precedence to the other churches in the formal etiquette.

The Orthodox Patriarchate of Jerusalem, as the only canonical local church, was the owner and protector of the shrines in the Holy Land before the schism. After the Crusades—which were not launched only against the Muslims, but against the Orthodox Christians as well—the majority of and the most important shrines remained under the Patriarchate's jurisdiction. Its rights concerning the foundations, the cult, and the shrines are based on various sources. Chronologically arranged, these sources include:

1. The edict of Khalif Umar Ibn al-Khatab in 636, granted to Sophro-

nius, "Patriarch of the imperial nation." This edict recognized, among other things, the ownership of the shrines—as, for instance, the Church of the Resurrection and the Church and the cave of the Nativity in Bethlehem. It provided that "our subjects the monks and priests and their churches and monasteries, and everything under their ownership, and other shrines situated within or outside Jerusalem shall be assured and the Patriarch shall be their head" (Moschopoulos 1948, 20; see also *Official Documents* 1944, 25–27; *Refutation* 1937, 51–52; Gaganiaras 1986, 145–309). Moreover, all Christian pilgrims, regardless of their country of origin and denomination—Armenians, Monophysites, and so on—would come under the jurisdiction of the Patriarchate (Moschopoulos 1948, 20, 26).

2. The *Hatt-i-Serif* of Sultan Mehmed II, the conqueror of Constantinople, issued in 1458 to the patriarch of Jerusalem Athanassios, confirmed the edict of 636 of Khalif Umar Ibn al-Khatab (Moschopoulos 1948, 27–29).

3. The *firman* (edict) of Sultan Selim, in 1517, issued to the patriarch of Jerusalem Dorotheos, provided that he should "have jurisdiction over . . . the shrines and inherit the deceased Metropolitans, Bishops and Monks" (Miliaras 1933, 3–5).

4. An edict of Sultan Suleiman the Magnificent, issued to the Patriarch Germanos, in 1538, recognized the patriarch's jurisdiction over the shrines (Miliaras 1933, 12–15).[1]

5. The order of Sultan Murad IV, in 1634, by which the keys to the shrines were to be handed over to the "Patriarch of the Romaioi [Greeks] and to the monks in Jerusalem and to their authority" (Miliaras 1933, 71–72).[2]

6. The *Hatt-i-Serif* of Sultan Murad IV, in 1731, provided that "the said places etc., and the keys to the two doors now in the hands of the monk and Patriarch of the Brotherhood of the Romans and of those who will succeed

1. At the time of Patriarch Germanos, the sultan recognized a host of other rights in favor of the Patriarchate, including the right to repair the bell tower of the Church of the Resurrection (in 1345) and even the church itself (in 1546).

2. In the Arab and Turkish languages, *Rum,*—that is, *Romaeoi* (meaning Romans)—refers to the Orthodox Christians whose mother tongue is Greek (see Moschopoulos 1948, 63–68).

him as Patriarchs, we have already recognized as theirs and they shall possess them" (see *Refutation* 1937, 53).

7. The order of Sultan Osman III, in 1757, repeated the text of the above grant because of disputes that arose between the Greeks and the Latins (Miliaras 1933, 296–303).

8. In 1809, Sultan Mahmoud II was issued a *firman* that granted to the Orthodox Greeks the right to rebuild the Church of the Resurrection, which had burned down the previous year. The construction was completed the following year (Miliaras 1933, 342–43).

9. In 1852, the Ottoman government, in its effort to put an end to the Greek-Latin dispute over the shrines, issued a *firman* addressed to Hafiz Ahmed Pasha (Noradounghian 1900, 407–10; Moschopoulos 1948, 41–44). According to the *firman:*

> Les Latins n'ont pas raison de prétendre à la possession exclusive, ni de cette coupole [du Saint-Sépulcre], ni de la petite coupole [sur l'endroit appelé le Tombeau de Jésus], ni de la Hadjir Moughtésil, ni du Golgotha, ni des voûtes de Sainte-Marie, ni de la grande église de Bethléem, ni de la Sainte-Crèche; il faut laisser tous ces endroits dans leur état actuel. . . .
>
> Les Latins, se basant sur quelques Firmans dont ils sont en possession, ont élevé la prétention que le Tombeau de la Bienheureuse Marie leur appartient exclusivement, mais ils n'ont pas raison en cela non plus
>
> . . . [J]e ne trouve pas à propos que les sujets de mon Empire qui professent la religion grecque soient privés de la faculté de pratiquer leur religion dans l'intérieur de l'oratoire sus-mentionné. Ainsi, on n'empêchera pas aux Grecs d'exercer leur culte dans l'intérieur du Coubel-el-Mess-ad (la Coupole de l'Ascension) (Noradounghian 1900, 408–9).

This firman, as regards the Orthodox Greeks, confirmed the status quo as it existed *ab antiquo*.

After the Crimean War, according to the Peace Treaty of Paris (1856), Ottoman Turkey, Russia, and France undertook jointly to rebuild the Church of the Resurrection, without any claim of possession. In 1869, the church was handed over to Patriarch Cyril, and the right to clean its cupola acknowledged to the Patriarchate.

10. Jurisdiction over the shrines was again established in 1875, in the Statute of the Patriarchate of Jerusalem, which constituted a law of the Ottoman Empire. The relevant text, in the official French translation, is as follows: "Le Patriarche de Jérusalem est, séparément ou en commun avec d'autres rites, le gardien de toutes les reliques de son ressort, dans l'église (Kumame) de Jérusalem; il est également le chef des églises, monastères, métropolitains, évêques, clercs et prêtres relevant du siège patriarcal et á la direction des écoles et des hôpitaux qui en dépendent" (Article 1 et seq., in Young 1905–6, 2: 36–37).

11. In 1939, when Palestine was under British Mandate, the king of England, George VI, confirmed the election of the new patriarch, which ended thus: "We . . . confirm him [the patriarch] in the exercise of the said rights, powers, jurisdictions, privileges and immunities, which are by law appurtenant to the said office, or are by ancient custom or practice held and enjoyed in conjunction therewith" (qtd. in Moschopoulos 1948, 83–84).

In 1958, Law No. 27 was issued by the Kingdom of Jordan, by which the organization, the representation, and the management of the property of the "Rum" Orthodox Patriarchate of Jerusalem are governed (Tzortzatos 1972, 151–63). This law is implemented, in Jordan as well as in Israel, in those areas that came under Israeli rule after the Six Day War. The protection of the Holy Land and of free access to it is provided for in a law issued by the State of Israel in June 27, 1967 (see Lapidoth and Hirsch 1994b, 166–69). The statement of Minister Moshe Arens on the respect of the legal rights and privileges of the Patriarchates of April 23, 1990, followed (Peters 1990).

Current Status of the Orthodox Patriarchate

The status of the Orthodox Patriarchate of Jerusalem is *ab antiquo* recognized, respected, and sufficient. It is satisfactory to the Orthodox Christians and is respected by Jordan and Israel. There have been, of course, unpleasant incidents—as, for instance in 1992, when some individuals damaged objects in the interior of the Church of the Resurrection or when the followers of a Judaic denomination squatted in a guest house of the Patriarchate. Such isolated trivialities, though, do not disrupt or even endanger the status quo.

Other events, however, cause apprehension and worries to the Orthodox. Their fears originate from the policy of the Holy See with regard to the status of Jerusalem.

At the end of World War II, the Vatican was opposed to the creation of a Jewish state in Palestine. This policy was founded on the determination to protect Roman Catholic interests in the Holy Land (Ferrari and Broglio 1988, 574). As one Catholic author stresses, the Vatican's aversion to a "Jewish Home" did not mean that it favored Arab domination in the Holy Land. The fear that either Arab or Jewish domination would prejudice Catholic interest lay behind the Vatican's concern regarding Palestine's future. According to the Holy See, its interests would be better protected through a solution in which "neither Jews nor Arabs, but a Third Power, should have control in the Holy Land" (Perowne, cited in Ferrari and Broglio 1988, 574).

Twenty-three years later, in June 1967, the Vatican official spokesman, Mgr. Vallainc, stated that the only solution for the protection of Jerusalem and the surrounding sites was to place them under an international regime. This internationalization meant a separate territory, a *corpus separatum* (see Ferrari and Broglio 1988, 577–78).

As far as I know, since the end of 1967, the demand for a special, internationally guaranteed status has no longer been accompanied by a request for the internationalization of the city, as one may assume from an allocution by His Holiness Pope Paul VI in December 1967 (see Ferrari and Broglio 1988, 579).

The problem has been how to secure the sacred and universal character of Jerusalem by providing a special status, internationally guaranteed, regardless of which state would be exercising sovereignty over the Holy City. This framework is acceptable to all religions concerned, at least as a basis for further negotiations.

On December 30, 1993, the Fundamental Agreement between the Holy See and the State of Israel was signed (1993, 153). Under Article 4, the State of Israel affirmed its continuing commitment to maintain and respect the status quo in the Christian Holy Places to which it applied and the respective rights of the Christian communities thereunder (Orthodox, Roman Catholic, and Armenian). The Holy See affirmed the Catholic Church's continuing commitment to respect the status quo and the said rights ("Fundamental Agreement" 1993, 155). Article 12 of the Fundamental Agreement, however, stipulates that the Holy See and Israel will continue to negotiate for a solution to those questions agreed on in the agenda of July 15, 1992. This agreement between the Vatican and Israel caused justifiable anxiety among Orthodox Christians and non-Roman Catholics in general.

Recently, the Holy See maintained that the Fundamental Agreement renewed the status quo. Despite this welcome assurance, the agreement contains a provision of unknown terms, which sanctions secret diplomatic proceedings between the Vatican and Israel, not of course to the prejudice of the conferring parties.

Furthermore, press reports claim that the Israeli-Palestinian agreements provide that the responsibility for the Muslim shrines of Jerusalem is to be entrusted to Saudi Arabia and for Christian shrines to the Vatican. The secrecy that cloaks the terms agreed on by the Holy See, Israel, and Palestine is ominous. The Conference on Christianism and Judaism, held in Jerusalem in February 1994, is a plain indication of these groups' respective intentions. As an eminent metropolitan of the Church of Greece pointed out in the press, "Neither the Orthodox nor the Armenian Patriarchs of Jerusalem were invited to take part to the Conference. This very sad omission does not obstruct our understanding of several goodwill gestures of the Roman Catholic Church towards the Jewish people which were intended to 'wash out mistakes of the past,' as Rabbi Rosen put it" (Christodoulos 1994).

Moreover, various relevant texts and statements from the conference include numerous references to the three monotheistic religions—Jewish, Christian, and Muslim—that regard Jerusalem as a Holy City. Nonetheless, the term *Christian* is never defined. Are all denominations being favored or only the most powerful one?

Clergymen and monks have publicized these fears through the media in the Orthodox countries. Unfortunately, competent officials have offered no denials or expectations. The message of the heads of the Orthodox Churches given on September 9, 1995, at the celebration of the Revelation in the church of Patmos expressed this concern. The message emphasizes that the Orthodox Church does not meddle in politics but cannot remain indifferent to political decisions that affect its existence. It concludes:

We consider that such a case is the matter of the future of the Holy Land, of the holy shrines and the Community living therein, which concerns the whole of Orthodoxy and more specifically the Patriarchate in Jerusalem. Therefore, any discussion regarding changes of the Holy Land's *status quo,* which was established through the ages by means of international decisions and treaties, cannot and should not be made without the knowledge of and in the absence of the Orthodox Patriarchate of Jerusalem, which has been based there for centuries. *(Orthodox Herald* 1995, 6)

Furthermore, the psychological factor is instrumental in relations between the Orthodox East and Frankish West, and has emerged in various forms over the centuries. For example, the Orthodox Arabs and the Greeks recall that the Crusaders of the Fourth Crusade, while guests in Constantinople, captured the capital of the Christian Roman Empire and divided its territories and treasures among themselves.

Let us also not overlook the very unpleasant fact that quite often the shrines become a field of conflict between the followers of different religions and even between different confessions of the same religion. For example, in April 1997, during renovations of the el-Khanka Mosque, the Jerusalem Waqf (Muslim religious trust), adjacent to the Church of the Holy Sepulcher, broke a common wall and took over two nearby rooms belonging to the Greek Orthodox Patriarchate *(Jerusalem Post,* Apr. 13, 1997, 1). On April 18, 1998, during the Ceremony of the Holy Fire in the same church, a dispute took place between Armenian and Syrian Orthodox Christians over who has the right to display religious joy *(Jerusalem Post,* Apr. 18, 1998, 3). The proliferation of such conflicts will be a natural outcome of the subjection of Jerusalem to the intrareligious administration.

Enhancing the presence and jurisdiction of the various cults or of some of these cults de jure in Jerusalem might lead to severe conflict. A relatively small number of Christian Arabs inhabit the wider area of Jerusalem, living among Jews and Muslim Arabs. Numerically, the non–Arab Christian population is almost nonexistent, so the "people" element of establishing a new regime in Jerusalem is missing. Thus, on the one hand, Christians of all denominations wish to impose a new situation from the top. On the other hand, fundamentalism has experienced a significant revival in recent years, although it has not yet spread to Israel and Jordan.

There is no reason to stir up the emotions and beliefs associated with these movements, particularly because Arabs and Israelis alike consider Christians of Europe as total strangers to the area of Palestine. Any attempt to alter the status of Jerusalem would constitute interference in Arab-Israeli domestic affairs and, for that reason, would be provocative. Christians would face violent reactions that might extend beyond the Holy Land. Therefore, there is no reason to create a new cause of local and international conflict in an already agitated world. The lessons of Bosnia are instructive. The haste of some European state and religious powers to dismantle Yugoslavia brought us to the brink of international conflict. The three parties at war in Bosnia belonged to the same nation and spoke the same language, but they followed different religions. Doubtless, the status quo in Jerusalem has its flaws. Nevertheless, it also has one great merit: it works. Let it then become the starting point of cooperation between Christian churches, not the beginning of trouble for all parties concerned.

PART THREE

The Temple Mount

10

Jewish-Muslim Modus Vivendi at the Temple Mount/al-Haram al-Sharif Since 1967

Yitzhak Reiter

The distinctiveness of the Temple Mount/al-Haram al-Sharif lies in its sanctity for both Muslims and Jews, and in its potent symbolic role in the historic, national, and cultural heritage of the two peoples and of the two faiths (its importance in Christianity is expressed mainly among neoevangelist groups; see Ucko 1993).[1] Its emotional, religious, symbolic, and national-political significance for Jews and Muslims—as for Israelis, Palestinians, and Muslim states—renders the Temple Mount a crucial element in any attempt to reach a settlement in Jerusalem.

This chapter analyzes Jewish-Muslim coexistence pertaining to the administration of the Temple Mount/al-Haram al-Sharif with regard to the arrangements developed since the Israeli takeover of east Jerusalem in June 1967 (table 10.1).[2] The current situation is examined with reference to five

---

1. Two names of the contentious site are used interchangeably: *Temple Mount,* the name Jews use, and *al-Haram al-Sharif,* its name for Muslims. For convenience and because it is better known to the English-speaking reader, the term *Temple Mount* is used more frequently.

2. In describing the situation at the Temple Mount after 1967 in various spheres, I have used the term *arrangements* rather than *settlements.* The latter are matters agreed on by different sides, whereas the arrangements on the Temple Mount were imposed by the balance of forces between the sides and cannot be considered settlements. I use the term *settlements* in reference to the practical aspects of the agreement that the parties will eventually reach.

TABLE 10.1

Summary of the Situation on the Temple Mount Since 1967

Subject	Secondary Subject	Official Authority	Situation in Practice
1. Freedom of access/worship	Freedom of access	For all, subject to limitations of visiting hours.	Palestinians dictate visiting hours.
	Freedom of worship for Jews	Natural right exists according to court ruling.	Not implemented. Previously: modest nondemonstrative individual prayer by prior coordination.
2. Sovereignty	Abstract	Israel	Universally not recognized.
	Jurisdiction	Israeli	Jordanian jurisdiction vis-à-vis Waqf employees.
	Control	Palestinian	Israel controls Mahkama building and Mughrabi Gate; Palestinians control other gates and access and visiting arrangements as well as site's character by ability to activate masses.
	Flags	No flags of any kind flown.	Palestinians hoist flags in demonstrations.
3. Security and policing	Overall security responsibility	Israel	Israel maintains security.
	Preserving public order and fighting terrorism	Israel	Palestinians and extremist Jews foment disturbances.
	Policing	Israel	Unofficial assistance of Waqf guards.
	Protection	Israel and Waqf guards	Division of roles between police (walls and posterns) and Waqf guards (internal).

fields of dispute or agreement between the Jewish and Muslim sides: sovereignty and political control, freedom of access and worship, administration, security and policing, and preservation of the character of the site.

The main questions to be answered are: How did these arrangements

TABLE IO.I, *(cont.)*

Summary of the Situation on the Temple Mount Since 1967

Subject	Secondary Subject	Official Authority	Situation in Practice
4. Administration	General	Palestinians, subject to Jordan	Palestinians, subject to Jordan and Palestinian Authority.
	Entry arrangements	Coordinated	Palestinian veto on visiting hours; Israeli veto for security.
	VIP visits	Coordinated	Same veto powers.
	Entry fee	Not collected because of freedom of access	Non-Muslims pay to enter mosques.
	Nonreligious use	Forbidden	Palestinians conduct political demonstrations.
	Rules of behavior	Coordinated	Muslims decide norms.
5. Preservation of character and making changes (planning and building, antiquities)	Preservation of character	Waqf responsibility, according to Israeli law	Site's character generally preserved.
	Building and demolition	Israeli Planning and Building Law; Israeli Antiquities Law	Palestinians effect changes without permits.
	Archaeological examination	Subject to Israeli law and implemented by Israeli authorities	Palestinians disrupt digs to prevent danger to buildings at site and to block opening of exit passages from Western Wall tunnel.

develop? What mechanisms were introduced to achieve them? And can this modus vivendi serve as a basis for a future settlement of the Jerusalem issue? By defining the principal interests of both parties, Israeli Jews and Palestinian Muslims, I reach a conclusion about some necessary elements that might serve as a bridge between the disputed positions.

The Religiopolitical Conflict: Historical Background

Since the 1920s, the Temple Mount/al-Haram al-Sharif has been a crucial symbolic focus in the political dispute between two national movements, the Zionist and the Palestinian Arab, which are locked in a struggle for national rights to the same territory. It is a salient example of the close affinity and mutual nourishment that exist between a religious focal point and a political center (for more details, see Reiter 1997, 88ff.).

The religious and political connection with the Temple Mount developed in Judaism and with al-Haram al-Sharif in Islam in different periods and different circumstances. Throughout the lengthy period of Muslim rule, Jews, most of whom lived in exile outside Palestine, bore the status of a recognized religious community. As a minority community under the Ottoman *millet* system, the Jews' only request was to be allowed to perform the prescribed religious rituals and to administer the Western Wall, which was then a relatively small area. Lacking external political support, they obtained only a *firman* (edict or decree) in 1840 and a decision by the District Council in 1911 granting them limited rights at the Western Wall (Porath 1974, 258).

Until the end of the Ottoman period, the Temple Mount was completely Muslim in character. Jews were denied access to the site, and testimonies from the Ottoman period claim that they were forbidden even to look in its direction (Cohen and Simon-Pikali 1993, 93, 114, 117; for examples of the punitive measures that were taken against non-Muslims who entered the Temple Mount precinct, see Shor 1982. It was not until 1885 that the site was opened to high-ranking non-Muslim visitors: the crown prince of Belgium (who later became King Leopold II), the emperor of Austria, the Prince of Wales, and Sir Moses Montefiore (Shor 1982).

The British Mandate authorities, who ruled in Palestine following the collapse of the Ottoman Empire in World War I, opted to maintain the previous situation in which the Temple Mount was totally controlled by the Muslim religious establishment, and non-Muslims could not enter its grounds until 1928. Indeed, as a non-Muslim government, the mandate authorities restricted its enforcement of law and order on the Temple Mount. British police, including Muslim members of the force, did not enter the

Temple Mount precinct in order to apprehend fugitives who found refuge there (see Kupferschmidt 1987, 55; Reiter 1996, 197–99). In 1928, the Muslim Council began charging non-Muslims an entrance fee to the Temple Mount in order to raise funds for the restoration of al-Aqsa Mosque (Kupferschmidt 1987, 132–33; Reiter 1996, 197–99). A British Muslim-staffed police base was established on the Temple Mount in 1938 and occupied itself primarily with keeping order and ensuring that the site's prescribed rules of behavior were upheld. During the mandate period, then, the Temple Mount was administered as a "quasi-extraterritorial" area.

In the two decades of Jordanian rule in east Jerusalem (1948–67), the Temple Mount remained under exclusive Muslim control and was administered by the Waqf (Muslim religious trust) Department within the framework of Jordan's Ministry of Religious Endowments.

From a Jewish-religious point of view, the existence of Muslim houses of worship on the Temple Mount is considered a gross defilement. However, Jewish law prohibits access of Jews to the area where the Temple was situated. After 1967, the Israeli Chief Rabbinate adopted the position that the entire Temple Mount precinct was subject to the principle of "fear of the sanctuary" because of the impossibility of ascertaining the precise location of the ancient Temple.[3] A sign was posted at the entrance to the Temple Mount that is reserved for Jews, stating: "Religious law strictly forbids entry to the Temple Mount area because of its holiness." This ruling in fact was a political boost to the Muslims in their efforts to retain control of the Temple Mount after the Six Day War.[4]

At its most basic, the Israeli-Jewish polemical view is that the Muslim claim of Jerusalem's sanctity in Islam is a political position. This reasoning is based on the relatively late emergence of the claim. Muslims take a similar stand regarding the Jews' connection to al-Haram al-Sharif. Islam recognizes

3. For the rabbinical ruling on entering the Temple Mount, see *Temple Mount Faithful et al. v. Attorney General*, HCJ 4185/90, *Piskei Din* 47 (5) (1993): 221–28.

4. More recently, it has been suggested from within the Jewish religious establishment that the Chief Rabbinate's position on the Temple Mount should be revised. Increasing numbers believe that Jews should implement in practice their right of worship at the site (see Ramon, chapter 11, this volume).

its precursor religions and their prophets, but maintains that the Jews falsi-fied the sacred texts and strayed from the path of God. Consequently, Mus-lims are highly skeptical of the Jewish claim regarding the location of the Temple. The Jews' identification with the site is perceived to be essentially political, with the religious grounds having been invented later in order to reinforce it.

But the facts on the ground are also meaningful. Jews acknowledge the Muslims' lengthy control of the site and understand the symbolic value it has acquired in Muslim consciousness. This value indeed was a major factor in Israel's decision not to take over the administration of the site in 1967. Mus-lims, for their part, until October 2000 accepted practically the Jews' right of access to the Temple Mount.

Arrangements Since the Advent of Israeli Rule in 1967

The arrangements that came into effect after June 1967 are the product of the new political balance of power—rule by Israel—and of the Israeli gov-ernment's concern that the introduction of radical changes would stir up public opinion and incense the Muslim world. The major change under Is-raeli rule was that adherents of all faiths—Jews included—have been given access to the Temple Mount during visiting hours agreed on with the Is-lamic clerics of the Waqf.

Political Powers: Sovereignty and Control

Following the Six Day War, Israel applied its law and jurisdiction to east Jerusalem and still considers itself the sovereign power over all of Jerusalem, including the Temple Mount precinct. Nevertheless, the Israeli government has not drastically altered the pre-1967 situation at the site. In consideration of its sanctity to hundreds of millions of Muslim believers throughout the world, Prime Minister Levi Eshkol of Israel stated in June 1967 that the Temple Mount's administration would rest with Muslim clerics.

Neither the international community nor the Jordanians and the Pales-tinians have accepted Israel's unilateral application of its sovereignty. The latter view Israeli rule in east Jerusalem as foreign occupation under international law, hence as an ephemeral situation. It is the Arab world's perception of such "ephemerality" that allows Israel, together with the Palestinians and Jordanians, to maintain various arrangements involving the site's administration. The Palestinians and Jordanians' passive consent to a number of Israeli-imposed arrangements enables the Israeli government to claim that Israeli sovereignty exists on the Temple Mount. In fact, Israel has exercised its sovereignty in several areas: by expropriating the building known as al-Mahkama (al-Madrasa al-Tankiziyya), taking possession of the keys to and controlling the Mughrabi Gate, maintaining overall responsibility for security and public order without permitting immunity, limiting entry to the site for reasons of security and upholding public safety, coordinating entry arrangements and visiting hours, coordinating VIP visits, applying Israeli law to anyone committing an offense at the site, partially enforcing Israeli planning and building laws, ensuring the right of free access to the Temple Mount, and to some extent upholding the principle of Jews' natural right to freedom of worship there.

Control of the Temple Mount is in the hands of Palestinian Muslims. Since 1994, there has been dual administration of the site by the Palestinians and Jordanians. The Palestinian Authority appointed the head of the Supreme Islamic Authority to hold the religious endowments portfolio and also named a mufti in an effort to undercut the Jordan-appointed mufti. Officials appointed by Jordan (which continues to pay the salaries of the Waqf Directorate staff in Jerusalem) are local Palestinians, and they receive orders from the Palestinian Authority as well. Since 1994, the Palestinian Authority has unofficially and gradually been taking over the power to administer the site.

Israel does not consider the Temple Mount to be a Muslim "quasi-extraterritorial" area as it was during the British Mandate period, or an area that automatically confers immunity. The Palestinians' control of the Temple Mount and their ability to fire up masses of believers at politically sensitive events limits Israel's ability to exercise its sovereignty in various spheres. True, Israel can send in armed police officers and in theory has the power to impose its will at its discretion. Nevertheless, the Israeli authorities must exercise caution in every confrontation with the Palestinians, asking themselves whether it is worth imposing sovereignty in a particular instance if this show of force risks public safety or if it will put Israel on the defensive vis-à-vis measures liable to be taken by the international community and the Islamic countries.

Flags symbolizing sovereignty have not been flown on the Temple Mount since 1967, when Defense Minister Moshe Dayan ordered the removal of the Israeli flag, which had been hoisted above the Temple Mount immediately after its capture (Dayan 1978, 390). Palestinians have raised Palestine Liberation Organization (PLO) flags in political demonstrations on al-Haram al-Sharif and in a few cases have burned Israeli and U.S. flags there. The police did not intervene, citing considerations of public safety—i.e., fear that bloodshed would ensue (see, e.g., *Knesset Record* 21, Apr. 11, 1989, 1830–33).

Despite its sanctity, then, the Temple Mount has occasionally served as a venue for political demonstrations by Palestinians and in some cases by Israeli nationalists. From time to time, Jewish groups such as the Temple Mount Faithful and the Hai Vekayam movement try to hold demonstrations, marches, and prayers adjacent to the gates of the Temple Mount and to enter the site demonstratively. In the name of upholding the right of free access and worship, the police are forced to negotiate with such extremist groups, which the Muslim establishment interprets as Israeli government support for the groups' activities (interview by the author with the then director-general of the Waqf, Hassan Tahbub, 1989).

On particularly sensitive occasions and after receiving intelligence warnings about probable violence, the security forces have curtailed the right of access of non-Jerusalem Muslims to the Temple Mount. In one instance, when Israeli security forces collected the ID cards of Muslims entering the Temple Mount for prayer, the Muslims interpreted this action as another attempt by Israel to reinforce its rule of the site *(Haaretz,* July 10, 1988; interview with Hassan Tahbub,1989).

Following a serious incident in January 1988, when Muslims seized a security man who was dispersing demonstrators on al-Haram al-Sharif and spirited him into al-Aqsa Mosque, relieving him of his firearm and beating him vigorously, the mayor of Jerusalem met with the head of the Supreme Muslim Authority and reached an understanding (which the Palestinians did not publicly acknowledge), according to which the security forces would not enter the Temple Mount precinct on Fridays if no demonstrations were held, no flags were hoisted, and no stones were thrown. The unofficial understanding has remained in force apart from specific events that have temporarily frozen its application.

The violence that followed the opening of the exit to the Western Wall tunnel in early September 1996 furnished additional proof that Israeli sovereignty on the Temple Mount and at the other holy sites in the vicinity is limited: Israel cannot change the existing arrangements unilaterally without paying a steep political and security price.

Right of Access and Right of Worship

Israeli government policy, set shortly after the Six Day War, was that the Muslim authorities would determine the internal procedures on the Temple Mount and that Jews would be allowed to visit the site but not to pray there. In fact, the government decided to prevent Jews from praying on the Temple Mount in groups but did not adopt an explicit decision prohibiting Jewish prayer there as such. Nevertheless, nowadays even nondemonstrative prayer by individuals is prevented.

In June 1967, the site's administrators began to collect an entry fee from tourists and non-Muslims; Israelis had to pay half the amount charged to tourists. In reaction, the police seized the keys to the Mughrabi Gate and permitted Jews free entry through it because a fee contradicted the freedom of access to Holy Places mandated by law. The Waqf Directorate countered by setting up a ticket booth (formally to sell the *Guide to al-Haram al-Sharif*) inside the precinct. The result is that non-Muslims wishing to visit the Dome of the Rock and al-Aqsa Mosque must purchase a ticket, but may visit the open area free of charge (Benziman 1973, 134–36).[5]

A major change relating to the Temple Mount after the Six Day War was the Knesset's enactment of the Protection of the Holy Places Law

5. For the High Court of Justice stand on the collection of an entry fee to the Temple Mount, see *Shabtai Ben-Dov v. Religious Affairs Minister,* HCJ 223/67, *Piskei Din* 22 (1): 440–48.

(1967) guaranteeing free access to Holy Places (including the Temple Mount). Although the law does not mention freedom of worship, the Israeli Supreme Court has had occasion several times to explain that freedom of worship is a natural right implicit in freedom of religion and that freedom of access to the Holy Places is purposeless if it does not include freedom of worship.[6]

As noted, the Israeli Chief Rabbinate has placed signs at the Mughrabi Gate warning that "Religious law strictly forbids entry . . . because of [the site's] holiness." However, certain religious groups and individuals reject this interpretation. Fearing a breach of public order, the Israeli police and courts have generally prevented Jewish worship on the Temple Mount, with a few exceptions until the 1980s involving private, nondemonstrative prayer by individuals under police control (interview with Hassan Tahbub, 1989; see High Court of Justice 4868/95, *Piskei Din* 74[5], 221).

In the coalition negotiations for the Israeli government, which was established in June 1996, the National-Religious Party pressed for the inclusion in the Government's Policy Guidelines the following statement: "The government will make prayer arrangements for Jews at holy sites in accordance with the guidelines of Jewish religious law" *(Haaretz,* May 13, 1996). However, following negotiations, a more general and more vaguely worded text was approved: "Freedom of worship and access to the Holy Places will be guaranteed to members of all faiths" (ibid.). Publication of the text and the attendant commentary led the Palestinian mufti of Jerusalem, 'Ikrima Sa'id Sabri, to react in a threatening tone against any attempt by the Israeli

6. Justice Agranat, *Nationalist Circles v. Minister of Police,* HCJ 222/68, *Piskei Din* 24 (2) (1970), 141: "It goes without saying . . . that the Jews' freedom of worship is their natural right which is deeply rooted in the lengthy history of the Jewish people." In *Cohen v. Minister of Police,* HCJ 99/76, 30 *Piskei Din* (2), 505, the court accepted as part of its judgment the reply of the State Attorney's Office that every Jew has a substantive legal right to pray on the Temple Mount, provided it is not "demonstrative prayer which is liable to cause the disruption of public order." Justice Menachem Elon (an observant Jew) stated in *Temple Mount Faithful et al. v. Attorney General,* HCJ 4185/90, *Piskei Din* 47 (5) (1993): "and the right of every person to freedom of worship, freedom of access to the Holy Places, and protection against their desecration is equally valid on the Temple Mount." He also noted that despite the court's nonintervention in the question of realizing the right of worship, that right per se is eternal.

government to permit Jewish worship on the Temple Mount. At the signing ceremony of the Policy Guidelines, various religious and nationalist groups urged the new minister of religious affairs (who had not yet been named) to introduce regulations that would enable Jews to assert their claim to pray on the Temple Mount. However, the minister of internal security rejected any possible change of the status quo.

Muslims viewed Israeli court decisions to uphold the basic right of Jews to freedom of worship on al-Haram al-Sharif as an affront to their sensibilities and as encouragement of serious disturbances, particularly in cases of demonstrative prayers by groups or individuals. However, until the events of 1996, the police permitted individuals to pray quietly on the Temple Mount without being interrupted by Muslim officials.

The Israeli authorities walk a thin line, whereas the High Court, in deliberating Jews' complaints against the police for barring them from praying on the Temple Mount, have chosen a middle ground and have attempted to strike a balance between two obligations: to guarantee freedom of access and to ensure the preservation of public order.

Ongoing Administration

As noted above, from an Islamic viewpoint, al-Haram al-Sharif is a Muslim religious endowment that until 1994 was administered by the Waqf Directorate under the responsibility of Jordan's Ministry of Religious Endowments and since that year also with the unofficial involvement of the Palestinian Authority. Recently, Waqf staff have begun to consider themselves subordinate to the Palestinian Authority as well, even though they receive their salary from Jordan in accordance with an agreement between Jordan and the Palestinian Authority. By recognizing the title and function of the "Waqf director in Jerusalem," the Israeli courts have acknowledged the holder of that position as the head of all the Muslim public endowments in the city, including the Temple Mount (Reiter 1997, 44).

The Israeli Religious Affairs Ministry has posted signs in Hebrew, English, and Arabic at the entry gates to the Temple Mount apprising prospective visitors of the site's holiness and of the requisite behavior, including modest clothing and a ban on photography inside al-Aqsa and the Dome of the Rock. The site's Muslim administrators dictate those rules, and Israeli police officers stationed at the gates to the Temple Mount and the Israeli judicial system enforce them.

Muslim administrators decide entry arrangements, too. In the past, they coordinated the opening and closing hours with the Israeli authorities (municipality and police), but after the events of October 8, 1990, when seventeen Palestinians were killed in rioting that erupted on al-Haram al-Sharif after Jewish worshipers at the Western Wall below were stoned, the Muslim authorities themselves decided on early closing hours without prior coordination. Israel did not try to hold them to the previous schedule.

The preachers of al-Aqsa Mosque and the Muslim religious establishment strongly resisted attempts by the Israeli military government immediately after 1967 and afterward by the Religious Affairs Ministry to obtain in advance the texts of sermons delivered by the preachers of al-Aqsa Mosque in order to delete inflammatory passages. The Friday sermons in al-Aqsa Mosque, which are broadcast over the loudspeaker system, often contain political views and expressions of incitement. Muslim officials on the Temple Mount, although recognized de facto by the Israeli authorities, do not enjoy clerical or other immunity in the performance of their duties.

Maintaining Security, Policing, and Preserving Public Order

Maintaining security on the Temple Mount is divided between the Muslim Waqf Directorate, which employs more than one hundred guards for that purpose, and the Israeli police, which maintains a permanent "point" at the site, conducts patrols around the perimeter, and stations police officers at the entrances. Despite this arrangement, overall responsibility for security, prevention of terrorism, and preservation of public order rests with the Israeli police. The Israeli police generally coordinate policing missions and the maintenance of public order with Muslim officials, with the exception of some cases of Palestinian mass demonstrations. They have not been able to prevent all Jewish extremists' attempts to wreak havoc on the Temple Mount—perhaps the two most dramatic incidents being the torching of al-Aqsa on August 21, 1969, by a deranged visitor from Australia (Benziman 1973, 141–54) and the April 11, 1982, shooting rampage perpetrated by

Allan Goodman, an American immigrant serving in the Israeli army
(Haaretz, Sept. 29, 1989). However, Israeli security and Waqf guards have
had some successes, notably in foiling the plots to blow up the Muslim
shrines on the Temple Mount by the Jewish Underground (apprehended in
1984), the "Lifta Gang" (January 21, 1984), and Yoel Lerner (1989).

Preserving the Character of the Temple Mount

According to Israeli law, the Israeli planning and building laws are in force
on the Temple Mount. However, the Israeli authorities' supervisory capabilities are limited. The Israeli Supreme Court has upheld the selective enforcement of the Planning and Building Ordinance and of the Antiquities
Law on the Temple Mount, at the same time acknowledging the discretion
exercised by the enforcement authorities because of the site's extraordinary
sensitivity and the need to preserve public order.

The Israeli government did not prevent the Muslim authorities from
renovating the Dome of the Rock and al-Aqsa. Indeed, the government exempted the Muslim establishment, at its request, from payment of customs
duties on some construction materials and on carpets imported from abroad.
The Waqf Directorate has on several occasions also carried out building and
restoration work on the Temple Mount without first obtaining the permits
required by Israeli law.

As a result of a suit filed in the mid-1980s by the Temple Mount Faithful against the attorney general and Israeli enforcement officials, it emerged
that the Waqf Directorate had for years executed various types of work without legal authorization.[7] Examples of such work include construction in ancient buildings; tiling or elevating ground for use as a prayer area, including a
prayer platform to commemorate the victims of the Sabra and Shatilla
refugee camps massacre (a private initiative by a Waqf staff member in November 1982, three months after the incident); covering antiquities with

7. Documentation of Prof. Asher Kaufmann of the Hebrew University relating to findings that were destroyed, covered with earth, or covered irrecoverably. Submitted to HCJ
193/86 *(Temple Mount Faithful v. the State of Israel, Takdin Elyon* 88 [3] [1988], 313) and HCJ
4185/90 *(Temple Mount Faithful et al. v. the Attorney General).*

earth; and building sidewalks and prayer platforms over earth-covered sites and planting trees in them. Justice Menachem Elon ruled that there was no proof that antiquities had been damaged and pointed out that the earth could be removed in the future, and, in any event, a great deal of time had passed since the changes had been effected. In his decision, he revealed that it is doubtful whether a building permit was required for some of the work, and the construction and restoration had contributed to the preservation of the antiquities, so there was no need to order the reinstatement of the status quo ante. Representatives of the Jerusalem municipality and the director of the Antiquities Authority testified that the Waqf administration had carried out certain projects without a permit; however, they added, the character of the changes that had been introduced and the site's religious and political sensitivity dictated that the matter be handled by direct contact with the Waqf Directorate and not necessarily by the regular legal and police agencies. Justice Elon quoted the attorney general as saying that, with the aim of reaching an understanding that would induce members of all nationalities and religions to respect the law and not turn ancient stones into the cornerstone of a conflict, he accepted the approach that the authorities had taken. Elon cite a previous stand according to which flexibility and pragmatism based on leniency were preferable to the rigid, unbending line represented by justice and the law.

The major reason for the court's decision not to intervene in the decision of the local authorities was the latter's pledge that in the future they would monitor events on the Temple Mount more closely and fully. The court's impression was that the authorities had tended to turn too much of a blind eye to violations of the law.[8]

Israeli works in the Temple Mount vicinity were also a cause of friction. Tension between the Jewish and Muslim authorities mounted as a reaction to the archaeological digs at the site and particularly to the excavation of the Western Wall tunnel. Muslims believe that the excavation of the Western Wall tunnel beneath the Temple Mount has nonscientific ulterior motives and is jeopardizing the physical safety of the Muslim buildings above. Their

---

8. *Temple Mount Faithful et al. V. Attorney General,* HCJ 4185/90, *Piskei Din* 47 (5) (1993): 221–28.

objection to the opening of the tunnel's new exit was motivated by their perception that it was an Israeli challenge to their authority.

Israeli authorities have also taken other actions. In 1978, they had the Mughrabi Gate repainted. The Muslim Council protested the project, claiming it was "aggression against al-Haram al-Sharif and an attempt to alter its character" (al-Alami 1984, 197–98).

In January 1986, members of the Ateret Kohanim group discovered the continuation of the Western Wall adjacent to the Street of the Iron Gate. They began holding prayers at the site, which became known as the Small Wall, and the Waqf discovered a breach in one of the entrances leading from the Small Wall to the Temple Mount. The misunderstanding between the sides came close to erupting into bloodshed (Shragai 1995, 202).

In 1993, the Western Wall Directorate prepared a plan to remove the earth ramp from beneath the Mughrabi Gate in order to expose the entire Western Wall, including Barclay's Gate beneath the Mughrabi Gate, and to install steps made of transparent material (Shragai 1995, 249). The Jerusalem Municipal Planning Committee has not yet approved the plan, apparently because of its political ramifications.

In September 1996, the renovation of Solomon's Stables and the site's preparation for Muslim worship furnished additional proof of the Israeli government's inability to supervise and enforce the Antiquities Law or the Planning and Building Laws without the cooperation of the Muslim establishment that administers al-Haram al-Sharif. In this case, as in the past, the Waqf administration unilaterally introduced physical changes within the Temple Mount precinct. The heads of the Waqf Directorate have announced publicly and in writing that they do not recognize Israeli authority with respect to Solomon's Stables, a site they consider to be the bottom section of the al-Aqsa Mosque (the Marwani Prayer Hall, named for the Caliph Marwan, son of 'Abd al-Malik); consequently, they refused to accept or obey a cease-work order issued on September 3, 1996, by the Local Affairs Court of the Jerusalem municipality, following a petition to the High Court of Justice by the Temple Mount Faithful demanding that the legal authorities be obligated to enforce the law. The case was overruled (High Court of Justice [HCJ] 6403/96 and HCJ 7128/96).

The scale of the government's impotence in supervision and in enforcing the law is strikingly apparent in the efforts the Antiquities Authority and the Jerusalem Municipality undertook after the events of September to downplay the report on violations of the law—the complete reverse of their previous positions. Press reports stated that the prime minister had ordered that the law not be enforced for fear of renewed rioting. Moreover, in his grounds for rejecting the petition of the Temple Mount Faithful, one Supreme Court justice remarked that at a sensitive site the law should be enforced leniently *(Haaretz,* Oct. 14, 1996).[9]

In 1998, the Muslim administration of al-Haram al-Sharif began renovating the lower part of al-Aqsa Mosque in order to make it an additional prayer hall. On this occasion, the police, for the time being, succeeded in putting a stop to the work. Here again, the renovations were carried out at an important archaeological site (in addition to its holiness) without permission being sought according to Israeli law.

In August 1999, the police sealed an opening in the lower part of al-Aqsa Mosque at the southern wall, an opening that had been worked by the Waqf unilaterally. In December 1999, the Waqf received a government agreement to open a small emergency doorway to Solomon's Stables. However, the Waqf dug a huge hole, explored three ancient monumental gates that could become a main entrance to that prayer hall. Archaeologists complained about the damage done to potential findings, but the attorney general admitted that not much could be done because of the fear of bloodshed *(Haaretz,* Dec. 3, 1999, A3; Dec. 8, 1999, A3; Dec. 26, 1999, A8).

The Nature of the Arrangements

The post-1967 modus vivendi was achieved owing to two factors: first, that in the new balance of power each party is aware of its vulnerable points; sec-

---

9. The mufti of Jerusalem and of the Palestinian areas on behalf of the Palestinian National Authority, 'Ikrima Sa'id Sabri, stated in a Friday sermon at al-Aqsa Mosque (September 6, 1996) that the Waqf did not intend to honor the cease-work order issued by the Jerusalem municipality. "al-Aqsa Mosque is outside the authority of this municipality and Waqf officials do not have to obtain its approval to carry out renovations at the place" *(Haaretz,* Sept. 8, 1996).

ond, that understandings between the parties, whether active or passive, should assume an unofficial, oral form.

The following is an example of a failure to reach an agreement as a result of the attempt of one side, the Israelis, to formalize an understanding in a letter to the other side.

In 1996, an understanding between the Israeli government and the Muslim establishment was almost achieved, according to which the Waqf Directorate would take no action against the opening of the exit to the Western Wall tunnel in return for the Waqf being permitted to renovate the Solomon's Stables area of al-Haram al-Sharif to serve as a prayer hall for Muslims, with no Israeli intervention.

Israeli government officials had tried in January 1996 to tie the opening of Solomon's Stables for prayer (initially without renovations) in the month of Ramadan to an unofficial understanding with representatives of the Waqf Directorate, just as other arrangements had been worked out in the past in meetings between the two sides. The Israeli minister of internal security, Moshe Shahal, in concurrence with Prime Minister Shimon Peres, ordered his representatives to meet with officials of the Muslim establishment on the Temple Mount to approve their request and at the same time to inform them of Israel's intention to open the exit to the tunnel (the opening of the tunnel's exit was delayed for a period of few years because of the fear of the Palestinian reaction). The Israeli authorities took the view that the tunnel is not a Holy Place and is not connected to the Temple Mount; consequently there was no need to get the Waqf's consent, and therefore the subject was raised separately and in the form of an announcement. The point of raising the two issues at the same meeting was to obtain an understanding similar to the other understandings prevailing since 1967 in connection with the Temple Mount. In the case of the tunnel, though, the Israelis did not request Muslim consent—it was clear that it would not be given—but only that they not foment disturbances after the fact (conversation between the author and Moshe Sasson, the then advisor to the minister of internal security and a participant in the meeting, Oct. 25, 1996).[10] According to an Israeli source,

10. A large number of police officers and representatives of the Muslim religious establishment attended the meeting. The latter included Shaykh Hassan Tahbub, minister of Waqf

none of the Muslim representatives at the meeting expressed a reaction, either positive or negative, to the announcement.

The attempt to reach an understanding failed because the commander of the Jerusalem District Police (apparently acting at the behest or concurrence of the minister of internal security) tried to deviate from the custom of fixing arrangements between the Israeli authorities and the Waqf, a custom that had been used since 1967, according to which all such contacts and understandings were conducted on an informal, oral basis. On January 24, 1996, he sent a letter to Shaykh 'Abd al-'Azim Salhab, the chairman of the Waqf Council appointed by Jordan (the letter states his title incorrectly as the president of the Supreme Muslim Authority), and to 'Adnan al-Husayni, the director of the Waqf in the Jerusalem District—both Jordan appointees but taking their orders from the Palestinian Authority's minister of Waqf Affairs, Hasan Tahbub, who was also at the meeting but did not receive the letter. The letter stated, among other things, "In the course of the meeting you put forward a request to open Solomon's Stables because of the forecast of heavy rain and concern for the worshipers on the Fridays of the blessed month of Ramadan this year. . . . In reply to your request, I agreed to the opening of the place to worshipers during the blessed month of Ramadan this year, in accordance with your undertaking to limit the number of worshipers who will enter the place. In addition, that you assume responsibility for the events there, given the difficult conditions, which may endanger the worshipers, by appointing ushers who will limit the number of worshipers at the site. In the meeting, I said that the atmosphere of peace which prevails in the region paves the way to the opening of the Western Wall tunnels [*sic*] in order to achieve economic goals and to increase the flow of tourists, a development which will serve the general interest, and I shall implement this soon" (letter in author's files).

This letter prompted a reply from Shaykh Salhab, who wrote, on February 6, 1996, "This place [Solomon's Stables], like the mosque [i.e., the gates

Affairs in the Palestinian National Authority and head of the Supreme Islamic Authority; Shaykh 'Abd al-'Azim Salhab, chairman of the Waqf Council; engineer Adnan al-Husseini, director of the Waqf in Jerusalem; and Shaykh 'Azzam al-Khatib, assistant to the director of the Waqf in Jerusalem; and Muhammad Nusseibeh.

of the Temple Mount], is opened at times and under conditions at the discretion of the Muslim Waqf Directorate, and they are not limited by time or by particular circumstances, as stated in your letter. . . . The position of the Muslim Council and the Waqf concerning the opening of the Hashemonean [Western Wall] tunnel is clear. It will generate an atmosphere of tension and dissatisfaction and will be harmful to the city's economy and to its image in the eyes of visitors from every corner of the world, and therefore we demand that this tunnel not be opened" (letter in Arabic in author's files).

The minister of internal security recommended that the exit from the tunnel not be opened during the month of Ramadan, the more so because his representatives had not heard agreement to such a move from anyone in the Muslim religious establishment. The tunnel was not opened then because this action was deemed inappropriate in the wake of the terrorist attacks perpetrated by the Hamas (Palestinian radical Islamic movement) and Islamic Jihad immediately after the exchange of the above-mentioned letters (conversation with Moshe Sasson, Oct. 1996). However, when the newly elected Israeli prime minister, Benjamin Netanyahu, considered the opening of the tunnel's exit, he was misled into believing that an agreement existed and that the action would not be met by Palestinian anger.[11]

The Israeli authorities did not fully grasp the implications of the letter from the Waqf authorities. And, in September 1996, the unilateral opening of the tunnel's exit sparked riots and large-scale violence between Palestinians and Israelis in the West Bank and the Gaza Strip.

The Role of Jordan and Other Islamic Countries

Because of the sanctity of Jerusalem to the world's Muslims, Islamic Arab countries such as Jordan, Saudi Arabia, Morocco, and Egypt aspire to be involved in the Jerusalem issue in general and in the future administration of

11. An unknown Israeli source released false information about such a deal. See, for example, Nadav Shragai's article "Who Owns the Temple Mount?" *(Haaretz,* Sept. 19, 1996), which appeared five days before the opening of the exit to the tunnel: "The Waqf promised to preserve the quiet of this time," and the understanding with the Waqf "is intended to avert a recurrence of the disturbances."

al-Haram al-Sharif in particular. The Jerusalem issue was raised in the Organization of the Islamic Conference (OIC), whose Jerusalem Committee was headed by the late King Hassan II of Morocco and by the Arab League. The royal families of Jordan and Morocco are descendants of the Prophet Muhammad. Egypt, the largest Arab nation, hosts the headquarters of the Arab League, and Saudi Arabia, a puritanical Islamic state headed by the House of Saud, is the birthplace of Islam and the site of the most important Islamic shrines, at Mecca and Medina. Jordan has the strongest claim owing to its control of the site from 1948 to 1967, its departure in circumstances of military occupation, and the continued administration to this day of the Temple Mount by its personnel via its Religious Endowments Ministry. This claim led to the inclusion of Article 9 of the Israel-Jordan peace treaty (October 26, 1994), which states:

> 1. Each Party will provide freedom of access to places of religious and historical significance.
>
> 2. In this regard, in accordance with the Washington Declaration, Israel respects the present role of the Hashemite Kingdom of Jordan in Muslim Holy Shrines in Jerusalem. When negotiations on the permanent status will take place, Israel will give high priority to the Jordanian historic role in these shrines. ("Israeli-Jordan Treaty of Peace" 1994; see also Merhav and Giladi 1999)

By means of Article 9, Jordan sought to ensure its standing with respect to the administration of the Temple Mount, whereas Israel's aim was to affirm in an international document a separation between political sovereignty and religious status at the Holy Places of Jerusalem. In 1994, Israel believed that assuring religious status to a Muslim element such as Jordan at the Islamic Holy Places and to the Vatican at Christian holy sites would reinforce its claim to sovereignty in Jerusalem because the relevant institutions would effectively administer the non-Jewish sites.

Article 9 infuriated the PLO, which was in possession of a letter from Shimon Peres, the foreign minister of Israel, dated October 11, 1993, and addressed to Peres's Norwegian counterpart, Johan Jürgen Holst, affirming that "all the Palestinian institutions of east Jerusalem, including the economic, social, educational, cultural, and the holy Christian and Moslem places, are performing an essential task for the Palestinian population. Needless to say, we will not hamper their activity; on the contrary, the fulfillment of this important mission is to be encouraged" *(Yediot Achronot,* Feb. 15, 1987). The PLO and the Islamic states construed Article 9 to mean Jordanian recognition of Israeli sovereignty in Jerusalem. Consequently, the subject was referred to the Conference of Islamic Countries, which was held in Casablanca in December 1994, where the Jordanian position was roundly defeated (Klein 1995, 43–56; Klein 1999, 124).

The Jordanian stand following the signing of the Israel-PLO Declaration of Principles in September 1993 was that a situation of "suspended sovereignty" should prevail on the Temple Mount (in the words of King Hussein, "Sovereignty is of Allah alone") and that Jordan's association with the Holy Places in Jerusalem should be preserved.

Following a meeting held in Cairo in May 1996—attended by President Husni Mubarak of Egypt, King Hussein of Jordan, and Yasir Arafat, the chairman of the Palestinian Authority—King Hussein declared his recognition of the Palestinian Authority's right to be granted political sovereignty in east Jerusalem as part of a permanent settlement, and Arafat agreed that Jordan should resume its administration of the Holy Places on a temporary basis until the Palestinian Authority achieved sovereignty in Jerusalem.

On the basis of Article 9 of the peace accords between Israel and Jordan, Israel should make an effort to give priority to the Jordanian role in Jerusalem's Holy Places while negotiating the permanent settlement with the Palestinian Authority. However, because of the current Palestinian Authority position, it is unlikely that Jordan will receive more than a symbolic representation in an administrative body of al-Haram al-Sharif. The Hashemite monarchy renounced its claim to sovereignty, and Jordan under King Abdallah II's leadership probably harbors less of an emotional obligation to Jerusalem than it did under the rule of the late King Hussein. It might accept a symbolic position and role.

Options for a Permanent Settlement

The above-mentioned arrangements could serve as a source of inspiration for future discussions on the permanent settlement for the Holy Places in Jerusalem. In negotiations for a permanent settlement on the Temple Mount, several basic interests are likely to guide the parties. In this section, I consider the basic interests of both sides and adduce some provisions by which the disputed issues might be bridged.

Israeli Interests

Israel desires continued sovereignty, within the current limitations, including the following: (1) right of access to the Temple Mount at precoordinated times; (2) recognition in principle of Jews' right of worship in a coordinated arrangement; (3) overall responsibility for security if public safety is jeopardized; (4) continued application of Israeli law and jurisdiction; (5) prohibition of nonreligious uses, including demonstrations or use for incitement; and (6) preservation of the site's character and prohibition of unauthorized building or demolition.

Palestinian Interests

Palestinian concerns revolve around the symbolic and concrete expressions of Palestinian (or inter-Muslim) sovereignty on al-Haram al-Sharif, including the following: (1) the right to fly the Palestinian flag; (2) Palestinian policing; (3) nonsubordination to Israeli laws; and (4) nonlimitation on the site's use or entry to it. In addition, the Palestinians seek elimination of Israeli-imposed arrangements, including return of the Mahkama building and of the keys to the Mughrabi Gate to Palestinians and prevention of Jewish worship and of excavations or digging beneath the Temple Mount and in its surroundings.

Disputed Issues and Bridging Possibilities

Political powers: sovereignty and control. The claim to sovereignty on the Temple Mount involves mainly symbolic expressions. From the Israeli viewpoint, however, two concrete expressions of sovereignty are essential:

1. Jurisdiction or the ability to bring to justice anyone who commits a crime at the site. If Israel agrees to the continuation of Muslim rule on the Temple Mount—as it almost certainly will—it is important that it be able to put on trial inciters or rioters, Jewish or non-Jewish, who endanger public safety. Israel will not be able to rely on the Palestinians here and will find it difficult to agree to Palestinians trying Jews who have committed offenses at the site.

2. Responsibility for security: Israel will not agree to relinquish overall security responsibility, which is part of its comprehensive security conception and certainly with regard to the heart of the capital city, and the need to protect Jewish worshipers at the Western Wall.

It is highly unlikely that the Israeli government will be able to forgo jurisdiction or responsibility for security, but it may agree to other expressions of authority for the Palestinians, such as the right to raise national or religious flags, despite the objections of religious Jews.[12]

In order to circumvent the symbolic-sovereignty obstacle inherent in the jurisdiction issue, agreement could be reached for Israelis and tourists who commit a crime on the Temple Mount after entering from Israeli territory to be tried in an Israeli court. Palestinian offenders and tourists entering from the area of the Palestinian Authority (state) would be tried in a Palestinian court. Such an arrangement would obligate the site's guards to turn

---

12. It is noteworthy, in this connection, that at the Camp David talks in 1978 then-prime minister Menachem Begin refused to accept President Sadat's demand that a religious flag fly over the Temple Mount, which, he believed, would be tantamount to agreeing that the site belonged to the Muslims. On the other hand, a proposal formulated by Gad Ya'akobi, Avraham Tamir, and Emanuel Sivan during the period of the national unity government (1984–88) would have permitted a Muslim flag to be raised over the Temple Mount without Israel forgoing its sovereignty therein (Shragai 1995, 378).

over the suspects to the relevant authority. Moreover, any international force to be stationed at the site would need to be strong, and each sovereign authority would have to undertake to carry out a speedy investigation and, if necessary, to place offenders on trial and inform the other side of its actions within a reasonable time.

Right of access and right of worship. The Palestinians probably will not object to the continuation of the current situation in which the site is open to everyone at hours the Palestinians themselves have determined. Israelis and Palestinians are likely to accept the existing arrangements of access and worship as a permanent settlement.

It is possible that in the course of the final-status talks Jewish religious groups will demand that the government allow them to realize the right of worship within the Temple Mount precinct, even if it requires concealing the act from the view of Muslim worshipers. Possible venues are the Mahkama building or another building, one of the spaces beneath the Temple Mount, or a designated area that would be blocked off by a high partition. The Palestinian leadership will certainly object to this demand. One reason for their opposition will be the precedent of Me'arat Hamachpela (the Cave of Machpela, or the Tomb of the Patriarchs) in Hebron. From the moment Jews were given the right to visit the site, in a letter to Moshe Dayan from the then-mayor Muhammad 'Ali al-Ja'bari, the Jewish side has not ceased to chip away at the Muslims' exclusivity, and today the site is a precedent for cooperation and division (coerced and problematic) between the followers of the two religions. Still, if the Palestinians show readiness to accept organized, modest, small-scale Jewish prayer somewhere on the Temple Mount or below the existing level, the Israeli government will the more easily be able to agree to the Palestinians' receiving more extensive control on the Temple Mount, including some emblems of sovereignty.

Ongoing administration. The Jewish public will prefer that a permanent settlement give expression to the site's standing in Judaism and that Jewish religious figures be involved in its administration. The Muslim public will prefer exclusive control and administration by Muslim clerics. Because of the importance of al-Haram al-Sharif to eight hundred thousand Israeli Muslim citizens, the future administration could include official clerics of this population alongside Palestinians and representatives from other Islamic nations. Certainly the status and religious significance of the Temple Mount justify its control and administration by religious authorities. The site will not serve political needs, and political bodies will not operate there or be granted rights at the site. Religious practices only will be permitted: prayer and ritual, religious studies, pilgrimage, etc. No political or governmental use will be made of the site, and no political demonstrations or incitement will be tolerated there.

Security, policing, and public order. Israel, as explained earlier, will not agree to relinquish overall responsibility for security, for preventing terrorism, and for preserving public order and safety. The current coordination between the Israeli police and the Waqf guards in the realms of protection and of policing and enforcing the appropriate rules of behavior on the Temple Mount could serve as a model for mutual cooperation in the future. Alternatively, a joint police force could be stationed at the site.

Preserving the character of the Temple Mount. It is in Israel's interest that whoever controls the Temple Mount not alter its character by turning it into a pantheon or making it an anomalous site in the heart of Jerusalem, and, most important, that it not be destroyed and that no harm come to ancient remnants of Jewish culture. Israel, therefore, will wish to maintain the site's subordination to the Israeli planning, building, and antiquities laws with an effective monitoring tool. One possible compromise is to work out an agreed system of planning and building laws and to set up a joint or multilateral committee to approve every action or project. Another method might be to make every change subject to bilateral agreement or, in the absence of agreement, to the decision of an external supervisory body.

Table 10.2 summarizes the interests and the bridging possibilities described in this section.

Conclusion

There is mutual nonrecognition between Israel and the Palestinians (and other Muslims) regarding the rights of the other side. This situation enables the two sides to maintain arrangements, in part coordinated and in part dictated by the balance of powers, wherein each side safeguards its perceived vital interests and creates "red lines" around them that the other side is

TABLE 10.2

**Israeli and Palestinian Interests on Controversial Issues
and Bridging Possibilities**

Disputed Issue	Israeli Interest	Palestinian Interest	Bridging Possibility
Jewish right of worship	Extension of status quo	Total cancellation	Continuation of status quo
Flying of flags	Prohibited	Permission for Palestinian flag	Religious flag on mosques only
Jurisdiction	Israeli	Palestinian-Jordanian or Palestinian	Divided
Overall security	Israeli	Palestinian	Joint, with the aid of external observers
Preserving public order	Israeli	Palestinian	Joint, with the aid of external observers
Policing	Israeli	Palestinian	Joint
Site's administration	With Israeli participation	Palestinian or inter-Muslim	Interfaith committee
Building, demolition, antiquities	Subordination to Israeli laws and Israeli bodies	Nonsubordination to Israeli laws and bodies, but agreement not to effect unilateral changes	Special laws and special supervisory authority to approve changes

forced to respect. Because of the political struggle and the mutual non-recognition of the other party's powers, the arrangements between the Israeli Jewish government and the Palestinian-Jordanian Muslim officials took an unofficial, oral form. Although unofficial, the set of arrangements developed since 1967 turned into a modus vivendi and brought about a dynamic new status quo.

An analysis of the existing arrangements on the Temple Mount and of the basic interests of the sides suggests that agreement is reachable on a large number of questions, based on the post–1967 model. These subjects include: freedom of access; administration; entry arrangements; VIP visits; entry fees; use of the site solely for religious needs; prevention of incitement; maintenance of agreed and appropriate rules of behavior; preservation of the site's character; implementation of changes involving building, demolition, and excavations with mutual consent only; and joint protection and security.

The disputed issues on which agreement will be difficult to reach are Jews' right of prayer and sovereignty-related subjects such as the right to fly flags; jurisdiction; and responsibility for overall security and maintenance of public order. However, it is likely that during negotiations between Israel and the PLO over the permanent-status settlement, the status of the Temple Mount, as one of many issues to be agreed on, may be traded off with other relevant issues.

Since 1996, the northern faction of the Islamic Movement fills a dominant role in *al-Haram al-Sharif*. The movement has organized the renovation works and the preparation of the two subterranean prayer halls on the site (The Marwan Hall and *al-Aqsa al-Qadima*). It also organizes mass gatherings under the slogan "Al-Aqsa is in Danger," whose purpose is to glorify the status of *al-Haram al-Sharif* and to deny any Jewish claim to the Temple Mount. The movement's contacts aid in disseminating this message over the whole Muslim world, and to mobilize donations for continuation of the building and renovation works of *al-Aqsa*.

The demonstrative visit of Ariel Sharon, then head of the Likkud Party, together with other Knesset members of the Temple Mount at the end of September 2000 sparked widespread violent disturbances in Israel and the Palestinian areas. It provided a religious dimension to the PA's turning towards a violent struggle after the failure of the Camp David peace summit in July 2000. President Clinton's proposal ignored the existing state on the Temple Mount—those arrangements presented in this chapter. The Palestinians rejected his proposal of a vertical division of sovereignty on the site, and refused to recognize any Jewish claim to it.

Since Sharon's visit to the Temple Mount, the site has been closed to non-Muslim visitors at the initiative of the Waqf administration; but security coordination between the Waqf and the Israeli police continues. In January 2000, the press reported that Prime Minister Sharon considered compelling the opening of the Temple Mount to visitors. Both the General Security Service and the Attorney General were of the opinion that the existing state would eventually lead to the loss of the principle of free access to a Holy Site.

11

Delicate Balances at the Temple Mount, 1967–1999

Amnon Ramon

Since Israel's conquest of the Temple Mount in 1967, both the state and the Jewish population have displayed ambivalence about control of the site. On the one hand, the Temple Mount is the holiest and most important site in Judaism. It was there, in 1967, that the commander of the Israeli paratroopers, Mordechai Gur, uttered his famous declaration, "The Temple Mount is in our hands!" Yet within hours of the Temple Mount's conquest, Moshe Dayan, the defense minister at the time, decided to place the Waqf (Muslim religious trust), which administered the site before 1967, in charge of its administration (apart from overall Israeli responsibility for public order) and to prohibit prayer by Jews there.

The Halakhic Prohibition on Jews Entering the Temple Mount

Implementation of Dayan's policy was facilitated by the halakhic decree issued by the Chief Rabbinate and other eminent Judaic authorities prohibiting Jews from entering the Temple Mount and certainly from praying there. The decree was based on the Halakhah (Jewish religious law) precept stipulating that all Jews are ritually unclean because they have come in contact with a corpse or been in the presence of a corpse at some time in their lives.

296

During the Temple period, Jews could purify themselves of such ritual uncleanness by mixing the ashes of a red heifer with special water. Because it is no longer possible to obtain the ashes of a red heifer (the breed is extinct), all Jews are held to be ritually impure and therefore may not ascend the Temple Mount (Benziman 1973, 136; Shragai 1995, 28).

On the face of it, it might still be possible to visit much of the Temple Mount precinct because the Temple stood on only a small portion of its area. (The present dimensions of the Temple Mount date from the major expansion project undertaken during the late Second Temple period, largely by King Herod.) However, neither the exact size nor the location of the Temple is known, so the Chief Rabbinate barred Jews from entering it altogether, citing the principle of *morah hamikdash* (fear of the sanctuary); in other words, whoever does not fear the possibility that he may tread on holy ground while in an impure state is violating a severe prohibition, even if it should later turn out that he walked only on permissible ground (Shragai 1995, 29). Another concern is that granting Jews permission to visit the margins of the site will result in the breaching of all prohibitions. Most will not be able to distinguish between the different areas and will not undergo ritual purification or fulfill the other precepts that are binding on visitors to the Temple Mount (Bakshi-Doron 1995).

Some rabbis (e.g., Rabbi Avigdor Nebenzahl, the rabbi of the Old City's Jewish Quarter) add to the halakhic strictures the fear that Jewish prayer on the Temple Mount would provoke a jihad (Islamic holy war), which would cause bloodshed and deaths of Jews in every corner of the world (Shragai 1995, 72).

Another reason (theological in character) that some rabbis (including disciples of Rabbi Zvi Yehuda Kook) cite in this regard is that where the Temple Mount is concerned, it is forbidden to "hasten the End." The Temple Mount is the exclusive domain of God, as Rabbi Menachem Froman, today the rabbi of the settlement of Tekoa, near Bethlehem, wrote: "The Temple is the ideal of sanctity, of absolute perfection, and must not be desecrated by taking the road of practicality, which is inherently partial and relative. The Temple is not another step on the way, it is the gift of grace at road's end" (qtd. in Shragai 1995, 73).

This viewpoint holds that the more sacred a place and its symbolic importance are, the greater the obligation to keep one's distance from it. In the case of the Temple Mount, the emphasis should be placed on the distance between the Jewish people and the site, according to Rabbi Shlomo Aviner, one of the eminent pupils of Rabbi Zvi Yehuda Kook and head of Ateret Kohanim Yeshiva in the Old City's Muslim Quarter: "Our ownership and belonging are manifested in the fact that we do not touch that place, and our national genius shines forth in the fact that we show the entire world: There is one place which we do not enter. . . . The distance does not separate; on the contrary, it joins" (Aviner 1989, 29). And he added: "On the question of the Temple Mount, our approach is like that of the [ultraorthodox] haredis" (qtd. in Shragai 1995, 73).

Another reason, not halakhic in character, may be the fear—to which the rabbinical establishment is especially prey—of the revolutionary potential latent in performing an act on the Temple Mount that would appear to be a step toward rebuilding the Temple. Most of the rabbis who permit Jews to visit the Temple Mount do not advocate building a new temple at this time, but even Jewish worship at the site or the establishment of a synagogue could be interpreted in revolutionary terms against the background of Judaism's development as a religion without a shrine since the destruction of the Second Temple. An echo of this reasoning can be heard in Prof. Israel Eldad's stinging rebuke to the Chief Rabbinate: "They acted in concert: a cringing, hesitant, conservative-exilic rabbinate went along with Israeli [government] policy, which was forced unwillingly to deal with the subject. . . . Now architects will come forward and design the Western Wall Plaza for anti-pilgrims who will [ascend] to the Temple Mount, there to enjoy the wonders of Muslim mosques" (Eldad and Eldad 1978, 244).

The Chief Rabbinate's most important halakhic ruling, based largely on the first two grounds cited above, was issued a few months after the Six Day War. Fifty-six of the country's preeminent rabbis signed a warning against Jews visiting "the entire Temple Mount" (Shragai 1995, 61). The signatories included the two chief rabbis of the time, Unterman and Nissim; the president of the Committee of Yeshivas, Rabbi Yehezkel Abramsky; and Rabbis Yosef Shlomo Elyashiv, Shlomo Zalman Auerbach, and Zvi Yehuda Hacohen Kook.

Representing virtually the entire gamut of opinion in the Jewish-religious population, those spiritual leaders were joined by more than three hundred additional rabbis who added their signatures to the ruling (Shragai 1995, 61). The result was a rare consensus in the schismatic world of Judaism.

In addition to issuing a halakhic prohibition, the Chief Rabbinate posted a sign by the walkway leading to the Mughrabi Gate to the Temple Mount, stating: "Religious law strictly forbids entry to the Temple Mount area because of its holiness" (Schiller 1989, 37). In the first months after the Six Day War, tens of thousands of Israelis streamed past the sign to visit the Temple Mount and its Muslim shrines. The religious affairs minister at the time, Dr. Zerah Wahrhaftig, told the chief rabbis that their sign constituted an edict that was beyond the public's endurance to obey. To avert the violation of Chief Rabbinate decrees adjacent to the Western Wall, Wahrhaftig tried to establish the Gate of the Chain as the general entry site to the Temple Mount, but without success (U. Benziman 1973, 136).

It is important to point out that at no time in their deliberations did the rabbis, rabbinic authorities, and religious politicians abjure their firm stand that the Jewish people have the right of eternal ownership of the Temple Mount—even if that right was not being realized because of the halakhic prohibition or because of fear of a Jewish-Muslim confrontation or both. Already on June 18, 1967, Religious Affairs Minister Wahrhaftig stirred a public furor when he stated in an interview: "There is no doubt that the Jewish people have the right to the Temple Mount, for it is the Holy of Holies of the Jewish people. However, as I understand it, the Jewish people do not intend to claim that right in our time by destroying those [Muslim] places" (qtd. in M. Benvenisti 1973, 238).

Was there any connection between the Chief Rabbinate's halakhic ban and the decisions taken by Moshe Dayan? Did the two sides hold prior negotiations? To this day, we do not know the answer. What is undeniable is that the religious prohibition remains the underlying stabilizing factor of Dayan's 1967 status quo.

Challenges to the Halakhic Prohibition

The majority of Israel's religious population supported the ruling of the Chief Rabbinate and of the major *haredi* (ultraorthodox) rabbis forbidding

Jews to enter the Temple Mount. However, some rabbis and groups, primarily from the national-religious camp and veterans of the prestate Lehi underground organization, refused to accept the Chief Rabbinate's decision.
Immediately after the Temple Mount was captured by Israeli forces, they
began to propose various ideas to consolidate the Jewish presence there. Dr.
Haim Moshe Gevaryahu, the chairman of the Biblical Research Society,
suggested that an *ohel moed* (the biblical "tent of congregation"—the shrine
before the building of the First Temple) be set up on the Temple Mount. His
colleague Ben-Zion Luria recommended building a synagogue (U. Benziman 1973, 136). But the personality who tackled the subject most intensively was the chief rabbi of the Israeli Defense Forces (IDF), Shlomo Goren,
who in 1973 became Israel's Ashkenazi chief rabbi.

Relying on measurements the IDF Engineering Corps made under his
guidance, Rabbi Goren ruled that Jews might enter and pray in those areas
of the Temple Mount that were added to the original site toward the end of
the Second Temple period during the reign of the Hasmoneans and especially under King Herod. Accordingly, Goren declared that no halakhic violation would occur if entry was made from the Mughrabi Gate in a straight
line to the east and south; prayer was permissible there, and a synagogue
could be built. Using the same method, Goren permitted entry to the
area of the northern gate of the Temple Mount from the Antonia Fortress to
near the platform on which the Dome of the Rock stands (Goren 1992, 53;
Shragai 1995, 62). He also adduced historical evidence for a Jewish presence
and Jewish pilgrimage to the Temple Mount from the destruction of the
Second Temple until the sixteenth century, including evidence of a Jewish
prayer site there (Avraham Ber Haya, Benjamin of Tudela, and Maimonides
in the twelfth century, and David Ben Zimra in the sixteenth century, although some historians today do not accept the claim of a permanent Jewish prayer site).

Goren also tried to explain that the tradition of the Western Wall as a
Jewish prayer site is only three hundred years old and had its origins in restrictions imposed by the Ottoman authorities on Jewish worship elsewhere
in the Temple Mount area. "We cannot claim rights at the Western Wall,"
Goren wrote to Prime Minister Yitzhak Rabin in August 1994. "Its sanctity
lies entirely in the fact that it demarcates the Temple Mount, in being a sub-

stitute for the Mount of the Lord. . . . As for the haredi rabbis, whose lack of topographic and halakhic knowledge makes them afraid to ascend the Temple Mount and worship there—good luck to them. But we and the entire nation should be permitted to pray freely on the Temple Mount and the Muslims given free access and control of their mosques" (qtd. in Shragai 1994a).

Rabbi Goren's findings generated extensive halakhic research on the boundaries of the Temple and on the areas in which prayer is permissible. The result was that a small minority of rabbis ruled that Jews should be permitted to visit certain parts of the Temple Mount after fulfilling the ritual conditions for entering the site. Among the major advocates of this approach was the Sephardi chief rabbi in the 1980s, Rabbi Mordechai Eliahu; while still in office, he urged that a synagogue be built in the southeastern corner of the Temple Mount, behind al-Aqsa Mosque, though stipulating that it be higher than the mosque (Shragai 1995, 65). His colleague, Ashkenazi Chief Rabbi Avraham Shapira, also supported in principle the idea of building a synagogue on the Temple Mount but argued that it is a political question in which the rabbinate should not intervene (Shragai 1995, 65).

Other leading rabbis who maintained that Jews could visit the so-called permissible areas under certain conditions included Eliezer Waldman; Haim Druckman; Yosef Kapah, member of the High Rabbinic Court; Dov Lior, head of the *hesder* yeshiva (combining religious studies with military service) in Kiryat Arba; Itzhak She'ar Yashuv Hacohen, chief rabbi of Haifa and member of the Chief Rabbinate Council; Yehuda Amital, head of the *hesder* yeshiva in Allon Shevut and chairman of the dovish religious Meimad movement; Zalman Koren, a leading expert on the boundaries of the Temple; David Chelouche, chief rabbi of Netanya and member of the Chief Rabbinate Council; Haim David Halevy, Sephardi chief rabbi of Tel Aviv and member of the Chief Rabbinate Council; and Yehuda Getz, rabbi of the Western Wall (Shragai 1995, 69).

In 1986, Rabbi Goren convened the largest forum of rabbis ever to address the issue, at Ha-idra Raba Yeshiva, adjacent to the Western Wall. The more than seventy rabbis who attended ruled that "Jews may enter and pray on the Temple Mount in most of its area" (Shragai 1995, 70) and added that, halakhically speaking, a synagogue could be built at the site. This forum, which called itself the Supreme Rabbinic Council for the Temple Mount, included Shalom Mashash, the Sephardi chief rabbi of Jerusalem; Yehiel Bouhbout, the Sephardi chief rabbi of Kiryat Shemona; Yitzhak Shilat, head of the *hesder* yeshiva at Maaleh Adummim; and Rabbi Meir Haeitan from the settlement of Kedumim in Samaria (Shragai 1995, 70).

Many other rabbis also held that Jews could visit the Temple Mount, but refrained from publicizing their opinion for fear of being denounced by the rabbinic and *haredi* establishment (Shragai 1995, 56). Indeed, even Rabbi Goren was originally reluctant to publish his research; he did so only in 1992, for fear that "the Temple Mount will be transferred to Moslem control" (Goren 1992, 10). Israel Medad, a Temple Mount activist, relates in the settlers' journal *Nekuda* that an important rabbi told him "that the halakhic problem of entering the permissible areas on the Temple Mount is less complicated than the solution that was found for milking cows on the Sabbath." He also quotes Rabbi She'ar Yashuv Hacohen as having written that "entry to the Temple Mount is not primarily a matter for rulings by religious authorities, but is first of all a question for engineers, geographers, archaeologists, and historians" (Medad 1995, 75).

On the second night of the Sukkot festival in 1991, Rabbi Menachem Mendel Shneersohn, the Lubavitcher rebbe and head of the Habad movement, instructed his disciples to hold the *Beit Hasho'evah* (water libation ritual) celebrations on the Temple Mount itself. However, the grave incident that occurred two days later at the site, in which seventeen Muslim worshipers were killed, aborted the Habad movement's plans (Shragai 1995, 60–61). Still, this was the first time that a major *haredi* rabbi had ignored the prohibition on Jews visiting the Temple Mount.

More recently, we are witnessing a gradual process in which growing circles in the national-religious camp (including its mainstream) take a positive view of visits by Jews to the Temple Mount. Fear of losing Jewish sovereignty on the Temple Mount and incidents in which the police have forcibly ejected radical activists in groups such as the Temple Mount Faithful (Neemanei Har Habayit) and Hai Vekayam generate solidarity within the national-religious camp and add new recruits for the stand that Jews should be allowed to exercise their right to pray on the Temple Mount.

However, the Chief Rabbinate replies to requests that it reconsider its stand by continuing to cite the 1967 warning that anyone entering the Temple Mount precinct in an unpurified state and in ignorance of the exact location of the Holy of Holies is committing a mortal sin for which divine punishment will be exacted (Shragai 1995, 70).

Haredi rabbis and politicians react virulently to attempts by Jews to visit the Temple Mount and to rabbinic rulings permitting such visits. Their position, which draws on a ruling *haredi* spiritual leaders (headed by Rabbi Yosef Haim Sonnenfeld) issued during the British Mandate period, absolutely forbids Jews to enter the Temple Mount and warns that anyone entering the Temple Mount in this era is violating a mortal prohibition entailing divine punishment" (Shragai 1995, 57). The *haredi* view is that the situation in which Jews refrain from visiting the Temple Mount does not infringe on Jewish sovereignty there. *Haredi* rabbis enjoin those who insist on their right to visit the site to study Torah and perform the commandments instead of trying to hasten the End of Days.

What are the prospects that the Chief Rabbinate will change its stand in the near future? Despite the pressures on the rabbinate to modify its sweeping ban on Jewish entry to and prayer at the site (Bakshi-Doron 1995), and notwithstanding the increasing number of religious Jews who visit the Temple Mount, the halakhic prohibition remains potent. The important *haredi* rabbis—the late Eliezer Shach, the late Shlomo Z. Auerbach, Yosef S. Elyashiv, Ovadiah Yosef, and the late Gur rebbe—as well as the chief rabbis and most of the rabbis in the national-religious camp have not altered their position (Shragai 1994a). Given the rising political power of the *haredim* and their growing influence on the chief rabbis and on the Chief Rabbinate Council, no new ruling by the Chief Rabbinate is likely in the foreseeable future.

The prohibition against entering the Temple Mount declared by the Chief Rabbinate and the major religious authorities is a decisive factor in the political-public struggle to change the status quo at the site. The majority of the national-religious public, which might have been the spearhead of the campaign, obeys the halakhic ruling. As such, it is effectively neutralized in terms of the ability to effect concrete changes vis-à-vis the Temple Mount, even though the Mount is held to be Judaism's most sacred place.

Activists Seeking to Change the Status Quo

In recent years, a number of groups have tried to change the status quo on the Temple Mount. Most of them have formed around a central figure who is obsessed with the subject, and each has a slightly different motivation from the others. Recently these groups have begun cooperating, and in the largest event of its kind since 1967, some fifteen hundred people attended the first Annual Conference of the Friends of the Temple on September 15, 1998, at the Jerusalem Convention Center. All the groups actively engaged with the Temple Mount took part in the gathering, together with many "new faces" from the mainstream of the national-religious movement. Among the most prominent of the activist groups seeking to change the status quo on the Temple Mount are the Temple Mount Faithful and Hai Vekayam.

Temple Mount Faithful

The group most strongly identified in the public mind with the Temple Mount controversy is the Temple Mount Faithful, led by Gershon Salomon.[1] One of the first activists to advocate a change in the status quo, Salomon took up the cause within a few months of the Six Day War. During the intervening years, movement activists, with Salomon in the forefront, have patiently and persistently requested permission from the police to visit the Temple Mount and pray there on certain fixed dates in the Jewish calendar: Rosh Hashanah (New Year), Yom Kippur (Day of Atonement), eve of Sukkot (Tabernacles), Pesah (Passover), Shavuot (Pentecost), Israeli Independence Day, Jerusalem Day, and the Ninth of Ab mourning-and-fast day. Their activity sometimes includes ceremonies such as laying the cornerstone for a new temple, performing the water libation ritual at the Gihon Spring, holding a Jewish wedding at the Mughrabi Gate, and so forth.

Gershon Salomon is an Orientalist by profession. His core of activists number a few dozen, though a few hundred more registered supporters can usually be counted on to turn up for a demonstration or a visit to the Tem-

---

1. The Temple Mount Faithful maintain an Internet site at http://www.templemount-faithful.org.

ple Mount. Funding comes from donations, and some claim that the donors include Christian fundamentalist groups in the United States (Milner 1990; Rabihiya 1992).

Many of the key activists in the other Temple Mount groups were at one time or another members of the Temple Mount Faithful but left because of its leader's "excessive centralization." Salomon appeals to teenagers, but opinion holds that few remain when they become mature and can think for themselves (Shragai 1995, 292–93).

Although the police rarely permit the group to pray on the Temple Mount, members nevertheless try to enter through the Mughrabi Gate— the only gate, next to the Western Wall, that is open to tourists. Invariably, they are stopped, offer up a prayer standing next to the gate, and say their piece to the many journalists and television crews that always accompany Salomon and his group. The movement's attempts to enter the Temple Mount grounds are always public and highly demonstrative. Their purpose is to arouse public opinion to the struggle for Israeli sovereignty at the site. Salomon believes in a public campaign and is unwilling to accept secret "under the table" arrangements for Jewish prayer on the Temple Mount.

The movement's objective is " 'to realize the historic belief and aspiration of the Jewish people, which is rooted in the Torah of Israel, that the Temple Mount is the national, religious, and spiritual center of the people of Israel and the Land of Israel' " (platform qtd. in Housen-Couriel and Hirsch 1990, 121). The movement is driven more by nationalist than religious motivations. Many of its activists, including Salomon, are not observant Jews— a fact that draws on them the wrath of *haredi* circles. Salomon's ambition is for the elected Knesset (Israeli Parliament) to hold its opening session on the Temple Mount every four years and for the Supreme Court to be located there. The site should also be the venue for the IDF's solemn ceremonies (Shragai 1995, 288). "Once the Temple Mount becomes the center of the Jewish nation," Salomon argues, "the Israeli government will move the mosques to Mecca and in their place the Third Temple will be built" (qtd. in Rabihiya 1992). Like other zealots, Salomon believes that "whoever holds the Temple Mount holds the title deed to the entire Land of Israel" (qtd. in Shragai 1995, 288).

According to the movement's platform in its unsuccessful run for the

Knesset in 1992, Israel should apply its sovereignty immediately in Judea and Samaria. Similarly, the Sinai Peninsula is an integral part of the Land of Israel and should be restored to the national fold. The movement would expel most of the Arabs of east Jerusalem from the city and so forth (Rabihiya 1992).

In contrast to Hai Vekayam (discussed below), the Temple Mount Faithful accept the legal rules of the game. Every action is preceded by a request for a police permit, and redress is often sought from the courts. The movement's legal battles have produced some significant achievements, such as the right to pray at the Mughrabi Gate (provided it does not endanger public safety), the right to visit the Temple Mount, and tighter supervision by the Israeli authorities over construction activity on the Temple Mount (which the court ordered in the wake of the movement's petition against illegal building by the Waqf). Leaflets announcing a visit to the Temple Mount note that the group has coordinated the event with the security authorities and approved by the police. The Waqf construes such announcements to mean that tacit cooperation exists between the state authorities and the Temple Mount Faithful. Former Jerusalem mayor Teddy Kollek's attempts to get the police to prevent Salomon and his group from praying at the Mughrabi Gate failed because it was clear that the High Court of Justice would overturn any such order.

Since the beginning of the Intifada (the Palestinian uprising) in December 1987, Salomon and his followers' visits to the Temple Mount have often provoked serious disturbances by the Muslim population. The Muslim public and the leaders of the Waqf view Salomon as the incarnation of the Israeli desire to seize control of the Temple Mount.

On October 8, 1990, during the Sukkot festival, the most serious incident on the Temple Mount since 1967 took place. The Temple Mount Faithful had received a police permit to perform the water libation ritual—dating from the Temple period—at the Gihon Spring below the Temple Mount. However, a rumor spread among the Muslim population that Salomon and his group were going to lay the cornerstone for a new temple on the Temple Mount. Hundreds of Muslims streamed to the site just as thousands of Jews gathered at the Western Wall directly below for the traditional *birkat hakohanim* (priestly benediction). A member of the Border Police accidentally dropped a tear-gas canister, setting off a riot in which Muslims rained down stones on the jammed Western Wall Plaza below. Police stormed the Temple Mount and opened fire indiscriminately, killing seventeen Muslim worshipers. More than ten years later, the impact of the event and the mutual suspicion to which it gave rise have not diminished.

After the incident, the police prohibited Salomon's entry to the Temple Mount. The High Court of Justice rejected his appeal against the order. Justice Mishael Heshin recently likened the effect of Salomon's entry to the Temple Mount precinct to an encounter between a lit match and gas fumes *(Haaretz, May 15, 1996)*.

The calculated and stubborn actions of Gershon Salomon and his group—their repeated attempts to enter the Temple Mount grounds and pray there, and their persistent and sophisticated legal battle—ensure that the Temple Mount Faithful will continue to be a cardinal factor in attempts to change the status quo at the site. The group's major achievement has been to keep the issue on the Israeli and Palestinian public agenda as one of the central bones of contention in the Arab-Israeli conflict (Shragai 1995, 291).

In recent years, Temple Mount Faithful publications have shown a pronounced shift from nationalist messages to blatantly religious ones, centering around the building of the Third Temple (with assistance by Gentiles). They also describe Salomon's recovery from a serious wound he suffered in a clash in 1958 while serving in the army in terms of a miracle and as "God's choice": the Syrian soldiers did not kill Salomon because they saw thousands of angels hovering around him. It was then that Salomon heard the voice of God, who saved him so that he might devote himself to redeeming the Temple Mount.

Hai Vekayam Movement

The second activist group whose members have tried dozens of times in the past year to enter the Temple Mount and pray there is called Hai Vekayam (meaning "alive and enduring"). The seven years of imprisonment its founder, Yehuda Etzion, served—as one of the leaders of the Jewish underground in the 1980s, which planned to blow up the Dome of the Rock on the Temple Mount—did not weaken his resolve. He refused to express contrition for his deeds or to request presidential amnesty. The principal modification in his thinking that occurred during his prison term was his conclusion that any activist operation concerning the Temple Mount must be preceded by the preparation of all segments of the public, however long that may take. In a letter he sent from prison to a friend, Etzion wrote:"I do not intend to act after my release for the immediate detonation of the Dome of the Rock or to encourage others to take action. Henceforth we must examine our steps in a full, broad perspective, as part of the thrust toward a comprehensive moral and cultural transformation. The movement of redemption must be established from concept to deed and not vice versa" (qtd. in Segal 1988). Following his release from prison, Etzion tried to establish a "movement of redemption" but found few kindred spirits. He devoted his energy at the time to helping the settlers' movement Gush Emunim (Bloc of the Faithful) to bring members of the Ethiopian Falas Mura community to Israel.

During the Hanukkah festival in December 1991, about two years before the signing of the Israel-PLO Declaration of Principles, Etzion founded the Hai Vekayam movement. His partners were Major (Res.) Motti Karpel and Haim Nativ, both "penitents" and members of the Bat Ayin settlement west of Gush Etzion between Bethlehem and Hebron; Noam Livnat of the Nablus settlement group; Yinon Mevorakh from the settlement of Berakha, adjacent to Nablus; and Haim Odem, builder of the Temple menorah (seven-branched candelabrum) that is on public display at the Jewish Quarter of the Old City of Jerusalem. Also close to the group is Rabbi Yitzhak Ginsburg, head of Joseph's Tomb Yeshiva in Nablus. Over time, the core of the movement expanded to comprise several dozen activists. An outer circle of supporters and sympathizers numbers a few hundred people (Shragai 1994b).

Following two years of ideological and organizational crystallization, the movement made itself known to the public by its participation in the first demonstrations against the Declaration of Principles in September 1993. The ideas and vision of Hai Vekayam are influenced by the doctrine of Shabtai Ben Dov, an activist in the prestate Lehi underground organization; the radical poet Uri Zvi Greenberg; and the writings of Rabbi Avraham Yitzhak Hacohen Kook. Etzion set forth the four cardinal tenets of the new movement in the first issue of its journal, *Labrit* (For the Covenant):

[1.] The movement of redemption arose in order to articulate an old-new national culture for the Jewish people: the culture that is taught by the Torah of Israel. That culture will give rise to the Kingdom of the House of David, which is the structure of regime and government that befits us, as the political expression of our national culture. The movement is the core of the purposed regime—already now, from the outset, from its inception.

[2.] The movement of redemption will make manifest the vision of the complete life of the people in its land—beneath the *shekhinah* [Divine Presence]—a life that is a constant, ascending dialogue between the God of Israel and His people. That dialogue, which was revealed in the biblical substantiality, was curtailed with the destruction of the Temple. Its renewal is the challenge for the sake of which we exist.

[3.] The movement of redemption treats the in-the-meantime State of Israel—fruit of the return of a part-people to a part-land with an imported, internalized gentile-concocted culture—as a partial achievement that can develop only by its radical transformation. Zionism's internal reservoir has dried up, from the outset it was limited and defective, and now the sons have reached the critical stage, but there is no strength to deliver the birth. The feeling of a dead end, the absence of purposefulness and meaning, pervades every sensitive heart. We owe our existence to the Zionism that has brought us this far, but additional momentum is possible only through an internal revolution: from the unconscious to what is consciously directed and desired from the outset.

[4.] Into our conscious will we inject the striving for a framework—the Kingdom of Israel and its supreme leadership institution, the Great Court in the Chamber of Hewn Stones [seat of the Sanhedrin, the supreme religious and judicial body, in the Temple period]—and the aspiration to fill the content of Israeli life. The Great Court will rejuvenate the rules of the Torah of life for the nation, the Oral Torah that shall be brought back to life as a binding order. Prophecy is the summit of such a life, which is a constant dialogue between He who chose His people and His chosen people. (Etzion 1993, 4)

The movement also called for the formulation of a new Declaration of Independence. The old one, in its view, was based on "relativistic human values derived from the gentile world, hence the root of the cultural and practical kowtowing to the nations of the world, which embitters the life of the people, violates its honor, and suppresses its creative spirit" *(Labrit* 1, [Jewish month of] Nisan 5753 [1993], back cover).

The harsh criticism Yehuda Etzion and his movement leveled against secular Zionism and the state did not spare religious Zionism or Gush Emunim, either. Etzion decried the continued sanctification of the State of Israel according to the tradition of Rabbi Zvi Yehuda Kook and Merkaz Harav Yeshiva. The sanctification of secular Zionism was justified while the state was being built, Etzion argued, but had become meaningless once the state had developed and especially after the Six Day War (Etzion 1985). Gush Emunim had been dragged in the wake of secular Zionism and refused to believe that the process of redemption was "stuck" because of the state's failure to understand the expectations of the Holy One in the world of redemption (Sprinzak 1995, 109). The "Emuni public" (i.e., supporters of Gush Emunim, with a play on the Hebrew word for "belief" or "faith"— *Emuna*), Motti Karpel (one of the founders of Hai Vekayam) wrote in *Nekuda,* "is incapable of putting forward either a political or a security alternative, still less an ideological alternative. We want this government [the Rabin government] to fall, but we [the national-religious public] lack the moral courage to topple it" (Karpel 1995, 60).

Karpel urged the Emuni public to abandon the historic alliance with secular Zionism, which was based on the values of decadent Western culture. The leaders of the national-religious camp, he stated, who until now had blindly followed the leaders of secular Zionism (which had reached the end of its tether), must assume the burden of responsibility. The profound crisis of values being experienced by the secular public obligates a so-called Hebraic revolution: the rebuilding of the state not according to the Western democratic tradition but as the continuation of the ancient, millennia-old Jewish tradition of the "Kingdom of the House of David," which will be "translated" into present-day reality according to the ideas of Shabtai Ben-Dov (author's interview with Motti Karpel, June 28, 1995).

Such messages—referring to the Kingdom of the House of David, the Sanhedrin, and prophecy, and emanating from a marginal, "eccentric" group headed by Yehuda Etzion, who is considered an oddball among the national-religious public—made little impact and won few followers. Nevertheless, the new reality created in Judea and Samaria in the wake of the

Oslo Accords between Israel and the PLO and the severe crisis that struck the settlers, gained Hai Vekayam public and media attention. The movement urged a civil revolt and called on Israelis to refuse to do military service either in the regular army or in the reserves. A few of the movement's activists (including Motti Karpel, a major in the Armored Corps reserves with a rich combat history) were convicted three times and served prison sentences for refusing to do reserve duty. The background to this refusal—also having the support of other radical settlers' groups—was the disinclination to obey laws that would promote an Israeli withdrawal from the territories or the application there of Palestinian (i.e., foreign) sovereignty. Members of the movement began a national registration of call-up books of reservists "whose loyalty to the people overrides their loyalty to the regime and its lackeys" (Dror 1993). Hai Vekayam announced that it would support any soldier or citizen who might be harmed by refusing to serve (Dror 1993). Yehuda Etzion also advocated civil disobedience and nonpayment of taxes (Sprinzak 1995, 109).

But the movement's principal channel of action continued to be the Temple Mount. Its activists tried dozens of times to enter the Temple Mount precinct (often three times a week) for prayer. On some occasions, foreign and local media representatives accompanied them. Their major goal, they say, is not to provoke the Muslim public or the Waqf authorities, but to arouse the Jewish public, especially the national-religious community, in order to generate a renewal of values that will foment the Hebraic revolution. Movement members have produced a videocassette documenting their attempts to pray on the Temple Mount and of both police and state efforts to thwart them—again, their purpose to awaken and "educate" the national-religious sector. Some activists have been repeatedly arrested. They refuse to sign a commitment not to visit the Temple Mount for thirty days or to report to the police for questioning as a condition of their release. An indictment has been filed against Yehuda Etzion, and he is forbidden to leave his settlement, Ofra. The movement has distributed leaflets urging police to refuse to obey any order entailing the prevention of Jewish worship on the Temple Mount (*Haaretz,* June 28, 1995). The movement's leaders want to bring the issue of prayer by Jews on the Temple Mount before the courts in order to arouse a wide public response, but so far they have had no success.

To date, the intensive activity of Hai Vekayam has produced two major results:

1. Its members' constant attempts to enter the Temple Mount have resulted in even more restrictions on religious Jews' visits there. They are allowed to enter as individuals or in groups of two or three but must be escorted by a Waqf guard and by a policeman in order to prevent any act of prayer (even mumbling a prayer aloud). These restrictions have affected mainly groups and individuals who had visited the Temple Mount for years, quietly and without prior coordination with the police and the Waqf. The police have "blacklists" of the movement's activists, and these activists are checked thoroughly before being allowed into the Temple Mount grounds.

2. Media images of Jews being forcibly ejected from the Temple Mount have brought home to the Jewish public (and particularly to the national-religious camp) the reality that prevails at the site: broad Muslim autonomy and a prohibition on Jewish prayer. The situation, which the public only vaguely understands, became much clearer in the wake of Hai Vekayam and the Temple Mount Faithful activity and prompted many—including supporters of the halakhic prohibition on visits of Jews to the Temple Mount— to protest the denial of the Jews' right to pray at their holiest site, when Muslims may do as they please. The result has been an increase in public support for Jewish prayer on the Temple Mount. Hai Vekayam activity has also had the effect of placing the Temple Mount issue higher on the agenda of the national-religious public. Additional groups and public figures, such as the Zo Artzeinu (This Is Our Land) movement and Prof. Hillel Weiss from Bar-Ilan University, have accepted Hai Vekayam's stand on the Temple Mount and its members' struggle for Jewish prayer there.

The entire subject of the Temple Mount, which in the past was considered "untouchable due to its sanctity" (Shragai 1995, 133), has in recent years become a widespread topic of study and contemplation in the religious Zionist yeshivas. As a result, the subject has also gained greater exposure among the secular public.

In an article entitled "The Temple Mount First," published within the framework of a personal column in the local weekly Jerusalem, Professor Hillel Weiss wrote on August 25, 1995:

Not a few rabbis, whose voices are being increasingly heard, know that the Temple Mount is the place from which the whole land of Israel is amenable to conquest, and if we do not fight for our rights there, we will not be able to smash this government and all the mediocrities who plan to replace it and then follow in its footsteps. This week I had the privilege of accompanying a group of youths, lion cubs among Israel's youth, and of clinging to the fringes of their robes, the heroes of Hai Vekayam, potent heroes who do His will. Whoever wants to set a limit to the destruction, let him hold on to the Temple Mount with all his might because it stands behind our [Western] Wall and without it there will be no peace. (13)

The growing number of Temple Mount activists within the national-religious camp in the past few years is one reflection of the radicalization that camp is undergoing. In the face of the Labor government's "way of withdrawal," the actions of Hai Vekayam and Zo Artzeinu have shown the readiness of much of the national-religious public to adopt a new approach in their relations with the state, which in their view has betrayed its mission. "The withdrawal from the depth, breadth, and heights of the Land of Israel is nowhere better symbolized than in the process of unwillingness and mental inability to arrange the situation on the Temple Mount," wrote Israel Medad, one of the leaders of the El Hahar ("To the Lord's Mountain Association) (Medad 1995, 75). Despair over the path of secular Zionism and the spectacle of the state withdrawing from Judea and Samaria provide fertile ground for the sprouting of Hai Vekayam's ideas concerning "Zionism that will transcend the Western Wall," a concept in which the Temple Mount occupies a major place as the symbol of control over the whole Land of Israel.

"The importance of the Hai Vekayam group," Prof. Sprinzak sums up, "lies . . . not in the number of its supporters but in the leadership quality of its few adherents, the systematic challenge it poses to trends toward pragmatism and acceptance which characterize the majority in Gush Emunim, and the serious questions it raises for those who have not yet lost their faith in the legitimacy of the State of Israel and its army but who are liable to despair when the moment of evacuation arrives" (1995, 190).

The murder of Prime Minister Yitzhak Rabin on November 4, 1995, which sent powerful shock waves through Israeli society and the national-religious public, drew an interesting reaction from Yehuda Etzion in the movement's journal *Labrit*. Etzion condemned the conception of the assassin, Yigal Amir, arguing that "no new creation will come forth . . . as a result of the physical liquidation of the leaders of the regime of *tohu* as long as the culture of *bohu* prevails [*tohu vebohu* means "chaos"; see Genesis 1:2]. He emphasized that his movement's educational mission, which seeks to build an ideological and conceptual infrastructure for "the fitting Kingdom of Israel," is a lengthy and arduous process: "It is impossible to move people forward by means of artificial pressures and one-time acts." Etzion saw Amir as a "product of the confusion" that marks the transition between "Israel's foreign, imported democratic culture," and "the culture of the Third Temple, which is struggling to be born" (Etzion 1995, 40–43). Indeed, in accordance with their conception of a lengthy and stubborn "educational process," Hai Vekayam activists tried again during Passover 1995 to enter the Temple Mount and pray.

More recently, a decline has been discernible in Hai Vekayam activity on the Temple Mount because of budget shortfalls and orders prohibiting its activists from approaching the area of the Mount. As a result, their work (and particularly that of Yehuda Etzion, its moving force) is currently concentrated in the educational-information sphere.

Other Groups

Apart from the Temple Mount Faithful and Hai Vekayam, several other groups that are active in connection with the Temple Mount deserve mention.

Yoel Lerner and Yemin Yisrael (Right of Israel). This group was founded by former Knesset member Prof. Shaul Guttman, who had resigned from the ultranationalist Moledet Party, and by Yoel Lerner, Guttman's parliamentary aide. Every few weeks, the two try to enter the Temple Mount and pray, are ejected by the police, and draw media attention. An order was once issued against Lerner prohibiting him from entering the Temple Mount for half a year (later reduced to three months). In contrast to his past underground operations, Lerner now declares that in recent years he has sought to change the status quo on the Temple Mount using open methods and especially through education (Shragai 1989; Shragai 1995, 179). Yemin Yisrael has not been active since 1996, though Lerner continues to be occupied with the Temple Mount in various groups.

Kach and Kahane Hai (Kahane Lives). These groups emphasize the nationalist aspect of the Temple Mount issue. Although they subscribe to the idea of establishing a new temple, in the here and now they are perturbed mainly by the presence of the Waqf and by the autonomy it enjoys in the center of Jerusalem. Among these groups' other motivations is a readiness to destroy the Muslim shrines on the Temple Mount in revenge for terrorist attacks on Jews and in order to prevent an Israeli withdrawal from Judea and Samaria. During Meir Kahane's funeral, held in Jerusalem in November 1990, public calls were heard for the first time urging the liberation of the Temple Mount and the demolition of the mosques. The police have "marked" some of the movements' activists, whose names appear on lists in the possession of the police at the gates to the Temple Mount and whose entry is prohibited or restricted (Shragai 1995, 181). Some of them attended the Temple Mount Yeshiva headed by Rabbi Avraham Toledano (the deposed successor of Meir Kahane), which was closed following the massacre perpetrated against Muslims at Me'arat Hamachpela (the Cave of Machpela, or Tomb of the Patriarchs) in Hebron in February 1994. One of the students at the yeshiva, Eyal Kenan, was arrested in December 1995 on suspicion of plotting to attack the Temple Mount mosques with an RPG mortar or a shoulder-fired missile (Sarna 1995). The potential danger latent in the members of these groups and in their periphery (which includes many "penitents") is considerable.

Another group that is close to Kach consists of pupils headed by Rabbi Yitzhak Ginsburg. They are influenced by Cabalistic ideas according to which man is responsible for helping God to bring about the process of redemption. One possible direction of activity of this group could involve "cleansing the defilement" from the Temple Mount (Shragai 1995, 180–81).

Temple Institute headed by Rabbi Israel Ariel (formerly head of Yamit Yeshiva). Located in the Jewish Quarter of Jerusalem's Old City, this institute manufactures and exhibits objects for use in a third temple and engages in extensive educational activity on the subject of the Temple. The institute also weaves vestments for the high priest, is engaged in a quest for a red heifer to solve the problem of defilement that prevents entry to the Temple Mount (see the beginning of this essay), and recently has introduced the Temple Display, which uses multimedia and other sophisticated computer technology to take the viewer on a "guided tour" of the Temple. More than one hundred thousand people have visited the institute, among them tens of thousands of pupils from state-religious schools. The institute does not try concretely to alter the status quo on the Temple Mount. Rabbi Ariel has explained that the temple he is laboring to build can be established only with the agreement of the people and the government, not by scheming to circumvent them. Ariel also maintains that the Halakhah permits the new temple to be erected alongside the mosque on the Temple Mount without having to destroy it. As for democracy, Rabbi Ariel maintains that democracy that operates contrary to the Torah is bad democracy (Shragai 1995, 146).

Movement to Establish the Temple. The moving spirit behind this group is the Elboim family. This *haredi* family, followers of the Belzer rebbe, visits the Temple Mount once a week, in defiance of the many warnings and leaflets issued against its members in *haredi* neighborhoods. The movement's founder, Rabbi David Elboim, also weaves vestments for the high priest; its secretary is his son, Yosef. The movement maintains a computerized office and issues a regular monthly bulletin, and its one hundred activists (all of them observant Jews) are committed to pay twenty shekels per month in dues and to visit the Temple Mount at least twelve times a year (Segal 1990).

Once a year the movement holds a Temple Banquet attended by some five hundred guests, including the activists from most of the Temple Mount groups. The movement coordinates its visits to the Temple Mount with the police and does not seek media publicity. This quiet approach has enabled it to perform the water libation ritual on the Temple Mount (Shragai 1995, 154). In recent years, it has cooperated closely with Yehuda Etzion and the Hai Vekayam group, as a result of which the movement's modest Temple Banquet turned into the gathering of fifteen hundred people mentioned earlier.

Ateret Kohanim Association. The association was founded in 1978—in the building that housed the Torat Hayim Yeshiva in the Muslim Quarter of Jerusalem's Old City—in the form of a yeshiva for the study of the lore of *ko-*

hanim (priests) and sacrifices. Its aim was to prepare priests for activity in the Temple. Twice a year, at Sukkot and Passover, Ateret Kohanim, in cooperation with the Ministry of Religious Affairs and other bodies, holds conferences to study the sacred rules of the Temple. Because these gatherings are described as "theoretical studies," rabbis from across the spectrum are able to attend. However, the original fervor of the association's founders to address the customs of the Temple gradually cooled following the appointment of Rabbi Shlomo Aviner as its yeshiva head. Under his tutelage, the study of Temple procedures was defined as mental, emotional, and intellectual—as distinguished from practical—preparation; one result of this change was that most of the pupils no longer concentrated their studies on the Temple rules (Shragai 1995, 152–53). The association devotes most of its energy to purchasing houses, land, and other property in the Muslim Quarter with a special emphasis on buildings close to the Temple Mount (mainly in the Via Dolorosa and on El-Wad Street).

Summary

Four of the seven groups mentioned above should be followed up. The Temple Mount Faithful erodes the status quo by attempting to worship demonstratively on the Temple Mount and by waging persistent legal battles. Its efforts have an impact on public opinion and put pressure on the Supreme Court to rule in favor of the struggle for Jewish prayer on the Temple Mount. Hai Vekayam, led by Yehuda Etzion, delegitimizes the governing authorities and transforms the stand of the national-religious public on the question of the Temple Mount.

With regard to Yemin Yisrael, special attention should be paid to the activity of Yoel Lerner, who has already been convicted three times for planning to blow up the Temple Mount mosques. His blatant contempt for democracy and for secular law, his tenacity on the Temple Mount issue, and his creative ideas make it imperative to keep a close watch on his activities (Shragai 1995, 179).

The mosques face concrete danger from activists and sympathizers who belong to Kach, Kahane Lives, and the pupils of Rabi Ginsburg. These groups and their peripheries contain penitents, eccentrics, and former criminals, all of whom are liable to do the unexpected. Potentially, they could produce a "lunatic" who will consider himself God's messenger on a mission to remove the "abomination" from the Temple Mount.

The final-status negotiations in which Jerusalem and the Temple Mount will be on the agenda could prove volatile (Shragai 1995, 181). The fear that Israel will give up its sovereignty on the Temple Mount or on parts of east Jerusalem can bring these groups to act. Any action by one of the groups (or even the rumor of an impending action) could spark a conflagration with the gravest consequences.

The Jewish Public and the Temple Mount

The Nonreligious Public

What is most striking about the entire Jewish public in Israel in connection with the Temple Mount is its ignorance of the status quo that has prevailed at the site since June 1967. For much of this public, the Temple Mount is terra incognita. Many have never visited it or not since immediately after the Six Day War. As a result of the intense media coverage of every incident at the site, many Israelis consider the Temple Mount the most dangerous place in Jerusalem and believe that because it is in Muslim hands, Jews cannot enter.

This situation accounts for the everyday reality on the Temple Mount: the mosques are packed with tourists enjoying the tranquil atmosphere; a few Israelis are also visible (usually organized groups such as army "educational seminars" or courses given by educational institutions of various types). Perhaps the Chief Rabbinate's halakhic edict against Jews entering the Temple Mount has also played a part in thrusting the subject out of the consciousness of the Jewish public (including the nonreligious public). The government's decision in 1967 to prevent Jewish worship on the Temple Mount has rooted itself deeply in the minds of Israelis. The Western Wall and the Western Wall tunnel that the Religious Affairs Ministry excavated have become the central sites of ritual for the Jewish public, whereas the Temple Mount—the site of the First and Second Temples—has been shunted aside.

Hence, perhaps, the indifference that the vast majority of the Israeli

Jewish public manifested for Article 9(2) of the Israel-Jordan Treaty of Peace (1994), which states that "Israel respects the present special role of the Hashemite Kingdom of Jordan in Muslim holy shrines in Jerusalem. When negotiations on the permanent status will take place, Israel will give high priority to the Jordanian historic role in these shrines." Most Israelis accepted this stipulation without objection. The Temple Mount has become a point of dispute between Jordan and the PLO, and very few Israeli Jews seem concerned about the place the Jewish side will have in the final settlement pertaining to the Temple Mount.

Should we therefore assume that the majority of the nonreligious Israeli Jewish public will also accept complacently a settlement that will institutionalize Muslim autonomy on the Temple Mount by, among other things, permitting a Palestinian or Muslim flag to be raised above the Dome of the Rock, as various individuals and groups (Israeli and foreign) have suggested since 1967 (Shragai 1995, 367–82)? The answer will depend on the political framework of the settlement. Within the nonreligious public, opposition to such an arrangement could arise on nationalist rather than religious or moral grounds. Many nonreligious Jews, be their politics Likud or Labor, will not easily swallow the sight of a Muslim or Palestinian flag flying above the Dome of the Rock and overlooking the Western Wall Plaza. They will take it as a blow to national pride. (In this connection, we should note Menachem Begin's firm refusal to accept Anwar Sadat's suggestion of raising a Muslim or Saudi flag above the Dome of the Rock.)

A comprehensive public opinion survey conducted at the end of 1995 by Professor Elihu Katz, Dr. Shulamit Levi, from the Guttman Institute of Applied Social Research in Jerusalem, and Prof. Jerome M. Segal, from the University of Maryland, subsequently reinforced this conclusion. Their findings, based on face-to-face interviews with a representative sample of 1,500 Jews in Israel and 121 Jewish settlers living across the Green Line, showed a strong affinity of all sections of the Jewish public in Israel for the Temple Mount (Katz, Levi, and Segal 1997). Fully 93 percent of the respondents said that the Temple Mount was important to them as part of Jerusalem, as compared with 99 percent who cited the Western Wall (ibid., 13). The Temple Mount was popular even among residents of Tel Aviv (where 82 percent of the respondents said it was extremely important) and among nonobservant Jews (of whom 65 percent said it was extremely important). Surprisingly, a relatively low proportion of Jerusalem residents (59 percent) ranked the Temple Mount as an extremely important site for them (ibid., 17).

A large majority (84 percent of the respondents) said it was important for them that Jews should be able to worship on the Temple Mount. Even among nonobservant Jews, a high proportion of the respondents (73 percent) stated that it was important or very important that Jews should be able to pray on the Temple Mount (ibid., 13, 39).

Sixty percent of those polled said they were unwilling to consider—within the framework of negotiations with the Palestinians—the transfer of the Temple Mount to the control of the Waqf, meaning that they effectively oppose the institutionalization of the current situation (ibid. 14, 18). In reply to another question, 79 percent of the respondents said they were not ready to entertain seriously the idea that Israel, as part of settlement with the Palestinians, will recognize Palestinian sovereignty over the Temple Mount in return for Palestinian recognition of Israeli sovereignty over the Western Wall. And 65 percent stated that they could not seriously consider the idea, once broached by King Hussein, that the two sides will drop their claims of sovereignty to the Temple Mount and leave sovereignty there in the hands of God (ibid., 14, 40).

Overall, the findings of the survey show that the Temple Mount occupies an important place in the consciousness of all sections of the Jewish public in Israel. An overwhelming majority actually supports the right of Jewish worship within the Temple Mount precinct and opposes any arrangement in which the site would be transferred officially to the control of the Waqf or to Palestinian sovereignty. These data are of critical importance. Their publication could serve as additional "ammunition" for those who advocate changing the status quo in the direction of granting Jews the right to pray on the Temple Mount. The survey also shows that there is little inclination within the Jewish public to agree to any concessions with respect to Israeli sovereignty and Israeli control over the Temple Mount.

The *Haredi* Public

The major factor that unites the *haredi* public on the question of the Temple Mount is its total acceptance of the rabbinic injunctions forbidding Jews to enter the site and pray there. The *haredim* strongly reject, on religious and ideological grounds, any intervention by the "Zionist state" on an issue as sacred and fundamental to Judaism as the Temple and everything pertaining to it. This sphere, they believe, is reserved exclusively for divine activity. Apart from the late Lubavitcher rebbe, all the important *haredi* religious authorities have objected to Jews visiting the Temple Mount—hence the sharp attacks on the Temple Mount Faithful in the *haredi* press whenever that group tries to enter the Temple Mount and pray there. An example is the editorial that appeared on August 7, 1995, in *Yated Neeman,* the paper of the *haredi* Lithuanian stream led by the late Rabbi Eliezer Shach:

> The true Temple Mount faithful—those who understand the sanctity of the site and are aware of the prohibition on visiting it in our time—naturally feel no grief that Jews are prevented from entering the Holy Place. Since the Temple Mount passed into Israeli hands, the greatest Torah sages have warned against Jews visiting the site on pain of committing a grave mortal sin. The group known as the "Temple Mount Faithful" does not aspire to enter the site because of love of the sacred but for "nationalist" reasons that are void of Jewish faith. They release all their supposed Jewish energy in abortive attempts to enter the Holy Place, though their "observance" of the other commandments is highly dubious. Therefore we are not sorry that they are unable to visit the Holy Place. Whoever does not heed the directives of the Torah sages will end by submitting to the dictates of the Palestinian *shebab* [street youth]. (2)

The *haredi* stand exercises a decisive impact on the chief rabbis. Sephardi Chief Rabbi Eliahu Bakshi-Doron, who is close to the Shas (Sephardi Torah Guardians) Party, is deeply influenced by the ruling of Shas's patron, Rabbi Ovadiah Yosef, against Jews visiting the Temple Mount. Nor is it likely that Chief Ashkenazi Rabbi Israel Lau, whose formative years were spent in *haredi* educational institutions, will defy the central *haredi* religious authorities in this matter. In short, it is difficult to imagine that the Chief Rabbinate will revise its 1967 ruling, despite pressures from various quarters in the national-religious camp.

But the fact that the *haredim* absent themselves from the Temple Mount and sharply condemn Jews who visit it should not be construed to mean that they will accept passively a settlement that institutionalizes Muslim autonomy at the site. The rightward political radicalization of the *haredi* population in recent years and the increasingly hawkish views espoused at both its grassroots and leadership levels will undoubtedly generate fierce opposition to any attempt to transfer Jewish sanctities to Muslims. The *haredi* leaders perceive the halakhic question of entry to the Temple Mount as an internal Jewish affair that has no bearing on "our right to the Mount." In the same vein, the *haredi* press views Muslim control of the Temple Mount, in continuation of the halakhic tradition, as illegitimate. Witness the statement in the daily *Hamodia* of August 7, 1995: "The description 'foxes prowl over it' [Lamentations 5:18] has been superseded by the mosques that were erected on the Temple Mount by the Muslims, who provoked the Jews and made constant efforts to offend their deep sensibilities and even had the audacity to tell all kinds of tales about the Muslims' attachment to that sacred Mount" (2).

The Washington Declaration, in which Israel recognizes Jordan's special role on the Temple Mount, induced the chief rabbis to seek clarifications from the late Prime Minister Yitzhak Rabin: Rabbi Bakshi-Doron demanded that Israel preserve the status of the Temple Mount as the holiest site for Jews and that nothing should be done to modify its status without prior consultation with the chief rabbis; and Rabbi Lau explained that a halakhic ruling cannot be changed by a political decision and that the Chief Rabbinate would oppose any sign of foreign sovereignty over the Temple Mount, whether by internationalizing it or by declaring it extraterritorial. Rabin accepted these importunities, which also had the support of the National-Religious Party (NRP) (Shragai 1995, 389).

Another reason for *haredi* opposition to the formalization of Muslim autonomy on the Temple Mount could be the fear that it would have an adverse effect on the status of the Western Wall, where many of the worshipers are *haredi*.

The National-Religious Public

In contrast to the situation in the *haredi* camp, there is no uniform position among the national-religious public on the question of whether Jews can visit and pray on the Temple Mount. Much of the national-religious community, probably the majority, accepts the ruling of the chief rabbis and the opinion of its important spiritual leaders, barring their view of visits by Jews to the Temple Mount. However, an increasing number of rabbis believe that Jews should be allowed to visit the permissible areas of the site and pray there, and that a synagogue could be built there. Lessons on the subject are given in several *hesder* yeshivas, and more members of the national-religious population are visiting the permissible areas. Thus, a large minority of rabbis, together with various groups within the national-religious camp, would like to revise the arrangements Moshe Dayan introduced on the Temple Mount in 1967. Even among those who accept the prohibition on entering the Temple Mount, there are many who claim that the government has no right to prevent prayer by rabbis and individual Jews who believe that it is permitted.

The shifting stands in the national-religious camp concerning prayer on the Temple Mount are discernible in statements some of its mainstream figures have made. For example, the former deputy president of the Supreme Court, Justice Menachem Elon, has publicly urged a revision in the stand of the Chief Rabbinate and the government on this question:

> Reconsideration should be given concerning the rightness of the government's stand which absolutely prohibits even one Jew from praying on the Temple Mount while holding a *siddur* [prayer book], even where entry is permitted according to many religious authorities, whereas prayer ritual is permitted everywhere on the Temple Mount only to the adherents of the Muslim religion. . . . Similarly, the Chief Rabbinate should consider the possibility of annulling the prohibition on entering the Temple Mount, which extends even to places where this is permissible according to many great halakhic authorities, a view which I also accept." (Unpublished speech by Justice Elon in a ceremony at Yad Ben-Zvi Institute, Jerusalem, June 21, 1995)

Journalist Israel Harel, former editor of *Nekuda* and a former leading member of the Yesha (Judea-Samaria-Gaza) Council, denounced Israel's decision in the Washington Declaration to recognize the special status granted to Jordan in administering the Temple Mount:

> Halakhic and political cowardice has prevented the religious establishment from ever giving serious thought to the Temple Mount issue, and in effect has created a factual, educational, and psychological situation that enabled Israeli statesmen to make the concession to Jordan. . . . The only ones who have fought tirelessly for years over the Temple Mount question are marginal groups to which no one—neither the religious establishment nor the establishment of the nationalist parties, nor even Gush Emunim and the settlers' establishment—attached any importance. Today we see how wrong we were not to speak out about sovereignty on the Temple Mount, which unfortunately has officially been transferred to the hands of gentiles. (Qtd. in Shragai 1995, 390)

These recent trends were given expression in the NRP platform in the 1996 general elections, which urged that "the status of the Temple Mount as the holiest place of the Jewish people be ensured and arrangements made concerning the religious and national rights of the Jewish people there [i.e., Jewish prayer]" (*Haaretz,* May 10, 1996).

A variety of reasons account for the growing numbers of individuals and groups within the national-religious camp that advocate Jewish prayer on the Temple Mount: shock at media images of Temple Mount Faithful and Hai Vekayam activists being ejected from the Temple Mount; religious and nationalist radicalization among sections of this population since the start of the peace process; a decline in the status of the Western Wall as the central site of ritual; and, above all, the awareness that continuation of the policy under which Jews do not visit the Temple Mount will result in the loss of Israeli sovereignty there.

Incipient signs that politicians are responding to the pressure to permit Jewish prayer at the site may be found in a preelection letter from Likud leader Benjamin Netanyahu to Yehuda Etzion declaring that the right of Jewish prayer on the Temple Mount should be arranged after the Likud reassumes the leadership of the state *(Jerusalem,* Apr. 28, 1995). Following Netanyahu's victory in the May 1996 elections, Etzion and his movement sent letters to the prime minister and to the new justice minister requesting the implementation of Netanyahu's pledge (Shragai 1996a). In addition, then-religious affairs minister Prof. Shimon Shetreet stated, after Temple Mount Faithful activists were prevented from visiting the site on the Ninth of Ab in 1995, that arrangements for Jewish prayer on the Temple Mount should be introduced.

Given this state of affairs, the national-religious public and the NRP leadership can be expected to mount trenchant opposition to any attempt to formalize Muslim autonomy on the Temple Mount by acts such as raising Palestinian or Islamic flags. Muslim demands along those lines will probably only heighten the pressures from various groups within the national-religious population to permit Jewish prayer on the Temple Mount and even to build a synagogue there.

Recent Developments

The most important recent development regarding Jewish prayer on the Temple Mount is a ruling issued in February 1997 by the Committee of Yesha Rabbis—a central body in the national-religious camp, which encompasses sixty rabbis of settlements and yeshivas in the West Bank and the Gaza Strip—permitting every rabbi who believes that it is permissible to enter the Temple Mount area to do so himself and to instruct his congregation on how to enter the compound while following halakhic strictures (Shilo 1997). This halakhic ruling, which was widely distributed in synagogues, effectively opens the way for larger sections of the national-religious public to visit the Temple Mount. I believe that it is a watershed in rabbinical pronouncements on the Temple Mount and that it will have far-reaching influence. The Chief Rabbinate's reaction was republication of the decree prohibiting Jews from entering the Temple Mount, but the pressure on them to change their ruling continues.

The major underlying factor that prompted the ruling is the Palestinian Authority's creeping takeover of the Temple Mount and the feeling of the rabbis that even Israel's de jure sovereignty at the site is being eroded.

The rabbinical ruling also reflects the national-religious public's grow-ing interest in the Temple and the religious rules related to it, an interest that has been manifested in a number of events: the preoccupation with the red heifer that was born in the village of Kfar Hasidim in March 1997, but was disqualified because it had several black hairs on its neck (Shragai 1997b); the "training" and study that advocates of building a third temple have under-gone in performing sacrifices (such as the ceremony held in Jerusalem's Abu-Tor neighborhood in April 1997); the renewal of customs that were practiced during the Temple period (such as the intercalation of the month, which has been carried out at the Western Wall excavations in recent months); and the large gathering held in September 1998, in which many families also took part (Shragai 1998c). The point is that occupation with the Temple is no longer confined to marginal groups but is attracting large sections of the national-religious mainstream.

These developments in the halakhic-religious sphere naturally have repercussions in the political and judicial realms. An Israeli cabinet discus-sion in early 1998 revealed that six ministers (Limor Livnat, Tzachi Hanegbi, Moshe Katsav from the Likud; Yitzhak Levy of the NRP; Rafael Eitan of Tsomet; and the nonparty Finance Minister Yaakov Neeman) advocated changing the status quo to permit Jews, including individual worshipers, to pray on the Temple Mount. Prime Minister Benjamin Netanyahu stated that the inner cabinet would discuss the subject but did not keep his promise (Shragai 1999).

In the judicial sphere, several important developments have exposed the flimsy basis for the government's decision of summer 1967 to prohibit Jew-ish worship on the Temple Mount. For example, a hitherto unknown opin-ion, delivered in 1986 by the jurist Aryeh Zohar of the cabinet secretariat, came to light, which stated that the government had never taken a decision of principle to prohibit Jewish worship on the Temple Mount. Only an ad hoc decision was made—following the attempt by Rabbi Goren to organize a mass prayer at the site on August 20, 1967—stating that "when Jewish worshipers come to the entry of the Temple Mount, they will be directed by the security forces to the Western Wall" (qtd. in Shragai 1997a). That tem-porary measure thus became the foundation of the policy that the govern-ment, the State Attorney's Office, and the police pursued regarding Jewish worship on the Temple Mount. Since then, successive Israeli governments have clung tenaciously to this order and have refrained from taking a principled, explicit decision on the subject. A similar approach appears in a letter the legal adviser to the Prime Minister's Office, Shimon Stein, sent in March 1997 to Israel Medad, of the To the Lord's Mountain Association, stating that to the best of his knowledge "worship of Jews on the Temple Mount was never prohibited." Stein referred the group to the police in order "to receive guidelines as to the dates of entry to the site and the procedure for behavior there" (qtd. in Shragai 1997b). In reply to a question by the reporter Nadav Shragai, the legal adviser explained that his reply referred to individual worship. Nevertheless, this official response is of great importance with respect to the political and judicial struggle to change the status quo on the Mount.

New attitudes regarding the possibility of Jewish worship on the Temple Mount have also appeared in recent years in court declarations and judgments. Judge David Frankel, of the Jerusalem Magistrate's Court, noted in a public lecture he delivered at a seminar called "Jerusalem, City of Law and Justice" that "if the rulings by the majority of Israel's rabbis were different, the policy of the Israeli government would also be different, and the courts would come under pressure to alter their attitude. If it is a matter of individuals, it is a need from the court's point of view, but if it is a matter of tens and hundreds of thousands, it becomes a public interest and then the attitude would certainly be different" (unpublished lecture delivered in Jerusalem on June 11, 1996). Against this background, it is possible to understand the crucial significance of the Yesha rabbis' ruling (Frankel 1998, 42).

The former deputy president of the Supreme Court, Justice Menachem Elon, has expressed himself in favor of a revision of the government's decision on Jewish worship on the Temple Mount (Ramon 1997, 25–26), as has former Supreme Court justice Eliezer Goldberg (now the state comptroller). In connection with Muslim building in the area of the Mount known as Solomon's Stables, Goldberg wrote that the expansion of the Muslims' area of worship on the Temple Mount "is a genuine affront to the religious and national sensitivities of a large Jewish public regarding the holiest place in Judaism" (HCJ 7128/96, judgment of Mar. 12, 1997, 20–21). Nor did Justice

Goldberg hesitate to urge the political level "to fill with content and meaning the historic call: the Temple Mount is in our hands."

Conclusion

Clearly, then, the Temple Mount issue is not only one of the major barriers to the resolution of the Arab–Israeli conflict; under certain circumstances, it could also become one of the deepest issues of contention within the Israeli Jewish society. The attitudes of different groups within the Jewish public and of the state authorities toward the Temple Mount reflect stands relating to Israel's Jewish identity, state-religion relations, and the spiritual image of the state in the near and more remote future.

Against this background, we can understand why the government and the Knesset have not to this day formally approved the arrangement on the Temple Mount Moshe Dayan made in 1967, in particular the ban on Jewish prayer. Nor has the Israeli Supreme Court, which has addressed the question on many occasions, succeeded in placing the 1967 arrangement on solid legal foundations and in resolving the contradiction between the government's decision to prohibit Jewish prayer and the principle of freedom of access to the Holy Places as formulated in the Protection of the Holy Places Law (1967) and in paragraph 3 of the Basic Law: Jerusalem, Capital of Israel (1980). The major stabilizing element has been the Chief Rabbinate's halakhic ruling and the leading religious authorities' prohibiting observant Jews from visiting the Temple Mount, a prohibition accepted by the overwhelming majority of the religious public.

That ruling has also dealt a mortal blow to the political-public struggle to alter the status quo of 1967. The ostensible vanguard of the campaign for Jewish prayer on the Temple Mount—the national-religious camp—has for the most part accepted the halakhic judgment. Even Gush Emunim, the spearhead of the activist drive for Jewish settlement in Judea and Samaria, has not engaged the Temple Mount front.

The failure of the political and legal campaign to change the status quo that was fixed by the government, the Supreme Court, and the Chief Rabbinate has engendered attempts by individuals (of differing levels of sanity), underground organizations, and other groups to transform radically the situation on the Temple Mount. They have sought, by their own methods, to create facts and to hasten the process of redemption. They have not hesitated to use violence at one of the most sensitive sites on earth. The tremendous attention they have attracted and the apocalyptic potential of their actions have acted as a magnet for additional "eccentrics" and the unhinged to try and leave their mark on the Mount. In some cases, the latter have come perilously close to success. Other efforts have not gone beyond the planning stage. Even now, schemes are perhaps being hatched to demolish the mosques on the Temple Mount.

Recent years have seen a gradual increase in the number of those—particularly from the national-religious camp—who favor Jewish prayer in the permissible areas on the Temple Mount and even in the building of a synagogue at the site. The force of the halakhic prohibition, which has been the greatest single factor in stabilizing the status quo, is slowly being undermined, and individuals and groups are beginning to pray on the Temple Mount despite the great efforts of the police. The activities of Hai Vekayam and the Temple Mount Faithful are helping to keep the subject under the public spotlight. Growing numbers in the national-religious camp now believe that the fact that Jews shunned the Temple Mount was a severe blow to Israeli sovereignty there and helped entrench Muslim control of the site. The remedy, they say, is to permit Jewish prayer on the Temple Mount and to formulate a new status quo. In 1996, a Temple Mount lobby was formed, and its secretaries, Rabbi Dr. Itamar Wahrhaftig and Rabbi Dr. Daniel Meir Weill, urge that the religious rights of the Jewish people at this Holy Place be ensured in any political settlement that may be worked out with the Palestinians (*Haaretz,* Apr. 25, 1996).

The ruling of the Committee of Yesha Rabbis, the importance of which has already been indicated, might serve as a major halakhic basis for permitting Jews to pray on the Temple Mount.

The fear that Israel will lose its sovereignty on the Temple Mount in the wake of its agreements with Jordan and the Palestinian Authority is generating additional political pressure to permit Jews to visit the site and pray there. At the same time, ideas are being broached for a new arrangement on the

Temple Mount to institutionalize Muslim autonomy and to raise Muslim or Palestinian flags above the mosques in return for Palestinian recognition of Israeli sovereignty in various parts of Jerusalem.

Such proposals will encounter strong resistance from the *haredim,* from the national-religious community, and even from considerable sections of the nonreligious public. Indeed, the publicity given to these ideas may well have the effect of intensifying the demands to permit Jews to pray on the Temple Mount and to revise the rules of the status quo of 1967.

Apprehension over the negotiations on the status of Jerusalem might well induce various political elements in the Jewish public—in the national-religious community especially—to step up their demands to ensure the right of Jewish prayer and ritual on the Temple Mount. Indeed, the NRP platform in the 1966 elections called, as we saw, for "arrangements [to be] made concerning the religious and national rights of the Jewish people at this Holy Place" (National Religious Party 1996). This call was echoed in the Policy Guidelines of the Netanyahu government, in which paragraph III/4 states: "The Government will make proper arrangements for Jews at holy sites in accordance [with] the guidelines of religious law" (*Haaretz,* June 17, 1996). The NRP, a member of Netanyahu's coalition, had wanted the Temple Mount to be mentioned by name, but Netanyahu decided otherwise, and he also moved the statement from the "Jerusalem" section to the "Religion and State" section (Shragai 1996b).

A different response came from Shaykh Ikrima Said Sabri, the mufti of Jerusalem, who is close to the PLO. He stated that Muslims everywhere and in Jerusalem especially oppose changing the situation on the Temple Mount and warned against the consequences of such a decision (Shragai 1996a). Opening the Temple Mount to Jewish prayer can also be expected to generate fierce resistance from the rabbis and political leaders of the *haredi* population, particularly the Shas Party and its spiritual leader, Rabbi Ovadiah Yosef.

Given the intensifying demands to modify the status quo on the Temple Mount and the far-reaching consequences any such change would have, balanced judgment and maximum caution are required from all those involved—in word or in deed—with this most sensitive of issues. The opening of the Western Wall tunnel and the renovation of Solomon's Stables in September–October 1996 show again the great public sensitivity and the far-reaching consequences of any change in the status quo in the area of the Temple Mount.

The chain of events concerning the Temple Mount that took place between June and December 2000 brought the processes and phenomena discussed in this article to the surface. First, the construction-related activities of the Waqf and the Islamic Movement–the opening of the "monumental" entrance to the mosque in King Solomon's Stables–was met in June by the protest of wide circles within the Israeli public.[2] Personalities from all ends of the political spectrum joined the committee formed to prevent the destruction of the Temple Mount antiquities, including archaeologists, jurists, writers, educators, and researchers. One of the causes of the extensive protest was the stubborn activity of the Temple Mount groups, who organized a joint staff intended to raise the level of public consciousness of the issue.

Muslim construction, pressure by the Temple Mount movements, and the letter from Sephardi Chief Rabbi Bakshi-Doron, opposing a change in the status quo on the Temple Mount and Jewish ascent to the Mount, also brought about a certain change in the position of the Supreme Rabbinical Council, which established for the first time a six-member special rabbis' committee to examine the possibility of establishing a synagogue on the Mount.[3]

The discussions at the Camp David conference (July 2000), at which the Temple Mount occupied a central place, the events of the al-Aqsa Intifada (which broke out after Ariel Sharon's visit to the Mount on September 28, 2000), the prohibition of non-Muslim visitors to the Temple Mount, and the negotiations between Israel and the Palestinians during those bloody events—from which the various ideas were leaked concerning Israeli agreement to transfer sovereignty over the Mount to the Palestinian Authority—awakened harsh reactions within Israeli public opinion, including persons

2. Nadav Shragai, "Protest Against the Destruction of Antiquities by the Waqf on the Temple Mount" [Heb.], *Ha'aretz,* 12 June 2000.

3. Nadav Shragai, "This Week the Rabbinate Will Begin Discussing the Establishment of a Synagogue on the Temple Mount" [Heb.], *Ha'aretz,* 3 September 2000.

and groups that do not belong to the right-wing camp or the national-religious public. A public opinion survey conducted in December 2000 (in the framework of the "peace index" project headed by Prof. Ephraim Ya'ar and Dr. Tamar Hermann of Tel-Aviv University) revealed a clear majority of 66 percent of the Jewish-Israeli public which opposed the Clinton proposal (27 percent agreed and 7 percent had no opinion). According to the Clinton proposal, the Temple Mount would be transferred to Palestinian sovereignty, while the Western Wall and the Jewish Quarter of the Old City would remain under Israeli sovereignty.[4]

The sharpest reactions were those of the "Yesha" Rabbis' Committee, Rabbi Mordecai Eliyahu, and the Temple Mount groups that support Jewish worship on the Mount.[5] The Temple Mount activists have been caught in a paradoxical situation: on the one hand, in light of the events referred to above, they have succeeded in getting large portions of Israeli society to support their struggle; on the other hand, the realization of their goal—enabling Jews to worship on the Mount or to establish a synagogue there—seems further away than ever, considering the anticipated Muslim reaction in Israel and abroad. The expectation that the Temple Mount will become one of the rockiest points of dispute in the Israeli-Palestinian/Jewish-Muslim conflict has thus been completely fulfilled.

4. Efraim Ya'ar and Tamar Hermann, "A Clear Jewish Majority Against the Main Sections of the American Bridging Proposal" [Heb.], *Ha'aretz*, 4 January 2001.

5. Nadav Shragai, "Rabbis: We Must Fight Until the Land Burns" [Heb.], *Ha'aretz*, 29 December 2000.

PART FOUR

Issues of Governance

12

The Municipal Organization
of the Jerusalem Metropolitan Area

Conceptual Alternatives

Shlomo Hasson

The aim of this essay is to present a conceptual framework of and several alternatives for the municipal organization of the Jerusalem metropolitan area. These alternatives may help outline a policy for the future of the city and serve as a basis for public discussion of the issue. Obviously, the most difficult dilemma in the case of the Jerusalem is sovereignty. My argument is that on the issue of Jerusalem a compromise must be reached between two extreme stances: preservation of the status quo and radical change. The status quo approach, which is Israel's official position, maintains that the solution to the problem of Jerusalem consists of freezing the present situation, which implies preserving Israeli sovereignty over the area currently in Israeli hands. The radical change approach, postulated by the Palestinian Authority, maintains that the solution to the problem of Jerusalem requires (1) handing over all the West Bank, including the areas around Jerusalem, to Palestinian control; (2) giving the eastern part of the city to the Palestinian Authority; and (3) establishing an eastern capital in east Jerusalem. The working assumption underlying the essay is that neither of these alternatives will be acceptable to the other side. Each alternative is based on an absolute concept of sovereignty, which in my view will not be acceptable to the other side. In line with recent theories, I would like to suggest new concepts of sovereignty that may help outline a policy for the future municipal organization of the city.

Sovereignty

Sovereignty in its classic connotation of total and indivisible state power, writes Lapidoth (1995), has been eroded. Modern economic developments, innovations in transportation and communications, and new rules of modern constitutional and international law have brought about profound changes in the meaning and implication of sovereignty. Participation in international organizations with wide powers has greatly reduced the substantive powers traditionally reserved for the state. The ethnic revival presents yet another challenge to the old notion of sovereignty. Because several thousand peoples or ethnic communities exist in the world and the planet is too small to provide each of them full sovereignty over a piece of land, compromises must be found to satisfy at least partially the aspirations of these various groups.

The search for a compromise has led to the development of new concepts of sovereignty. Among them are the concepts of pluralistic sovereignty, divided sovereignty, shared sovereignty, and functional sovereignty. The functional approach to sovereignty, for example, is based on the existence of a multilayered reality consisting of a variety of authoritative structures.

Geopolitical Complexity

The extreme sensitivity of the region in terms of religion and culture as well as its geopolitical complexity militate against any simplistic approach based on the concept of absolute sovereignty. As map 12.1 clearly shows, Jerusalem lies at the intersection of two national axes. The Jewish population distribution is from west to east (from Tel Aviv in the west to Ma'ale Adummim in the east), whereas the Arab population distribution is from north to south (from Nablus in the north to Hebron in the south). As a result, the Palestinians immediately interpret any development plan under-

Two Geopolitical Axes

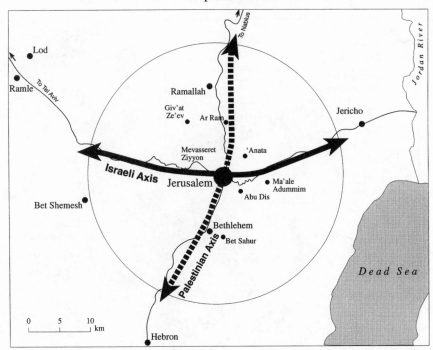

Map 12.1

taken by the Israeli government along the east-west axis (e.g., expansion of Ma'ale Adummim or the building in Har Homa) as a deliberate attempt to cut through their national settlement axis that runs from north to south. The Israelis, on the other hand, view with suspicion any Palestinian building along the north-south axis (e.g., building in the villages surrounding Jerusalem from the north, such as Ar Ram), which in their view may lead to encirclement of the city.

Within the city of Jerusalem, the settlement issue is no less problematic. As map 12.2 illustrates vividly, both Jews and Arabs inhabit the eastern part of the city because new Jewish neighborhoods built after 1967 border with Arab neighborhoods. Any attempt to separate the two groups either by territorial partition or population transfer is doomed to fail.

Finally, the Old City of Jerusalem with its mosques, churches, synagogues, and other holy sites is an area that every party wishes to claim for itself.

Distribution of Population by Religion, 1995

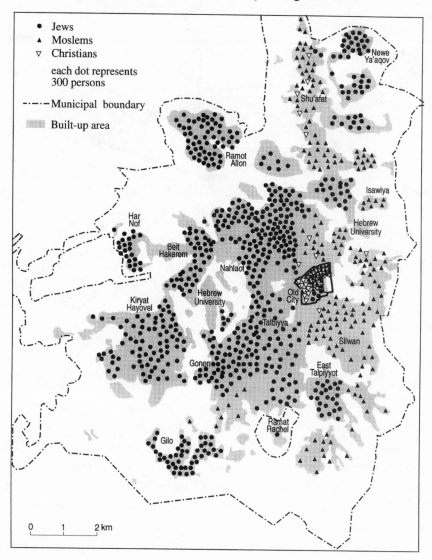

Map 12.2

Divided Regions and Cities: Lessons of Experience

Lessons accumulated in ethnonationally divided regions around the world
clearly point to the existence of territorial and institutional alternatives for

conflict regulation. The territorial alternative is based on land division be-tween the competing nations. This alternative might involve population transfer or ethnic cleansing or war and may eventually lead to the creation of homogeneous ethnonational regions. The institutional alternative, in con-trast, is based on the creation of new administrative and political structures without necessarily leading to territorial division. This method is expressed in the setting up of new organizations that act as coordinating bodies and in-volves new patterns of cooperation between national groups, decentraliza-tion of power, and higher levels of citizen participation in decision-making processes (McGarry and O'Leary 1993).

Although a territorial solution to the problem of Jerusalem is possible, the preferred option is an institutional one. In other words, a viable solution to the Jerusalem problem should rely on the creation of new institutional structures and new concepts of sovereignty. In developing the conceptual alternatives, I have benefited from different ideas and proposals that have come from various academic researches and politicians over the years. Sir William Fitzgerald suggested in 1945 that the city of Jerusalem be divided into Jewish and Arab quarters. Each quarter, he maintained, would be ad-ministered by a separate council, and the two councils would be under the authority of a citywide council (Ginio 1980). Benvenisti (1988) proposed in 1968 the setting up of a binational metropolitan council administered by Is-rael and Transjordan. Albin, Amirav, and Seniora suggested in 1991–92 the creation of a metropolitan city in the Jerusalem area. Heller and Nusseibeh (1991) put forward a proposal to create two distinct municipal organs under the auspices of an umbrella city council. Although these proposals have never been realized, they affected the municipal thinking within Jerusalem. In 1982, Teddy Kollek, then the city mayor, introduced the concept of neighborhood administrations and claimed that these organizations might eventually play a leading role in the solution of the Jerusalem problem (Kollek 1988–89). In 1998, there were twenty-eight such councils in Jerusalem, and a recent proposal suggested clustering these councils in four distinct groups: Arab, *haredi* (ultraorthodox) Jew, nonorthodox Jew, and the Old City. The Beilin-Abu Mazen plan attempted to solve the problem of Jerusalem by expanding the boundaries of the city and then dividing it into two sove-reign areas, one at al-Quds and the other in Jerusalem, but the plan was not daring enough to examine new ways of sharing the city and its metropolitan area.

It is evident that each proposal has focused on a specific geographic level: the metropolitan area, the municipal city, and the subsections of the city (i.e., areas that encompass several neighborhoods). With the exception of Elazar (1991), there has been no attempt to develop a comprehensive approach to the Jerusalem problem that relates to the different geographic levels. I would like to suggest several institutional alternatives to the Jerusalem problem that, on the one hand, relate to different geographic levels and, on the other, adopt new concepts of sovereignty.

Framework Principles

Given the geopolitical complexity, a new conceptual framework with respect to sovereignty and municipal organization of the city and its environment seems to be required. The conceptual framework should be based on several principles involving space, time, and the linkage between arrangements in Jerusalem and other components of an agreement between Israel and the Palestinian Authority.

Space

Any discussion of Jerusalem must transcend the municipal boundaries and consider the Jerusalem metropolitan area in its entirety. In addition to the city of Jerusalem, this area includes the cities and settlements of Ramallah to the north, Bethlehem to the south, Ma'ale Adummim to the east, and Mevasseret Tzion to the west. A metropolitan approach to Jerusalem is obligatory for the following reasons:

1. In the wake of the Oslo Accords, the territory of the Palestinian Authority will be situated next to Jerusalem, and its presence will have an impact on the lives of the Jewish and Arab residents of the city.

2. Outside the Jerusalem city limits are Jewish localities that must be considered in any scenario that deals with municipal organization of the Jerusalem area.

3. The city is an economic, cultural, and service center for the population of the metropolitan area; therefore, any discussion of Jerusalem must address the system surrounding it.

4. Continued population growth (both Jewish and Arab) in the city will be manifested in a westward and eastward spillover of population beyond the present city limits.

Time

It will take a long time to conclude arrangements for Jerusalem and its metropolitan area because of the centrality of the city in the Israeli and Palestinian ethos, the intensity of emotions regarding the city on both sides, the sociodemographic complexity of the city, and the affinity of nations around the world for the city. It is assumed that instead of reaching a permanent agreement in a single step, the Israelis and Palestinians will develop a series of interim arrangements that reflect the evolving system of relations between Israel and the Palestinian Authority. These arrangements will not be linear; there will be ups and downs, and solutions that cannot be foreseen will develop on the basis of them. The incremental approach will allow both parties to devise confidence-building measures to alleviate existing tensions—for example, changing the existing Israeli housing policy and withdrawing the residence limitations set on Jerusalem's Palestinian citizens.

Linkage

It is a fundamental principle that arrangements in Jerusalem must be packaged together with spatial and social arrangements outside Jerusalem. The arrangements outside Jerusalem would relate to the geographical area adjacent to the city (the Jerusalem metropolitan area) and to all of Judea and Samaria. They would also relate to arrangements concerning cooperation between Israeli and Palestinian authorities in the area and the use of transportation routes and water resources.

Compromise

The fundamental principle behind the proposal that follows is that on the issue of Jerusalem a compromise must be reached between the two extreme stances outlined above. The two sides will present their claims for sovereignty over the city as starting positions, but during the process they will reach compromises that diverge from their initial positions. The development of alternatives must therefore address the extreme point of departure, and a series of alternatives must be constructed that can serve as a conceptual foundation for discussing the question of Jerusalem.

Political Organization of the Metropolitan Area: Examples and Lessons

The discussion of Jerusalem should not be isolated from the metropolitan context. As stated in the list of fundamental principles, the city will be a center for the metropolitan area that takes shape around it, and most of the population that spills out of the city in the future will live in the city's metropolitan area. Moreover, establishment of a Palestinian local authority that serves as a center for the national institutions of the Palestinian Authority will require coordination between the cities on various physical and social matters.

Coordination between the localities in the city's metropolitan area can take several forms:

1. *Agreements and contracts:* informal agreements and ad hoc contracts between the localities in the region to deal with specific needs, such as the use of joint water resources, maintenance of roads, and treatment of waste.

2. *Municipal corporations:* establishment of joint municipal corporations for coordination, planning, management, and development in the form of intercity corporations responsible for infrastructure (e.g., roads, water, electricity), environment (e.g., protection of water and air quality), and economic development (e.g., job creation).

3. *Metropolitan government:* establishment of a metropolitan government for joint management and planning of the area.

A metropolitan government is the broadest and most comprehensive of the three frameworks. Its main contributions would be in the areas of development of a comprehensive perspective, environmental planning and development, and development of the transport system. In the specific case of Jerusalem, the framework of the metropolitan government might also help with coordination, planning, and development of the water and infrastructure systems, the labor market, and tourism.

My argument is that Israel and the Palestinian Authority can learn from the experience of various cities that are ethnically divided (Montreal and Brussels) and of cities that are not ethnically divided (Toronto and San Francisco) with respect to metropolitan government. Therefore, I have chosen to present examples from these cities and to note several lessons that can be learned from their experience.

The example cities are in Canada, the United States, and Europe. Canada and the United States have different approaches to the development of umbrella municipalities. Metropolitan governments in Canada are stronger. They have a wide variety of functions, are statutory bodies, and are more involved in physical and economic spatial design and in the provision of services than are those in the United States—mainly because of the Canadian federal system, which gives the provincial governments more power than the U.S. federal system gives state governments. Another difference has to do with the relatively high sociodemographic homogeneity of the Canadian municipal system. In the United States, the large disparities between the poor central city and the affluent suburbs makes coordination and joint work difficult. The disparities between the central city and the suburbs are immeasurably smaller in Canadian cities, where the ethnic concentrations, especially the concentrations of blacks, are low.

Brussels is an example of a city with two different ethnic groups, French speakers and Flemish speakers, who have managed to develop a metropolitan government that allows for collaboration and separation between the groups. Table 12.1 sums up the findings about metropolitan governments in Montreal, Toronto, San Francisco, and Brussels.

Several lessons can be learned from the data on metropolitan governments. First, a metropolitan government is created because of the need to coordinate development in the metropolitan area and to prevent harm to the population of the area as a whole. The main problems that require coordina-

TABLE 12.1

Metropolitan Governance: Comparative Perspective

Main Features	Montreal	Toronto	San Francisco	Brussels
Name	Montreal Urban Community	Metropolitan Toronto	Association of Bay Area Governments	Brussels Capital Region
Established	1970	1954	1961	1989
Population in metropolitan area (1990, thousands)	3,068	4,200	6,253	1,000
Population served by metropolitan government (1990, thousands)	1,700	2,200	6,253	1,000
Number of municipal authorities	102 in M.A., 29 in M.G.★	30 in M.A., 6 in M.G.★	9 counties, 100 municipal authorities	19
Procedure of establishment	Government law	Government law	Voluntary association	Change of constitution
Structure	General council, executive council, permanent committees	General council, executive council, permanent committees	General council, executive council, permanent committees	Council and executive at the regional level, council and executive serving each ethnic group
Elections	Representatives of Montreal and suburbs	Direct elections of local authorities and metropolitan government	Representatives of the municipalities and the counties	Direct elections from two lists: French speaking and Flemish speaking
Spheres of responsibility	Transportation, police, and planning	Transportation, police, education, social services, and planning	Regional planning, social services	Regional planning and development
Decision Making	Double majority: entire council and representatives of the suburbs	Majority decision	Double majority: representatives of the counties and representatives of the suburbs	Decisions arrived through discussion and consensus
Main problems	Struggle between Montreal and the suburbs	Metropolitan government serves only a small segment of the metropolitan area	Limited steering capacity	Permanent need to achieve consensus between the two communities

★ M.A. = metropolitan area, M.G. = metropolitan governance

tion are development of the transport system, development of physical infrastructure, preservation of the environment (including protection of water and air quality), creation of jobs, planning of the spatial distribution of the population, and spatial planning of land use. These problems will confront policymakers and planners in the Jerusalem area; therefore, it would be wise to prepare for them by creating models for cooperation in the Jerusalem area.

Second, a metropolitan government serves only some of the residents of the metropolitan area. In an ideal situation, it would serve approximately 60 percent of the residents, which is a direct outcome of the ceaseless suburbanization process that has led to a mismatch between the built-up area and the administrative boundaries of the metropolis. What this means for the Jerusalem area is that an administration can be created that relates only to part of the area, for example, towns and villages adjacent to Jerusalem.

Third, the authorities in each metropolitan area are ranked hierarchically. In Canada, for example, there are four levels. At the top is the federal government; below it is the province, which established the metropolitan government; next is the metropolitan government itself; and finally comes the local government. In Belgium, there are three levels: a federal government, the government of the Brussels area, and the boroughs that make up the government of the Brussels area. Each level has its own unique powers, but the different geopolitical levels coordinate their activities with each other and sometimes even share powers. The powers are scattered throughout the hierarchy. Low-level units deal with basic needs and functions. As one climbs higher in the hierarchy, the scope of services becomes broader. For example, planning functions exist on every level, but the higher one goes in the hierarchy, the larger the range of planning becomes and the more space it encompasses. What these principles mean for the Jerusalem area is that a hierarchical structure of municipal systems can be created in which the powers of each stratum in the system are clearly defined, as are the patterns of coordination among the various municipal strata.

Fourth, in ethnically divided areas, geographical or functional solutions and arrangements have been developed to cope with the groups' aspirations for cultural and administrative autonomy. In Montreal, a geographic division has developed: the Francophones are concentrated chiefly in Montreal and in some of the suburbs, whereas the Anglophones live mainly in the suburbs.

In Brussels, a functional division has developed: the council and the executive of the Brussels area handle general issues, whereas the assemblies of French—and Flemish-speaking communities handle education and culture. The lesson this system can teach Jerusalem is that functional and territorial solutions can be adopted for the political organization of the metropolitan area and of the city of Jerusalem.

Fifth, in all of these metropolitan areas, conflicts exist between the central city and the local governments of the surrounding localities. In all of them, there is a tendency to curtail the decision-making power of the central city by granting greater representation to small local governments.

Finally, the nature of the metropolitan government in terms of organizational structure, electoral processes, and division of powers is not fixed. It tends to change over time and to adapt itself to the needs of its constituent units. What this means for the Jerusalem area is that flexible approaches should be adopted that allow for freedom of action and a possibility of future change in the organizational and political structure.

The Conceptual Framework Underlying the Proposal

The hierarchical principle explained in the previous section underlies the conceptual framework. Specifically, the conceptual framework says that municipal organization in Jerusalem and the surrounding area should be based on a hierarchy of several geographical levels: international, metropolitan, municipal, and submunicipal.

What is the purpose of an approach based on a spatial hierarchy? Why not settle for alternatives that focus on the municipal organization of the city itself? The answer is complex.

International Considerations

On the international level, Jerusalem is a spiritual center for the three monotheistic religions. Within the walls of the Old City of Jerusalem are many religious sites—among them the Western Wall, the Dome of the Rock, al-Aqsa Mosque in the Temple Mount/al-Haram al-Sharif area, and the Church of the Holy Sepulcher. Any arrangement in the city requires attention to many players, including the Christian, Jewish, and Muslim worlds. To this end, it is necessary to create arrangements on the international level that take into account the various players and their interests in the region. International arrangements between Israel and the Palestinian Authority are required in order to coordinate metropolitan issues associated with economic development, transportation, and the construction of water and sewage systems.

Metropolitan Considerations

On the metropolitan level, the Jerusalem area is one of Jewish and Arab settlement, both of them umbilically linked to the city. Any municipal arrangement in Jerusalem requires thinking about the nature of the political, economic, and environmental ties between Jerusalem and its surroundings. In particular, one must address issues related to transport, preservation of the environment, development of physical infrastructure (water and sewage), tourism, and economic development. Therefore, there must be a supermunicipal entity that takes a comprehensive view, such as a district authority or a metropolitan government. The alternative to metropolitan government and coordination is perpetuation of the present situation, which would mean a lack of frameworks for coordination and cooperation on the supermunicipal level in environmental, economic, and settlement matters. Without coordination and cooperation frameworks on the metropolitan level, the costs to both sides may increase owing to the development of duplicate infrastructure systems, and the environment, water sources, and air quality may be harmed. Most serious would be the economic damage caused by lack of cooperation between the two sides, especially in the field of tourism. Finally, uncoordinated development may lead to uncontrolled settlement in the Jerusalem area, accompanied by extensive friction between the two sides.

Municipal Considerations

On the municipal level, a municipal system must be developed that will serve fairly the diverse population groups that inhabit the city. This system should provide the municipal services (water, sewage, maintenance, and cleaning), help with the provision of state services (education, health, welfare, and religious services), carry out urban planning, and manage the city. The need for a fair municipal system is salient in view of the enormous disparity that exists between western and eastern Jerusalem in terms of planning, housing, development of physical infrastructure, provision of physical and social services, investment, and the overall attitude toward residents. On the municipal level outside the Jerusalem city limits, a Palestinian local authority can be formed in which the Palestinian Authority institutions would be concentrated. If a Palestinian national center develops outside the city limits, it will be necessary for the two cities to coordinate the various aspects of physical infrastructure, transport, and planning.

Submunicipal Considerations

On the submunicipal level, the model of neighborhood administrations must be improved, expanded, developed, and made a component of municipal arrangements in Jerusalem. The idea of neighborhood administrations as a solution to the problem of Jerusalem first emerged in the late 1970s. Teddy Kollek, then the city's mayor, proposed maintaining the city unity by displaying sensitivity and open-mindedness toward local cultures. According to this conception, neighborhood administration *(minhalot* in Hebrew, which means "administration") can encourage values of self-expression and local management. In Kollek's words, "an expanded system of *minhalot* could eventually play a role in the permanent arrangements by becoming the framework for self-administration by the different autonomous communities within one municipality" (1988–89, 163). The administrations of the Jewish and Arab neighborhoods in their present form are a perversion of the original idea, and their impact on the municipal system is contingent on functionaries and elected officials' goodwill. They are not statutory bodies, and their formal powers are few. This situation is the result of a deliberate municipal policy that never intended to grant the administrations political power or authority or to include them in any real way in decision making. The creation of a submunicipal level therefore requires a new way of thinking that would involve the institutions of the central government, the municipality of Jerusalem, and the inhabitants of the city. The administrations in their new form would be more like the model of submunicipalities developed in Rotterdam. The new model would give the city residents a large degree of self-management and participation in decision-making processes.

The result would be a hierarchical system of institutions that have different functions on different geographical levels: international, metropolitan, municipal, and submunicipal. On each geographical level, there would be a specific organization with clear powers; its nature would vary in keeping with the alternatives.

In a functional arrangement, the following forms of organization would operate on the different geographical levels:

1. On the international level, there would be a supreme committee comprising representatives of the Israeli and Palestinian governments. This committee would deal with such critical issues as demography and housing in the Jerusalem area. In addition, an organizational arrangement for the administration of the holy sites would be drawn up, and it would involve players from the Christian community and the Muslim world as well as from the Israeli and Palestinian governments.

2. On the metropolitan level, a metropolitan government would be established. This organization would deal with the metropolitan area and would comprise representatives of the local governments in the area. Outside the Jerusalem city limits, a Palestinian municipal authority might be formed that would serve the Palestinian Authority.

3. On the municipal level, the Jerusalem municipality would be in charge.

4. On the submunicipal level, administrations or submunicipalities would be established.

Table 12.2 presents the municipal hierarchy under a functional arrangement. Although this functional arrangement does not address the issue of sovereignty directly, there is no doubt that the arrangement would require both sides to make concessions and to restrict their sovereignty in certain areas. (On the various models of sovereignty, see Lapidoth 1995.) In other words, the scattering of powers over various geographical levels in which Israelis, Palestinians, and other countries take part clashes with the principle of absolute sovereignty. The scattering of powers limits both internal sover-

TABLE 12.2

Multilayered Approach to the Jerusalem Problem

Geographic Level	Institutions	Procedures	Criteria
International			
Israel and the Palestinians	Israeli–Palestinian joint committee	Coordination and cooperation	
Multinational	Formal and informal arrangements concerning the Holy Places	Formal and informal division of authority	Recognition of international interests
Regional-metropolitan	Formal or informal metropolitan council	Comanagement, coordination, and cooperation	Economic efficiency and equity
Municipal	An umbrella city council within the existing municipal boundaries	Power sharing	Democracy, respect for human and civil rights, equity, and effectiveness
	A Palestinian capital on the city's boundaries	Division of authority	
Submunicipal	Submunicipalities with budgets and powers	Empowerment, decentralization, and self-management	National and cultural identity, effectiveness

eignty (relations between the state and the community in its territory) and external sovereignty (relations between countries). In the case of Jerusalem, however, the functional approach would justify these restrictions because of the extreme sensitivity of the region and the geographical mix of population groups.

Supporters of the functional approach would justify the internal restrictions on sovereignty because there would be national communities in the metropolitan area and within the city limits that are linked culturally and socially to the entity over the border. They would argue that there is a need for sensitivity and consideration for the values of the national communities that live in the area and would recommend a high degree of power delegation. Furthermore, they would argue that the restrictions on sovereignty on the level of foreign relations are necessary because decisions regarding infrastructure, water, sewage, tourism, and the environment can have an impact on the neighboring entity. Supporters of the functional approach would prefer to accept restrictions on themselves and a greater degree of coordination and cooperation between the two entities in the area.

Three Alternatives: A Conceptual Proposal

The conceptual model proposed here does not directly address the issue of sovereignty. In essence, the issue enters the proposal by the back door, by means of the arrangements on the various geographical levels. Of course, one can consider sovereignty more directly and develop additional alternatives that deal with municipal organization in Jerusalem on the basis of various geopolitical assumptions. For this reason, I have developed three proposals for the hierarchical organization of the municipal system in the Jerusalem area based on different geopolitical assumptions: (1) functional sovereignty (scattered sovereignty over the metropolitan area and the city of Jerusalem, where functions are divided between Israeli and Palestinian authorities); (2) shared sovereignty (spillover of sovereignty over the metropolitan area and the city of Jerusalem, where the two authorities comanage certain areas); and (3) qualified sovereignty (setting limits on sovereignty within the metropolitan area and the city of Jerusalem).

Functional Sovereignty

This alternative proposes dividing the part of the metropolitan area located in Area C (the part of the Occupied Territories that are under Israeli civilian and military control) between Israel and the Palestinian Authority. Israel would have sovereignty over the Jewish localities in the metropolitan area, including Ma'ale Adummim and its surrounding localities, Givat Zeev, Har Adar, Efrat, Betar Illit, and the localities in Gush Etzion, thereby forming a continuous stretch of localities that abuts Jerusalem.

Sovereignty within the Jerusalem city limits would be made ambiguous by transferring broad, diverse powers to the institutions and organizations of the Palestinian community in the city. It would be possible to link the changes in sovereignty on the metropolitan level with those on the municipal level and, in the bargaining process, to resort to the municipal options described in the other two alternatives.

In the metropolitan area, an Israeli metropolitan umbrella municipality would be established as a statutory body. It would comprise representatives of the Jewish community in the metropolitan area. The Israeli government would delegate the umbrella municipality authority and budgets. The Israeli metropolitan umbrella municipality would deal with infrastructure issues that affect the Jewish localities in the area: roads, transport, water, sewage, drainage canals, main roads, garbage collection, telephone, electricity, and communication. It would also deal with the regional environment, including regional parks, air and water pollution, and environmental nuisances. And it would manage economic development from a comprehensive regional perspective, would emphasize tourism development, and would be responsible for all aspects of regional planning that affect planning in the Jewish localities.

The Israeli government and the Palestinian Authority would establish a supreme authority for coordination and monitoring of metropolitan issues. This authority would have powers in sensitive areas outside the purview of the metropolitan umbrella municipality, such as the demographic balance and construction, infrastructure, and pan-regional economic development. The authority would make decisions in matters not handled by the metropolitan umbrella municipality and would resolve conflicts when disagreements arise.

As for the Holy Places, the existing arrangements for the Temple Mount area would be made official, and the Christian Holy Places would be granted immunity. Israel would officially recognize Muslim control and administration of the Temple Mount and would retain supreme responsibility for security. The present situation regarding freedom of access and freedom of worship would be preserved.

Within the city of Jerusalem, Israel would retain its sovereignty over all parts of the city. The Palestinian capital would be located outside the present city limits. Within the city, powers would be distributed among Palestinian institutions and organizations. A municipality in which both communities are represented would administer Jerusalem. The Palestinian institutions in the city—administrations and educational and health institutions—would provide services; be involved in municipal activity and low-level political activity; and maintain educational, social, and cultural ties with the Palestinian Authority. The Arab administrations would have numerous powers with respect to social affairs, welfare, culture, and planning. The municipality would provide all local services and would supplement state services.

Shared Sovereignty

The model of shared sovereignty is based on a spillover of sovereignty in "seam" areas on the metropolitan and urban levels. In terms of daily life, the two communities share these areas (i.e., work across the border, consume services, use the transportation system, and confront common ecological problems). Shared sovereignty entails joint management of seam areas insofar as prosperity and growth necessitate binational management. According to this model, a variant can be developed in which the Palestinian Authority's supremacy would be recognized in the metropolitan area, and Israeli supremacy would be recognized within the Jerusalem city limits, but *sovereignty would not be complete* in that each side would have influence and a presence in the other side's area. According to this model, the Jewish community's connection to the State of Israel would be recognized, as would the connection of the Palestinian community in Jerusalem to the Palestinian Authority.

On the metropolitan level, a joint umbrella municipality would be established; this statutory body would comprise representatives of the Jewish and Palestinian communities in the area. The Israeli government and the Palestinian Authority would delegate the powers of the umbrella municipality. The Jewish localities in the area would form an association of Jewish localities, would receive educational, cultural, and social services from Israel, and would be represented in the umbrella municipality. The umbrella municipality would have a two-community, two-story structure: Israeli and Palestinian municipalities and local councils, with a statutory umbrella municipality above them. The functions of the umbrella municipality would be as described in the previous alternative.

The two governments would establish a supreme authority for coordination and monitoring of metropolitan issues. The authority would have powers in areas outside the purview of the metropolitan government, and it would make decisions on issues not handled by the metropolitan government.

The Holy Places would be treated as in the previous alternative. In other words, the principle of shared sovereignty would not apply to the Holy Places because it is not possible.

Within the city of Jerusalem, sovereignty would be blurred through the creation of a model of shared sovereignty, in which sovereignty spills over from one area to the other. The Palestinian capital would be established on the border of Jerusalem, and each side would interpret its significance and location differently (the Palestinians would play down the border and point to the sociocultural and functional connection, whereas the Israelis would point to the existence of a border and the formal political aspects). The Palestinian capital would contain a government center strongly associated with Jerusalem in terms of responsibility for Muslim religious affairs as well as provision of cultural and educational services.

A single municipality would function in the city, and alongside it would be Arab administrations with numerous social, welfare, cultural, and local planning powers. The administrations would be associated with the Palestinian Authority, whose territory would be adjacent to the city. The municipality of Jerusalem would provide local services, and the Palestinian Authority would provide most state services (education, culture, welfare, health, and religion) to the Palestinian residents. Taxes would be paid to the municipality of Jerusalem, and deductions and arrangements would be made for municipal and state taxes. The Palestinians would have a coordination and liaison office in the city, and low-level political institutions would operate in the city.

This alternative is based on recognition of the minority's right to meet its social and governmental needs itself by means of a *connection* to an adjacent political entity. This approach allows for the formation of a linkage between a solution to the problem of the localities outside the city limits and a solution to the problem of the Palestinian community in Jerusalem. The Arab administrations, which would have a large degree of autonomy, would correspond to the umbrella organization of the Jewish localities in the metropolitan area. The link between the Palestinian community in Jerusalem and the Palestinian Authority would correspond to the link between the Jewish community in the metropolitan area and the State of Israel. The Jewish lo-

calities' participation in the metropolitan umbrella municipality would correspond to the Arab population's participation in the Jerusalem municipality.

Qualified Sovereignty

Under this alternative, the Palestinians would have sovereignty in the metropolitan area, and Israel would have limited sovereignty in areas where Jewish
localities are located. The Jewish localities in the metropolitan area would
form an enclave within Palestinian Authority territory, and their connection
to Israel would be recognized. Symmetrically, the Palestinian community in
Jerusalem would have an enclave with limited sovereignty within Israel. Israel would have influence over the enclave in the Palestinian metropolitan
area, and the Palestinian Authority would have influence over the Palestinian enclave in the city. However, the Palestinian Authority's influence would
be qualified—that is, confined in terms of functions and responsibilities.
Thus, the Palestinian enclave in Jerusalem would include service-providing
institutions and municipal administrative institutions, and the branches of
the national government would not be represented there.

A metropolitan umbrella municipality would be established that would
include representatives of the Palestinian and Jewish localities. The Jewish
localities would form an association that would have numerous powers with
respect to planning and building. The association would maintain a close relationship with Israel and would receive numerous services from it. The association of Jewish localities would be represented in the metropolitan
government and would have veto power. The metropolitan government
would be a statutory body. The Palestinian Authority would delegate the
umbrella municipality's powers, and the Israeli government would authorize
the Jewish community's participation. The areas of responsibility of the metropolitan government would be like those described in the first alternative.
The Palestinian capital would be established in the metropolitan area adjacent to Jerusalem, and the central Palestinian Authority institutions would
be concentrated there.

In the Temple Mount area, the Palestinian Authority would have qualified sovereignty, including the right to maintain order and security within

the compound, but the overall responsibility for security around the area would lie with Israel. In the Christian Holy Places, the church would be given a degree of functional internationalization, which may imply the adoption of a special statute for the Holy Places, with some observation by an interreligious group or council.

Within the city of Jerusalem, the formation of a sovereign Palestinian enclave within the area of Israeli sovereignty would blur the issue of sovereignty. A Palestinian submunicipality would operate in the Palestinian enclave, and low-level government institutions would be situated there. The Palestinian submunicipality would provide local and state services to the Palestinian residents of Jerusalem, and the Palestinians would pay their taxes to their submunicipality. None of the branches of the Palestinian Authority—legislative, executive, and judicial—would be located in the Palestinian submunicipality in Jerusalem. There would be a single municipality in the city of Jerusalem, and it would include representatives of the Palestinian submunicipality.

This alternative is based on geopolitical and institutional symmetry. Geopolitically, the Palestinian Authority would maintain an enclave within Jerusalem, and Israel would maintain an enclave within the territory of the Palestinian Authority. The institutional organization is based symmetrically on two authorities on every geographical level: (1) a Palestinian metropolitan umbrella municipality alongside an umbrella organization representing the Jewish community, and (2) an Israeli umbrella municipality alongside a Palestinian submunicipality.

Israel would be involved in the development of the metropolitan area through representation of the Jewish localities in the metropolitan governing system. The Palestinian Authority would be involved in Jerusalem by means of the submunicipality and Palestinian participation in the umbrella municipality of Jerusalem.

The Geographical Model

The three geopolitical alternatives are manifested in the following geographical models:

1. *Functional sovereignty ("finger" model).* According to this alternative, Is-

rael would partially withdraw its forces from Area C and link Jerusalem with the nearby settlements. The areas linking these localities and the localities themselves would be under Israeli sovereignty.

2. *Shared sovereignty (shared space).* According to this alternative, the issue of sovereignty in the area would be blurred. Arrangements would be made in which Israeli sovereignty would spill over into the metropolitan area and Palestinian sovereignty would spill over into eastern Jerusalem.

3. *Qualified sovereignty (bloc model).* According to this alternative, Israel would withdraw its forces completely from Area C and would hand over the area to Palestinian Authority control. The Israeli localities would remain as isolated blocs in the area handed over.

Conclusion

This essay has presented three intermediate alternatives between freezing the present situation and changing it radically (that is, division of the metropolitan area, including Jerusalem, between Israel and the Palestinian Authority).

The alternatives do not cover all possibilities. Moving the center of gravity among the different levels can modify each. For example, the metropolitan and submunicipal governments can be strengthened at the expense of the municipal government, thereby reducing the importance of the municipality. Alternatively, the status of the municipality can be reinforced, thereby weakening the status of the other levels of government. This diversity makes it possible to bargain in keeping with the goals set—for example, consolidating one party's status in the metropolitan area as opposed to consolidating its status in the city. Parts of the alternatives can also be exchanged or certain segments in each alternative may be strengthened on the expanse of others. Table 12.3 sums up the three alternatives and clarifies the possible variations.

In theory, there are twenty-seven alternatives. If Israel's priority is sovereign contiguity with the Jewish localities, a new alternative can be created: 1A, 3B, and 3C (the numbers refer to the alternatives and the letters refer to the geographical levels). Under this alternative, Israel would make concessions in Jerusalem in order to retain sovereignty in the metropolitan area. Alternatively, if Israel's priority is keeping Jerusalem united, a different

TABLE 12.3

Municipal Organization of the Jerusalem Metropolitan Area:
Three Alternatives

Geographic Level	1. Functional Sovereignty	2. Shared Sovereignty	3. Qualified Sovereignty
A. Regional-metropolitan	An Israeli metropolitan government working in cooperation with a Palestinian one	One metropolitan government serving both Israeli and Palestinians	A Palestinian metropolitan government and participation of the association of the Jewish settlements
		An association of the Jewish settlements with a strong link to Israel	An association of the Jewish settlements with a strong link to Israel
B. Municipal	One municipality with direct Israeli and Palestinian participation	One municipality with direct Israeli and Palestinian participation	An umbrella municipality with direct Israeli and Palestinian participation
	A Palestinian capital on the city's boundaries	A Palestinian capital on the city's boundaries that provides state services to the Palestinians in Jerusalem	A Palestinian capital on the city's boundaries
C. Submunicipal	Arab self-administered councils with authority and budgets	Arab self-administered councils with authority, budgets, and a strong link to the Palestinian Authority	Two submunicipalities

alternative can be created: 3A, 1B, and 1C. Under this alternative, Israel would make concessions in the metropolitan area in order to keep all of Jerusalem under Israeli sovereignty.

The matrix may help decision makers while they are considering different options with respect to the municipal organization of Jerusalem and its environment. No matter which option is taken, one thing seems to be unquestionable: there are no easy, simple solutions to this issue. Each alternative is filled with tensions: separation of and coordination among municipal entities, concentration and decentralization of power, claims of sovereignty and its diffusion, the separation of identities and the creation of supra-identities, withdrawal to old divisions and creation of new united organs. It is in this uncharted and complex organizational terrain, which is filled with tensions and ambiguities, that the two parties may choose to move forward while devising new approaches to the Jerusalem problem. I strongly recommend that a special committee be established to examine new conceptual models pertaining to this issue, while suspending for some time the pragmatic and down-to-earth approaches. It seems to me that in this way the two parties may be able to create a new space for political maneuver, allowing greater flexibility for the political and legal discussions to follow. I also suggest serious consideration of intermediate alternatives like those I propose here. Such alternatives should be given priority over the polar choices of eternal unity under Israeli sovereignty or territorial division into two capitals. These intermediate approaches are much closer to the current reality than any of the polar choices. They reflect arrangements and compromises made informally since 1967; therefore, they may stand a better chance of being adopted and approved by the two communities.

13

Jerusalem Economy and the Peace Process

Abraham (Rami) Friedman

Jerusalem is a complex city because of its cultural heterogeneity, its religious importance to the three monotheistic religions, and its national-historical symbolism to both Israelis and Palestinians. Although in many respects, Jerusalem is perceived and acts as a united city, it is divided into semiseparate, relatively homogenous neighborhoods. Similarly, the economy of the city is partially unified and interdependent and partially separated, and each economic sector is independent of the other. Thus, some economic branches such as the public sector are separated for Israelis and Palestinians, whereas other branches, such as tourism and health, are and should be joint economic ventures.

The economy of a city is an outcome of many factors, some of them internal and some external. The economic system of Jerusalem has to be analyzed within the framework of its external environment. The city interacts with the rest of Israel, with the areas controlled by the Palestinian Authority, with the neighboring countries, and in many respects with the global economy as well as with the metropolitan area of the city. The internal environment of Jerusalem includes factors such as its physical structure (zoning), its historical cultural and religious heritage (the holy sites), its physical infrastructure (roads, water, and sewage), and its social composition and infrastructure (demography, educational and welfare systems).

Thus, plans for the improvement of Jerusalem's economy have to adapt the open-systems approach, taking into account the external and internal environments. Separate economic development plans should be conceived to strengthen the economy of Arab east Jerusalem, the economy of the Jewish sector, and the economy of the city as a whole. Because of data limitations, the discussion here focuses on the Jewish and joint parts of the city, and the discussion of the economy of the Arab part of the city is less extensive (see Choshen and Shahar 1999, 167, for a discussion of the difficulty encountered in trying to get labor-market data related to the population in east Jerusalem).

Current Status

Jerusalem is a unified city under Israeli sovereignty. Both Israeli and Palestinian peace plans declare that the city will remain united. The laws that are in power and that govern daily life in Jerusalem are Israeli laws, although in some aspects of daily life and for some parts of Jerusalem's society the traditional religious laws and even religious courts are the relevant ones. For all practical purposes, the regulation of economic activities in Jerusalem is mostly under Israel's jurisdiction. The municipality of Jerusalem is one. The mayor and the city council members are Jews because most of the Arab residents boycott the municipal elections. Municipal laws and bylaws apply in the same manner to the Jewish and Arab quarters of the city, although there are some claims that they do not apply and are not enforced equitably all over the city.

There is no approved general zoning plan for Jerusalem, only partial zoning plans for the west side of the city and for the east side. The Israeli government recently adapted a controversial, well-advertised program for strengthening Jerusalem, but the resources necessary for the implementation of the program were only partially appropriated. In May 1999, the Israeli government decided to appropriate in the next three years 500 million shekels for different development programs in Jerusalem. The program recommends a change in the municipal boundaries, mainly to the west side of the city *(Committee* 1998, sect. A). The areas to be added, according to the program, include some of the small semiurban residential areas and open spaces in the neighborhood of Jerusalem. Even if this program is applied, it is expected to take several years to complete. The program also calls for the establishment of a roof municipality for the metropolitan area of Jerusalem *(Committee* 1998, sect. B; see also Decision No. 3913 1998, sect. B).

There is no general economic master plan for the city of Jerusalem, for either the long run (i.e., ten to fifteen years) or the short run (i.e., three to five years). Some pragmatic, usually industry—or area-specific plans have been made, though. The most recent one among them is a specific program for strengthening the economy of Jerusalem, proposed by the municipality and adapted by the Israeli government. The program recommends:

1. Encouraging the development of the high-tech industry

2. Reducing the cost of housing by making more land available at lower prices

3. Improving railway services to the city from Tel Aviv

4. Establishment of a new system of public transportation within the city, especially the light rail system

5. Developing the main roads and arteries in the city

6. Speeding urban renewal projects

7. Increasing the pace of development of social services in the city

8. Increasing governmental development budgets for the needed infrastructure in the tourism industries for the year 2000.

The strategic unit of the municipality of Jerusalem had established several blue ribbon committees to propose programs for the development of different economic and social aspects of Jerusalem's economy and quality of life. These programs are part of the general strategic master plan for Jerusalem for the year 2010.

None of the programs offered was developed beyond the level of general principles. Thus, their impact was very limited; they did not lead to any serious economic activity.

General Economic Situation

Jerusalem is the poorest of the large towns in Israel and one of the poorest of all the towns in the country. The data on poverty in Jerusalem is an underestimate because very limited statistics are available on the economic conditions of the Arab population in the city. It is known that the general economic conditions of the Arab population in the city are worse than that of the Jewish population (Choshen and Shahar 1999, 132).[1] The level of poverty in Jerusalem results from (1) the large *haredi* (ultraorthodox) Jewish sector, which does not participate in economic activities and devotes most of its time to the study of the Jewish Torah,[2] and (2) the low level of participation of Arab females in the labor force and the high level of unemployment among male and female Arabs (see the next section).

Data on the level of poverty in a geographical area are presented by a poverty incidence index, which shows the extent of poverty in terms of the level of poverty of the relevant population. By incidence of poverty, reference is made to the proportion of the population—families, individuals, or children—below the poverty line. The poverty line is personal income that is half the median personal disposable monthly income in Israel. In 1996, the poverty line per standardized individual was NIS (new Israeli shekels) 1,173 (about U.S.$295) (Choshen and Shahar 1999, 129–30).

The poverty incidence index for families, individuals, and children in Jerusalem is higher than those for Tel Aviv, Haifa, and Israel as a whole. In Jerusalem, 20.9 percent of families were below the poverty line, compared with 16.8 percent for Tel Aviv, 16.3 percent for Haifa, 46.1 percent for Benei-Beraq, and 23.3 percent for Israel.[3] Thus, we can conclude that out of three large towns in Israel, Jerusalem is the poorest. As mentioned above, the main reason for this phenomenon is the relatively large proportion of the Jewish *haredi* population of Jerusalem. (Jerusalem's Arab population is also very poor and contributes to the fact that Jerusalem is so poor. Because the official Israeli statistics do not include the Arabs, they were not included in this part of our discussion. I present Palestinian statistics and the low income level of the Arab population of Jerusalem.) Most of the male adults in the

1. The data on household income and poverty levels in Israel in general and in Jerusalem in particular are based on a survey that does not include east Jerusalem's Arabs.

2. A similar situation exists in Benei-Beraq, Israel, where the level of poverty is even larger than in Jerusalem because most of its population is *haredi*.

3. These data come from the Central Bureau of Statistics. The data for 1997 are NIS 2,460 for Israel and NIS 2,620 for Jerusalem.

haredi population devote their time to the study of the Holy Scriptures, resulting in a very low level of disposable income. The median personal monthly disposable income for 1996 was NIS 2,000 (U.S.$500) for Israelis and NIS 2,068 (U.S.$517) for Jerusalem Jews (Choshen and Shahar 1999, 105, table VI/1); by contrast, the median personal monthly disposable income for Jerusalem Arabs was NIS 655 (U.S.$139) (Palestinian Central Bureau of Statistics [PCBS] 1997, quoted in Hazboun 1999, 4, table 1).

The average uncommitted income per family in Jerusalem is 103.4 percent of the average for Israel. In Tel Aviv, the ratio is 116.8 percent, in Haifa 110.5 percent, and in Benei-Beraq 68.4 percent (Choshen and Shahar 1999, 105, table VI/1). From the data presented above, it is clear that aside from its share of poor people, Jerusalem also has a large population that is at least semiaffluent. This segment of society has to bear the larger share of the costs of the municipal services. This polarization of income and poverty is contributing to the tension between the general Jewish population of Jerusalem and the Jewish *haredi* community.

Jerusalem's Labor Force

The most updated data on Jerusalem and Israel's labor force is obtained through the periodical labor-force surveys conducted by the Central Bureau of Statistics (CBS) of Israel (Choshen and Shahar 1999, 166–67). More detailed data, pertaining to different demographic segments of society, can be obtained from the national census conducted once every ten years. The most recent census was conducted in Israel in 1995. The coverage of the census in Jerusalem, including the Arab sector, was quite good. Thus, the findings of the census, especially regarding demographic and labor-force characteristics, are reliable.

The data on the Arab labor force in Jerusalem and the West Bank is based on two sources: labor-force surveys conducted quarterly by the PCBS and the 1997 census, also conducted by the PCBS (see Hazboun 1999; Awartani 1999).

The methods and definitions used in the labor-force surveys and the census were almost identical to those the CBS used. Thus, the Palestinian data is compatible with the Israeli data. The problem is that the Israelis and the Palestinians use different definitions of the Jerusalem area. The Israelis refer to the city of Jerusalem, whereas the Palestinians refer to Jerusalem District, which is larger.

In 1996–97, the size of the potential labor force (i.e., the population age fifteen and above) in Jerusalem was 390,100, which constitutes 9.6 percent of the potential labor force for Israel as a whole, although Jerusalem's population accounts for 10.5 percent of the population of Israel. These statistics indicate the relatively large proportion of children in Jerusalem's population (Choshen and Shahar 1999, 168–69, table VII/1).

The relative share of the potential labor force of Jerusalem in the Israeli labor force stabilized itself since 1997, after declining for about a decade. The decline was the result of the relative decrease in the inflow of new immigrants to the city. As a result, since 1995, the rate of growth of the potential labor force was lower in Jerusalem (8.6 percent) relative to Israel as a whole (13.2 percent).

The rate of participation in the labor force measures the propensity of the potential labor force to participate in the labor force—that is, to take active part in the labor market. The participants in the labor market include those individuals who are gainfully employed and those who actively seek employment.

The data from the labor-force surveys show that the rate of participation in the labor force is lower in Jerusalem (49.6 percent) than in Israel as a whole (53.6 percent). A similar result is observable for males (58.2 percent for Jerusalem compared with 61.9 percent for Israel) and for females (41.4 percent versus 45.7 percent). The rate of participation for males in Jerusalem is higher than for females, a pattern similar to that found in Israel as a whole (Choshen and Shahar 1999, 168–69, table VII/1).

The rate of participation of Arabs in the labor force in Jerusalem District was 32.6 percent in 1997 (Hazboun 1999, 11, table 10). The average rate of participation in Jerusalem District for 1998 was 36.4 percent compared with 43.5 percent for the West Bank (Awartani 1999, 24, table 19).

By *the rate of unemployment,* we refer to the proportion of the participating population that actively seeks employment and is not able to find it. According to labor-force survey data for 1996–97, the rate of unemployment for Jerusalem (6.1 percent) is lower than for Israel as a whole (7.2 percent) (Choshen and Shahar 1999, 168–69, table VII/1).

The rate of unemployment of Arabs in Jerusalem District was 7.4 percent in 1997 (Hazboun 1999, 11, table 10). The average rate of unemployment for 1998 was 10.4 percent for Jerusalem District compared with 11.6 percent for the West Bank (Awartani 1999, 23, table 17).

Thus, we can conclude that (1) the rates of participation and of unemployment in Jerusalem are lower than the rates in Israel as a whole, (2) the rate of participation of Jews in Jerusalem is higher than that for Arabs in Jerusalem District, and (3) the rate of unemployment of Jews is lower than that of Arabs.

The labor-force survey data show that the rate of unemployment for Jews in Jerusalem (5.3 percent) is much lower than for Jews in Israel as a whole (7.2 percent). This might be an indication that Jerusalem "exports" some of its unemployed Jews to other parts of Israel, mainly to the greater Tel Aviv area. In order to understand this phenomenon, an analysis by demographic characteristics is needed. The 1995 census data is detailed enough to offer an analysis of the labor force by demographic characteristics.[4] Table 13.1 presents data on the rate of participation by demographic

TABLE 13.1

Labor-Force Participation by Gender and Demographic Characteristics in Jerusalem

	Total	Male	Female	Population (age 15 years and older)
Total population	48.9%	57.2%	41.0%	401,460
Jews	54.2%	55.4%	53.0%	284,275
Haredi	39.3%	37.4%	41.2%	60,065
Nonorthodox	58.2%	60.7%	56.0%	224,210
Arabs	36.1%	61.4%	11.3%	117,185

Source: 1995 Census (State of Israel 1997).

4. The 1995 census data, though conducted by the Israeli Central Bureau of Statistics, supplies reliable data on the Arab population labor-force characteristics. The Arab east

TABLE 13.2

**Unemployment by Gender and Demographic
Characteristics in Jerusalem**

	Total	Male	Female
Total population	7.6%	7.2%	8.1%
Jews	6.6%	5.8%	7.4%
Haredi	8.2%	7.7%	8.6%
Nonorthodox	6.3%	5.5%	7.2%
Arabs	11.1%	10.1%	11.3%

Source: 1995 Census (State of Israel 1997).

characteristics, and table 13.2 presents similar data on the rate of unemployment. The source for both tables is the 1995 census.

Arabs. The rate of participation for Arabs in Jerusalem (36.1 percent) is much smaller than the rate for Jews (54.2 percent). The rate of participation for Arab males (61.4 percent) is higher than the rate for Jewish males (55.4 percent); by contrast, the rate for Arab females (11.3 percent) is much lower than the rate for Jewish females (53.0 percent). There are several explanations for the difference between the labor-force behavior of Arabs and Jews.

First, it might be that job opportunities available to the Arabs are more limited than those open to the Jews. This explanation is the *demand-deficiency hypothesis,* according to which the supply of labor is adequate from the point of view of the workers' capabilities, but there is not enough demand for their work. This deficiency can be caused by (1) decline in the demand in product market for the commodities that the place of employment of the unemployed produces (usually owing to depression in the economy), or (2) the existence of administrative restrictions on the workers' participation in the labor market. The relevant aspect for the Palestinians is that they do not have free access to all the available jobs (see, e.g., Bellmonte and Jackson 1983, 298–301).

Second, when openings in the labor market are limited, some of the un-

Jerusalem population participation in the census was good because of social security and the residency implications of not participating.

employed might be discouraged from continuing their search for employment. According to this *discouraged workers hypothesis,* we can expect a large promotion of so-called hidden unemployment, by which members of the labor force are willing to work, become discouraged about finding a job, and stop searching for a job and thus are statistically not counted members of the labor force (see, e.g., Bellante and Jackson 1983, 74–75).

Third, it might be that many Arabs are members of the so-called shadow economy, which refers to those segments of the economy that are engaged in either illegal activities (e.g., drugs and protection) or economic activities that are not reported to the legal authorities, especially to the tax authorities. The latter is more relevant to our discussion. Thus, the statistics on the Arab labor-force participation is an underestimate. It is known that many difficulties were encountered while trying to establish a reliable database on the Arab population of Jerusalem, especially regarding economic variables. This explanation can be termed the *shadow economy hypothesis.*

Fourth, it might be that the propensity of Arabs, especially females, to participate in the labor force, is significantly lower than that of Jews—the result of tradition or religion that dictates a code of social behavior that discourages females from working outside the household. This explanation can be called the *cultural-tradition hypothesis,* which refers to external factors that influence the propensity of relevant segments of the society to participate in the labor market. Those factors are social norms that forbid married women from working or that pressure students of the Holy Scriptures to continue their studies and not work.

In my opinion, all four explanations are viable and in reality each has its merit, but each explains the behavior of a different segment of Jerusalem's Arab population.

The discouraged worker hypothesis and the cultural-tradition hypothesis hold mainly for the labor-market behavior of Arab females. The fact that it is very difficult for Arab females to find jobs is supported by the high rate of unemployment among this group (11.3 percent), compared with the rate (7.4 percent) for Jewish females. The fact that Muslim tradition and culture discourage females from working outside the home is well known and is represented by the low level of labor-force participation. The shadow economy hypothesis might also hold for this group. Some Arab females produce traditional craft and other products at home.

The rate of unemployment for Arab males (10.1 percent) is much higher than the rate for Jewish males (5.8 percent), as is the rate of participation. This finding could be explained by the *additional worker hypothesis,* which states that as employment becomes scarcer, more and more of a household's members join the labor force in an effort to maintain the household's income. Most of the household's members will be unemployed; thus, the rate of unemployment is an overestimate of the natural labor-market behavior. Many Arab males work at short-term jobs that are not reported and are part of the shadow economy.

In summary, the labor-market behavior of Jerusalem's Arab population is highly influenced by gender. The behavior of Arab males can be explained by the demand-deficiency, discouraged worker, additional worker, cultural-tradition, and shadow economy hypotheses. Thus, in order to elevate their situation, new jobs must be created, vocational training and education programs must be established to help match market quality demands, and special workplaces must be created that will allow Arab females to join the labor force.

Jews. The labor-market behavior of Jerusalem's Jewish *haredi* community is unique. Their rate of participation is very low (39.3 percent) compared with the rate for Jerusalem's nonorthodox Jews (58.2 percent).

The pattern of labor-force behavior of the *haredi* Jews has special characteristics. First, the rate of participation of the males (37.4 percent) is lower than the rate for females (41.2 percent), which is opposite to the trend for nonorthodox Jews and Arabs in Jerusalem and for Israel as a whole. This finding might be the result of the fact that *haredi* males' exemption from military service is dependent on their not working and devoting all their time to the study of Torah.

Second, the rates of participation of male and female *haredi* Jews are lower than those of male and female nonorthodox Jews.

Third, the rate of unemployment among *haredi* Jews is higher (8.2 percent) than the rate for nonorthodox Jews (6.3 percent) and smaller than that for the Arabs (11.1 percent).

Fourth, the rate of unemployment for *haredi* females is higher than the rate for males, a similar phenomenon to that found in the general population.

Regarding the low rate of participation of the *haredi* Jews, the cultural-tradition hypothesis holds. The high employment rate indicates that once *haredi* individuals enter the labor market, their commitment to stay in the labor force is high, and they will continue to look for a workplace if they become unemployed. This behavior has some similarities to that predicted by the additional worker hypothesis.

There is a claim that the size of shadow economy in the Jewish *haredi* community is much larger than that of the general Jewish population. Thus, the shadow economy hypothesis might also be a partial explanation of the labor-market behavior of the *haredi* Jewish community.

As was mentioned earlier, young *haredi* male Jews have a major incentive not to work, or at least not to report it, in order to maintain their exemption from the draft.

A new trend is developing. *Haredi* leaders have started sending less-talented scholars to learn an occupation and work in order to support their families and community. If this trend continues and increases, it might help raise the level of income in Jerusalem in general and in the community in particular, which will demand the creation of a new type of workplace that will allow opportunity for prayer, study of the Torah on site, and modest dress at the workplace, especially for females. A newer trend is to allow less-talented *haredi* students to enlist for military service in special religious units, which will allow these individuals to join the labor force after finishing their military tour of duty.

The labor market for nonorthodox Jews in Jerusalem also has certain characteristics. First, the rate of participation (58.2 percent) is higher than the rate for Israel as a whole (53.9 percent). Second, the rate of participation of nonorthodox Jewish males in Jerusalem is lower (60.7 percent) than it is for Jewish males in Israel as a whole (62.5 percent). The rate for Jerusalem's nonorthodox Jewish females is higher (56.0 percent) than the rate for Jewish females in Israel as a whole (45.6 percent). Third, the rate of unemployment of Jerusalem's nonorthodox Jews (6.3 percent) is lower than the rate for Jews in Israel as a whole (6.8 percent). Fourth, the rate of unemployment of Jerusalem's nonorthodox Jewish males is lower (5.5 percent) than the rate for

Jewish males in Israel as a whole (5.7 percent). The female nonorthodox Jewish population shows similar rates (7.2 percent for Jerusalem and 8.2 percent for Israel).

The behavior of the nonorthodox Jewish population in Jerusalem can be characterized as regular labor-market behavior. Because many of the job openings in Jerusalem are in the service industries, nonorthodox Jewish females can have higher participation and employment rates.

There is a claim that the lower rate of unemployment for Jerusalem's nonorthodox Jewish population is the result of the fact that a relatively large proportion of the young unemployed are leaving the city and looking for jobs in the Tel Aviv area. We might label this phenomenon the *Jerusalem discouraged worker hypothesis,* indicating that some of the unemployed are not discouraged from finding a job in general, but are discouraged from finding a job in Jerusalem.

In summary, the labor-market behavior of the *haredi* Jews in Jerusalem can be explained by the large impact of traditional-cultural factors and through some impact of the shadow economy. In contrast, the nonorthodox Jewish population exhibits regular labor-market behavior.

Workplace Characteristics

Most (88 percent) of those employed in Jerusalem, regardless of their demographic characteristics (Jews, Arabs, *haredi,* and nonorthodox) are wage earners. The proportion of wage earners among females is higher (93 percent) than among males (83 percent).

Most of the self-employed work alone. This trend is stronger among Arabs (70.2 percent) than among Jews (59.8 percent). They are mostly small shopkeepers and professionals.

Jewish employment in Jerusalem concentrates in the public-service sector (45.5 percent of the employed). The non-public-service sector is about one third (38.1 percent) of the workforce. Industry employs a small share (9.9 percent), and construction even smaller (6.5 percent).

The proportion of employment in the public sector in Jerusalem is much higher (45.5 percent) than in Israel as a whole (31.4 percent) because Jerusalem is the capital of Israel. Employment in industry is relatively low in

Jerusalem (9.9 percent) compared to Israel (20.0 percent) (Choshen and Shahar 1999, 178–79, table VII/9).

Arab employment in the Jerusalem District concentrates in wholesale and retail and repair (35.6 percent, compared with 10.6 percent for Jews) and in manufacturing (32.5 percent, compared with 16.6 percent for Jews). Although those industries that employ most of the Jewish labor force employ a lesser proportion of the Arab labor force, there is no Palestinian public sector in Jerusalem by law. The public-service sector accounts for 16.1 percent of the Arab labor force, compared with 45.5 percent of the Jewish labor force; and the non-public-service sector accounts for 43.7 percent of the Arab labor force, compared with 38.1 percent of the Jewish labor force. Only 0.8 percent of the Arab labor force is in construction, compared with 9.9 percent of the Jewish labor force (Hazboun 1999, 5, table 2).[5]

There are more than five hundred industrial establishments in Jerusalem, employing about 16,000 workers. The number of people employed in industry has been decreasing. The industries that employed the largest number of employees were printing and publication, food products, electronics, and metal products.

Most of the industrial establishments in Jerusalem are small (less than 50 employees). The small establishments employ about 40 percent of the industrial employees, the medium-size establishments (50–299 employees) employ 35 percent, and the large ones (more than three hundred employees) employ about 25 percent.

The total revenues from industry in Jerusalem in 1994 were about 4 billion NIS (U.S.$1 billion); 43.4 percent of which was from exports. The main income-generating industries are electronics (30 percent), chemicals (12.9 percent), food (12.7 percent), and printing (12.4 percent) (Choshen and Shahar 1999, 202–3, table VIII/2).

The data presented above indicate the importance of high-tech industry to Jerusalem. The gross value added of industry in Jerusalem was about 1.7 billion NIS (U.S. $425,000). The electronics industry's share in the value

5. The data presented here are derived from one of several different official surveys available. The differences between the results of the surveys are large. Thus, the data should be handled cautiously.

added is 42.4 percent; by comparison, the printing industry's share is 15.1 percent, and the food industry's share is 9.0 percent (Choshen and Shahar 1999, 209, table VIII/7).

Thus, if the large industrial establishments, especially in electronics, move out of Jerusalem, the implications for both employment and income will be grave. The loss of these industries would mean major employment and income loss for Jerusalem. The large establishments are currently threatened by a new zoning code that will create a *haredi* neighborhood in their proximity, which, according to past experience, will encourage these industries to move out of Jerusalem.

Approved Projects for Investment

The data in this section come from Choshen and Shahar (1999, 212–13, table VIII/10).

Industry and building for industry. In 1996, there were thirty-six approved programs for establishment of industrial plants, or of building for industry, which is 6.7 percent of the total number of projects approved for Israel. The expected investment in industry for Israel is about 11 billion NIS, 1.6 percent of which will be invested in Jerusalem.

These new establishments are expected to employ 1,433 workers, to have a turnover of U.S.$390 million, $355 million of which will be exports. Most of the new establishments are export oriented.

Tourism. In 1996, twenty new tourism projects were approved for Jerusalem. These projects constitute one-quarter of the total number of tourism projects approved for the country as a whole. The investment in these projects will be approximately $710 million, 26.6 percent of the total investment in tourism for Israel. Expected employment in these projects is 1,620 workers.

Other industries. Three other projects were approved for Jerusalem out of fifty-nine for Israel (5.1 percent). The expected investments are $684 million for Israel and about $18 million in Jerusalem (2.6 percent).

It is clear that the approved projects for Jerusalem concentrate in industry and tourism. It looks, however, as though Jerusalem has a problem in attracting industry.

Needs and Goals

In order to develop a master plan for the economic development of Jerusalem, we have first to set the demographic, social, and economic goals for the future of the city. We should thus have a clear vision about the size of the city in geographical area and population. The plan also has to specify the average per capita income that it expects to achieve. Currently the emphasis in public policy is on raising the household income in Jerusalem. The discussion presented here assumes that we want to raise the average income and the rate of participation in the labor force. Jerusalem has to become a more affluent city so that it can offer better services. It has to become a place that offers jobs for young professionals and thus can attract them. The city has to become more viable and offer a high quality of life and affordable, good housing.

The economic master plan has to cater to all parts of the city (east and west) and to all segments of society. The advancement of peace negotiations and a peace agreement that will settle the status of Jerusalem will help solidify the city's economy.

The question is which industries will help to meet these goals and can be developed in Jerusalem, which should be developed separately for the Arabs and for the Jewish population, and which should be developed jointly for both Jews and Arabs.

Jerusalem as the Capital

There is no question that Jerusalem will serve as a capital of one or more states; thus, public-sector employment will serve as one of the major sources of employment and income for the people of Jerusalem. The issue is what part of the economy of Jerusalem should be based on government employment? Obviously, most of the employees in this sector will be Jews in the near future. Yet, in east Jerusalem, there are several semigovernmental Palestinian agencies, and many Palestinian governmental agencies and ministries operate in the adjoining towns that are controlled by the Palestinian Authority.

It looks as though the governmental sectors will be the major employment sector for Jews in both the present and in the future and for the Palestinians in the future.

Jerusalem has to exploit the fact that it is the capital of Israel and will remain so. More government offices and functions should be moved to Jerusalem, as should nongovernmental offices and policy research institutions.

For example, there is a plan to open in Jerusalem the central college (university) for the public sector. Because Jerusalem is the capital of Israel and the public sector employs about one-fifth of the Israeli labor force, it is natural that the training institutions for the public sector will be concentrated in Jerusalem. The previous central training school, a nonacademic institute for government employees, existed in Jerusalem until it closed in the mid-1990s. Currently there is growing demand for college degrees in the labor market.

Education and Research

Jerusalem used to be one of the major centers of higher Jewish education in Israel. Jerusalem lost its primacy. Yet in the Jewish community, Jerusalem can serve as the major center for Jewish studies and for Diaspora-Israel relationships and studies. The same goes for theological seminars and other religious institutions. A similar program should be developed for the non-Jewish community.

Jerusalem should be the center for policy and public administration studies for Israel, for the Palestinian Authority, for both together, and maybe for the entire region.

When peace comes, these academic research and teaching institutions should be joint Jewish and Arab ventures with international connections. By its religious, traditional, national, and historical status, Jerusalem can serve as the major place for research and study on peace issues in general and on living together peacefully in the Middle East in particular.

An international business school that will cater to the development of business leadership for the Near East is one of the most obvious joint ventures. Joint research on environmental issues in the Middle East is another venue for research and teaching.

These are but a few examples of a general program that has to be developed jointly with international help and support.

Jerusalem as a Medical Center

Jerusalem (east and west) has several of the best medical centers in the country. These centers should develop into an "export" industry, attracting patients from the whole region and even from other parts of the world, mostly from former Iron Curtain countries.

Because many non-Jewish staff members are employed in Jewish hospitals, cooperation and coordination between the health centers in the city can be achieved, and a joint effort to market these services is possible. This development can promote cooperation between Jerusalem's Jews and Arabs.

Jerusalem can serve as *the* medical center for the Middle East. It is near many Muslim countries, and the high level of available services is known in the region. With the help of the Palestinians, the demand for medical services will increase. Currently Jerusalem has a relative surplus of hospital beds; thus, it can cater to more patients.

Joint medical ventures between Israelis and Palestinians already exist. The cooperation of the Soroka hospital with hospitals in Gaza is one example. This cooperation should be expanded with international help and investment.

Jerusalem as a Tourist City

Many see the tourism industry as one of the major economic areas in Jerusalem. Current statistics reveal that approximately 80 percent of the tourists who visit Israel stay in Jerusalem. The problem with this industry is that it is a labor-intensive, low-income industry.

Jerusalem is the diamond in the crown of tourism to the Holy Land. This asset should be developed, not only by building more hotels but also by creating more attractions.

There is an urgent need to establish a master plan for the development of tourism in the Holy Land to clarify and define whether the goals of the development of the tourist industry are mainly employment or income. The role that Jerusalem will play in such a plan is obvious, but because tourism is a regional venture, cooperation should be promoted.

Jerusalem as an Industrial City

High-tech industry can attract young professionals to Jerusalem, although Jerusalem's share in the country's industry will remain relatively small because of geographical and urban problems. For example, industries must be clean from an environmental point of view.

Jerusalem needs industry, but it is difficult to imagine that it will develop into one of the country's industrial centers. The printing industry and the mass media industries are likely candidates for development in the city.

Conclusion

Jerusalem is a unique city. It has a unique labor force and needs to develop a unique economy. The city has three different economies: Jewish, Palestinian, and joint Israeli-Palestinian. The economic future of the city depends on the development of all three economies. It has to use its advantage as a capital and as a historical and religious city to develop its economy and to promote cooperation and understanding between the different segments of society.

The main Israeli-only economy that has to be developed is in the public administration area: the administration college for the public sector, government ministries, and other public-sector institutions. A research and educational center is needed for the Jewish people of the Diaspora as well as for Israelis. Also, international religious centers that attract believers from all over the Jewish world have to be encouraged.

The main Palestinian-only economic sector has to develop the following industries: public institutions (semigovernmental), Palestinian education and research institutions, and Muslim and Christian religious educational and functional institutions.

The joint economic branches to be developed have to concentrate on industry (mainly the high-tech industry), commerce (e.g., Jerusalem can serve as the commercial center of the Palestinian Authority), health, and tourism.

Peace will help Jerusalem to develop as an economically viable city. Foreign embassies will move to Jerusalem. A major international community will develop. Foreign investment and support will be obtained for cultural, religious welfare, and tourism projects. If the peace agreement concerning Jerusalem is not delayed for many years, the natural tendency of the Palestinians to see Jerusalem as a center of their national life will be very powerful. Thus, newly developed alternatives to Jerusalem as the center of the Palestinian economic life will either decline or move to Jerusalem, or if they are in Jerusalem's neighborhood, they will become part of Jerusalem's metropolitan area and thus part of its economy.

14

Environmental Issues in the Jerusalem Metropolitan Area

Qasem Abdul-Jaber and Deborah F. Mir

This chapter focuses on environmental problems and management practices in the Jerusalem metropolitan area (JMA), emphasizing issues of shared resources, pollution, and cooperation. The JMA encompasses the Jerusalem municipality (including east Jerusalem and the Old City), Palestinian communities (Ramallah, Bethlehem, Beit Jala, and Beit Sahur), and adjacent villages. The area is mostly urban and includes suburbs, rural communities, and open spaces of ecological, tourist, historical, and to a lesser extent agricultural importance.

Although environmental issues in the JMA affect both the Israelis and the Palestinians, environmental policies are often not implemented because of their low priority; that is, a political solution to the territorial disputes has taken precedence. There is also a significant developmental gap between the Israeli and Palestinian sectors as expressed in the level of physical and management infrastructure. The JMA is under intense development pressure owing to rapid population growth and conflicting political agendas.

The Environmental Unit in the Jerusalem municipality and the Israel Ministry of Environment—Jerusalem Region (MOE) are working to re-

This is a joint research paper. Dr. Abdul-Jaber researched the Palestinian content, and Dr. Mir, with the Jerusalem Institute for Israel Studies, researched the Israeli content.

duce environmental impacts in the planning and operational stages, within the constraints of political and financial priorities. Although progress has been made in some areas (e.g., constructing a sewage treatment plant, reducing industrial pollution), implementation is less stringent outside the city and where special interests are involved. Environmental management is minimal in the Palestinian–controlled sector, partially because of limited infrastructure and because they are in the early stages of developing government institutions and practices that were formally under Israeli jurisdiction.

In 1998, approximately 120 Jews and Arabs representing twenty-five nongovernmental organizations (NGOs) established the Sustainable Jerusalem Charter. Key issues they have addressed include the deteriorating environment; loss of open spaces, forest, and landscapes; heavy traffic and air pollution; illegal dumping; littering; and disregard for the historical value of the city's building and character. Although a system has been established to examine environmental concerns in the planning process, the charter addresses the apparent anarchy in its implementation.

The most important issues are the water distribution network; solid waste collection and treatment systems; preservation of open spaces; and the lack of infrastructure for sewage collection, treatment, and disposal. The JMA is characterized by high water demand and sewage and solid waste production in the domestic sector versus relatively low water demand and waste production in the agricultural and industrial sectors. Air pollution is mostly from traffic because Jerusalem is traditionally a tourist, religious, and government center and not an industrial city. Most of the municipal industries have a low potential to affect the environment, and they comply with regulations or were closed down or transferred from residential areas to industrial parks where pollution control infrastructure can be concentrated and environmental enforcement may be facilitated. The Palestinian sector of the JMA has fewer industries, so the emphasis is on economic development and not on environmental compliance.

Intense residential, industrial, and infrastructure development is threatening the surrounding open spaces, which also receive sewage and solid waste. Illegal dumping of construction and other wastes is considered a serious problem and is a by-product of the current focus on economic development. The political emphasis of the Israelis and the Palestinians is on establishing a "concrete presence in the region" (e.g., buildings), which leads to many environmental planning considerations being ignored or not enforced.

Population Trends and Water and Sewage Infrastructure in the Jerusalem Metropolitan Area

The annual population growth in the Jerusalem municipality, 1.0 percent for Jews and 3.6 percent for Arabs in 1996 reflects the high birthrates and the cultural norms of the large Arab and ultraorthodox Jewish sectors (Choshen 1998a, 1998b). Water demand is increasing with population growth and improved economic standing, and is also affected by the type and integrity of the water distribution system. Sewage volume depends on water use and on the extent and integrity of the collection system; sewage quality depends on the source (i.e., domestic versus industrial sewage) and on treatment practices. Israel controls most major water sources in the JMA, though control is being transferred to Palestinian authorities as they obtain jurisdiction over land. According to ARIJ (1996c) water sources include:

• Groundwater wells within the municipality and its surroundings

• Groundwater wells in the Ein Samya spring field, which are used to supply Ramallah

Groundwater wells in Beit Fajjar and Herodion, which are used to supply Bethlehem, Beit Jala, and Beit Sahur

• Israel integrated water grid, known as the National Water Carrier (NWC)

The Jerusalem municipality is supplied by the NWC and by local wells within the city limits (MOE 1997). The water distribution and sewage collection infrastructure is more developed in west Jerusalem and in the newer Jewish communities, although infrastructure and services have been improved in east Jerusalem and in other Palestinian communities. The Gihon Jerusalem Water and Sewage Company controls water management in the Jerusalem municipality, and there are three management bodies in the Palestinian communities outside the Jerusalem municipality:[1] (1) Jerusalem Water

---

1. The Gihon spring was the biblical water source for Jerusalem.

Undertaking (JWU); (2) Water Supply and Sewerage Authority (WSSA) of Bethlehem, Beit Jala, Beit Sahur; and (3) West Bank Water Department (WBWD).

The main objective of the JWU—a public, nonprofit establishment with financial and administrative autonomy—is to supply drinking water. The JWU's income covers regular expenses, and development and capital expenses are financed largely through other sources that contribute toward costly activities such as drilling wells and establishing reservoirs (JWU 1991).

The WSSA, a nonprofit establishment with financial and administrative autonomy, is responsible for water supply in the municipal areas of Bethlehem, Beit Jala, and Beit Sahur and for the collection and disposal of wastewater in the same areas. Most of its income is used to cover operating expenses.

The WBWD was part of the military governing body in the West Bank (Civil Administration) and reported directly to the Israeli military water officer. It obtains its drinking water supply from wells. It formerly monitored the water quantity and quality of wells and springs in the West Bank, but both the Israeli and Palestinian health authorities now carry out monitoring.

Water Management and Use in the Jerusalem Municipality

This section focuses on the managerial and technical aspects of the Jerusalem municipality water system, including both east and west Jerusalem. The city purchases water from Israel's national water company, Mekorot, through the Gihon Company, which is responsible for providing water throughout the city and for maintaining and expanding the water network. Jerusalem receives more than 50 million cubic meters (MCM) of water annually, of which some 12 percent is lost, mostly from leaking pipes, or is not paid for because of poor monitoring (MOE 1997, 97–98). The Gihon Company sells some 2 MCM of Jerusalem water to neighboring communities, including Palestinian communities east and north of the Jerusalem municipality.

The annual average water use of approximately 72 cubic meters per capita per year in Jerusalem is 10 percent lower than the Israel national average, including water for residences and gardening, industry, institutions and hotels, public works, and to a lesser extent agriculture (Feitelson and Abdul-

Jaber 1997, 5–6; interviews at the Gihon Company and Environmental Unit at the Jerusalem municipality in 1998). Interestingly, this quantity compares closely to the 70 cubic meters per capita per year calculated for the pipe-fed municipalities in the Palestinian sector. Table 14.1 illustrates the distribution of water use in 1994–95, by category. Because of the historic difficulties in water supply and other factors (e.g., limited industry and agriculture, large families with low income in the Arab and ultraorthodox Jewish sectors), Jerusalem traditionally uses less water than the rest of Israel. Water demand is seasonal, varying between 110,000 cubic meters per day in winter and 180,000 cubic meters per day in summer (MOE 1997, 93).

The water distribution network is divided into pressure zones to account for the mountainous topography. Reservoirs are used not only for water storage but also to reduce water pressure. The Jerusalem reservoir system has a capacity of approximately 260,000 cubic meters, including an 88,000-cubic-meter reservoir installed in 1970, partially to solve the water problems of east Jerusalem. Two new projects under construction are a water reservoir in west Jerusalem and a water tower in the southeastern part of the city. The quality of the water distribution system varies mostly with the age of piping, a small amount of which was installed toward the end of the Ot-

TABLE 14.1

Water Distribution in the Jerusalem Metropolitan Area, 1994 and 1995

	Quantity of Water (m³/year)		Percentage	
Type of Use	1994	1995	1994	1995
Homes and gardens	24,800	26,300	59.3	59.8
Public institutions	5,500	5,700	13.2	13.0
Hotels	2,200	2,200	5.3	5.0
Offices and businesses	5,000	5,300	12.0	12.0
Industries (rationed)	1,600	1,600	3.8	3.6
Construction	700	700	1.7	1.6
Agriculture	200	400	0.5	0.9
Outside communities	1,800	1,800	4.3	4.1
Total	41,800	44,000	100	100

toman period or during the British Mandate (World War I to 1948) to the present. New communities and more established areas have modern piping systems, whereas older areas, especially in east Jerusalem, have pipes with a smaller diameter and in poorer condition. In 1994, approximately 21.5 kilometers (2 percent) of the old pipes were replaced, out of approximately 980 kilometers of existing piping (MOE 1997, 97).

When the eastern part of the Jerusalem municipality was under Jordanian rule, the Old City (historic Jerusalem) received its water on a biweekly basis, augmented by local well water and rainwater rooftop harvesting, and many people in east Jerusalem were without a piped water supply. After 1967, Israel installed temporary small-diameter gravitational lines, pending development of a comprehensive road, water, and sewage plan. Piping was added on request and depending on funding. In 1983, a road plan with matching pipes was proposed, and larger-diameter pipes were installed in many areas. Road and piping work suffered a setback during the Palestinian uprising (Intifada) in 1988 and as a result of operational difficulties in the field and of a decrease in funding. Construction restarted in 1997 and continues intermittently depending on political priorities and safe working conditions.

The Gihon Company checks water quality routinely for bacteria and residual chlorine, with additional testing as needed. The Ministry of Health checks water quality at least once a month. In 1994, only 0.5 percent of samples indicated substandard drinking water. The water is treated with both chlorine and fluoride. Calcium deposits and biological growth are problematic in some rooftop water storage systems, and the city routinely sends out flyers instructing people how to maintain them.

The lack of a comprehensive water management master plan for the Jerusalem municipality makes it difficult to plan and budget for the long term, a situation complicated by differences in interpreting the geographic boundaries of the city's area of jurisdiction. This lack is especially worrisome given the increasing water demand in the domestic sector owing to population growth and improved living standards. Water stealing is also a problem, especially in east Jerusalem; water meters are tampered with or broken, people hook into the water system illegally, and payment collection is difficult (interviews with officials in the Gihon Company and Environmental Unit in the Jerusalem municipality in 1998).

Water Management and Use in the Palestinian Communities Outside the Jerusalem Municipality

The domestic sector is the largest consumer of water; industrial use is less, and agricultural use minimal. Average water use is 70 cubic meters per capita in areas with a pipe-fed supply (interviews at the Gihon Company and Environmental Unit at the Jerusalem municipality in 1998). In some areas and especially during the dry summer months when water demand is highest, pipe flow is often restricted to a few days per week. People depend on alternate water sources, such as rain-fed cisterns, which may not be safe. Industries are especially vulnerable to uncertain water supplies and quality (e.g., trucked-in water to dairies). The largest industrial water demands come from the textile industry and laundries (in Ramallah); the food and beverage sector, including dairies (in Ramallah and Bethlehem); stone-cutting enterprises (in Anata, Ramallah, and Bethlehem); and olive presses. Other industries or services (e.g., garages) use water in smaller amounts.

The quality of water distributed by the JWU and the WSSA in Ramallah and Bethlehem districts is good from a chemical point of view. Although the water distributed by both the JWU and the WSSA is chlorinated, sampling in Bethlehem, Beit Sahur, and Beit Jala has indicated occasional contamination with fecal bacteria, possibly from corroded pipes.

In general, the Palestinian communities lack a comprehensive water management master plan, partly because of uncertainties in the geopolitical arena that make long-term planning difficult. The development of the Ramallah and al-Birah water distribution system is typical of the JMA Palestinian community. The integrated network connects to several reservoirs that are used for water storage or to facilitate gravity-driven distribution. The original pipe network was laid out without a comprehensive plan, starting in the early 1950s. Street limits as well as town and country planning were not taken into account, and houses were connected individually or not at all. The network experiences high water losses. The pipe network is not stan-

TABLE 14.2

Estimates of 1994–1995 Water Supply for Some Palestinian Localities in the Jerusalem Metropolitan Area

Locality	Population	Annual Consumption (m^3/capita)	Supply (m^3/year)	Sewage (m^3/year)**	Administrative Body
al-Birah	33,539	109	3,661,759*	2,528,231	JWU
Ramallah	20,561	109	2,244,832	1,571,382	JWU
Beitunya	7,544	50	378,597	265,018	JWU
Qalandia refugee camp	4,275	31	132,859	93,001	JWU
Bir Nabala	3,661	50	181,755	127,228	JWU
ar-Ram and Dahyat al-Barid	23,740	43	1,031,128	721,790	JWU
Hizma	2,779	35	97,070	67,949	JWU
Beit Hanina	20,284	29	585,558	409,891	JWU
Beit Sahur	12,258	120	1,472,197*	1,030,537	WSSA
as-Sawahra ash-Sharqiyyah	4,325	23	100,000	70,000	WBWD
Bethlehem	21,697	120	2,605,829	1,824,080	WSSA
Beit Jala	12,795	120	1,536,691*	1,075,684	WSSA
Average		70		49	

Source: Modified after CDM/Morganti 1997b.

* Calculated according to size of population.
** 70 percent of the supplied water.

dardized, and larger-diameter pipes were generally secondhand. Subsequently, larger and better-condition pipes were connected to the system. Financing is also a serious problem, with nonpayment of water bills, illegal hooking into the water system (i.e., water stealing), and faulty water metering. Because of the network's poor situation and management, water losses are relatively high and can exceed 25 percent.

For the most part, the Palestinians in the JMA have a sufficient water supply, especially in villages. The water problem appears to be more severe during summer but is less critical at other times of the year. Palestinians living in the JMA have adapted their lifestyles to a restricted water supply by limiting their water consumption to fulfill minimum needs. However, in times of scarcity, such as drought, the water problem can become acute.

Sewage Management in the Jerusalem Metropolitan Area

In this semiarid region, wastewater is a precious resource, and future agricultural production in the JMA will be based largely on reclaimed water (Feitelson and Abdul-Jaber 1997, 1). Most Jerusalem sewage continues to flow untreated and infiltrates sensitive aquifers that are the main reservoirs of the high-quality water available to both sides; other Jerusalem sewage flows with inadequate treatment, either west to the Mediterranean Sea or east to the Dead Sea. Untreated sewage has serious environmental and health impacts. Approximately 60 percent of the Jerusalem municipality (including most of the western sector) and 70 percent of Ramallah, al-Birah, Bethlehem, Beit Jala, and Beit Sahur are connected to sewer systems; the remaining waste flows to septic tanks, cesspools, or, in some cases, open sewers. The sewage is either disposed of at sewage treatment plants or dumped into seasonal intermittent streams.

Although sewage from the western part of the municipality and neighboring communities, including some Palestinian communities, will soon be treated, no decision has been made regarding joint or separate sewage treatment for the eastern part of the JMA, including both Jewish and Arab communities. Several options under review in Israel focus on engineering, economic, and environmental considerations. Other possibilities for joint treatment are being considered with the Palestinians, international experts, and potential donors, but little progress has been made despite the urgency of the situation. Complications result from nationalistic sensitivities, security issues, high financial costs, and reluctance on the part of donor countries to finance a joint project shared with Israel, a developed country.

Sewage Management in the Jerusalem Municipality

The Gihon Company is responsible for maintaining and operating the sewage collection and treatment system for the Jerusalem municipality and adjacent communities. Until recently, Jerusalem was the only major Israeli metropolitan area whose wastewater flowed untreated through neighboring valleys (Feitelson and Abdul-Jaber 1997, 1). The raw, filtered sewage had a strong odor and was unsightly. On June 6, 1999, the new Jerusalem Wastewater Treatment Plan began serving the western part of the city and neighboring communities, including parts of Palestinian communities (e.g., Bethlehem and Beit Jala). The modern energy-intensive plant is designed to provide high-quality effluents for irrigation as well as dry sludge for use as fertilizer (interview at ATAT Project Management 2000). The trial-year operations have shown good results to date.

According to the Environmental Unit in the Jerusalem municipality, the most serious problem in east Jerusalem is untreated sewage. Plans are under consideration to connect the sewage stream from Bethlehem and Beit Sahur to the Kidron Wadi for future joint sewage treatment.[2] Presently the sewage undergoes only primary treatment and, after screening, flows to the Dead Sea in a corroded, leaking pipe, contaminating the groundwater. Approximately half of the sewage is treated in settling and treatment ponds near the Dead Sea and is used for irrigating date crops. Plans to treat all the eastern watershed sewage for use in irrigation are being considered, subject to political, environmental, and economic assessments.

Sewage Management in the Palestinian Communities Outside the Jerusalem Municipality

Because the Ramallah sewage treatment plant is too small for the current load, sewage is only partially treated. The wastewater collected from al-Birah flows untreated. The sewage system in both cities receives untreated industrial and medical wastewater in addition to domestic wastewater. The planned expansion to the Ramallah sewage treatment plant was canceled because of construction of a bypass road across the proposed site. Instead, the city is considering plans for two new sewage treatment plants. The al-Birah municipality is constructing a wastewater treatment plant designed to serve forty thousand people in its first phase and could be expanded to serve approximately eighty thousand inhabitants in the future (Arij 1996b; CDM/Morganti 1997a).

The WSSA is responsible for the sewage system in the municipal areas of

2. Wadis are intermittent rivers or streams that flow only when sufficient precipitation is present.

Bethlehem, Beit Jala, and Beit Sahur. Until the early 1990s, the Bethlehem district sewage system served less than 20 percent of the city of Bethlehem and 60 percent of the residents of al-Daheisha refugee camp. A new wastewater collection network serves 70 percent of the inhabitants in the municipal area of Bethlehem, Beit Sahur, and Beit Jala as well as the refugee camps of al-Daheisha, Beit Jebren, and Aida. In the second phase, the network will be expanded to reach 90 percent of the population. The remaining 10 percent of the population will dispose of their wastewater in cesspools until they are able to connect to the sewage system.

The sewage system was designed to collect domestic wastewater through two pipelines. The first pipeline connects to the west Jerusalem collection network, serving mainly Beit Jala and the western part of Bethlehem. According to the Gihon Company, the pipes were poorly connected without approval from Israel, and sewage is leaking and infiltrating the aquifer. The wastewater is treated in the Israeli sewage treatment plant. The Palestinians will pay for sewage collection and treatment but will not use the treated effluents (Arij 1996a). The second pipeline will collect sewage from Palestinian communities east of the surface water divide[3] and join the east Jerusalem collection system, where options for an eastern sewage treatment plant are under consideration.

Municipal Solid Waste Management in the Jerusalem Municipality

A serious problem associated with rapid growth in the Israeli and the Palestinian sectors of the JMA is illegal dumping of construction wastes, abandoned vehicles, and goods in open spaces along roads as well as the burning of trash in open dump sites. In 1993, Israel decided to close four hundred improperly operated garbage dumps and authorized a restricted number of national sanitary landfills to be established or modified in accordance with modern standards. The policy provided subsidies to local councils for transportation and monetary awards for waste minimization through incineration or recycling. Since 1983, the municipality disposes solid waste to the nearby

3. Line of high land separating two river systems or watersheds.

Abu Dis landfill. Construction, abandoned vehicles and other large garbage, and gardening wastes are supposed to be disposed of separately, but in the absence of a designated site they are frequently brought to Abu Dis. The landfill is expected to come under the jurisdiction of the Palestinian authorities in the near future and will reach capacity in three to five years unless it is expanded and developed as a sanitary landfill.

The Jerusalem municipality is preparing a solid waste master plan to the year 2010 for municipal solid waste (MSW) collection, transport, and disposal. The plan will assess the relative merits of transporting wastes to distant sites versus enlarging the existing Abu Dis landfill or establishing an alternative site close to Jerusalem. Although recycling is laudable, the current municipal debt, lack of funding, and the low national priority for recycling make this option unlikely. The municipality is looking for economically attractive solutions for composting gardening waste. Of special interest is a plan to optimize the distribution and type of waste collection receptacles in order to reduce transportation costs.

The quantity and diversity of MSW in the JMA has increased dramatically with the increase in population and growing standard of living. In 1998, the amount of MSW collected was approximately 1,400 tons for a population of 600,000 (1.5 kilograms per capita per day), excluding solid wastes collected from 150,000 businesses and institutions. Abu Dis receives 800–1,000 tons of waste daily from the JMA and from other Israeli and Palestinian communities. This amount is expected to increase at a rate of 2–3 percent annually (interview at Environmental Unit in the Jerusalem municipality in 1998). Environmental impacts associated with solid waste collection and disposal depend on the type of garbage and containers; the waste program infrastructure, equipment, and operations; and the level of residential cooperation. Some issues related to solid waste in Jerusalem include:

- The variety of container sizes and types
- Waste collection and transportation within the city
- Transfer stations and garbage compression
- Special short-term events such as festivals that temporarily increase the population and amount of wastes produced.
- Special wastes, including cartons, batteries, construction and gardening wastes, abandoned vehicles and goods, and hazardous wastes

A family of four in the JMA produces an average of thirty liters of garbage per day, collected at least three times per week. Most refuse containers are located in public areas, along roads, on sidewalks, or in parking lots, depending on the population density and land availability. Problems with maintenance and sanitation, which occur when containers overflow and garbage is dumped next to them, are associated with a lack of responsible behavior in public areas. Residents in some older areas that have narrow roads, including parts of east Jerusalem and the Old City, dispose of garbage in plastic bags that are carted out on wagons pulled by tractors or donkeys. A recent article referring to the unequal services in parts of Arab east Jerusalem described residents in Silwan regularly dumping garbage out their windows, causing an unbearable stench along the Qidron River (Rubinstein 1999). Until recently, the new Jewish neighborhood of Pisgat Zeev used plastic bags in order to avoid unsightly garbage containers and the attendant sanitation and aesthetic problem. However, the plan didn't work because it depended on taking out the bags only at fixed times and locations, and a lack of cooperation led to unsanitary and unsightly conditions (e.g., spills, strewn garbage).

For historical and political reasons, the city uses a variety of container types and sizes ranging from large roll-off containers to plastic bags. This lack of uniformity is problematic. Smaller containers are generally more labor intensive because they have to be emptied and returned, and large roll-on containers require special trucks that may cover the same routes where smaller containers are also used. Some containers are less volume efficient than others. Access is also a serious problem. Garbage trucks may have trouble accessing containers, and the trucks sometimes block traffic. In some industrial parks, waste is collected for a fee in special large containers situated on the company's land, and the companies are responsible for maintenance and sanitation.

Compactor trucks were introduced around 1994 to reduce MSW volume. In addition, fixed compactors are used at three transfer stations. Compacting increases the amount of garbage in each truck and reduces the number of trips to the landfill. However, some collection trucks drive directly to the landfill without first compressing the wastes. Both transportation and equipment maintenance are costly owing to the slow speeds of the collection trucks and to the frequent stops they must make.

Because of the city's special religious, historical, and political importance, large-scale group events frequently produce large quantities of waste.
A sufficient pool of manpower and equipment must be maintained in order
to handle the waste generated by such events.

Special wastes—including cardboard (20–25 tons per month), batteries
(50 tons per year), and hazardous wastes—are collected in authorized disposal containers found in various private and public locations. The city collects gardening wastes at scheduled times, using special shredding equipment
to reduce volume (when the machinery is working). A municipal program
for abandoned vehicles (1,300 tons per year) involves attempts to identify the
vehicle owners and subsequent disposal at the Abu Dis landfill.

Solid Waste Management in the Palestinian Communities Outside the Jerusalem Municipality

The amount of solid waste Palestinians generate in the JMA ranges from 0.5
to 2.5 kilograms per capita per day (compared to 1.5 kilograms per capita per
day in the Israeli sector). The municipalities in the Palestinian communities
outside Jerusalem are responsible for solid waste collection, storage, and disposal. These municipalities collect solid wastes from residential areas and
from commercial, industrial, and medical centers. Generally, solid waste is
not sorted or recycled except in individual cases; for example, small businesses collect metals (especially aluminum) and glass on a very small scale.
Bulk containers provided by the municipalities are not standard at the
household and street level. The system suffers from a shortage of containers,
uneven distribution, and infrequent collection. As a result, people dump
garbage next to overflowing trash containers, which causes health and environmental problems (Monjed 1997).

Dumpsites are not selected according to any planning, environmental,
or economic considerations. All types of solid waste (domestic, commercial,
industrial, and medical) are dumped in open garbage sites. The entrances to
the dumps are littered with construction debris, scrap metal (mostly from
old vehicles), and other waste.

A representative example is the al-Birah municipality, which collects 105
tons of garbage per day (2.5 kilograms per capita per day) in some 450 small

(1,100-liter) and 50 large (6,000-liter) containers. The small containers are distributed in the residential areas, and the large containers serve the commercial and industrial areas. Most of the containers are emptied daily, but those in the main streets are collected twice daily. The solid waste is transported to an open dump located a few kilometers east of the city, where the waste is covered with construction debris. The site was selected randomly in the early 1980s, without any environmental impact assessment (EIA) study. The dump receives approximately 300 tons of solid waste per day and is expected to reach capacity in two years. No solution is planned for the future, and the option of using the Abu Dis landfill or another sanitary landfill in Israel is problematic because of the relatively high cost (compared to the present situation) of disposal to the landfill (tipping fee) of approximately U.S.$4.00 per ton.

Open Spaces in the Jerusalem Metropolitan Area

By 2020, approximately 90 percent of Israelis will live in urban environments, and their contact with nature will depend primarily on so-called urban preserves. Open spaces framing the city and its treasures are uniquely important because of the city's international, historical, and religious value. The Jerusalem municipality and the major Palestinian communities in the JMA were traditionally designed and built on hilltops interspersed with green valleys. Bordering on a desert, the city delineates the range of many plants and fauna, and has special tourism and recreational value. Many of the threatened open spaces are designated nature reserves or national gardens. However, the threats to open spaces, through government and private-investor initiatives, have increased in the last few years and are expected to continue in the near future. Examples of development plans threatening open spaces in Jerusalem include:

• Residential development in the Valley of the Cedars, which is the northwestern gateway to the city—an area that has ecological value and is extremely sensitive to development.

• Road numbers 4, 9, and 16 and the east Jerusalem ring road, some of which lie in ecologically sensitive areas. For example, the ring road crosses several wadis. The plan includes four bridges and three tunnels to minimize the environmental impact.

- Expansion or establishment of new communities and settlements.
- Construction of high-rise buildings and their impact on the historic Jerusalem skyline.
- Construction of bypass roads around Ramallah, al-Birah, and Beit Jala.

Intense development in the JMA is undertaken in response to the needs of the growing population and in order to establish a concrete presence in the region, pending resolution of the geopolitical conflicts. The Jerusalem District Planning Committee can require EIAs during the planning phase to assess potential environmental impacts, but often fail to do so.[4] Some projects have been implemented without or before completion of an EIA. For example, the expansion of road number 1 through the nature reserve in the Refaim Wadi caused irrevocable but avoidable damage. In many cases, the value put on open spaces also depends on their potential use (e.g., a forest adjacent to an orthodox Jewish neighborhood, where local residents prevent travel and recreation in the park on Saturdays and on religious holidays). As a result, some of this parkland will be rezoned for residential development and will no longer be protected. In Rumema, the wadi was filled with building debris instead of being preserved as an open space because the area was not used by the population for recreation and there were strong pressures for residential development (interviews with officials in the Jerusalem municipality in 1998).

Open Spaces in the Jerusalem Municipality

The statutory plan titled "Outline Scheme for west Jerusalem" dates from 1959, and the "Outline Scheme for east Jerusalem" was never approved. The 1959 scheme refers to the pre-1967 borders of the city, when east Jerusalem was under Jordanian rule and when the western area was less developed. Currently, planning is conducted in the absence of an approved overall city zoning plan, based on partial zoning plans for the west and east sides. However, municipal laws and bylaws apply equally to the entire city. The Jerusalem City Engineer commissioned a 2020 master plan for open spaces

4. The committee is comprised of civil servants from various ministries, the Jerusalem municipality, and representatives from the architects union.

in the Jerusalem municipality, evaluating the demand for open areas (Faludi 1997). The extensive study and its recommendations under review defined three principal types of open spaces:

• *Surrounding outside lands between the built-up areas and the city border.* These open areas include large nature areas that frame the city in a green landscape, including man-made forests, natural forests, scrub, olive groves, home orchards, and other cultivated land.

• *Contact areas (i.e., barrier lands between the surrounding outside land and the built-up areas).* These areas include rivers and valleys that penetrate into the developed areas, some of which serve as large city parks and are characterized either by their natural beauty or by their neglected state.

• *Internal areas.* These smaller open areas in the built-up parts of the city are used for leisure, welfare, and play areas for the local populations. These areas can be subdivided into developed areas (i.e., playgrounds, gardens, and paths) and undeveloped areas.

The published study focused on size, availability, use, image, and contribution to public welfare. The report found that the use and demand for open spaces varies because of the physical and cultural diversity of the Jerusalem municipality. According to the study, the city should preserve an optimum of 25 square meters of open space per person (from World Health Organization standards) and should provide a suitable response to tourism needs, including developing statutory city parks. The average area of public open spaces in 1990, including parks, was 11.3 to 11.9 square meters per person and was expected to decline to 7.7 square meters by 2020.

According to the study, the border areas should encompass a larger area of 85 square meters per person to preserve the special character and appearance of the city at its periphery, excluding roadside buffer zones. The study indicated a lack of and poor accessibility to parks, particularly in the newer neighborhoods and older parts of the city. In addition, less than half of the open spaces has been developed as natural or recreation areas, which affects their general use and value. Many of the developed areas are deteriorating, and funding is needed for their maintenance and management (Eshkol 1996).

The city's open spaces are being whittled away in small and large projects. The public values open spaces for various reasons, including recreation, exercise, and general welfare, but development threatens many historical sites and functional ecosystems. Government organizations and NGOs—such as the Green Forum, the Forum for the Future of Jerusalem, and the Society for the Protection of Nature (SPNN)—are discussing solutions and lobbying against threats to the Jerusalem environment. Because of the piece-meal destruction, the public is less aware and less involved, a phenomenon known as the salami effect, by which open spaces are constantly being sliced away. Some examples include extending an industrial zone, uprooting orchards for residential development, and putting roads through the remainder of the Jerusalem forest (interviews with government organizations and NGOs such as the Jewish National Fund [JNF] and SPNN, 1996–98).

In the late 1950s, the JNF approved a project to plant a green belt around Jerusalem, from north to south and from west to east through the Valley of the Cedars. The JNF's historic mission is to purchase land in trust for the Jewish people and to plant forests for ecological and recreational reasons. After 1967, the Jerusalem forest grew to include parts of east Jerusalem, including Gilo Park, which is adjacent to a large Jewish neighborhood opposite Beit Jala and Bethlehem. The expansion includes a biblical park in the Refaim Valley, a restored ancient farm, and a variety of recreation facilities (Orenstein 1996). Most of the forest was densely planted with fast-growing pine trees, native trees and shrubbery, and trees and vegetation associated with abandoned Palestinian villages. Currently, however, the trend is to clear large tracts of the forest for residential and industrial projects, including infrastructure (especially roads).

The Jerusalem forest originally covered 4,500 dunams (1 dunam = 1,000 square meters), of which only 1,250 dunams remain. A growing citizens' movement is fighting to preserve the remaining forest and open lands. A recent issue that fired up a public outcry was the plan to put a road through the Valley of the Cedars, which frames the entrance to Jerusalem and gives it a special atmosphere in keeping with the city's international and religious roles. The project would have destroyed the forest around Malcha, Lifta, and Ein Keren. As a result of organized protest movements, a decision was made to preserve the valley and for part of road to go through a one-kilometer tunnel. The surface road will be constructed along the side of the valley, and the rest of the area will be left as open space because of the special nature and view of the wadi. Lobbying is now under way to declare the Valley of the Cedars a national park, in opposition to political and economic interest groups that favor development.

Open Spaces in the Palestinian Communities
Outside the Jerusalem Municipality

The issue of open spaces was considered less important and problematic in the past because cultivated land, home orchards, and meadows served as open areas for both village inhabitants and urban dwellers. Currently, the only recreational areas in Ramallah and al-Birah are restricted parks belonging to the municipalities. Jewish settlements today occupy most of the open spaces, and roads cross fields and other cultivated areas in the JMA. The lifestyle of the population has changed since 1967, and open spaces adjacent to residential areas are needed. The geographic situation and the construction of bypass roads around Ramallah, al-Birah, and Beit Jala may impede planning of open spaces around or adjacent to these cities.

The new proposed plans of the Ramallah municipality provide for public areas covering 2.2 percent of the municipal land within the city and 8.5 percent of the agricultural land that borders the northern and northwestern parts of the city in a continuous strip.

Conclusion

Israel controls most of the water sources for the JMA, which is connected to the Israel National Water Carrier. The domestic sector is the main water consumer, and the water demand per capita in the Jerusalem municipality is 10 percent lower than the Israel average and is similar for both Israelis and Palestinians when a comprehensive water network is available. Water distribution is uneven in the JMA, especially in the summer when some Palestinian communities have running water only part of the week. Although the Jerusalem municipality is responsible for and is investing in improving the water distribution network, most of the older pipes are in east Jerusalem and have been under Israeli management since 1967. There are multiple reasons for the gap in investment in infrastructure between the eastern and western parts of the city, including the quality of or lack of existing infrastructure; political uncertainties and changing priorities for funding; and difficulties in working during the atmosphere of civil disobedience and violence during Palestinian uprisings.

Water use in the Palestinian sector of the JMA is lowest where the distribution network is poor or nonexistent, especially in outlying areas, and water must be brought in by tanker truck or in smaller containers. There are also problems with insufficient pressure for distribution, especially during periods of drought and when there are cutbacks in the amount of water supplied by Israel. The water network and administration in the Palestinian sectors of the JMA are affected by problems of tampering and water stealing because of civil disobedience and economic problems that are not expected to change in the near future. The relatively low per capita demand is offset by the high population growth, leading to a net increase in demand that is expected to further increase with improvements to the distribution network.

Some 70 percent of the sewage is collected from the JMA municipalities, whereas other municipal residents and communities use cess pools or open drainage. The quality of industrial sewage is generally less problematic because of reasonable environmental management in most of the Israeli sector and the low rate of industrial development in the Palestinian sector. Sewage treatment remains a serious problem, and untreated or partially treated sewage flows toward the Mediterranean and Dead Seas, polluting the aquifer system. Although a new state-of-the-art treatment plant is operational for the western part of the JMA, and the al-Birah plant is also under construction, other treatment facilities either operate poorly (being overloaded or offering only partial treatment) or are in the planning stage. The municipality has no solution for east Jerusalem, including the Jewish and Arab neighborhoods and adjacent communities, and several planning options are under review. This issue is a critical joint concern because of the negative impact of untreated sewage on the shared water resources and because of the loss of the treated influents that could be used in the agricultural sector. Resolution of the problem is pending a political decision either to construct a joint treatment plant or plants (more economical) or for Israelis and the Palestinians to operate independently. The solution is also affected by the reluctance of potential donor countries to contribute toward a project shared with a developed country.

Municipal residents have indicated they are upset by the amount of littering, but this problem is secondary to the ecological hazards posed by illegal dumping around the city. The amount of domestic waste produced per capita is similar for Israelis and Palestinians. Solid waste is a growing problem, and the active landfill used by the JMA is expected to reach capacity in several years, and existing landfills and dumps are poorly run and were chosen without conducting environmental site assessments. The future legal status of the landfill is also uncertain because it may be transferred to Palestinian control, and funding is needed for expansion and development as a sanitary landfill.

A common problem in the collection system is the nonuniformity of containers requiring repeat trips, and the Palestinian sector also suffers from infrequent collection. Except for some industrial hazardous waste in the Jerusalem municipality that is transferred to the Israel national hazardous waste site, all wastes are either buried in the Abu Dis landfill or buried or burned in open dumps. Although the Jerusalem municipality is preparing several options for the future (2010 plan), the Palestinian sector of the JMA has no program for this very important and costly problem. The 2010 plan is studying options to improve the efficiency of the municipal collection network, including recycling, though the latter is a low financial priority at this time. The Palestinians are considering waste disposal to an Israeli landfill, but the relatively high cost compared to the current open dumps is a deterrent. This issue is also a critical joint concern because of the negative impact of untreated solid waste infiltrating down to and polluting the shared water sources.

Open spaces in the JMA are suffering from development and from political efforts to establish concrete facts on the ground. Although open spaces are part of the planning process in the Israeli sector of the JMA, they are valued unevenly by different sectors of the population, and political and financial considerations often take precedence. Criteria for open spaces established in the master plan for open spaces are often ignored, and the city has a low ratio of parks per capita. The lack of open spaces and parks directly affects the population's quality of life, and there is a growing citizens' movement to resist development pressures and to preserve the remaining green spaces. Controversial areas include the valleys surrounding Jerusalem and the Jerusalem forest. The importance of parks and undeveloped open spaces is only recently being addressed in the Palestinian sector. These issues will receive more attention when the territorial and other high-priority issues are resolved, and they will be affected by the degree of joint cooperation to conserve natural areas.

15

Living Together and Apart in Jerusalem

Lessons Learned

Bill Hutman and Amir Cheshin

With great fanfare, on the eve of Israel's May 1999 national election, Jerusalem mayor Ehud Olmert warned that Israel's control over east Jerusalem was threatened by the repeated failure of the state to properly provide for the city's Palestinian residents. Olmert made a public appeal to Prime Minister Benjamin Netanyahu for an emergency budget allocation earmarked to improve living conditions in Palestinian neighborhoods.

"It will be impossible [for Israel] to continue to hold on to this city for very long if we continue as we are doing today and ignore the needs of the Arab neighborhoods of Jerusalem," Olmert warned Netanyahu (Olmert 1999a). "The key to the unity of Jerusalem lies in real equality between Arabs and Jews," he said. He demanded funds to improve and expand basic infrastructure in Arab neighborhoods, from roads and sewage systems to parks and school buildings, as well as services such as education and health care.

Only a year earlier, Olmert had accused officials in the Israeli Finance Ministry of being "racist" in their decision to hold up funds promised by the Netanyahu government for Jerusalem's Arab sector ("Olmert: Treasury Officials Racist," *Kol Hair,* Apr. 29, 1998). "Half of the [1998] budget that was approved by the government was not transferred because [treasury officials had the attitude that] 'after all it's just for Arabs,'" Olmert said. "The treasury

401

officials told us that we would get the money in 1999. If it would have been on their street, they would have run to get it done."

Much of what Olmert said was, of course, political grandstanding. Olmert and Netanyahu were both with the Likud Party, but they were also rivals. And although Olmert was probably not out to hurt Netanyahu's reelection chances, he knew that there were political points to be won by a politician in Israel who positions himself as a defender of Israel's claim to Jerusalem.

Whatever his intentions, Olmert's attacks on Netanyahu and his government reiterated perhaps the central issue of Israeli policy toward east Jerusalem: Israel's failure, in more than three decades rule of united Jerusalem, to provide properly for the city's Palestinian population. For Israel, this failure left the country in control of a city that de facto remained divided and with no one but itself to blame.

Israeli municipal officials estimated that it would cost at least U.S.$300 million to bring infrastructure in Arab neighborhoods in line with those in Jewish neighborhoods. This was a conservative estimate. It did not, for instance, include the public monies required to ease the Arab sector's severe housing shortage. Since 1967, the Israeli government has subsidized the construction of thousands of homes for Jews in Jerusalem, including a number of new Jewish neighborhoods built on land taken by Israel in the Six Day War. Only several hundred homes were built for Arabs with Israeli government help. The result was that by 1997 (the most up-to-date statistics available) there were nearly as many Jews as Palestinians in those parts of Jerusalem conquered by Israel in 1967, according to official Israeli statistics (Choshen and Shahar 1998, 46–52). Out of a total population in the city of approximately 646,000, there were 180,000 Palestinians and slightly fewer Jews living in east Jerusalem.[1]

---

1. The official figures showing that there are still more Palestinians than Jews in east Jerusalem would appear to be misleading. The figures are based on estimates and data gathered by the Israeli Interior Ministry. Palestinian Jerusalemites forced to move out of the city because of the lack of housing frequently do not report their change of address to the Israeli authorities because it might mean that Israeli identification cards—and the advantages that come with them—would be taken away. These Palestinians live in places such as Azariya, Abu Dis, A-Ram, and Dahiyat al-Barid, which are just outside Jerusalem's municipal boundaries,

In response to Olmert's demands for greater funding for Arab-sector projects, Netanyahu ordered the establishment of a special governmental committee and gave it the mandates of studying the problem and coming up with solutions. The prime minister reiterated his commitment to maintaining a unified Jerusalem under his control and said that he agreed with the mayor that doing so meant that Israel must treat the city's Palestinian residents better. Netanyahu even accused his political opponents in the Labor Party of planning to redivide the city and of caring less than he about the well-being of the city's Arabs.

Netanyahu and Olmert maintained that Israel's failure to provide for the basic infrastructure and services for Jerusalem's Palestinians created a vacuum, which the Palestinians, and in particular the Palestinian Authority, were quickly filling. For instance, because the state-subsidized public bus company, Egged, failed to provide adequate service in the Palestinian sector, local Palestinian entrepreneurs did so instead. Israel did not build enough schools for the Palestinian sector, so Palestinian parents sent their children to private schools in the city run by the Palestinian Authority and Muslim organizations. The Palestinians already had their own quasi court system and even a police force in Jerusalem. Palestinian parents for the most part took their newborn children to Palestinian Authority-sponsored infant care centers, where they received free health services. In the Old City, the Palestinian Red Crescent, headed by Yasir Arafat's brother Dr. Fathi Arafat, opened a clinic to serve the Palestinians living there. To Netanyahu and Olmert's thinking, the Palestinians were simply providing services for themselves where the Israeli authorities had not.

Netanyahu, however, never gave Olmert the special funding for services and infrastructure in the Palestinian sector that the mayor demanded. The committee he appointed never took concrete action, and the situation, in which gross discrepancies exist between living conditions in Arab and Jewish neighborhoods, was left to worsen.

It is important from the outset to understand that the issue of Israeli pol-

---

but they are counted as city residents in the official statistics. A more accurate count would likely show that Israel has already successfully created a strong Jewish majority in east Jerusalem, as the country's leaders have aimed to do since 1967.

icy in east Jerusalem has historically not been characterized by sharp divisions between the mainstream Israeli right- and left-wing parties. Netanyahu's decision not to approve the additional funding, or at least his decision to put off the matter indefinitely, was not surprising. All of his predecessors had acted similarly, as did his successor, Ehud Barak.

In his first months in office, Barak repeatedly stated that Israel would never give up any of its authority not only in Jerusalem, but also in the areas around Jerusalem that are loosely described as greater or metropolitan Jerusalem. He visited Ma'ale Adumim in September 1999 and told residents of the town, just to the east of Jerusalem, that it was part of the area he defined as greater Jerusalem and on which Israel would keep complete control. Barak also expressed support for plans to link Ma'ale Adumim physically to Jerusalem by building on the undeveloped lands that divided the two cities. He repeated the mantra of virtually every Israeli prime minister before him: "Jerusalem will forever remain the undivided capital of Israel." And like the prime ministers that came before him, he said little about the sharp divisions that existed between Jerusalem's Jewish and Palestinian populations, and how these divisions threatened the city's unity.

At Camp David, Barak offered unprecedented concessions on Jerusalem. Apparently for the first time, an Israeli prime minister in formal negotiations with the Palestinians agreed that Israel would give up control of certain Arab sectors of east Jerusalem, including the Old City. These concessions were extremely significant, and at the time of our writing this chapter it remained unclear exactly where this agreement would take the negotiations on Jerusalem between Israel and the Palestinians.

Camp David, however, did not, at least immediately, bring about a change in Israeli policy toward Jerusalem. Since 1967, all Israeli governments have shared the same priorities when it comes to Jerusalem: encourage Jews to live in the city and encourage Arabs to move away. Both the right-wing Likud Party and the left-wing Labor Party translated these priorities into policy that was best reflected each year when the Jerusalem municipal government and the national government decided on their budget allocations for the city. Vast sums were earmarked for projects that benefited the Jewish population. In comparison, the Arab population received little.

In May 1999, former Jerusalem city councilor Moshe Amirav published a report stating that Netanyahu's Likud-led government had allocated pro-portionally more to development in Arab east Jerusalem than previous Labor-led governments *(Haaretz,* May 10, 1999).[2] In 1997–98, the Ne-tanyahu government allocated to infrastructure projects (roads, sidewalks, sewage, and street lights) in Arab neighborhoods of east Jerusalem approxi-mately U.S.$52 million. Overall, during the Netanyahu-Olmert years, twenty times more money was allocated annually to basic infrastructure in Arab neighborhoods than during the previous Kollek-Rabin/Peres/Shamir years, according to Amirav's report. Nevertheless, Amirav noted, even the Netanyahu-Olmert government allocations fell far short of the Arab sector's requirements. According to the report, in a comparison of Arab and Jewish population sizes and infrastructures in their respective communities, gaps greater than 500 percent are found. For instance, in Jewish neighborhoods, 743 residents share one kilometer of sewage line. In Arab neighborhoods, 2,809 residents share each kilometer of sewage line. In Jewish neighbor-hoods, 447 residents share one public park, compared to 7,362 residents in Arab neighborhoods. Similar gaps exist in literally every area of life in Jerusalem, not just infrastructure, but also in education, community serv-ices, health care, and so on. Amirav's report did not go into details about these sectors, but other reports have. In 1999, the head of Jerusalem's Wel-fare Department reported that more than $13 million was needed to bring welfare services in Arab neighborhoods up to par with those in Jewish neighborhoods. *(Kol Hair,* Mar. 12, 1999). He noted that only two city wel-fare offices served Arab residents, whereas fourteen offices served Jewish neighborhoods.

Olmert has even published a report flaunting all that he had done for the Palestinian sector. "Since 1995, municipal departments have taken great steps to improve services in [Arab] east Jerusalem," states a municipal memo

2. The Likud and others on the right heralded Amirav's report (see Amirav 1999), par-ticularly given the fact that its author came from the left. Amirav sat on the city council as a member of the left-of-center Meretz Party. Previously, however, he was Likud. Amirav was expelled from the party after it became public that he had met with senior PLO officials (be-fore Oslo, at a time when it was illegal for Israelis to do so), despite the fact that he had done so at the request of Likud Party leaders.

that was distributed to the press. Steps taken by the municipality include "re-allocating funds earmarked for west Jerusalem [Jewish] neighborhoods for east Jerusalem [Arab] neighborhoods" (Olmert 1999b), the report states. Under Olmert, who became mayor in 1994, more than $130 million had been invested in Palestinian sector projects, according to the report.

But there is still a long way to go, Olmert admits in this same report. "The basic principal upon which the government of Israel and the municipality of Jerusalem operate is that there must be equality [between Arabs and Jews] in services and infrastructure. The principal that there must be equality with the Arab population is not a function of some political position, but rather of our basic values as a society" (Olmert 1999b), the report states. "In reality, there exists a great gap between the level of infrastructures in Jewish and Arab neighborhoods of Jerusalem. This is the result of historical, geographic, and cultural circumstances, and in order to lessen this gap there must be cooperation between the government of Israel and the Jerusalem municipality, including the allocation of the necessary monies [for the improvement of services and infrastructure in Arab east Jerusalem]." Olmert, like former Jerusalem Mayor Teddy Kollek, knew the problem centered on Israel's failure to make improving conditions in the Palestinian sector a priority and to allocate the funding necessary to do so.

Historical Perspective

During his twenty-nine years as mayor, Kollek often appealed for emergency funding for Jerusalem's Palestinian sector. Each time, his appeal was largely unanswered. There is an eerie similarity between Olmert's last-ditch appeal to Netanyahu and the demand for more money that Kollek made in 1992 to then-prime minister Yitzhak Rabin and members of Rabin's cabinet. "The level of services and infrastructure in the Arab sector is far below that of Jewish neighborhoods," Kollek told Finance Minister Avraham Shohat (Kollek 1992a). "There is a desperate need for emergency allocations to improve the physical and social infrastructure in east Jerusalem, and to begin doing so immediately," he said. The aging mayor used his hefty political clout to lobby Rabin and his ministers. Kollek even went so far as to threaten to retire from politics if Rabin didn't grant major funding for Arab east Jerusalem. He badgered Rabin on the issue at numerous meetings. He wrote letters to and met with government ministers, complaining about the lack of housing and schools, shoddy road system, poor services, and generally below-standard living conditions in Arab east Jerusalem. And Kollek, like Olmert after him, made clear that the funding needed was far beyond the municipality's means: the Israeli government, if not for humanitarian reasons then at least for the purpose of maintaining control of east Jerusalem, would have to pay for the improvement of living conditions of Jerusalem's Arab residents.

Kollek demanded an immediate government allocation of $12 million. He received a commitment from Rabin for only $4 million and agreed not to retire. At the same time, however, Kollek warned that the allocation would be "far from what is needed to solve the problems of such a complicated and sensitive city as Jerusalem," and that the continued lack of proper funding for Arab east Jerusalem threatened Israel's hold on the city (Kollek 1992b).

The Rabin government never made the full $4 million allocation, according to city officials. As in the past, an Israeli government had not even kept promises for major budget allocations to Arab east Jerusalem. Kollek was deeply disappointed and even angry. He had believed a government led by his own Labor Party would finally come through with the help needed for Jerusalem's Arab sector—a move that he believed was vital to Israeli interests. Kollek had put a great deal of hope in Rabin. He believed that the new prime minister was the Israeli leader who would finally understand the importance of improving conditions in the Palestinian sector. Perhaps not surprisingly, the mayor lashed out at Rabin and his government when he discovered that nothing was changing with regard to Israeli policy toward east Jerusalem. He accused the prime minister not simply of having a failed policy but of having no policy toward east Jerusalem (Kollek 1992c). In another letter, to a cabinet member, Kollek warned that the failure of the government to act threatened the continued "unity and standing of Jerusalem" (1992d).

Kollek and Olmert after him watched as the gap between living conditions in Jewish and Arab neighborhoods grew larger. There is no hiding the gap. A drive through east Jerusalem reveals the gross disparities in everything from roads and sidewalks to schools and parks. In Beit Hanina, many roads are still unpaved, and the roads that are paved are in poor condition. There are few street lights and sidewalks. In Pisgat Zeev, the newly built Jewish neighborhood next door, residents return home on well-paved roads, and their children have beautiful schools and parks. The same contrast can be seen elsewhere in east Jerusalem, between the Arab Shuafat and Jewish Neve Ya'akov, Arab Issawiya and Jewish Giva'a Tsarfatit (French Hill), or Arab Sur Baher and Jewish East Talpiot. A single public library serves Jerusalem's Palestinian population, and that was built not with public funds but with foreign contributions raised by the Jerusalem Foundation.

The library was built at Kollek's initiative, and it was Kollek, the founder of the Jerusalem Foundation, who personally raised much of the money. A charismatic and well-liked mayor known worldwide, Kollek was a great fund-raiser. The monies he and others at the Jerusalem Foundation raised were used in a number of projects aimed to improve services and living conditions for Jerusalem's Arab sector. Those projects included Sheikh Jarrah Health Clinic, the Beit Hanina Sports Fields, playgrounds in several Arab neighborhoods, and major improvements at Abdallah Ibn Hussein Technological School, which enabled the school to become an accredited technical college. But the foundation's good works in many ways served to accentuate the failure of the Israeli government to provide properly for Jerusalem's Arab residents. When foundation money went to help set up a library for the Jewish sector, it was meant to build an additional library or to improve an existing library. The library built by the foundation in the American Colony neighborhood in east Jerusalem stood out because neither the Israeli national or municipal government had built a library anywhere in east Jerusalem.

It shouldn't be surprising, then, that this library was opened with great fanfare. What is surprising is that Israeli policymakers believed that such fanfare would deceive the Arab residents and, for that matter, also the world into thinking that Israel was treating Jerusalem's Arab population fairly. Early on, Mayor Kollek and others at Jerusalem City Hall and in the Israeli government realized that given their goal of strengthening the Jewish presence in Jerusalem, there would be little available in the way of financial support for the Arab sector. Budget allocations for Jerusalem were earmarked almost exclusively for development aimed at bringing more Jews to the city. Kollek tried to make the most out of the little that went to the Arab sector. Israel must at least make it look as if it is taking significant steps to improve living conditions for the Arab residents, Kollek and others believed. "We must show them [the Arabs] we are doing something," the mayor told a forum of municipal and government officials in 1985. "Even if it is something small, it is important to make a big deal out of it to make it appear like we are working for them" [minutes from a meeting at the home of city manager Aharon Sarig, July 1985]. That meant holding big celebrations each time Israel embarked on a new public development, no matter how small, for the Arab sector.

The plan of at least making it look as if Israel was working hard to improve conditions in the Arab sector did have some effect. People, including Israelis themselves, are often shocked when they are shown the true situation. Many Israelis have not been in Arab sections of the city since the Palestinian uprising, or Intifada, of the late 1980s and early 1990s. Even before the Intifada, Israelis rarely ventured into the outlying Arab neighborhoods in the city, such as Umm Tuba and Jebel Mukabber. When they did, they were often struck by the poor conditions in which Jerusalem's Arabs largely lived and continue to live today.

Reasons for the Disparities

One of the reasons for these disparities is simply that many of the Jewish neighborhoods are newer. The Jewish neighborhoods built in east Jerusalem were built after 1967. In 1948, Jordan had driven all the Jewish residents from the Old City and subsequently ransacked the Jewish Quarter. Even many of the Jewish neighborhoods in what was formerly west Jerusalem are newer, built after the Jewish state was established in 1948.

But this is not the only reason. Israeli leaders have been keenly aware of the disparities in living conditions of Arabs and Jews in Jerusalem since the city's reunification. They have held countless symposiums and compiled numerous reports detailing the problem and its negative impact on Israeli-Palestinian relations in Jerusalem. Kollek, at a city council meeting in 1987 just after the outbreak of the Intifada, gave a particularly frank analysis of Israeli policy toward east Jerusalem. "I no longer want to give them [Palestinian east Jerusalemites] the feeling of equality. I know that we cannot give them this feeling. But I want here and there, when it doesn't cost so much money, only effort and a little money, to nevertheless give them the feeling that they can live here. If we don't give them that feeling, we will suffer," Kollek said *(Maariv,* Dec. 23, 1997).[3] "My concern is for the Jewish majority. . . . That's the reason we are sitting here. . . . For Jewish Jerusalem, I have done much over these past 25 years. For east Jerusalem? Nothing. What have I done? Schools? Nothing. Sidewalks? Nothing. Cultural institutions? Nothing," said Kollek, clearly upset by the violence that had broken out in east Jerusalem in the first days of the Intifada. He believed strongly that Israel's failure to provide adequately for Jerusalem's Palestinian residents was one of the reasons they were so quick to join the uprisings.

"Yes, we built them a sewage system and improved their water system. Do you know why? Do you think this was for their benefit, to make their lives better? You've got to be kidding. There were several instances of cholera, and the Jewish residents were concerned that they would catch it. So we built them a sewage and water systems, to prevent the spread of cholera," Kollek told the city council *(Maariv,* Dec. 23, 1997).

In 1990, an Israeli official ordered the recall of a particularly embarrassing municipal report because it showed that Israel was not only failing to make improvements in closing the gap between the Arab and Jewish sectors in Jerusalem, but also was not allocating to the Arab sector what was required to ensure that the gap did not grow. The report stated that Palestinians made up 28 percent of Jerusalem's population but received only between 2 and 12 percent of the municipal budget in the various city departments ("Advisor to the Mayor" 1994).

The actual size of Israeli allocations to Arab neighborhoods were probably even less than in the report Israeli officials had covered up. In many cases, money earmarked for the Arab sector ended up in programs that at best only peripherally helped Arab residents. Route One, one of the city's major road projects in the 1990s, came from funds earmarked for the Arab

---

3. The quote itself was taken from recorded minutes of a city council meeting on December 27, 1987.

sector and, indeed, in part served Arab residents. But it's main purpose was to ease traffic to the center of the city from the new Jewish neighborhoods in north Jerusalem. Jerusalem's new soccer stadium, "Teddy Stadium," is a more extreme example. It too was paid for in part by government funding earmarked for the Arab population. City officials justified this allocation by arguing that Arab residents would also be using the stadium, although few Arab residents have gone there because most events cater to the Jewish population. Thus, when Israeli officials provide totals for money allocated to the Arab sector, those figures are often misleading. The investment Israel makes toward improving conditions for Arab residents is even lower than the low amounts admitted officially.

Israel's neglect of the city's Arab neighborhoods appears to result at least in part from the Jewish state's aim of encouraging Arabs to leave the city while at the same time increasing the Jewish population. The development policies implemented by Israel in united Jerusalem reflect this aim. State funds for Jerusalem development went largely to the development of new Jewish neighborhoods and improvement as well as the expansion of older ones. A table in a Jerusalem 1999 municipal report graphically displays this gap: 680 kilometers of roads in west Jerusalem, only 86 kilometers in east Jerusalem; 700 kilometers of sidewalks in west Jerusalem, 73 kilometers in east Jerusalem; 1,079 public gardens in west Jerusalem, 29 in east Jerusalem; and 650 kilometers of sewage lines in west Jerusalem, but only 76 kilometers in east Jerusalem.[4]

The municipality admits that the homes of 80,000 Palestinian Jerusalemites—or nearly one half of the city's total Palestinian population—are still without proper sewage *(Kol Hazman,* June 11, 1999). For some, septic tanks are an alternative. For others, the sewage from their homes spills untreated into nearby wadis and streams.

The disparities are in virtually every sector—from housing and infrastructure to education and welfare. Only two small government-supported

4. The cover page of this 1999 municipal report simply carries the statement, in quotations, "The unity of Jerusalem, under the sovereignty of the Israeli government, depends, to a large extent, in the equality of municipal services for all residents, in both the [Arab] eastern and [Jewish] western sectors of the city" (Amirav 1999).

welfare department offices serve Jerusalem's Arab sector, compared to two large "district" offices and ten smaller neighborhood offices for the Jewish sector *(Kol Hair,* Mar. 12, 1999). Government social workers in the Arab sector normally work approximately 350 cases at a time, whereas in the Jewish sector they work approximately 150 cases *(Kol Hair,* Mar. 12, 1999). Similarly, there are few public infant care centers serving the Arab population, and, as noted above, many Palestinian parents take their newborns to centers run by Palestinian welfare organizations.

In 1999, the Jerusalem municipality approved an allocation of approximately $4,000 for teenage sports programs, a figure that was matched by the municipality. Thirty-two city community centers were awarded the funding, but only two of those were in the Arab sector *(Kol Hazman,* June 11, 1999). Palestinian elderly fare no better when it comes to the services Israel provides. Thirty-five public care centers serve the city's Jewish neighborhood, compared to seven that serve Arab neighborhoods *(Yerushalayim,* Feb. 5, 1999). The centers in the Jewish neighborhoods are also far better funded.

From an Israeli perspective, what makes these discrepancies the most troubling is that they don't always seem to be justifiable, even by its own reasoning that everything possible had to be done to strengthen Israel's hold on Jerusalem, even when it meant providing less for the city's Palestinians. Such reasoning might be used to defend Israel's policy of building homes nearly exclusively for Jews in Jerusalem and not for Arabs or to defend the other discrepancies in budget allocations, but it would clearly be inappropriate for the numerous occasions when the issue was not money.

In 1993, for instance, the Education Ministry of the State of Israel produced a book on Jerusalem, titled *Our Town,* and like similar books produced for Israeli schoolchildren from other cities, it was aimed at teaching them about the communities in which they live. Chapter 1 opens with the question, "Who is a Jerusalemite?" and gives the answer: "Three friends, Yaron, from the Morasha neighborhood, Yael, who lives in Kiryat Hayovel, and Rami from Ramot." There is no Ahmed from Sheikh Jarrah or Mahmoud from A-Tur. They aren't presented as being part of what makes up Jerusalem. When he first saw the book and noticed that the Palestinian population had been ignored, Kollek protested and demanded changes. They were never made.

Disparities in Housing Development

The disparity between the Jewish and Arab sectors is perhaps the most glaring with regard to housing development. Of the 64 square kilometers Israel added to the municipal boundaries after the 1967 war (M. Klein 1999, 11), 24.8 square kilometers was expropriated (ibid., 18). Most of that land was taken from Arab landowners and went to building new Jewish neighborhoods. At the same time, Israel used the expropriations to limit Palestinian growth. For instance, in 1970, Israel expropriated 550 acres for the construction of the Jewish neighborhood of East Talpiot, but only 445 acres was actually earmarked for the new neighborhood.[5] Similarly, 1,200 acres were expropriated for the construction of Neve Ya'akov, but only 790 dunams of this land actually went to the new neighborhood.[6] The unused land was meant to lay idle, until there was a need for additional expansion of the Jewish neighborhoods.

This is also one of the stories behind the Har Homa neighborhood. Jews had owned most of the land expropriated for the purpose of building this Jewish neighborhood. There was much discussion within the government on the need to expropriate the land and on the size of the final expropriation. In the end, Israel decided on a large expropriation of approximately 460 acres. A much smaller expropriation was all that was needed to get construction under way. But Israel decided to take the additional land in order to create a massive new Jewish neighborhood in southeastern Jerusalem and to prevent the expansion of nearby Palestinian neighborhoods, such as Sur Baher, that would link them to Beit Sahur, a Palestinian town just outside of Jerusalem, and Bethlehem.

Since 1967, Israel has helped build thousands of new homes for Jews in east Jerusalem and only several hundred for Arabs (in Beit Hanina and Wadi al-Joz). Israeli leaders did consider building more for Jerusalem's Arabs, but not in Jerusalem. Rather, in years following the 1967 war, there were dis-

5. "Proposed Program for Building at East Talpiot," Israel Housing Ministry internal memo, September 25, 1970.

6. "Proposed Program for Building at Neve Yaacov," Israel Housing Ministry internal memo, September 24, 1970.

cussions over building homes for Jerusalem Arabs in the West Bank as a means for encouraging Arab residents to leave the city. In the 1970s, Israel built a few dozen homes for Jerusalem Palestinians in Azariya, just east of the city, and there were plans to build more. But although in principal Israeli leaders backed the idea of building for Jerusalem Palestinians outside the city, they opted instead to concentrate the country's financial resources on building for Jews in Jerusalem and simply to allow the Palestinians to fend for themselves. When it came to building homes for Palestinian Jerusalemites, even locations outside the city were not a priority.

This is not to say that Palestinians did not build in Jerusalem. On the contrary, despite Israel's attempt to restrict the growth of the Palestinian population, Palestinian neighborhoods also expanded. According to one survey, based on an analysis of aerial photographs just after the 1967 war and again in the past few years, a total of 13,600 new buildings were built between 1968 and 1995 in east Jerusalem and the Arab communities that bordered the city (Kimhi 1998, 36). The Palestinian population boomed, as did the Jewish population.

The official Israeli statistics show that the percentage of Arabs in Jerusalem has grown since 1967, and the percentage of Jews has decreased. In 1967 (after reunification), Jews made up 74.2 percent and non-Jews 25.8 percent of Jerusalem's population. By 1996, the percentage of Jews had dropped to 70 percent (Choshen and Shahar 1998, 29). The official Israeli statistics, however, don't necessarily tell the whole story. It is indeed clear that the Palestinian population in the Jerusalem region has boomed since 1967, as has the Jewish population. But many of the Palestinians who claim Jerusalem residence and who even have Israeli-issued Jerusalem identity cards in fact live outside the city in towns such as A-Ram and A-Zayim. A true population count would likely show the Palestinian population in Jerusalem far lower than shown by the official statistics.

Disparities in Daily Living

The numbers tell only part of the story. The contrasts between the Arab and Jewish sectors are sharpest in the reality of day-to-day life in Jerusalem. The numbers that show infrastructure and services in Arab neighborhoods being far below that of Jewish neighborhoods are reflected in substandard living conditions in the Arab neighborhoods. For instance, in Sawahra, the trash piles up alongside the dirt roads. There are no sidewalks. There are also no sewage lines, and instead homeowners must use septic tanks, which are emptied every few months. The trucks that come to pump out the sewage tanks don't go far with their loads. The drivers pull up alongside city man-holes and dump the sewage into the municipal system, often causing back-ups and worse. Other times, the trucks dump the sewage in open areas just outside the neighborhood, where it wreaks havoc on the ecosystem. The Is-raeli authorities say it is up to the residents to come up with the funding for the sewage system—just as residents of Jewish neighborhoods must con-tribute to the construction of the sewage system if the neighborhood is new. Arab residents argue they can't afford such payments, which are com-pounded by the fact that they often live in single-family homes and not high-rise apartment units in which the expenses for infrastructure can be di-vided among many. But Israel has rejected their argument, and their sewage is left to flow unchecked.

The damage hurts Jew and Arab alike. Many of the wadis and streams flowing down from the hillsides of east Jerusalem, through the Judean Desert and into the Jordan River and Dead Sea, are to one degree or an-other polluted with the free-flowing waste from the city. Nahal Kidron, known in Arabic as Wadi A-Naar, is heavily polluted. So is Nahal Og (Wadi al-Mukhalib). Nahal Prat (Kelt), site of the majestic St. George Monastery built into the mountainside just above the stream below, has not escaped the damage. The untreated waste from Kalandia refugee camp and the nearby Palestinian town al-Birah, and from the Jewish communities Kokhav Yaa-cov and Ma'ale Mikhmash—all just north of Jerusalem—threaten Nahal Mikhmash (Wadi a-Tsunit). These once pristine homes of desert oasis have slowly been turned into open sewage lines, whose only hope for recovery is that they won't be forgotten in the conflict over Jerusalem's future. Until now, however, they have been forgotten by short-sighted leaders on both sides, who repeatedly fail to comprehend the long-term effects of their policies.

In the immediate aftermath of the first Oslo Accord in 1993, there was an attempt to bring the sides to their senses with regard to the issue of water and sewage in the Jerusalem area. Well-intentioned European leaders tried to bring together Palestinians and Israelis to address these issues. The Europeans offered to pay for the construction of a major sewage treatment plant for the waste flowing to the east. The idea was quite simple: the Palestinian authorities in Bethlehem and Beit Jala, as much as the Israeli authorities in Israel, would benefit from the project and, having to put up no money of their own, would have no reason to object to its implementation. The Israelis quickly accepted the proposal for the plant, which they knew should have been built years ago but wasn't because the country's priorities were elsewhere. The Palestinians, however, balked. They wanted political solutions first.

The sewage of east Jerusalem was left to flow untreated, but so too was the sewage of Beit Jala, Bethlehem, and Beit Sahur. Jerusalem was Israeli, whereas Beit Jala, Bethlehem, and Beit Sahur were Palestinian. But topographical lines crossed these artificial borders. Sooner or later cooperation would be required. There, of course, is also another possibility—that the Palestinians and Israelis will continue to ignore each other's common needs. The implications of such a course are clear: more polluted rivers, threatened water sources, and increased health hazards.

Cooperative Efforts

The irony is that, before Oslo, Palestinians and Israelis had on occasion found common ground to cooperate in such matters as infrastructure development. Given the times, they did so quietly, often in secret. Nonetheless, there appeared to be a realization that, at least in Jerusalem, there was little choice but to learn to get along. In A-Tur in the early 1970s, for instance, the Palestine Liberation Organization (PLO) helped fund the construction of a sewage system. The Jerusalem municipality had offered to provide the materials for the project and called on the residents of the Mount of Olives neighborhood to cover the costs of the work. The residents, however, were unable to pay the costs themselves, which is where the PLO's financial help came in. The PLO, with the help of Jordan, had set up a fund earmarked specifically for Palestinian projects in east Jerusalem, and the A-Tur sewage project became a major recipient. For their part, the Israelis knew quite well that the money was coming from the then–outlawed PLO, but they looked the other way. Israel set aside, at least in this instance, the short-sighted political reasoning that forbade any PLO activity in the city.

There were also other forms of cooperation—again dictated by a combination of political and physical motives. Between 1967 and 1987, electricity throughout east Jerusalem was provided by the Jerusalem District Electric Company (JDEC), and to this day the JDEC provides power to Arab neighborhoods of the city and surrounding villages. The JDEC was a Palestinian company that had operated in Jerusalem and the surrounding areas since the early 1900s. Before Israel's independence and the division of Jerusalem, the JDEC had provided electricity for Jews and Arabs alike. With the reunification of Jerusalem in 1967 and the return of Jews to the area, the JDEC again began providing both Jewish and Arab residents power in east Jerusalem. In west Jerusalem, however, the Israel Electric Corporation became the power source.

Not surprisingly, since 1967, the JDEC has been a center of Palestinian political power and pride in Jerusalem—a symbol of Palestinian independence in east Jerusalem. Long before Palestinians had their own parliament, the elections for the JDEC union were hotly contested battles pitting nationalist and pro-Islamic candidates against one another, even in the days when Israel outlawed such political affiliations by Palestinians.

Palestinians themselves saw the absurdity in their company trying to compete with the larger and better funded Israel Electric Corporation in fast-growing east Jerusalem. Over time, the JDEC ended up producing less electricity itself and instead purchasing it from the Israeli government-owned electric monopoly. On New Year's Eve 1987, the Jewish neighborhoods of east Jerusalem—their residents fed up with the frequent power outages and poor service of the JDEC—were switched over to the Israel Electric Corporation grid. The JDEC continues to operate in Jerusalem's Arab neighborhoods, although no longer producing its own electricity and instead itself a consumer of the Israel Electric Corporation.

The JDEC remains in operation owing to political, not market, forces. The Palestinians are loath to give up the symbolic value of having their own electric company in Jerusalem, even though that company doesn't produce any electricity. (The Israel Electric Corporation is also loath to take over the

Palestinian company, which has had difficulty obtaining payment from customers, particularly so in the refugee camps in the Jerusalem vicinity that the JDEC serves.) Israeli leaders in the first years after the 1967 war had pondered doing away with the JDEC, but even before Oslo they realized that the company had turned into a political live wire that they were better off not touching. So an antiquated system was allowed to remain in place. Perhaps it could be argued that this status was good in the short run because the symbolic power of the company outweighed the hardship it created for Arab residents in the way of poor service. But in the long run, development in a growing metropolis such as Jerusalem can only be ill-served by the outdated infrastructure and service represented by the JDEC.

The Palestinians also have their own water company in Jerusalem, although this fact has drawn less public attention. The Ramallah Water Company continues to provide water to the outlying Palestinian neighborhoods, such as Beit Hanina and Shuafat. Like its counterpart in electricity, the Ramallah Water Company is no longer a producer. It purchases water from Mekorot, the Israel state-owned water company, and then sells it to its customers. But unlike its electrical counterpart, the Ramallah Water Company operates and maintains an extensive network of water lines in east Jerusalem, often alongside those of the Israeli company. Again, the reasons are both political and practical. Since 1967, Israel, concentrating its financial resources on development of Jewish neighborhoods of east Jerusalem, was less than eager to commit funds to a vast overhaul of the entire water system in the Arab neighborhoods. It did make a major investment in establishing a modern water system in the Old City and in the Arab neighborhoods in its immediate vicinity. When Israel reunited the city in 1967, it acquired an area that still largely received its water from private wells and from water trucks and vendors—such as the vendors stationed just inside Herod's Gate, who would sell water to Old City residents. The residents would haul the water in containers, large enough to make their backs sore but still too small to last more than a short while.

In the years following the Six Day War, Israel built a water system in the Old City. It also did so in Wadi al-Joz, Sheikh Jarrah, Abu Tor, and other neighborhoods near the Old City. The neighborhoods to the north had water, which they received from the Ramallah Water Company, and Israel did not interfere in the company's operations. To this day, the Ramallah Water Company continues to provide water for most of the Palestinian businesses and residences in north Jerusalem. The Palestinians have de facto autonomy over their water system in Jerusalem, despite Israel's public stance of forbidding any form of Palestinian self-rule in the city. As with electricity, Israel leaves the Palestinians of north Jerusalem to themselves when it comes to their water needs.

Palestinian residents are not happy with this situation, but for political reasons they don't protest too loudly. The reason they are unhappy is simple: cost. Palestinian residents receiving their water from the Ramallah Water Company pay much higher rates than those residents supplied water by the Jerusalem municipality. But most Palestinians don't fight this situation for fear such protest might be misread as undercutting the position of a Palestinian company in Jerusalem—a situation similar to that of the Jerusalem District Electric Company, discussed above. In fact, in 1993, the JDEC raised its rates by 24 percent, which meant that Palestinian Jerusalemites were paying more for their electricity than Jewish residents, but Palestinian residents made no protest.

A few Palestinian residents have complained to the municipality about their high water rates and at one point demanded, as residents of the city, to receive their water from the Israeli water authority, as do all residents of the city. The municipality was about to comply with the residents' demand when attorneys with the city's legal department halted the changeover. They argued that the Ramallah Water Company had the right to provide water in north Jerusalem and that it would be illegal to attempt to infringe on that right.

Ironically, the Israeli attorneys may have in the end saved Palestinian residents some money. The municipality levies a heavy tax on new home builders when they hook up to the city's water system. Palestinians living in north Jerusalem who hook up to the Ramallah Water Company avoid this tax. For the present—with Jerusalem served by two separate Israeli and Palestinian water systems—Palestinians building their homes in Beit Hanina, Shuafat, and other area neighborhoods served by the Palestinian company will continue to receive this tax break but also pay higher water bills than Jewish residents.

In south Jerusalem, however, things worked out differently. In the early 1990s, residents of Beit Safafa requested to be hooked up to the Jerusalem municipal system and eventually got their way. Before 1967, Beit Safafa was a divided village. The Jordanian section received water from the Bethlehem Water Company, the Israeli section from the Jerusalem municipality. After the war, the city's boundaries were expanded to include both halves of Beit Safafa. However, residents of the formerly Jordanian side have continued to receive their water from the Bethlehem Water Company. But as in north Jerusalem, they paid higher prices than their fellow villagers that received water from the municipality. To make matters worse, they also received worse service. Bethlehem Water Company water lines were old and frequently leaked or exploded, and residents were left without water for days. Beit Safafa leaders approached the Jerusalem municipality and requested to be switched to the municipal water system. Kollek readily agreed, but as with other issues in Jerusalem, the matter had strong political implications, of which Kollek was well aware. He knew that Palestinian political sensitivities would have to be considered if the changeover was going to come about. Kollek also remembered what had happened when the municipality attempted a changeover in north Jerusalem. This time, he decided to leave the lawyers out of the picture.

Kollek held a private meeting with Bethlehem mayor Elias Freij at City Hall in Jerusalem. Great pains were taken to ensure the media did not find out about the meeting. Freij and Kollek were both elder statesmen by this time. Over the years, they had become friends, and they would visit each other in their respective cities. Freij readily agreed to the changeover. Like Kollek, he saw the move as making sense on a practical basis, but also as with the Jerusalem mayor, he knew the political implications could not be ignored. Thus, Freij and Kollek agreed that the changeover would be done quietly and that all effort would be made to ensure the move did not become public. And they succeeded.

Quiet cooperation also succeeded in other areas. In the early 1980s, when Israel built a small housing project for Jerusalem Palestinians in the nearby village of Azariya, city officials agreed to provide the residents with trash collection, even though they were moving outside of city limits. Village leaders requested from Kollek that the Jerusalem municipality sanitation trucks that came to pick up trash at the project also pick up trash of village residents and businesses on the way. The leaders, strapped for funding in the poor village, asked this as "a favor" from the Jerusalem mayor. Kollek readily agreed, taking advantage of an easy opportunity to improve relations with his Palestinian neighbors.

Shifting Borders

With or without cooperation between Israelis and Palestinians, Jerusalem grows. The city is no longer a city, but a metropolitan area sprawling beyond the artificial boundaries that Israel or the Palestinian Authority or, for that matter, anyone may place on it. From Bethlehem in the south to Ramallah in the north, armed Israelis and Palestinians have attempted to set up watch over the land that they have carved out as their own. But their checkpoints and outposts are lost in the ever-widening expanse of this metropolitan area. As in New York, Paris, and Beijing, the city's boundaries have become gradually more meaningless. Test yourself. Driving into Jerusalem from the north, you may or may not find comfort crossing the Israeli army checkpoint at A-Ram, widely seen as the border crossing into Jerusalem. But cross that border and turn either left or right, and you will quickly find yourself outside the city. For that matter, just a couple hundred meters before the checkpoint, you might be surprised to discover that you are already in areas that Israel has claimed as part of Jerusalem. Similarly, try the eastern entrance to the city along the old Jericho road. Where on the slopes of the Mount of Olives does Jerusalem begin and the West Bank end? Only the artificial lines drawn by generals and politicians can give you the answer. Why Israel in 1967 made some Mount of Olives villages part of Jerusalem and not others is a source of great debate. The only thing that is certain about this debate is that there was nothing sacred in the drawing of that line. Rather, the lines were drawn according to practical (and at times impractical) geopolitical considerations. Military men, not statesmen or even religious leaders, had much to say about the setting of Jerusalem's borders after the 1967 War. They aimed to establish secure borders for the city. They also wanted to include in Jerusalem as much undeveloped territory and as little Palestinian population as possible. There was nothing sacred about their work.

It is in these "unholy" gray areas that there would appear to be room for Palestinians and Israelis to come to an understanding over Jerusalem. The possibility for success of the various proposed agreements on the city's future is based to a large extent on the shared belief that despite the rhetoric, Jerusalem is not the all-sacred, no-compromise issue that both sides publicly claim. In fact, Palestinian and Israeli negotiators might have more wiggle room and an easier time at reaching an agreement on Jerusalem than on any of the other final-stage issues.

It is these same gray areas that also appear to suffer the worst from the lack of courage on both sides to move ahead with the dialogue on Jerusalem. The village of Zayim is one such area. Just to the east of the Maaleh Adummim-Jerusalem road, this small village did not even exist twenty years ago. In a few short years, it has grown into a symbol of the failure of Israeli policy-makers to deal with the needs of Palestinian Jerusalemites. The boundaries of Zayim are just inside the Israeli army checkpoint at the eastern entrance to the city. But the village itself is not within the city limits. Its residents are largely Jerusalemites, however. Jerusalem Palestinians from A-Tur, on the Mount of Olives, with no real possibility to obtain building permits on their lands within the city, began building homes on land they purchased just outside the city limits, on the slopes of the Judean Desert. By 1983, there were less than two dozen homes there. Today there are hundreds. In the early years, the Israeli military authorities in the West Bank threatened to tear down the few homes that had been built there, claiming they were built without permits. But at Kollek's insistence, the homes were allowed to stay. His reasoning: Palestinian Jerusalemites needed a place to build, and it was in Israel's interest that that place be outside the city.

To this day, Zayim has no zoning plan, and in effect all construction there is illegal. The JDEC provides electricity, but there is no sewage system, and residents instead use septic tanks. Israel also failed to put in a water system. In the early years, residents would take water from friends and family in nearby A-Tur. Eventually, however, a local businessman, Abu Dighram, convinced Kollek to run a water line to the edge of the city's eastern boundary at A-Tur and place a meter there. Abu Dighram took care of the rest. He extended the line into Zayim and charged the residents for this service. In effect, he became a one-man water company in the village.

Similarly, several dozen Palestinian families on a hillside in south Jerusalem lived for more than twenty years as if they were residents of the West Bank. Their "village," named Walaje—several dozen scattered homes connected by dirt roads—was founded in 1948 by refugees of a larger village of the same name several miles away, which fell into Israeli hands after the war. In around 1990, however, Jerusalem municipality building inspectors began enforcing building codes in the area, which until then had been treated as being outside of the city limits. The officials demanded the villagers provide housing permits or have their homes demolished. The villagers protested. On the one hand, they received nothing from the municipality. They had no roads, no sewage system, no municipal schools, no municipal services whatsoever. They weren't issued Israeli identity cards, but instead carried West Bank IDs, which greatly limited their freedom of movement into Jerusalem. Yet the municipality was demanding they obtain building permits. The villagers were willing to apply for permits, but here too they had a problem: the Jerusalem municipality itself had not previously recognized Walaje as part of the city, so there was no zoning plan for the area, which meant there was virtually no way for residents to obtain building permits. To this day, the Israeli authorities have yet to decide how to handle Walaje. The Palestinian Authority, however, has gone ahead and appointed a village council in hopes that one day Walaje will be part of a future Palestinian state.

It is within this state of contradictions—inside Jerusalem or outside Jerusalem? Jerusalem residents or not Jerusalem residents? illegally built homes or legally built homes?—that the residents of Zayim and Walaje have struggled to live. The residents of Zayim, with Israeli IDs, have been somewhat more successful. Not only do they have running water, but also a swimming club (also owned by Abu Dighram) that attracts Palestinians from the entire area. Run-down auto repair shops still line the entrance to the village, and the roads are in poor condition, but many of the homes in Zayim are larger and more luxurious than in neighboring A-Tur. Walaje residents, with West Bank IDs, have found conditions much more difficult. Unable to enter Israel, they have a difficult time finding work. They are even at risk of arrest when traveling in Jerusalem, where Israeli IDs or special permits are required.

It is within this state of contradictions that Palestinian and Israeli leaders must attempt to forge an understanding on Jerusalem. For more than three decades, Zayim, Walaje, and numerous other localities in similar situations have caused great tension. But these villages may also represent the possibilities for the future. When Prime Minister Barak says that Jerusalem will always remain under Israeli control, does he include Walaje, Zayim, Anata (in north Jerusalem), Mazmuriya (between Jerusalem and Bethlehem), and Bir Una (between Jerusalem and Beit Jala)—villages that straddle the present Jerusalem boundaries? These gray areas might offer some help in arriving at an understanding between Palestinians and Israelis on Jerusalem.

Opportunities for the Future

Jerusalem is no longer the tiny walled city crammed with holy sites and pilgrims that it was for most of its history, but rather a large metropolitan area spreading from Ramallah in the north to Bethlehem in the south. The old boundaries—Ottoman, British, Jordanian, and even Israeli post-1967—today exist largely on paper. On the ground, there is a mishmash of Palestinian and Israeli neighborhoods, villages, and other communities. There might exist some creative way to separate them: Palestinians on one side, Israelis on the other. But it seems unlikely that any such arrangement could really work. Instead, whether they like it or not, in Jerusalem the Palestinians and Israelis are stuck with each other.

The sooner they realize this the better. Roads and water systems and schools and parks need to be built, and both sides have a responsibility in seeing them built. There are projects that would benefit the entire population, making Jerusalem more livable for both its Palestinian and Israeli residents, as well as the millions of others who visit the city.

One such project is the eastern ring road, the proposed highway along Jerusalem's eastern boundary. Palestinian and Israeli planners agree that the highway would be a magnet for additional development in an area of Jerusalem that perhaps suffers the worst from lack of infrastructure (for a discussion of this project, see Rekhes, Eshkol, and Gilboa 1993). It would ease congestion in the center of Jerusalem by allowing commuters, Palestinian and Israeli alike, between areas north and south of the city to go around instead of through the crowded center city. Both Palestinians and Israelis have an interest in such projects and both should be required to make an investment in ensuring they are carried out.

Similarly, the Atarot Industrial Zone and nearby Atarot Airport are other points where Israeli and Palestinian interests might come together. Atarot is officially part of Jerusalem today. However, it is situated to the north of the Israeli checkpoint into the city, in an area populated exclusively by Palestinians. Today, there are few Palestinian businesses at Atarot, and the airport is used only by Israel. But the locations of the two sites, just minutes from Ramallah, naturally call for their being opened up to greater Palestinian use. Atarot would appear to be a natural location for Israeli and Palestinian interests in fostering economic development in the Jerusalem area to come together, perhaps as part of an early stage in the implementation of an agreement on Jerusalem.

At the same time, there must be a recognition that there are also areas in which Jewish and Arab needs in Jerusalem differ. They have different religions, languages, cultures, ways of life in general, and, perhaps most importantly, political aspirations. Jerusalem needs better roads, sewage systems, and public transportation for all of its residents together. Israel's failure to provide this basic infrastructure in Arab neighborhoods has been a major factor in Jerusalem's remaining a divided city to this day. But some divisions are necessary. Arab and Jewish children attend different schools with different curriculums—Israeli and Palestinian. In general, both communities and their leaders encourage this separation. They want to develop their respective national identities. In the not so distant future, Jerusalem Palestinians and Israelis might be residents of two different countries—Israel and Palestine. In the meantime, integration, at least in the areas of social services, is not an option. The political atmosphere greatly limits the possibilities for such mingling.

Yet for Palestinians and Israelis to live and work together in Jerusalem, they will have to overcome the psychology of demography that has dominated policymaking on both sides since 1967. The race of percentages—how many Jews to how many Arabs live in Jerusalem—has wrought havoc on development in the city and its environs. Both sides will wind up as losers if this competition is allowed to continue. Jerusalem's inspirational landscape has already suffered from the unchecked expansion caused by this numbers game. The city has become congested and overcrowded in parts, its hilltops and wadis ravaged by ever-expanding neighborhoods and villages. Building homes as quickly and inexpensively as possible has for too long been the main objective. Largely forgotten is the notion that to build a city is not simply to put up stone and concrete structures but also to create open spaces, parks, playgrounds, and gardens.

Teddy Kollek maintained that the competition between the Palestinians and Israelis over Jerusalem could ultimately be used to the city's overall benefit. Early on in his career, he realized that this competition was an excellent vehicle for raising contributions from Jews worldwide. Kollek and other Israeli leaders appealed to Jews living outside of Israel to make contributions to strengthen the Jewish state's standing in Jerusalem. In 1965, two years before Jerusalem was reunited, Kollek helped establish the Jerusalem Foundation largely to this end. Later, he would call on Arab leaders to set up their own fund to help their neighborhoods of the city. They have yet to meet the challenge. The time now may be the most ripe for them to do so.

The Jerusalem issue will likely take much time to resolve. Particularly sensitive points such as the status of the Old City and holy sites will be difficult to negotiate. But until an agreement is reached, the reality of life in Jerusalem demands greater cooperation and understanding from all the parties interested in the city's future. There would appear to be no alternative.

There are, however, groups on both sides for whom any type of compromise is not acceptable. For ideological and religious reasons, they want everything. For certain Jewish groups, even Walaje—which is already under de facto Palestinian control—must be under Israeli rule. Certain Palestinian groups maintain that any agreement on Jerusalem must put all of east Jerusalem, even Jewish neighborhoods such as French Hill and Pisgat Zeev. These hard-line positions offer little hope for the future. But the reality of life in Jerusalem does. In Walaje and Zayim, de facto compromises have already taken place. They've also taken place with the Jerusalem District Electric Company and with the Bethlehem and Ramallah Water Companies. Even on more "sensitive" issues such as the operations of the Palestinian police and the status of the Palestinian Authority on the Temple Mount/al-Haram al-Sharif and at Orient House, de facto understandings exist between the two sides. It is these understandings that Palestinians and Israelis must build on in order to establish the groundwork for a comprehensive agreement on Jerusalem.

Glossary

References

Index

Glossary

Beit Hashoeva: water libation ritual

birkat hakohanim: priestly benediction

corpus separatum: separate body

firman: edict or decree

Gebietshoheit: physical control

Halakhah: Jewish religious law

al-Haram al-Sharif/Har Habayit: terms used by Muslims and Jews, respectively, for the Temle Mount in Jerusalem

haredi: ultraorthodox

"Hatikvah": the Jewish national anthem

hesder **yeshiva:** combining religious studies with military service

jihad: Islamic holy war

Kedusha: holiness

Knesset: Israeli Parliament

Kofer Ha'Yishuv: voluntary defense tax

kohanim: priests

Manhi: Jerusalem Education Authority

midrash: a homiletical interpretation of a biblical passage

minhalot: administration (neighborhood government)

mishnah: the second-century law code composed by Judah Ha-Nasi

morah hamikdash: fear of the sanctuary

Moser: informer

Neturei Karta: guardians of the city

ohel moed: the biblical "tent of congregation"—the shrine before the building of the First Temple

Pesah: Passover

al-Quds: Arabic term for Jerusalem

Rosh Hashanah: New Year

Sharia courts: religious courts

Shavuot: Pentecost

shebab: street youth

shekhinah: the Divine Presence

siddur: prayer book

Sukkot: Tabernacles

territoriale Souveraenitaet: legitimate title to an area

tohu vebohu: chaos

Via Dolorosa: the Way of the Cross, commemorates the journey Jesus made through the city of Jerusalem

Waqf: Muslim religious trust

Yemin Yisrael: Right of Israel

Yerushalayim: Hebrew term for Jerusalem

Yerushalayim Shel Maalah: the spiritual Jerusalem

Yerushalayim Shel Matah: the earthly Jerusalem

Yom Kippur: Day of Atonement

Zeirei Agudat Israel: Agudat Israel's youth movement

References

Abell, Peter. 1995. "The Institutionalism and Rational Choice Theory." In *The Institutional Construction of Organizations: International and Longitudinal Studies,* edited by W. Richard Scott and Soren Christenson, 3–14. Thousand Oaks, Calif.: Sage.

"Absentees' Property Law." 1951 [5711]. *Laws of the State of Israel, Authorized Translation* 5 (1950–51): 63.

Abu Odeh, Adnan. 1992. "Two Capitals in an Undivided Jerusalem." *Foreign Affairs* 17: 183–88.

————. 1996. "Religious Inclusion, Political Inclusion: Jerusalem as an Undivided Capital." *Catholic University of America Law Review* 45, no. 3 (spring): 687–94.

Abu Odeh, Adnan. 1993. "The Origins and Relevance of UNSC Resolution 242." In *UN Security Council Resolution 242: The Building Block of Peacemaking,* 45–58. Washington, D.C.: Washington Institute for Near East Policy.

"Advisor to the Mayor of Jerusalem: Kollek Filed Away Critical Report on Services to Arab Population." 1994. *Haaretz,* May 4.

Agence France Presse. 2000. "Majority of Israelis Oppose Handover of Jerusalem Suburbs to Palestinians." May 16.

"Agreement on the Gaza Strip and the Jericho Area." 1994. Signed May 4, Cairo. UN Doc. A/49/180 S/1994/727 (Annex) of 20 June 1994. Reprinted in *International Legal Materials* 33 (1994): 626–720, and in *Israel Law Review* 28 (1994): 452–543.

al-Alami, Sa'd al-Din. 1984. *Wathaiq al-Hay'a al-Islamiyya al-'Ulya 1967–1984.* Jerusalem: Dar al-Tiba'a al-'Arabiya.

Albin, Cecilia, Moshe Amirav, and Hanna Seniora. 1991–92. *Jerusalem: An Undivided City as Dual Capital.* Israeli-Palestinian Peace Research Project, Working

Paper Series No. 16. Jerusalem: Harry S. Truman Research Institute for the Advancement of Peace and the Arab Studies Society.

Altel, Tarik. 1996. "Myth and Misunderstanding in Jordanian Palestinian Relations." *al-Siyasa al-Filastiniyya* 3, no. 12: 152–66.

"An Alternative to the Palestinian Authority." 1999. *Haaretz,* May 10.

American Consul in Jerusalem Burdett to the Secretary of State. 1949a. *Foreign Relations of the United States,* Jan. 13, 661–63.

———. 1949b. *Foreign Relations of the United States,* Jan. 29, 710.

———. 1949c. *Foreign Relations of the United States,* Jan. 29, 711.

———. 1949d. *Foreign Relations of the United States,* Feb. 5, 729–30.

Amichai, Yehuda. 1995. "Homage to Jerusalem: Jerusalem, 1967." In *The Jerusalem Anthology: A Literary Guide,* edited by Reuven Hammer, 362. Philadelphia: Jewish Publication Society.

Amirav, Moshe. 1992. "Blueprint for Jerusalem." *Jerusalem Report,* Mar. 12, 41.

———. 1999. "An Alternative to the Palestinian Authority." *Haaretz,* May 10.

Amman to Washington. 1949. *Foreign Relations of the United States,* Jan. 15, 667.

Applied Research Institute—Jerusalem (ARIJ). 1996a. *Bethlehem District.* Vol. 1 of *Environmental Profile for the West Bank.* Jerusalem: Applied Research Institute.

———. 1996b. *Ramallah District.* Vol. 4 of *Environmental Profile for the West Bank.* Jerusalem: Applied Research Institute.

———. 1996c. *Jerusalem District.* Vol 6 of *Environmental Profile for the West Bank.* Jerusalem: Applied Research Institute.

Arafat, Yasir. 1996. Letter. *al-Quds,* Nov. 11.

Arian, Alan [Asher]. 1994. *Security Threatened: Surveying Israeli Opinion on Peace and War.* JCSS Memorandum No. 43. Tel Aviv, Israel: Jaffee Center for Strategic Studies, Tel Aviv University.

Armstrong, Karen. 1996. *Jerusalem: One City, Three Faiths.* New York: Ballantine.

Aumann, Robert J. 1987. "Game Theory." In *The New Palgrave: Game Theory,* edited by John Eatwell, Murray Milgate, and Peter Newman. New York: W. W. Norton.

Aviner, Shlomo. 1989. *Shalhevt-ya: Chapters in the Sacred and the Temple* (in Hebrew). Bethel, Israel: Hava Library.

Awartani, Faisal. 1999. *Facts and Figures about the District of Jerusalem, 1998.* Jerusalem: IPCC.

Axelrod, Robert, and Robert O. Keohane. 1985. "Achieving Cooperation under Anarchy: Strategies and Institutions." *World Politics* 38: 1–24.

Bahat, Dan. 1987. *Carta's Historical Atlas of Jerusalem: An Illustrated Survey.* Jerusalem: Carta.

Baird, D. G., R. H. Gertner, and R. C. Picker. 1994. *Game Theory and the Law 50.* Cambridge, Mass.: Harvard Univ. Press.

Bakshi-Doron, Eliahu. 1995. "On the Climbers of the Mount" (in Hebrew). *Hatzofe,* May 26.

Barak, Aharon. 1994. *Interpretation in Law: Constitutional Interpretation* (in Hebrew). Vol. 3. Jerusalem: Nevo.

"Basic Agreement Between the Holy See and the Palestine Liberation Organization." 2000. Signed February 15. Available at: http://www.vatican.va, or in *Quaderni di Diritto e Politica Eclesiastico* 2 (2000): 593–97.

Baskin, Gershon. 1994. *Jerusalem of Peace: Sovereignty and Territory in Jerusalem's Future.* Jerusalem: IPCRI.

Beilin-Abu Mazen Proposal. 1995. "Draft Framework for the Conclusion of a Final Status Agreement between Israel and the Palestine Liberation Organization." Oct. 31 and Nov. 1. Published in *Haaretz,* English edition, Sept. 21, 2000, 3–4.

Bellmonte, Dan, and Mark Jackson. 1983. *Labor Economics Choice in Labor Market.* 2d ed. New York: McGraw-Hill.

Ben-Arieh, Yehoshua. 1989. *Jerusalem in the 19th Century: Emergence of the New City.* 1984. Jerusalem: Yad Yitzhak Ben-Zvi. Reprint. New York: St. Martin's.

Benvenisti, Eyal. 1993. "The Israel–Palestinian Declaration of Principles: A Framework for Future Settlement." *European Journal of International Law* 4: 542–54.

Benvenisti, E., and E. Zamir. 1993. *The Legal Status of Lands Acquired by Israelis Before 1948 in the West Bank, Gaza Strip, and East Jerusalem.* Jerusalem Institute for Israel Studies Research Series No. 52. Jerusalem: Jerusalem Institute for Israel Studies.

———. 1998. *Private Property and the Israeli-Palestinian Settlement.* Jerusalem Institute for Israel Studies Research Series No. 77. Jerusalem: Jerusalem Institute for Israel Studies.

Benvenisti, Meron. 1973. *Opposite the Closed Wall* (in Hebrew). Jerusalem: Weidenfeld and Nicholson.

———. 1988. *The Sling and the Stone* (in Hebrew). Jerusalem: Keter.

———. 1996. *City of Stone: The Hidden History of Jerusalem.* Berkeley: University of California Press.

Benziman, Uzi. 1973. *Jerusalem: City Without a Wall* (in Hebrew). Jerusalem and Tel Aviv: Schocken.

Berkovitz, Shmuel. 1978. "The Legal Status of the Holy Places in Israel" (in Hebrew). Ph.D. thesis, Hebrew University.

———. 1997. *The Legal Status of the Holy Places in Jerusalem.* Jerusalem Institute for Israel Studies Research Series No. 73. Jerusalem: Jerusalem Institute for Israel Studies.

———. 2000. *The Battle for the Holy Places: The Struggle over Jerusalem and the Holy Sites in Israel, Judea, Samaria, and the Gaza District.* Jerusalem: Hed Arzi and the Jerusalem Institute for Israel Studies.

Berman, Eli. 1998. *Sects, Subsidy, and Sacrifice: An Economist's View of Ultra-Orthodox Jews.* Jerusalem: Jerusalem Institute for Israel Studies, Maurice Falk Institute for Economic Research in Israel.

Bialer, Uri. 1985. "Haderech Labira: Hafichat Yerushalayim Limqom Moshava Harishmi Shel Memshelet Israel Bishnat 1949" (Establishment of Jerusalem as the Official Seat of the Government of Israel in 1949). *Qathedra* 35: 163–91.

Binmore, Ken. 1990. *Essays on the Foundations of Game Theory.* Cambridge, Mass.: Basil Blackwell.

Bin Talal, Crown Prince Hassan. 1979. *A Study on Jerusalem.* London: Longman.

Blau, Amram. 1947 [Kislev 5707]. "What Should Be Done?" (in Hebrew). *HaHoma* (The Wall, organ of Neturei Karta) (December).

———. 1948 [Shevat 5708]. "We Have to Declare." *HaHoma* (January).

Blum, Yehuda Z. 1968. "The Missing Reversioner: Reflections on the Status of Judea and Samaria." *Israel Law Review* 3: 279–301.

———. 1974. *The Juridical Status of Jerusalem.* Jerusalem: Leonard Davis Institute for International Relations.

Bollens, Scott A. 2000. *On Narrow Ground: Urban Policy and Ethnic Conflict in Jerusalem and Belfast.* Albany, N.Y.: State Univ. of New York Press.

Boxer, Barbara (Senator). 1995. Remarks. *Congressional Record* 141: S15483 (daily edition Oct. 23).

Boyle, Francis A. 1990. "The Creation of the State of Palestine: Too Much Too Soon?" *European Journal of International Law* 1: 301–6.

Brams, Steven J. 1975. *Game Theory and Politics.* New York: Free Press.

Breger, Marshall J. 1994. "Jerusalem Now and Then: The New Battle for Jerusalem." *Middle East Quarterly* (Dec. 23): 32–34.

Breger, Marshall J., and Thomas A. Idinopulos. 1998. *Jerusalem's Holy Places and the Peace Process.* Washington, D.C.: Washington Institute for Near East Policy.

Calvo-Goller, Karin N. 1993. "Le Régime d'autonomie prévu par la Déclaration de Principes du 13 septembre 1993." *Annuaire Francais de Droit International* 39: 435–50.

Campbell, John C., ed. 1976. *Successful Negotiation:Trieste 1954.* Princeton: Princeton Univ. Press.

Carleton, David, and Michael Stohl. 1985. "The Foreign Policy of Human Rights: Rhetoric and Reality from Jimmy Carter to Ronald Reagan." *Human Rights Quarterly* 7: 205–29.

Cassese, Antonio. 1981. "Legal Considerations on the International Status of Jerusalem." In *The Legal Aspects of the Palestine Problem with Special Regard to the Question of Jerusalem,* edited by Hans Koechler, 149–51. Vienna: International Progress Organization.

———. 1993. "The Israel-PLO Agreement and Self-Determination." *European Journal of International Law* 4: 564–71.

Cattan, Henry. 1976. *Palestine and International Law.* 2d ed. London: Longman.

———. 1981. *Jerusalem.* New York: St. Martin's.

———. 1988. *The Palestine Question.* London: Longman.

CDM/Morganti. 1997a. *Task 4, Comprehensive Planning Framework for Palestinian Water Resources Development.* Final Report. Vol. 2, text. Ramallah: CDM/Morganti.

———. 1997b. *Task 4, Comprehensive Planning Framework for Palestinian Water Resources Development.* Final Report. Vol. 3, appendices. Ramallah: CDM/Morganti.

Chafee, John (Senator). 1995. Remarks. *Congressional Record* 141: S15526 (daily edition Oct. 24).

Charnoff, Gerald, Charles J. Cooper, and Michael A. Carvin (Carvin, Shaw, Pittman, Potts & Trowbridge). 1995. Memorandum to American Israel Public Affairs Committee, June 27. *Congressional Record* 141: S15471, S15472 (daily edition Oct. 23).

Chazan, Naomi. 1991. "Negotiating the Non-Negotiable: Jerusalem in the Framework of an Israeli-Palestinian Settlement." In *Emerging Issues.* Occasional Paper No. 7. Cambridge, Mass.: International Security Studies Program, American Academy of Arts and Sciences.

Cheshin, Amir S., Bill Hutman, and Avi Melamed. 1999. *Separate and Unequal:The Inside Story of Israeli Rule in East Jerusalem.* Cambridge, Mass.: Harvard Univ. Press.

Choshen, Maya. 1998a. *Jerusalem: Facts and Trends 1997.* Jerusalem: Jerusalem Institute for Israel Studies.

————. 1998b. *Jerusalem on the Map: Basic Facts and Trends.* Jerusalem: Jerusalem Institute for Israel Studies.

————. 2000. *Migration from Jerusalem: Who Migrates, Why, and Where?* Jerusalem: Jerusalem Institute for Israel Studies.

Choshen, Maya, and Naama Shahar, eds. 1998. *The Statistical Yearbook of Jerusalem, 1997.* Jerusalem: Jerusalem Institute for Israel Studies.

————, eds. 1999. *Statistical Yearbook for Jerusalem, 1998.* Jerusalem: Jerusalem Institute for Israel Studies.

————, eds. 2000. *Statistical Yearbook of Jerusalem, 1999.* Jerusalem: Jerusalem Institute for Israel Studies and the Jerusalem Municipality.

Christodoulos (Metropolitan of Demetrias; presently Archbishop of Athens). 1994. "The Vatican and the Holy Land" (in Greek). *To Vima,* July 17.

Christopher, Warren (Secretary of State). 1995a. Letter to House Speaker Newt Gingrich, June 20. *Congressional Record* 141: S15469 (daily edition Oct. 23).

————. 1995b. Letter to Senator Robert Dole, June 20. *Congressional Record* 141: S15469 (daily edition, Oct. 23).

Clinton, William J. (President). 1999. Memorandum for the Secretary of State, June 18, *Weekly Documents of the President,* no. 99–29.

Cohen, A., and A. Simon-Pikali. 1993. *Jews in the Muslim Courts: Society, Economy, and Communal Organization in Ottoman Jerusalem* (in Hebrew). Jerusalem: Yad Yitzhak Ben-Zvi.

Cohen, Hilel. 1998. "The Eastern Section" (in Hebrew). *Kol-Ha-Ir* (Jerusalem weekly), July 17.

Cohen, Saul B. 1977. *Jerusalem: Bridging the Four Walls.* New York: Herzl.

Cohen, Stephen B. 1982. "Conditioning U.S. Security Assistance on Human Rights Practices." *American Journal of International Law* 76: 246–79.

Cohen, William (Senator). 1995. Remarks. *Congressional Record* 141: S15523 (daily edition Oct. 24).

Collin, Bernardin. 1974. *Pour une solution au probleme des Lieux Saints.* Paris: G. P. Maisonneuve et Larose.

Committee for Strengthening Jerusalem. 1998. Report of committee chaired by the director general of the prime minister's office and including the director generals of the Ministry of Internal Affairs, the municipality of Jerusalem, and the Authority for the Development of Jerusalem, June. Jerusalem, unpublished internal document.

Cotran, Eugene. 1996. "Some Legal Aspects of the Declaration of Principles: A Palestinian View." In *The Arab-Israeli Accords: Legal Perspectives,* edited by Eugene Cotran and Chibli Mallat, 67–77. The Hague: Kluwer.

Crawford, James. 1990. "The Creation of the State of Palestine: Too Much Too Soon?" *European Journal of International Law* 1: 307–13.

Cust, Lionel G. A. 1980. *The Status Quo in the Holy Places.* 1929. Reprint. Jerusalem: Ariel.

D'Amato, Alfonse (Senator). 1995. Remarks. *Congressional Record* 141: S15476 (daily edition Oct. 23).

Dann, Uriel. 1982. *The Transjordan Emirate 1921–1946* (in Hebrew). Tel Aviv: Silo'ah Institute for Middle Eastern and African Studies, Tel Aviv University.

———. 1990. *King Hussein's Solidarity with Saddam Hussayn: A Pattern of Behavior?* Tel Aviv: Moshe Dayan Center for Middle Eastern and African Studies, Tel Aviv University.

———. 1994. "The Hashemite Monarchy 1948–88: The Constant and the Changing—An Integration." In *Jordan in the Middle East: The Making of a Pivotal State, 1948—1988,* edited by Joseph Nevo and Ilan Pappé, 15–25. Essex: Frank Cass.

Daschle, Tom (Senator). 1995. Remarks. *Congressional Record* 141: S15534 (daily edition Oct. 24).

Dayan, Moshe. 1978. *Story of My Life.* London: Sphere.

Decision No. 3913. 1998. Government of Israel Secretariat, Prime Minister's Office, June 21.

"Declaration of Principles on Interim Self-Government Arrangements." 1993. Signed September 13, Washington, D.C. UN Doc. A/48/486-S/26560 (Annex) of October 11, 1993. *International Legal Materials* 32 (1993): 1525–44, and *Israel Law Review* 28 (1994): 442–51.

DellaPergola, Sergio. 1998. "Summary of Trends and Forecasts for the Population of Jerusalem: Strategic Plan for Jerusalem." Jerusalem Municipality, unpublished report.

Dellinger, Walter (Assistant Attorney General). 1995. Memorandum to Abner J. Mikva, Counsel to the President, May 16. *Congressional Record* 141: S15468 (daily edition Oct. 23).

Dinstein, Yoram. 1971. "Zion Shall Be Redeemed in International Law" (in Hebrew). *Hapraklit* 27: 5.

———. 1981. "Autonomy." In *Models of Autonomy,* edited by Yoram Dinstein, 291–303. New Brunswick, N.J.: Transaction.

"Documents Concerning the Accession of the Hellenic Republic to the European Communities, Final Act." 1979. *Official Journal* 291, part L: 180, 186.

Dole, Robert (Senator). 1995a. Remarks. *Congressional Record* 141: S15531 (daily edition Oct. 24).

———. 1995b. Remarks. *Congressional Record* 141: S15532 (daily edition Oct. 24).

Draper, G.I.A.D. 1981. "The Status of Jerusalem as a Question of International Law." In *The Legal Aspects of the Palestine Problem with Special Regard to the Question of Jerusalem,* edited by Hans Koechler, 154–56. Vienna: International Progress Organization.

Drayton, Robert Harry. 1934. *Laws of Palestine.* Vol. 3. London and Jerusalem: Waterlow and Sons.

Dror, Shlomo. 1993. "And Now the Withdrawal Refuseniks" (in Hebrew). *Hadashot,* Sept. 23.

Dubois, Marcel J. 1976. *Vigiles a Jerusalem.* Paris: Morel.

Eisner, Michael. 1994. "Jerusalem: An Analysis of Legal Claims and Political Realities." *Wisconsin International Law Journal* 12: 221–75.

Elaraby, Nabil. 1993. "Legal Interpretations of UNSC 242." In *UN Security Council Resolution 242: The Building Block of Peacemaking,* 35–44. Washington, D.C.: Washington Institute for Near East Policy.

Elazar, D. J. 1991. *Two Peoples, One Land: Federal Solutions for Israel, the Palestinians, and Jordan.* New York and London: Univ. Press of America.

Eldad, Arye, and Israel Eldad. 1978. *The Challenge of Jerusalem* (in Hebrew). Jerusalem: Maariv Library.

Eldar, Akiva. 1999. "EU Asserts Jerusalem Is Not Israeli." *Haaretz* (English edition), Mar. 11, 1.

Elon, Menachem. 1996. *"Temple Mount Faithful v. Attorney-General,* Decision of Supreme Court of Israel (1993)." *Catholic University Law Review* 45: 861–941.

Emmett, Chad F. 1996–97. "The Status Quo Solution for Jerusalem." *Journal of Palestine Studies* 26: 16–28.

Englard, Izhak. 1994. "The Legal Status of the Holy Places in Jerusalem." *Israel Law Review* 28: 589–600.

Eshkol, Shlomo. 1996. *Master Plan for Open Spaces in Jerusalem* (in Hebrew). Jerusalem: Reces Eshkol Architects.

Esposito, John C. 1984. *Islam and Politics.* Syracuse, N.Y.: Syracuse Univ. Press.

Etzion, Yehuda. 1985. "To Raise the Banner of Jerusalem at Last" (in Hebrew). *Nekuda* (Nov.): 93.

————. 1993. "Draft of the Four Points" (in Hebrew). *Labrit* 1 (Hanukkah).

————. 1995. "And It Came to Pass That Yigal Raised His Hand Against Yitzhak" (in Hebrew). *Labrit* 3 (Hanukkah).

Faludi, A. 1997. "A Planning Doctrine for Jerusalem." *International Planning Studies* 2, no. 1: 83–101.

Farhat, Edmond, ed. 1987. *Gerusalemme nei documenti pontifici*. Vatican City: Libreria Editrice Vaticana.

Feinstein, Dianne (Senator). 1995. Remarks. *Congressional Record* 141: S15521 (daily edition Oct. 24).

Feintuch, Yossi. 1987. *U.S. Policy on Jerusalem*. New York: Greenwood.

Feitelson, Eran, and Q. Abdul-Jaber. 1997. *Prospects for Israeli-Palestinian Cooperation in Wastewater Treatment and Re-use in the Jerusalem Region*. Jerusalem: Jerusalem Institute for Israel Studies.

Ferrari, Silvio. 1996. "The Religious Significance of Jerusalem in the Middle East Peace Process: Some Legal Implications." *Catholic University Law Review* 45: 733–43.

Ferrari, Silvio, and Francesco Margiotta-Broglio. 1988. "The Vatican, the European Community, and the Status of Jerusalem" (in Italian). In *Studi in memoria di Mario Condorelli*, vol. 1. Milano: Giuffré.

First Secretary McDonald to the Secretary of State. 1949. *Foreign Relations of the United States*, Feb. 2, 721, 740.

"For East Jerusalem? Nothing!" 1997. *Maariv*, Dec. 23.

Frankel, David D. 1998. "The Temple Mount: Access and Prayer." In *Jerusalem City of Law and Justice*, edited by Rakover Nahum, 35–42. Jerusalem: Library of Jerusalem Law.

Friedland, Roger, and Richard Hecht. 1996. *To Rule Jerusalem*. Cambridge: Cambridge Univ. Press.

Friedman, M. 1977. *Society and Religion: The Non-Zionist Orthodox in Eretz-Israel, 1918–1936* (in Hebrew). Jerusalem: Yad Izhak Ben-Zvi.

————. 1989. "The State of Israel as a Theological Dilemma." In *The Israeli State and Society: Boundaries and Frontiers*, edited by B. Kimmerling, 165–215. Albany: State Univ. of New York Press.

————. 1991. *Haredi ("Ultra-Orthodox") Society: Sources, Trends, Processes* (in Hebrew). Jerusalem: Jerusalem Institute for Israel Studies.

————. 1995. "The Structural Foundation for Religio-Political Accommodation in Israel: Fallacy and Reality." In *Israel: The First Decade of Independence*, edited by I. Troen and N. Lucas, 51–82. Albany: State Univ. of New York Press.

Fudenberg, Drew, and Jean Tirole. 1991. *Game Theory.* Cambridge, Mass.: MIT Press.

"Fundamental Agreement Between the Holy See and the State of Israel." 1993. Signed December 30. *International Legal Materials* 33 (1994): 153ff.

Gaganiaras, Archimadrite Damaskinos. 1986. *Disputes among Greeks and Armenians on the Shrines of the Holy Land* (in Greek). Thessaloníki: private publication.

Galilee, Orit. 1996. "Yerushalayim Shtey Panim La" (The Two Faces of Jerusalem). *Haaretz,* Aug. 5.

Garfinkle, Adam. 1992. *Israel and Jordan in the Shadow of War: Functional Ties and Futile Diplomacy in a Small Place.* New York: St. Martin's.

Garrett, Geoffrey, and Barry R. Weingast. 1993. "Ideas, Interests, and Institutions: Constructing the European Community's Internal Market." In *Ideas and Foreign Policy: Beliefs, Institutions, and Political Change,* edited by Judith Goldstein and Robert O. Keohane, 173–206. Ithaca, N.Y.: Cornell Univ. Press.

Ghanem, Asad. 1996. *The First Palestinian General Elections: A Challenge for Democracy* (in Hebrew). Guivat Havi'va: Institute for Peace Research.

Gibbons, Robert. 1992. *Game Theory for Applied Economists.* Princeton, N.J.: Princeton Univ. Press.

Giladi, Rotem M. 1995. "The Practice and the Case Law of Israel in Matters Related to International Law." *Israel Law Review* 29: 506–34.

Gilbert, Martin. 1985. *Jerusalem: Rebirth of a City.* London: Chatto and Windus.

———. 1992. *The Arab-Israeli Conflict: Its History in Maps.* 5th ed. London: Weidenfeld and Nicolson.

———. 1994a. *Jerusalem: Illustrated History Atlas.* 6th ed. Jerusalem: Steimatzky.

———. 1994b. *Jerusalem Past and Future.* Jerusalem: Institute of the World Jewish Congress.

———. 1996. *Jerusalem in the Twentieth Century.* London: Chatto and Windus.

Ginio, Alisa. 1980. "Plans for the Solution of the Jerusalem Problem." In *Jerusalem: Problems and Prospects,* edited by J. L. Kraemer, 41–71. New York: Praeger.

Glaubach, Eliezer. 1996. *Jerusalem: The Permanent Settlement.* Tel Aviv: Yediot Aharenot.

Golani, Motti. 1994. "Zionut Lelo Zion? Emdat Hanhagat Hayishuv Umedinat Israel Beshelat Yerushalayim 1947–1949 (Zionism without Zion? The Position of the Palestinian Jewish Leadership and the State of Israel on the Jerusalem Question)." In *Yerushalayim Hahazuya* (Divided Jerusalem), edited by Avi Bareli, 30–52. Jerusalem: Yad Yitzshaq Ben-Zvi.

———. 1999. "Jerusalem's Hope Lies Only in Partition: Israeli Policy on the

Jerusalem Question, 1948–67." *International Journal for Middle East Studies* 31: 577—604.

Gold, Dore. 1995. *Jerusalem—Final Status Issues: Israel-Palestinians.* JCSS Study No. 7. Tel Aviv: Jaffee Center for Strategic Studies, Tel Aviv University.

"Good Friday Agreement." 1998. Available at: http://www.nio.gov.uk/agreement.

Goren, Shlomo. 1992. *The Book of the Temple Mount: Fighting Back* (in Hebrew). Part 4. Jerusalem: Haidra Raba Yeshiva.

Greenspan, David J. 1986. "Bridging the Irish Sea: The Anglo-Irish Treaty of 1985." *Syracuse Journal of International Law and Commerce* 12: 585–99.

Greiesammer, Ilan, and Joseph Weiler. 1987. *Europe's Middle East Dilemma: The Quest for a Unified Stance.* Boulder, Colo.: Westview.

Gruhin, Mark I. 1980. "Jerusalem: Legal and Political Dimensions in a Search for Peace." Comment. *Case Western Reserve Journal of International Law* 12: 169–213.

Halberstam, Malvina. 1995. "Can the Congress Move an Embassy?" *Legal Times,* Oct. 9, 26. Reprinted in *Congressional Record* 141: S15177-S15179 (daily edition Oct. 13).

———. 1996. "The Jerusalem Embassy Act." *Fordham International Law Journal* 19: 1379–92.

Hasson, Shlomo, Nili Schory, and Hagit Adiv. 1995. *Neighborhood Governance: The Concept and Method* (in Hebrew). Jerusalem: Jerusalem Institute for Israel Studies.

Hazan, Anna. 1995. *Jerusalem Municipal Boundaries 1948–1993* (in Hebrew). JIIS Background Papers No. 17, edited by Amnon Ramon. Jerusalem: Jerusalem Institute for Israel Studies.

Hazboun, Samir. 1999. *Labor Profile.* Draft 2, July. Unpublished internal document.

Heap, Shaun H. 1992. "Rationality." In *The Theory of Choice: A Critical Guide,* edited by Shaun H. Heap and Martin Hollis, 3–25. Oxford: Blackwell.

Heap, Shaun H., and Yanis Varoufakis. 1995. *Game Theory: A Critical Introduction.* London: Routledge.

Heller, M. A., and S. Nusseibeh. 1991. *No Trumpets, No Drums.* New York: Hill and Wang.

Henkin, Joseph Eliahu. 1981. "Speak to the Children of Israel That They Go Forward (Exodus 14:15)" (in Hebrew). In *The Collected Writings of Rabbi Joseph Eliahu Henkin,* vol. 1, 93–94. New York: Ezras Torah (Torah Relief Society).

Hirsch, Moshe. 1996. "The Future Negotiations over Jerusalem: Strategic Factors and Game Theory." *Catholic University Law Review* 45, no. 3: 699–722.

———. 1998. "The Asymmetric Incidence of Rules of Origin: Will Progressive and Cumulation Rules Resolve the Problem?" *Journal of World Trade* 32: 41–53.

———. 1999. "Game Theory, International Law, and Future Environmental Co-operation in the Middle East." *Denver Journal of International Law* 27: 75–119.

Hirsch, Moshe, Devora Housen-Couriel, and Ruth Lapidoth. 1995. *Whither Jerusalem? Proposals and Positions Concerning the Future of Jerusalem.* The Hague and Boston: Martinus Nijhoff, with the Jerusalem Institute for Israel Studies.

Hoffman, David. 1994. "Fete in Amman Marks Restoration of Dome of the Rock in Jerusalem." *Washington Post,* Apr. 19, A11.

Hoppen, K. 1989. *Theodore Ireland Since 1800: Conflict and Conformity.* London: Longman.

Housen-Couriel, Deborah, and Moshe Hirsch. 1990. "The Religious Status Quo in Jerusalem" (in Hebrew). Jerusalem Institute for Israel Studies, unpublished manuscript.

———. 1992. *East Jerusalem and the Elections to Be Held in Judea, Samaria, and Gaza, in Accordance with the Israeli Peace Initiative of May 1989* (in Hebrew). Jerusalem: Jerusalem Institute for Israel Studies.

Hughes, Michael. 1994. *Ireland Divided: The Roots of the Modern Irish Problem.* New York: St. Martin's.

Hussein I. 1994. Speech before the U.S. Congress. *Congressional Record* 141: H6204, H6205 (daily edition. July 26). Reprinted in *Haaretz* July 7, 1994; *FBIS Daily Report* July 27, 1994.

al-Husseini, Faisal. 1996. Memorandum to Dennis Ross, U.S. Department of State, July 1, 1993. In *Documents on Jerusalem,* edited by Mahadi Abdulhadi, 55. Jerusalem: Palestinian Academic Society for the Study of International Affairs.

Ibrahim, Youssef M. 1994. "Confirmation of Jordan as Guardian of Shrines." *New York Times,* July 26, A8.

Idinopulos, Thomas. 1991. *Jerusalem Blessed, Jerusalem Cursed: Jews, Christians, and Muslims in the Holy City from David's Time to Our Own.* Chicago: Ivan R. Dee.

Ilan, Shahar. 1998. "Right from the Right Wing" (in Hebrew). *Haaretz,* Mar. 11.

Immanuel, Jon, and Bull Hutman. 1994. "Arafat Suggests Hussein Head Confederation." *Jerusalem Post,* Aug. 4.

"Initial Registration Canvass Agreement. 1995. Signed September 23. Unpublished document.

"I.R.A. and the Arms Principle." 2000. *New York Times,* Feb. 5, A4; Feb. 12, A1.

Irani, G. I. 1986. *The Papacy and the Middle East, 1962–1984.* Indiana: Univ. of Notre Dame Press.

"Israel Hints at Jerusalem Compromise." 2000. BBC News, Jan. 31. Available at: http://news2.thls.bbc.co.uk.

"Israel-Jordan Treaty of Peace." 1994. Signed Oct. 26. *International Legal Materials* 34 (1995): 43–66.

"Israeli-Palestinian Interim Agreement on the West Bank and the Gaza Strip." 1995. Signed September 28. Excerpted in *International Legal Materials* 36 (1997): 551–647. Also available at: http://www.mfa.gov.il/mfa/home.asp. Full text published in *Kitvei Amana* 33.

"Israelis May Be More Flexible on Jerusalem Poll." 1995. Reuters, May 31. Available in Lexis/Nexis Library, Curnws File.

"Italy and Yugoslavia Sign Accord on Trieste Region." 1975. *New York Times,* Nov. 11, 34.

"Italy—the Holy See: Agreement to Amend the 1929 Lateran Concordat." 1985. *International Legal Materials* 24: 1589–1596.

Jehl, Douglas. 1994. "Jordan and Israel Join in Pact Aimed at Broad Mideast Peace." *New York Times,* July 26.

Jerusalem Water Undertaking (JWU). 1991. *Programs and Future Development Preview, Annual Report 1991.* Ramallah, Palestine: JWU.

Johnson, Paul. 1992. *Ireland: Land of Troubles.* New York: Holmes and Meir.

Karpel, Dalya. 1995. "Toldoteiha Shel Fantasya (History of a Fantasy)." *Haaretz,* Oct. 13.

Karpel, Motti. 1995. "The Meaning of the Paralysis in Gush Emunim, Yesha Council, and the Religious-Ideological Right" (in Hebrew). *Nekuda* (April): 185.

Katz, E., S. Levi, and J. Segal. 1997. *The Status of Jerusalem in the Eyes of Israelis.* Jerusalem: Guttman Institute of Applied Social Research and the Center for International and Security Studies, Univ. of Maryland.

Keegan, John. 1992. "The Six-Day Miracle." *Daily Telegraph,* June 6, 1.

Keohane, Robert O. 1988. "International Institutions: Two Approaches." *International Studies Quarterly* 32: 379–96.

Keohane, Robert O., and Lisa L. Martin. 1995. "The Promise of Institutionalist Theory." *International Security* 20, no. 1: 39–51.

Khalidi, Walid. 1996. *Islam, the West, and Jerusalem.* Washington, D.C.: Center for Contemporary Arab Studies and Center for Muslim-Christian Understanding, Georgetown Univ.

Kimhi, Israel. 1993. *25 Years of Re-united Jerusalem.* JIIS Focus Series No. 3. Jerusalem: Jerusalem Institute for Israel Studies.

————. 1998. *Arab Building in Jerusalem 1967–1997*. Boston, Mass.: Committee for Accuracy in Middle East Reporting in America (CAMERA).

Kleiman, Aaron S. 1970. *Foundations of British Policy in the Arab World: The Cairo Conference of 1921*. Baltimore and London: Johns Hopkins Univ. Press.

Klein, Claude. 1992. "Constitutional Law in Israel." In *International Encyclopedia of Laws*, vol. 2, edited by R. Blanpain, 24. The Hague: Kluwer Law and Taxation.

————. 1994. "La nouvelle legislation constitutionelle d'Israel." *Jahrbuch Des öffentlichen Rechts der Gegenwart* 42: 553–70.

Klein, Menachem. 1988. *Du Siah Veshivro: Yahasei Yarden Ashaf 1985–1988* (Antagonistic Collaboration: PLO-Jordanian Dialogue 1985–1988). Jerusalem: Davis Institute at the Hebrew University.

————. 1995. *Jerusalem in Negotiations for Peace: Arab Positions* (in Hebrew). Jerusalem: Jerusalem Institute for Israel Studies.

————. 1996. "The Islamic Holy Places as a Bargaining Card (1993–1995)." *Catholic University of America Law Review* 45: 745–63.

————. 1999. *Doves over Jerusalem's Sky: The Peace Process and the City (1977–1999)* (in Hebrew). Jerusalem: Jerusalem Institute for Israel Studies.

————. 2000. "The 'Tranquil Decade' Reexamined: A New Assessment of Israel-Arab Relations During the Years 1957–1967." *Israel Affairs* 6, nos. 3–4 (spring-summer): 68–82. Also in *From War to Peace?* Vol. 2 of *The First Hundred Years*, edited by Efraim Karsh, 68–82. London: Frank Cass, 2000

Klinghoffer v. Achille Lauro. 1991. 937 F. 2d 44, 47 (2d Cir.).

Kokhanovski, Ad. M. (Legal Adviser of the Ministry of Defense). 1995. *Haaretz*, Oct. 27.

Kol Hair. 1999. "A Small Problem of 50 m. Shekels." March 12.

Kollek, Teddy. 1981. "Jerusalem: Present and Future." *Foreign Affairs* 59: 1041–49.

————. 1988–89. "Sharing United Jerusalem." *Foreign Affairs* 67, no. 2: 156–68.

————. 1992a. Letter to Finance Minister Avraham Shohat, September 18. From Teddy Kollek's personal archives.

————. 1992b. Letter to Housing Minister Binyamin Ben-Eliezer, November 15. From Teddy Kollek's personal archives.

————. 1992c. Letter to Prime Minister Rabin, December 29. From Teddy Kollek's personal archives.

————. 1992d. Letter to Prime Minister Rabin, Dec. 4. From Teddy Kollek's personal archives.

Kramer, Martin. 1986. *Islam Assembled: The Advent of the Muslim Congresses*. Boulder, Colo.: Westview.

Krystall, Nathan. 1998. "The De-Arabization of West Jerusalem 1947–50." *Journal of Palestine Studies* 17: 5–22.

Kupferschmidt, Uri M. 1987. *The Supreme Muslim Council, Islam under the British Mandate for Palestine.* Leiden: E. J. Brill.

Kyl, Jon (Senator). 1995a. Remarks. *Congressional Record* 141: S15470 (daily edition Oct. 23).

———. 1995b. Remarks. *Congressional Record* 141: S15532 (daily edition Oct. 24).

La Pira, Giorgio. 1979. *Il sentiero di Isaia.* Florence: Giventi.

Landau, Asher Felix. 1999. "The Constitutional Status of Basic Laws." In *Towards a New European Ius Commune,* edited by A. Gambaro and A. M. Rabello, 375–80. Jerusalem: Sacher Institute, the Hebrew Univ.

Lapidoth, Ruth. 1992a. "Security Council Resolution 242 at Twenty Five." *Israel Law Review* 26: 295–318.

———. 1992b. "Sovereignty in Transition." *Journal of International Affairs* 45: 325–46.

———. 1994. "Jerusalem and the Peace Process." *Israel Law Review* 28: 402–34.

———. 1995. "Redefining Authority: The Past, Present, and Future of Sovereignty." *Harvard International Review* 17, no. 3: 8–13.

———. 1996a. "Jerusalem: Past, Present, and Future." *Revue Internationale de Droit Compareé* 48: 9–33.

———. 1996b. "Jerusalem: Some Jurisprudential Aspects." *Catholic University Law Review* 45: 661–86.

———. 1999. *Commentary on the Basic Law: Jerusalem Capital of Israel* (in Hebrew). Jerusalem: Sacher Institute, Hebrew Univ.

———. 2001. "The EU, Jerusalem, and the Peace Process." In *Festschrift in Honor of Prof. Thomas Oppermann,* 267–83. Berlin: Duncker and Humblot.

Lapidoth, Ruth, and N. Karin Calvo-Goller. 1992. "Les éléments constitutifs de l'e-tat et la déclaration du Conseil National Palestinien du 15 Novembre 1988." *Revue Générale De Droit International Public* (1992): 777–809.

Lapidoth, Ruth, and Moshe Hirsch, eds. 1992. *The Arab-Israel Conflict and Its Resolution: Selected Documents.* Jerusalem: Jerusalem Institute for Israel Studies and Martinus Nijhoff.

———. 1994a. *Jerusalem: Political and Legal Aspects* (in Hebrew). Jerusalem: Jerusalem Institute for Israel Studies.

———, eds. 1994b. *The Jerusalem Question and Its Resolution: Selected Documents.* Dordrecht: Jerusalem Institute for Israel Studies and Martinus Nijhoff.

Lautenberg, Frank (Senator). 1995. Remarks. *Congressional Record* 141: S15532 (daily edition Oct. 24).

Lauterpacht, Elihu. 1968. *Jerusalem and the Holy Places.* London: Anglo-Israel Association.

Lauterpacht, Hersch, ed. 1957. *International Law Reports Year 1953.* Vol. 20. London: Butterworth.

"Law Implementing the Treaty of Peace Between the State of Israel and the Hashemite Kingdom of Jordan." 1995. *Sefer HaHukim,* no. 1503: 109–11.

Lee, J. J. 1989. *Ireland 1912–1985: Politics and Society.* Cambridge: Cambridge Univ. Press.

"Legal and Administrative Matters (Regulation) Law, Consolidated Version." 1970. *Laws of the State of Israel, Authorized Translation,* 24 (1969–70 [5730]): 132–52.

Leich, Marian Nash, and Geoffrey R. Watson. 1993. "Jerusalem." *Cumulative Digest of U.S. Practice in International Law 1981–1988* 1: 478–86.

Letter from 92 U.S. Senators to Secretary of State Christopher. 1995 (Mar. 20). *Congressional Record* 141: S15476 (daily edition Oct. 23).

Levi v. the Estate of Mahmoud Mahmoud. Piskei Din (Judgements) 40, no. 1: 374. 1986.

Levush, Ruth. 1995. "Moving the United States Embassy to Jerusalem: A Legal Analysis." *World Law Insight* (Sept.): 1–36.

Lewis, Samuel W. 1996. "Reflections on the Future of Jerusalem." 45 *Catholic University Law Review* (1996): 695–98.

Luce, R. Duncan, and Howard Raiffa. 1957. *Games and Decisions: Introduction and Critical Survey.* Mineola, N.Y.: Dover.

Lustick, Ian. 1997. "Has Israel Annexed East Jerusalem?" *Middle East Policy* 5: 34–35.

Lyons, Bruce. 1992. "Game Theory." In *The Theory of Choice: A Critical Guide,* edited by Shaun H. Heap and Martin Hollis, 93–129. Oxford: Blackwell.

Makovsky, David. 1996. "Time for Beilin to Disclose Agreement in Full." *Jerusalem Post,* Feb. 28, 2.

Malanczuk, Peter. 1996. "Some Basic Aspects of the Agreements Between Israel and the PLO from the Perspective of International Law." *European Journal of International Law* 7: 485–500.

Mallison, Sally V., and W. Thomas Mallison. 1981. "The Jerusalem Problem in Public International Law: Juridical Status and a Start Towards Solution." In *The Legal Aspects of the Palestine Problem with Special Regard to the Question of Jerusalem,* edited by Hans Koechler, 98–119. Vienna: Braumueller.

Mallison, W. Thomas, and Sally V. Mallison. 1986. *The Palestine Problem in International Law and World Order.* London: Longman.

Mansi, S. S. 1980. *Sacrorum conciliorum nova et amplissima collectio.* Reprint. 1901. Paris: n.p.

al-Maqadme, Ibrahim. n.d. *Itifaq Ghaza Waarikha Ruya Islamiyya* (Gaza and Jericho Accord: An Islamic Vision). N.p.: n.p.

McCurry, Mike (Press Secretary). 1995. Statement, Oct. 24. Available on Westlaw (1995 WL 622772), the White House.

McDowell, Eleanor C., ed. 1977. *Digest of U.S. Practice in International Law 1976.* Washington, D.C.: U.S. Department of State.

McGarry, J., and B. O'Leary, eds. 1993. *The Politics of Ethnic Conflict Regulation.* New York and London: Routledge.

———. 1995. *Explaining Northern Ireland.* Oxford: Blackwell.

McKittrick, David. 1996. *The Nervous Peace.* Belfast: Blackstaff.

Medad, Israel. 1995. "Relevant History" (in Hebrew). *Nekuda* 188 (September): 74–75.

Meeting of Dean Rusk with Shertok. 1949. *Foreign Relations of the United States,* Apr. 4, 890.

Meigham, Katherine W. 1994. "The Israel–PLO Declaration of Principles: Prelude to Peace?" *Virginia Journal of International Law* 34: 435–68.

Merhav, Reuven, and Rotem M. Giladi. 1999. *The Role of the Hashemite Kingdom of Jordan in a Future Permanent Status Settlement in Jerusalem: Legal, Political, and Practical Aspects* (in Hebrew). Jerusalem: Jerusalem Institute for Israel Studies.

Metropolitan Washington Airports Authority v. Citizens for the Abatement of Aircraft Noise. 1991. 501 U.S. 252, 271.

Meyer, Jeffrey A. 1988. "Comment: Congressional Control of Foreign Assistance." *Yale Journal of International Law* 13: 69–110.

Miliaras, Archimandrite Kallistos. 1933. *The Holy Land in Palestine and the Rights of the Greek Nation on Them* (in Greek). Vol. 2. Jerusalem: Fraternity of the Holy Sepulcher, Sept.-Oct.

Milner, Iris. 1990. "Making History" (in Hebrew). *Haaretz,* Nov. 2.

Ministry of the Environment (MOE). 1997. *Environmental Quality in Jerusalem* (in Hebrew). Edited by Amira Halper and Edna Meemran. Jerusalem: Ministry of the Environment, Education Authorities in Jerusalem, Development Group for Jerusalem Ltd., and Department of Environmental Quality in the City of Jerusalem.

Mohn, Paul. 1950. "Jerusalem and the United Nations." *International Conciliation* 464: 421–71.

Monjed, T. M. 1997. "Strategies for Solid Waste Management in the West Bank– Palestine." Unpublished master's thesis in science, Delft, the Netherlands.

Morgenstern, Oskar. 1968. "Game Theory: Theoretical Aspects." In *International Encyclopedia of the Social Sciences,* 6: 62. New York: MacMillan.

Morris, Benni. 1996. *Israel's Border Wars 1949–1956.* Oxford: Clarendon.

Moschopoulos, Nic. 1948. *La question de Palestine et le Patriarcat de Jèrusalem: Ses droits, ses privileges.* Athens: n.p.

Mu'asher, Marwan (Jordanian Minister of Information), to Eldar Akiva. 1996. "Mi Makir et Hayardenim? (Who Knows the Jordanians?)" *Haaretz,* Nov. 14.

Mubarak Awad v. Itzhak Shamir et al. 1988. *Piskei Din* 42, no. 2: 424.

Musallam, Sami F. 1996. *The Struggle for Jerusalem: A Programme of Action for Peace.* Jerusalem: PASSIA.

Narkiss, Uzi. 1975. *Ahat Yerushalayim* (One Jerusalem). Tel Aviv: Am-Oved.

———. 1991. *Hayal Shel Yerushalayim* (Jerusalem's Soldier). Tel Aviv: Misrad Habitakhon.

National Planning and Building Council. 1991. *Combined National Master Plan for Building, Development, and Immigration Absorption, NMP 31. Interim Report, Summary of Phase I.* Vol. 1. Jerusalem: National Planning and Building Council.

National Religious Party (NRP). 1996. *NRP Platform for the Fourteenth Knesset* (in Hebrew). Jerusalem: NRP, May 12.

Nevo, Joseph. 1994. "Jordan and Saudi Arabia, the Last Royalists." In *Jordan in the Middle East: The Making of a Pivotal State: 1948–1988,* edited by Joseph Nevo and Ilan Pappé, 103–18. Essex: Frank Cass.

———. 1996. *King Abdalla and Palestine: A Territorial Ambition.* Oxford: St. Antony's College.

Nolte, Georg. 1995. "Ems-Dollard." In *Encyclopedia of Public International Law,* vol. 2, edited by Rudolf Bernhardt, 78–80. Amsterdam: North Holland.

Noradounghian, Gabriel E. 1900. *Recueil d' actes internationaux de l' Empire Ottoman.* Paris: F. Pichon.

Novak, Bogdan C. 1970. *Trieste, 1941–1954: The Ethnic, Political, and Ideological Struggle.* Chicago: Univ. of Chicago Press.

Nuofal, Mamduh. 1995. *Qissat Itifaq Oslo: al-Ru'ya al-al-Khaqqiqyya al-Kamila, Tabakhat Oslo* (The Story of the Oslo Accords: The Full True Version, the Oslo Meal). Amman: al-Ahaliya.

Nusseibeh, Sari. 1993. *Jerusalem: Visions of Reconciliation.* New York: UN Publications.

Official Documents about the Shrine-Worshipping and Administrative State of the Church of Jerusalem (in Greek). 1944. Jerusalem: Fraternity of the Holy Sepulcher.

O'Leary, Brendan, and John McGarry. 1997. *The Politics of Antagonism: Understanding Northern Ireland.* 2d ed. London: Athlone.

Olmert, E. 1999a. "The Key to the Unity of Jerusalem: Real Equality Between Arabs and Jews." *Havetzelet* (neighborhood newspaper), April.

———. 1999b. *Physical and Cultural Infrastructure in East Jerusalem: Central Policy Tenets.* Jerusalem: Jerusalem Municipality, March.

Orenstein, Shmuel Even-or. 1996. *A Crown for Jerusalem: Jewish National Fund Endeavors in and Around Jerusalem.* Jerusalem: Jewish National Fund.

Palestine National Council. 1988. Palestine National Council Declaration of Independence, November 15, UN GAOR Official Record, 43rd Session. U.N. Doc. A/43/827, S/20278. Also published in Lapidoth, Ruth, and Moshe Hirsch, eds. 1992. *The Arab-Israel Conflict and Its Resolution: Selected Documents,* 344–56. Jerusalem: Jerusalem Institute for Israel Studies and Martinus Nijhoff.

Palestinian Academic Society for the Study of International Affairs (PASSIA). 1996. *Jerusalem: Documents.* 5th ed. Jerusalem: PASSIA.

Palestinian Central Bureau of Statistics (PCBS). 1997. *Population, Housing, and Establishment Census.* Ramallah, Palestine: PCBS.

Papastathis, Charalambos K. 1993. "The Status of Mount Athos in Hellenic Public Law." In *Mount Athos and the European Community,* edited by Anthony-Emil N. Tachiaos, 55–75. Thessaloniki, Greece: Institute for Balkan Studies.

———. 1996. "A New Statute for Jerusalem? An Eastern Orthodox Viewpoint." *Catholic University Law Review* 45: 723–31.

Pappé, Ilan. 1994. "Jordan Between Hashemite and Palestinian Identity." In *Jordan in the Middle East: The Making of a Pivotal State: 1948–1988,* edited by Joseph Nevo and Ilan Pappé, 61–94. Essex: Frank Cass.

Parks, Michael. 1994. "Israel Suggests Shared Control of Holy Sites." *Jerusalem Post,* July 20.

Patchen, Martin. 1987. "Strategies for Eliciting Cooperation from an Adversary." *Journal of Conflict Resolution* 31: 164–81.

Pedahzur, Reuven. 1995. "Segirato Shel Ma'agal, Bahazara El Haopziya Hafalastinit (Closing the Circle: Back to the Palestinian Option)." *Medina Mimshal Veyahasim Benleumiyim* 40: 31–66.

Peres, Shimon. 1994. Letter to the minister of foreign affairs of Norway. *Jerusalem Post,* June 7, 1.

Peters, Ann. 1990. "Islamic Group Joins Christians Against Jewish Settlement." UPI, Apr. 24, available in Lexis/Nexis Library, UPI file.

Pfaff, William. 1995. "Jerusalem's Future Will Hinge on 'Second Choices.' " *Chicago Tribune,* June 12.

Porath, Y. 1974. *The Emergence of the Palestinian Arab National Movement 1918–1929.* London: Frank Cass.

Pundik, Ron. 1994. *The Struggle for Sovereignty: Between Great Britain and Jordan 1946–1951.* Oxford: Blackwell.

Putnam, Robert D. 1988. "Diplomacy and Domestic Politics: The Logic of Two-Level Games." *International Organization* 42: 427–60.

Quigley, John. 1991. "Old Jerusalem: Whose to Govern?" *Denver Journal of International Law and Policy* 20: 145–56.

———. 1996. "Sovereignty in Jerusalem." *Catholic University Law Review* 45: 765–80.

Rabihiya, Yitzhak. 1992. "Our Father Abraham Was Also a *Nudnik*" (in Hebrew). *Jerusalem,* Feb. 21.

Rabin, Yitzhak. 1996. "Inaugural Speech to the 13th Knesset, July 13, 1992." In *Documents on Jerusalem,* 117–118. Jerusalem: Palestinian Academic Society for the Study of International Affairs.

Rabinovich, Itamar. 1991. *The Road Not Taken.* New York: Oxford Univ. Press.

Rahall, Nick (Representative). 1995. Remarks. *Congressional Record* 141: H10685 (daily edition Oct. 24).

Raiffa, Howard. 1982. *The Art and Science of Negotiation.* Cambridge, Mass.: Belknap, Harvard Univ. Press.

Rajewski Brian, ed. 2000. *Countries of the World.* Detroit: Gale Group.

Ramon, Amnon. 1997. *The Attitude of the State of Israel and the Various Sections of the Jewish Public Toward the Temple Mount 1996–1997* (in Hebrew). Jerusalem: Jerusalem Institute for Israel Studies.

Refutation of the Allegations Put Forward by Sir Anton Bertram Against the Patriarchate of Jerusalem (in Greek). 1937. Jerusalem: Patriarchate of Jerusalem.

Reisman, Michael. 1970. *The Art of the Possible: Diplomatic Alternatives in the Middle East.* Princeton, N.J.: Princeton Univ. Press.

Reisner, Daniel. 1995. "Peace on the Jordan." *Justice* 4: 3–22.

Reiter, Yitzhak. 1996. *Islamic Endowments in Jerusalem under British Mandate.* London and Portland: F. Cass.

————. 1997. *Islamic Institutions in Jerusalem: Palestinian Muslim Organizations under Jordanian and Israeli Rule.* The Hague and London: Kluwer, with the Jerusalem Institute for Israel Studies.

————, with Marlen Eordegian and Marwan Abu Khalal. 2000. "The Holy Places: Between Divine and Human: The Complexity of Holy Places in Jerusalem." In *Jerusalem: Points of Friction—and Beyond,* edited by Mosher Maoz and Sari Nusseibeh, 95–164. The Hague: Kluwer Law International.

Rekhes, Eli, Shlomo Eshkol, and Razia Gilboa. 1993. *The Eastern Ring Road.* Jerusalem: Jerusalem Municipality.

"Resolution of 22 March 1990." 1991. In *American Foreign Policy: Current Documents, 1990.* Washington, D.C.: Department of State.

Riphagen, W. 1975. "Some Reflections on 'Functional Sovereignty.' " *Netherlands Yearbook of International Law* 6: 121–65.

Robb, Charles (Senator). 1995. Remarks. *Congressional Record* 141: S15523 (daily edition Oct. 24).

Romann, Michael, and Alex Weingrod. 1991. *Living Together Separately: Arabs and Jews in Contemporary Jerusalem.* Princeton, N.J.: Princeton Univ. Press.

Rosenne, Meir. 1993. "Legal Interpretations of UNSC 242." In *UN Security Council Resolution 242: The Building Block of Peacemaking,* 29–34. Washington, D.C.: Washington Institute for Near East Policy.

Rosenne, Shabtai. 1951. *Israel's Armistice Agreements with the Arab States.* Tel Aviv: Blumstein.

Ross, Denis. 1993. "UNSC 242 and Arab-Israeli Peacemaking." In *UN Security Council Resolution 242: The Building Block of Peacemaking,* 59–68. Washington, D.C.: Washington Institute for Near East Policy.

Rostow, Eugene. 1993. "The Intent of UNSC Resolution 242: The View of Non-Regional Actors." In *UN Security Council Resolution 242: The Building Block of Peacemaking,* 5–20. Washington, D.C.: Washington Institute for Near East Policy.

Rubin, Benjamin. 1995. "The Law of the State and the Territory of the State: Margins of Difference" (in Hebrew). *Mishpatim* 25: 215–39.

Rubinstein, Amnon, and Barak Medina. 1996. *The Constitutional Law of the State of Israel* (in Hebrew). Vol. 1. 5th ed. Tel Aviv: Schocken.

Rubinstein, Danny. 1997. "Khai Minuyim Lehar Habayit (Eighteen Appointments in the Temple Mount)." *Haaretz,* Jan. 26.

————. 1999. "Investment in East Jerusalem? Ha!" *Haaretz* (English edition), Mar. 29.

Rubinstein, Elyakim. 1998. "Israel and Jordan on Road to Peace" (in Hebrew). *Mehkarei Mishpat* (Bar-Ilan University Law Review) 14: 521.

Salmon, Jean. 1989. "Declaration of the State of Palestine." *Palestine Yearbook of International Law* 5: 48–82.

Sarna, Yigal. 1995. "The Deep Intoxication of the Suspect Kenan" (in Hebrew). *Yediot Ahronot,* Dec. 8.

Satloff, Robert B. 1994. *From Abdulla to Hussein: Jordan in Transition.* New York and Oxford: Oxford Univ. Press.

———. 1995. "The Jordan-Israeli Peace Treaty: A Remarkable Document." *Middle East Quarterly* 2: 47–51.

Savir, Uri. 1988. *The Process* (in Hebrew). Tel-Aviv: Yediot Aharonot and Hemed.

Sayegh, Selim. 1971. *Le statu quo des Lieux-Saints: Nature juridique et portée internationale* (in Italian). Rome: Libreria Editrice della Pontificia Universita Lateranense.

Schach, Eliezer Menachem. 1988. *Letters and Articles* (in Hebrew). Parts 1 and 2. Bene Beraq, Israel: n.p.

Schelling, Thomas C. 1980. *The Strategy of Conflict.* 1960. Reprint. Cambridge, Mass.: Harvard Univ. Press.

Schiff, Zeev. 1996. "Beilin and Abu Mazen Drafted a Document on Final Status; Agreed to Establish a Palestinian State." *Haaretz,* Feb. 22, 1.

Schiller, Eli. 1989. "The Temple Mount and Its Sites" (in Hebrew). *Ariel* 64–65 (Jan.): 37.

Schueftan, Dan. 1986. *A Jordanian Option: The "Yishuv" and the State of Israel vis-à-vis the Hashemite Regime and the Palestinian National Movement* (in Hebrew). Jerusalem: Yad Tabenkin.

Schwebel, Stephen M. 1970. "What Weight to Conquest?" (editorial comment). *American Journal of International Law* 64: 344.

Segal, Haggai. 1988. "Prisoner Number 2 Is Free" (in Hebrew). *Yediot Ahronot,* Dec. 30.

———. 1990. "Elboim Works Quietly" (in Hebrew). *Yediot Ahronot,* Oct. 19.

Sela, Avraham. 1990. "Yahasey Hamelekh Abdallha Vememshelet Israel Bemilkhemet Haatzmaut: Behina Mehudeshet (Relations Between King Abdullah and the Government of Israel: A Reassessment)." *Qathedra* 57: 120–162, 172–93.

———. 1992. "Transjordan, Israel, and the 1948 War: Myth, Historiography, and Reality." *Middle Eastern Studies* 28, no. 4: 623–88.

Shabbat, Yehezkel. 1997. *Hamas Vetahalikh Hashalom* (Hamas and the Peace Process). Private publication by the author.

Shahar, Ilan. 1998. "Further to the Right Than the Right" (in Hebrew). *Haaretz,* Mar. 11.

Shaltiee, Eli, ed. 1981. *Jerusalem in the Modern Period:Yaacov Herzog Memorial Volume.* Jerusalem: Yad Izhak Ben-Zvi and Ministry of Defense.

"Sharm el-Sheikh Memorandum on Implementation Timeline of Outstanding Commitments of Agreements and the Resumption of Permanent Status Negotiations." 1999. *International Legal Materials* 38 (1999): 1465.

Shehada [Shehadeh or Shihadeh], Raja. 1993. "Can the Declaration of Principles Bring about a Just and Lasting Peace?" *European Journal of International Law* 4: 555–63.

———. 1997. *From Occupation to Interim Accords: Israel and the Palestinian Territories.* London: Kluwer.

Sheinfeld, Moshe. 1948. "The Recruitment for Zion" (in Hebrew). *Diglenu la'Meguyasim* (Our Flag for the Soldiers) (May, Tel Aviv).

Shilhav, Yosef. 1988. "Changes in the Religious-Haredi Space." In *Twenty Years In Jerusalem: 1967–1987,* edited by Joshua Prawer and Ora Ahimeir, 82–94. Jerusalem: Jerusalem Institute for Israel Studies.

Shilo, Daniel. 1997. "Regarding the Ascent to the Temple Mount and Prayer There" (in Hebrew). In *Yibaneh Hamikdash* (The Temple Shall Be Built), pamphlet, 111–12. Jerusalem: Movement to Establish the Temple.

Shlaim, A. 1988. *Collusion Across the Jordan: King Abdullah, the Zionist Movement, and the Partition of Palestine.* Oxford: Clarendon.

Shor, Nathan. 1982. "Forbidden Visits on the Temple Mount. *Kardom* (Year 21–23, July 4): 90–96.

Shragai, Nadav. 1989. "The Temple Mount, Source of Calamity" (in Hebrew). *Haaretz,* Sept. 29.

———. 1994a. "Waiting for Red Heifer No. 10" (in Hebrew). *Haaretz,* Aug. 4.

———. 1994b. "Delusions from the Extreme Right" (in Hebrew). *Haaretz,* Dec. 9.

———. 1995. *The Temple Mount Conflict* (in Hebrew). Jerusalem: Keter.

———. 1996a. "Hai Vekayam Movement Asks Netanyahu to Permit Jewish Prayer on Temple Mount" (in Hebrew). *Haaretz,* June 26.

———. 1996b. "The Salon Beyond the Corridor" (in Hebrew). *Haaretz,* July 4.

———. 1997a. "Entry Prohibited, But Why?" (in Hebrew). *Haaretz,* Feb. 25.

———. 1997b. "Ladder to the Altar" (in Hebrew). *Haaretz,* Apr. 17.

————. 1997c. "Legal Adviser in PM's Office: Jewish Worship on Temple Mount Was Never Prohibited" (in Hebrew). *Haaretz,* Mar. 9.

————. 1998a. "The Committee of Director Generals Recommends . . ." *Haaretz,* May 21, A2.

————. 1998b. "The Plan for the Extension of Jerusalem . . ." *Haaretz,* May 20, A1, A4.

————. 1998c. "To Bring Elokim Home" (in Hebrew). *Haaretz,* Sept. 17.

————. 1999. "Temple Mount in the Hands of the Status Quo" (in Hebrew). *Haaretz,* Feb. 2.

Shultz, George P. 1990. "A Chance of Some Serious Diplomacy in the Middle East" (editorial). *Washington Post,* Mar. 6, A23.

Singer, Joel. 1994a. "Aspects of Foreign Relations under the Israeli-Palestinian Agreements on Interim Self-Government Arrangements for the West Bank and the Gaza Strip." *Israel Law Review* 28: 268–96.

————. 1994b. "The Declaration of Principles on Interim Self-Government Arrangements." *Justice* 1: 4–13.

————. 1995. "The West Bank and Gaza Strip: Phase Two." *Justice* 7: 5–17.

Slonim, Shlomo. 1998. *Jerusalem in America's Foreign Policy.* The Hague: Kluwer.

Snidal, Duncan. 1985. "The Game Theory of International Politics." *World Politics* 38: 25–57.

Sprinzak, Ehud. 1995. *Between Extraparliamentary Protest and Terror: Political Violence in Israel* (in Hebrew). Jerusalem: Jerusalem Institute for Israel Studies.

State of Israel. Central Bureau of Statistics. 1995. *Labour Force Surveys.* Publication no. 24. Jerusalem: Central Bureau of Statistics.

————. Central Bureau of Statistics. 1997. *Residential Units and Buildings: Summaries from Records of the Census-Takers.* Publications of the Housing and Population Census 1995. Jerusalem: Central Bureau of Statistics.

"State Property Law." 1951. *Laws of the State of Israel, Authorized Translation* 19.

Stevens, R. P. 1981. "The Vatican, the Catholic Church, and Jerusalem." In *The Legal Aspects of the Palestine Problem with Special Regard to the Question of Jerusalem,* edited by H. Kochler, 172–80. Vienna: Wilhelm Braumuler.

Stone, Julius. 1981. *Israel and Palestine: Assault on the Law of Nations.* Baltimore: Johns Hopkins Univ. Press.

Stoyanovsky, J. 1928. *The Mandate for Palestine: A Contribution to the Theory and Practice of International Mandates.* London: Longman.

Susser, Asher. 1994. "Jordan, the PLO, and the Palestine Question." In *Jordan in the*

Middle East: The Making of a Pivotal State, 1948–1988, edited by Joseph Nevo and Ilan Pappé, 211–28. Essex: Frank Cass.

————. 1995. "Demographiya Vepolitiqa Beyarden (Demography and Politics in Jordan)." In *Demographiya Vepolitiqa Bemedinot Arav* (Demography and Politics in the Arab States), edited by Ami Ayalon and Gad Gilbar, 131–51. Tel Aviv: Merkaz Moshe Dayan Beuniversitat Tel Aviv and Hakkibutz Hameukhad.

al-Tafukji, Khalil. 1996. "al-Istitan fi Madinat al-Quds" (The Settlements in Jerusalem). In *al-Quds, Dirasat Filastiniyya Islamiyya Wamasihiyya* (Jerusalem, Palestinian Islamic and Christian Studies), edited by Jiryes Sa'ad Khuri, Adnan Musallam and Musa Darwish, 359–74. al-Quds: al-Liqa.

al-Tal, Tariq. 1996. "al-Astira Wsumua al-Fahm fi al-Alaqat al-Urdiniyya al-Filas-tiniyya (Myth and Misunderstanding in Jordanian Palestinian Relations)." *al-Siyasa al-Filastiniyya* 3: 152–65.

"Treaty of Peace between the State of Israel and the Hashemite Kingdom of Jor-dan." 1994. Signed Oct. 26. *Kitvei Amana* (Israel Treaty Documents) no. 1069, vol. 32, 271. Reprinted in *International Legal Materials* 34 (1995): 43–66.

Turner, Vernon. 1993. "The Intent of UNSC Resolution 242: The View of Non-Regional Actors." In *UN Security Council Resolution 242: The Building Block of Peacemaking,* 21–28. Washington, D.C.: Washington Institute for Near East Policy.

Tzortzatos, Varnavas. 1972. "Translation of *Official Gazette of the Kingdom of Jordan*" (in Greek). 1958. Reprinted in *The Basic Administrative Institutions of the Ortho-dox Patriarchates,* 556–564. Athens: Institute for Balkan Studies.

Ucko, Hans, ed. 1993. *The Spiritual Significance of Jerusalem for Jews, Christians, and Muslims.* A Report on a Colloquium Convened by the World Council of Churches, Glion, Switzerland, May 2–6. Geneva: World Council of Churches.

Unger, Leonard, and Kristina Šegulja. 1990. *The Trieste Negotiations.* Washington, D.C.: Univ. Press of America.

United Mizrahi Bank Ltd. et al. v. Cooperative Village Migdal el al. 1995. Civil Appeal 6821/93, *Piskei-Din* 49, no. 4: 221.

United Nations. 1979. *The Status of Jerusalem.* New York: United Nations.

"United Nations Convention on the Continental Shelf." 1958. Art. II, 499 *United Nations Treaty Series,* 311, Apr. 29.

"United Nations Convention on the Law of the Sea." 1982. *UN Publication Sales No. E.83,* vol. 5 (1983): 1–157.

"United Nations Convention for the Protection of Cultural Property in the Event of Armed Conflict." 1954. 249 *United Nations Treaty Series,* 240, May 14.

United Nations Educational, Scientific, and Cultural Organization (UNESCO). 1968. Resolution 3.343 (no title). General Conference Fifteenth Session, Oct., Paris. Published in *United Nations Educational, Scientific, and Cultural Organization Records of the General Conference,* 53. Paris: UNESCO.

———. 1985. *Conventions and Recommendations of UNESCO Concerning the Protection of Cultural Heritage.* Paris: UNESCO.

United Nations General Assembly. 1947. Resolution 181(II) U.N. GAOR, 2d Sess., at 131, UN Doc. A/64 (1947).

———. 1966. "International Covenant on Civil and Political Rights." Resolution 2200A (XXI), Official Record, 21st Sess., Supp. No. 16, at 52, UN Doc. A/6316 (1966), 999 U.N.T.S. 171, entered into force Mar. 23, 1976. *International Legal Materials* 6 (1967): 368.

———. 1981. "Declaration on the Elimination of All Forms of Intolerance and of Discrimination Based on Religion or Belief." Resolution 36/55, Official Record, 36th Sess., Supp. No. 51, at 171, UN Doc. A/36/55 (1981).

United Nations. Trusteeship Council. 1950. *Question of an International Regime for the Jerusalem Area and Protection of the Holy Places: The Holy Places.* Working Paper prepared by the Secretariat, T/L.49, Mar. 7. New York: United Nations.

U.S. Congress. 1974. *Foreign Assistance Act.* 88 Stat. 1795, 22 U.S.C. §2304(a)(3).

———. 1986. *Anti-Drug Abuse Act.* Section 2005. *U.S. Code and Administrative News* (100 Stat.), 3207–262.

———. 1995. *Jerusalem Embassy Act.* Public Law 104–45, 109 Stat. 398., Nov. 8, 1995. Reprinted in *Statutes at Large* 109: 398.

United States v. Butler. 1936. 297 U.S. 1, 73–74.

United States v. Palestine Liberation Organization. 1988. 695 F. Supp. 1456 (S.D.N.Y.).

United States. v. Pink. 1942. 315 U.S. 203, 229.

Vance, Cyrus. 1986. Statement. *U.S. Middle East Policy: Hearing Before the Senate Committee on Foreign Relations.* 96th Cong., 2d sess., 1980. Excerpted in *Digest of U.S. Practice in International Law 1980,* edited by Marian Nash Leich. Washington D.C. Office of the Legal Advisor, U.S. Department of State.

Van Dusen, Michael. 1972. "Jerusalem, the Occupied Territories, and the Refugees." In *Major Middle Eastern Problems in International Law,* edited by Majid Khadduri, 37–63. Washington, D.C.: American Enterprise Institute.

van Genugten, Willem J. M. 1999. "Jerusalem, City in Need of a Special Legal Regime?" In *Realism and Moralism in International Relations: Essays in Honor of*

Frans A. M. Alting von Guesau, edited by Willem J. M van Genugten, Ernst M. H. Hirsch Ballin, Eric J. Janse de Jonge, and Pieter H. Kooijmans, 223–33. The Hague: Kluwer.

"Vienna Convention on Diplomatic Relations." 1961. 500 *United Nations Treaty Series* 95, 23; *United States Treaties* 3227; *Treaties and International Agreements,* no. 6702, Apr. 18.

"Vienna Convention on the Law of Treaties." 1969. May 23. Reprinted in *International Legal Materials* 8: 679–713.

Von Neumann, John, and Oskar Morgenstern. 1953. *Theory of Games and Economic Behavior.* 3rd ed. Princeton, N.J.: Princeton Univ. Press.

Walker, Christopher. 1994. "PLO Hails Jordan's Pledge on Jerusalem Holy Sites." *London Times,* Nov. 2, 15.

Walker, Clive, and Russel L. Weaver. 1994. "A Peace Deal for Northern Ireland? The Downing Street Declaration of 1993." *Emory International Law Review* 8: 817–44.

"Washington Declaration Signed by Jordan and Israel." 1994. *New York Times,* July 26.

Watson, Geoffrey R. 1996. "The Jerusalem Embassy Act of 1995." *Catholic University Law Review* 45: 837–50.

———. 2000. *The Oslo Accords: International Law and the Israeli-Palestinian Peace Agreement.* Oxford: Oxford Univ. Press.

Werblowsky, R. J. 1988. *The Meaning of Jerusalem to Jews, Christians, and Muslims.* Jerusalem: Israel Study Group for Middle East Affairs.

Wolfrum, Ruediger. 1995. "Internationalization." In *Encyclopedia of Public International Law,* vol. 2, edited by Rudolf Bernhardt, 1395–98. Amsterdam: North Holland.

Young, G. 1905–6. *Corps de droit ottoman.* Vols. 1–7. Oxford: Clarendon.

Youngstown Sheet and Tube Co. v. Sawyer. 1952. 343 U.S. 579, 635–37.

Zak, Moshe. 1996. *Hussain Oseh Shalom* (Hussain Makes Peace). Ramat Gan: Bar-Ilan Univ. Press.

Zander, W. 1971. *Israel and the Holy Places of Christendom.* London: Weidenfeld and Nicolson.

Zeuthen, Frederik. "Economic Warfare." In *Bargaining: Formal Theories of Negotiation,* edited by Oran R. Young, 145–63. Urbana: Univ. of Illinois Press.

Index

Abdallah Ibn Hussein Technological
School, 408
Abdallah (Abdullah) I, King of Jordan,
138–44, 183, 184, 219, 238
Abdallah (Abdullah) II, King of Jordan,
172, 204, 213, 289
Abdul-Jaber, Qasem, 379–400
Abidin, Shaykh Abd al-Qadir, 164, 182,
187
Abramsky, Rabbi Yehezkel, 298
Abu Dis, 8; landfill, 390, 392, 393
Abu Odeh, Adnan, 152–53, 233
Abu Tor, 140–41, 418
additional worker hypothesis, 369, 370
Agreement of Principles, 150
agricultural sector, 380, 383 table 14.1,
387, 388
Agudat Israel: composition of, 250; as
faction of *haredi* politics, 254;
opposition to Jewish state, 243–44;
political involvement of, 249, 251; post
independence changes in, 245;
proposed alliance with Arabs, 238–41;
world movement of, 236
Ahmed, Abd al-Aziz al-Haj, 169
al-Ahram, 162
Albin, Cecilia, 339
Alexander the Great, 258

American Colony, 408
Ami, Rabbi, 235
Amichai, Yehuda, 1
Amir, Yigal, 314
Amirav, Moshe, 405
Amital, Rabbi Yehuda, 301
Amman Agreement (1984), 166, 168
Annual Conference of The Friends of the
Temple, 304
antimilitarist tendencies: of Hai Vekayam,
311; of Neturei Karta, 237, 241–42,
244, 246, 247–48; of third century
Jews, 235–36
Antiquities Authority, 282, 284
Antiquities Law, 281, 283
anti-Zionists, 235–41. *See also* Neturei
Karta (Guardians of the City)
Applied Research Institute—Jerusalem
(ARIJ), 381
al-Aqsa Intifada. *See* Intifada
al-Aqsa Mosque: access fees to, 277;
administration of, 104n. 12; funds for
restoration of, 273; as payoff in
negotiations, 102; refurbishing of, 168;
renovation of, 281, 284; requisite
behavior in, 279–80; significance to
Jordanians, 184; torching of in 1969,
280